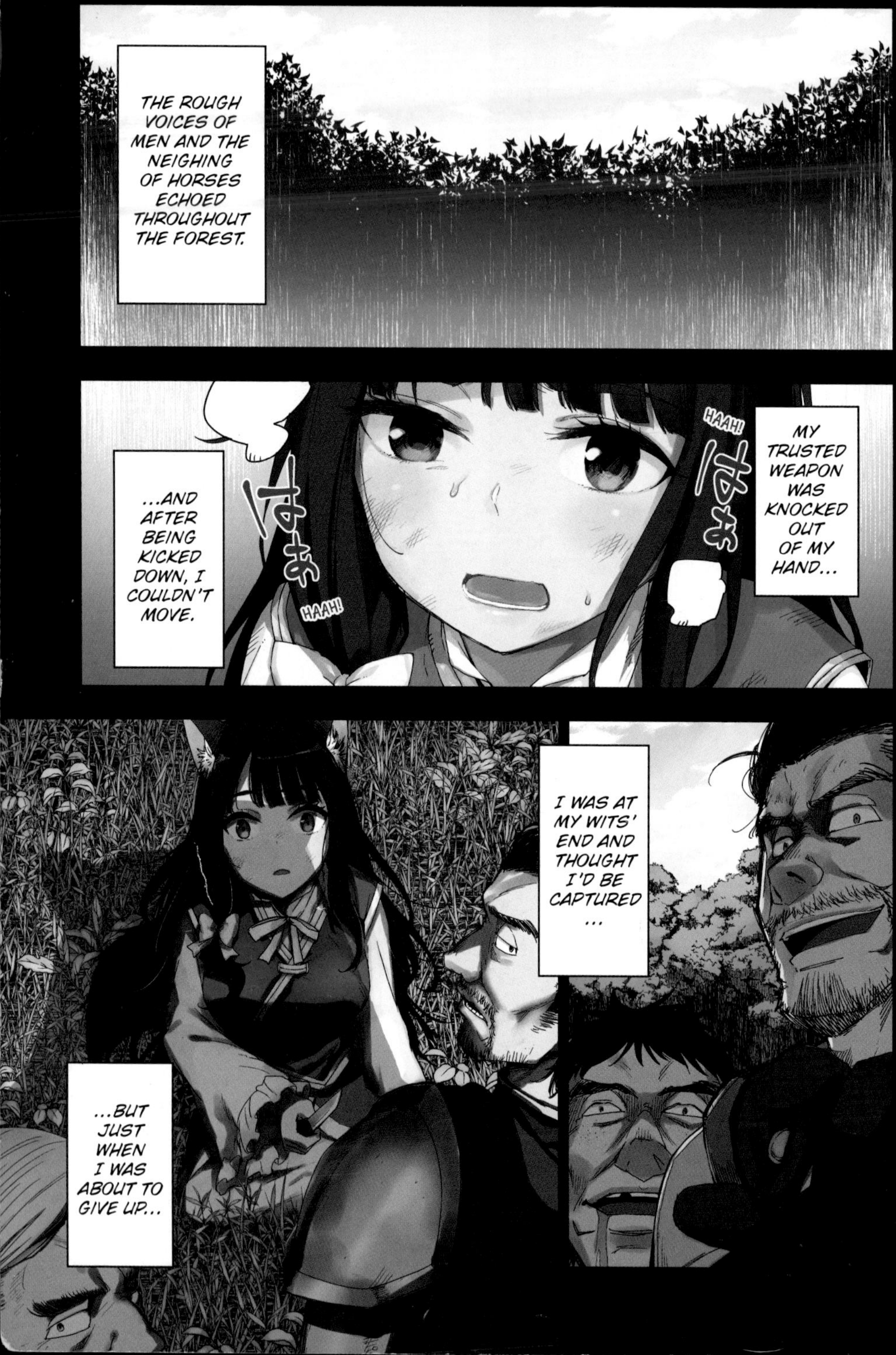
THE ROUGH VOICES OF MEN AND THE NEIGHING OF HORSES ECHOED THROUGHOUT THE FOREST.
MY TRUSTED WEAPON WAS KNOCKED OUT OF MY HAND...
HAAH!
はぁ
はぁ
HAAH!
...AND AFTER BEING KICKED DOWN, I COULDN'T MOVE.
I WAS AT MY WITS' END AND THOUGHT I'D BE CAPTURED...
...BUT JUST WHEN I WAS ABOUT TO GIVE UP...

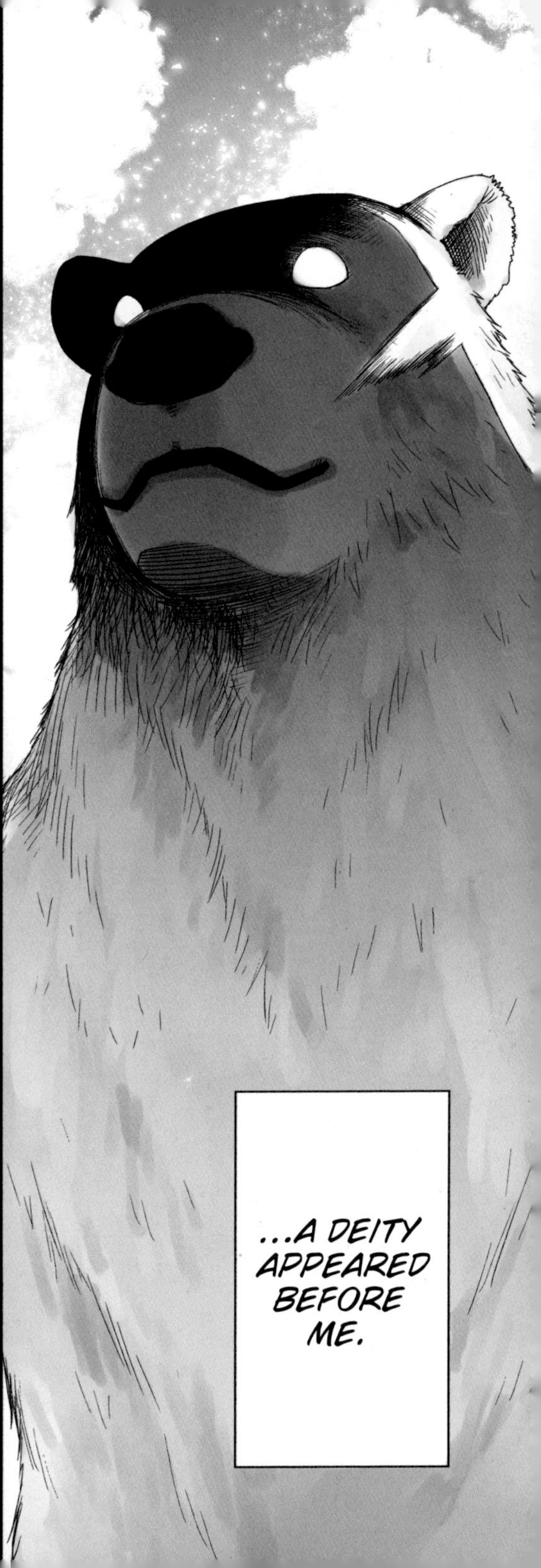
...A DEITY APPEARED BEFORE ME.
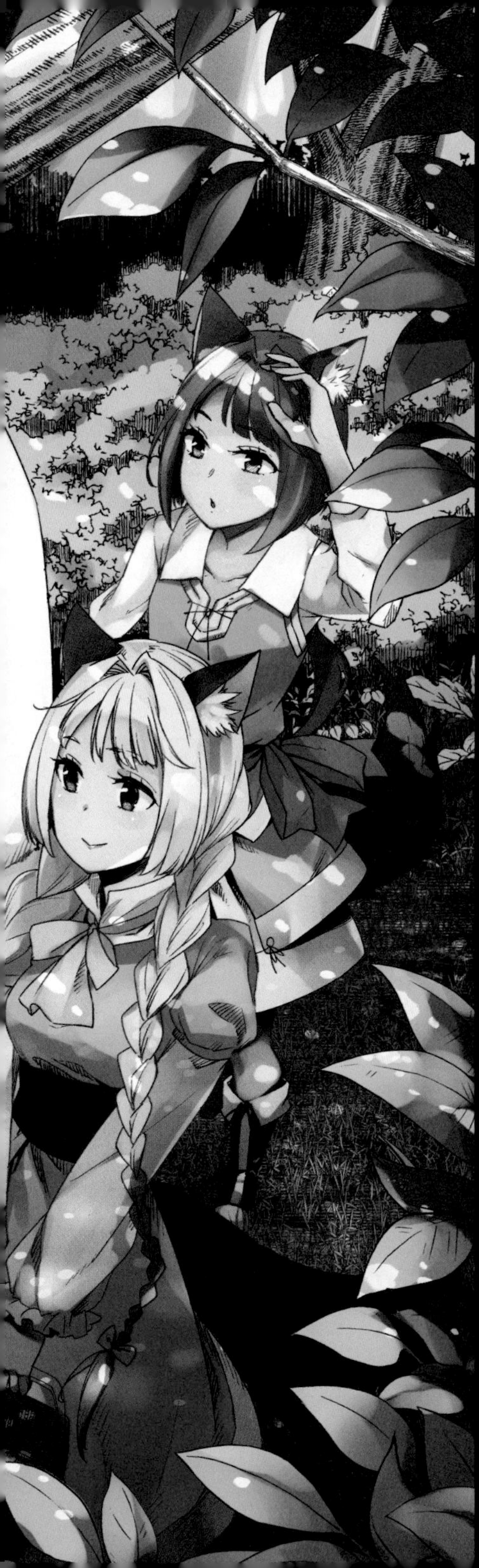

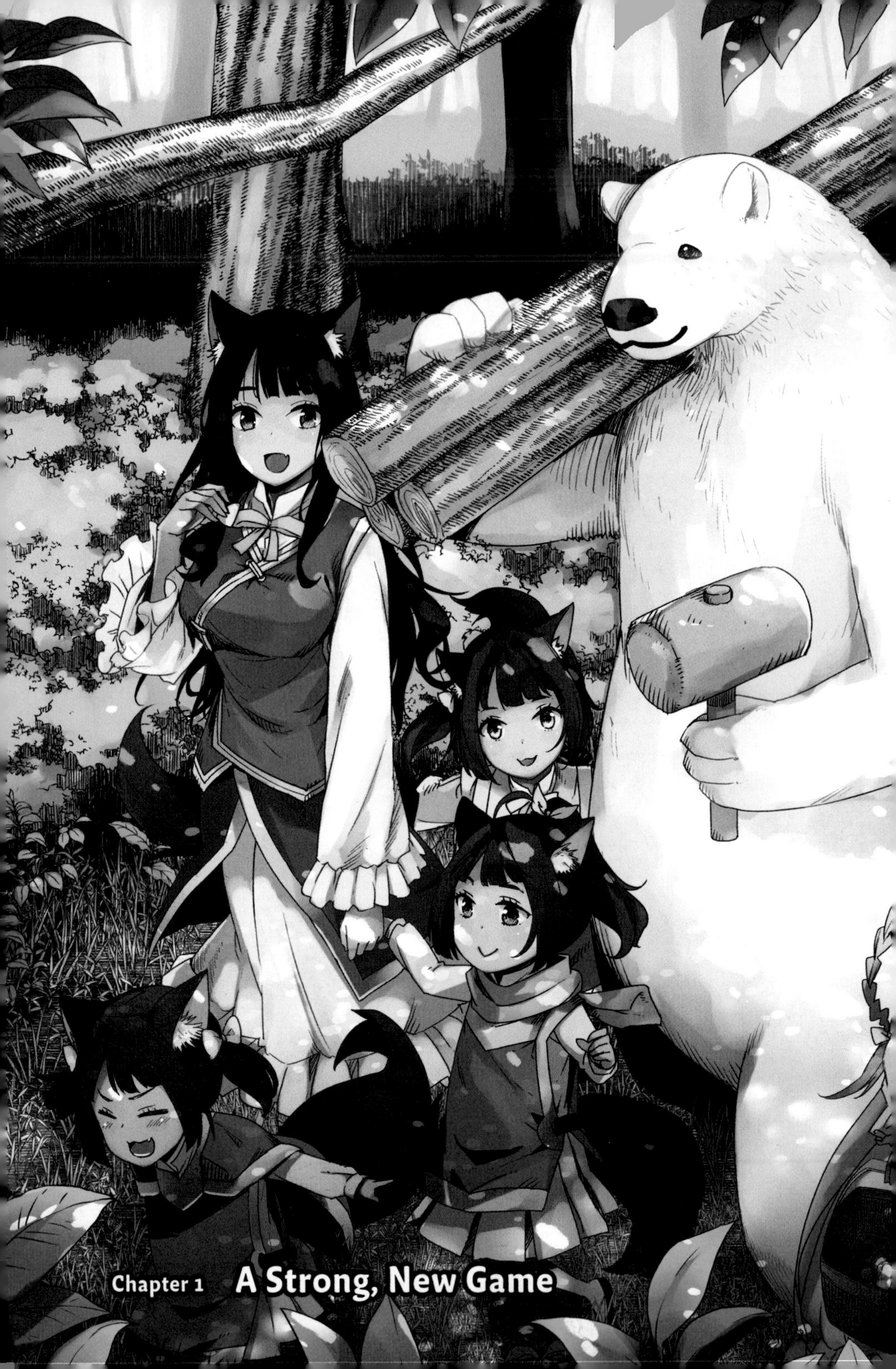

Chapter 1 A Strong, New Game

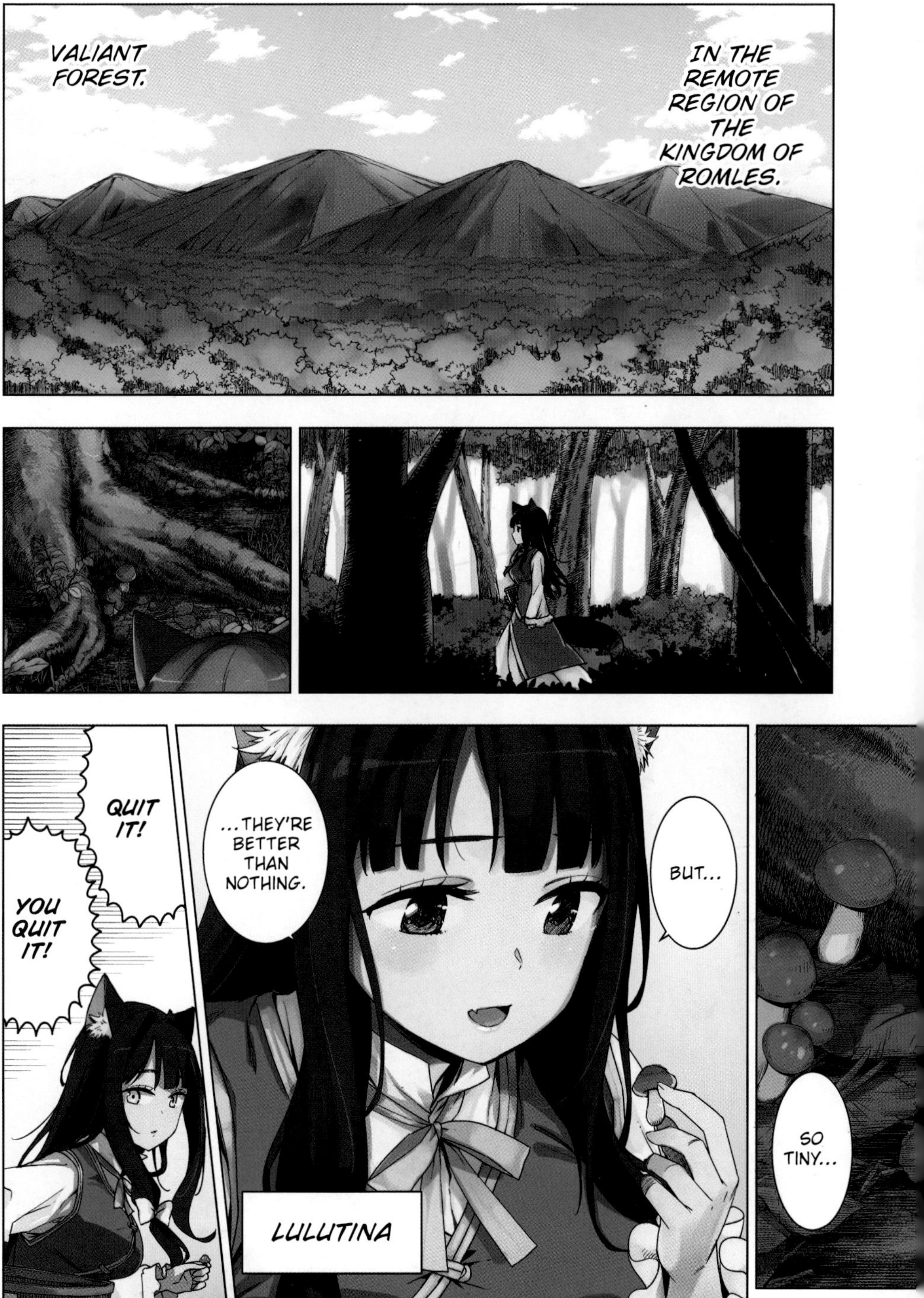
IN THE REMOTE REGION OF THE KINGDOM OF ROMLES.
VALIANT FOREST.
SO TINY...
BUT...
...THEY'RE BETTER THAN NOTHING.
LULUTINA
QUIT IT!
YOU QUIT IT!

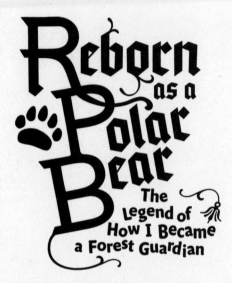

Reborn as a Polar Bear
The Legend of How I Became a Forest Guardian

ART: Houki Kusano
ORIGINAL STORY: Chihiro Mishima
CHARACTER DESIGN: Kururi

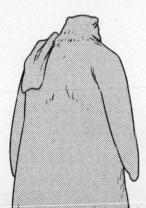

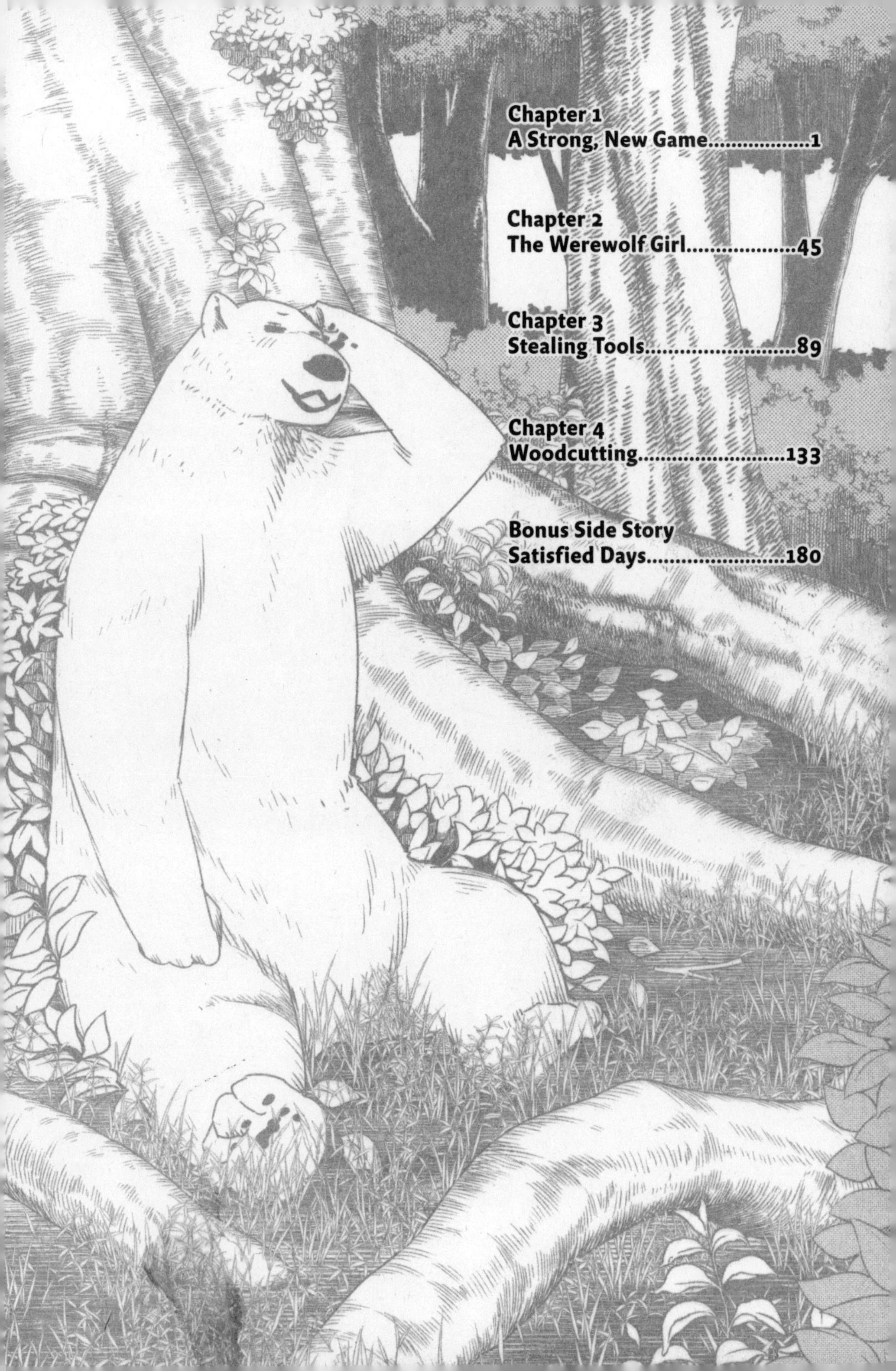

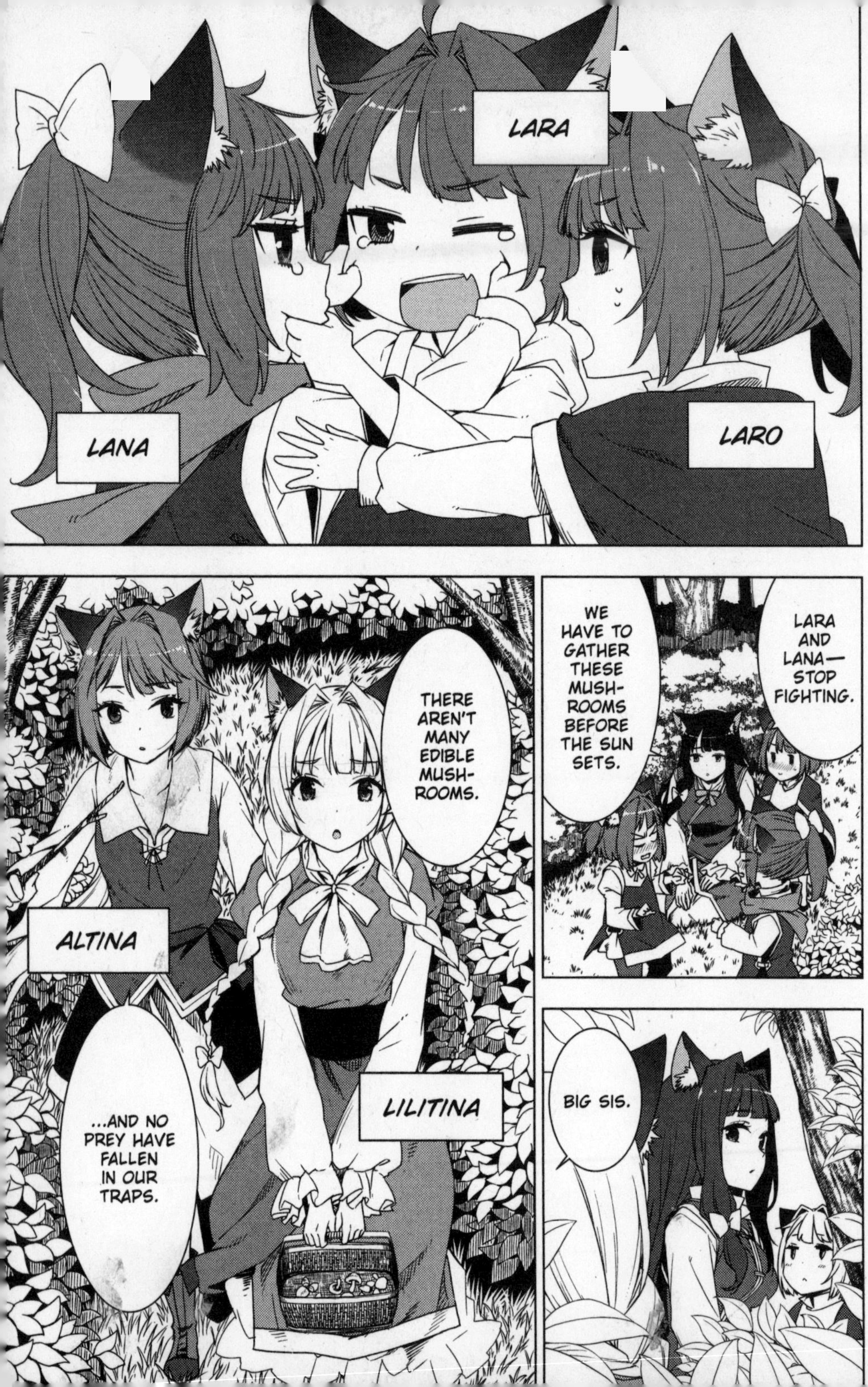
LARA
LARO
LANA
LARA AND LANA—STOP FIGHTING.
WE HAVE TO GATHER THESE MUSHROOMS BEFORE THE SUN SETS.
BIG SIS.
THERE AREN'T MANY EDIBLE MUSHROOMS.
ALTINA
LILITINA
...AND NO PREY HAVE FALLEN IN OUR TRAPS.

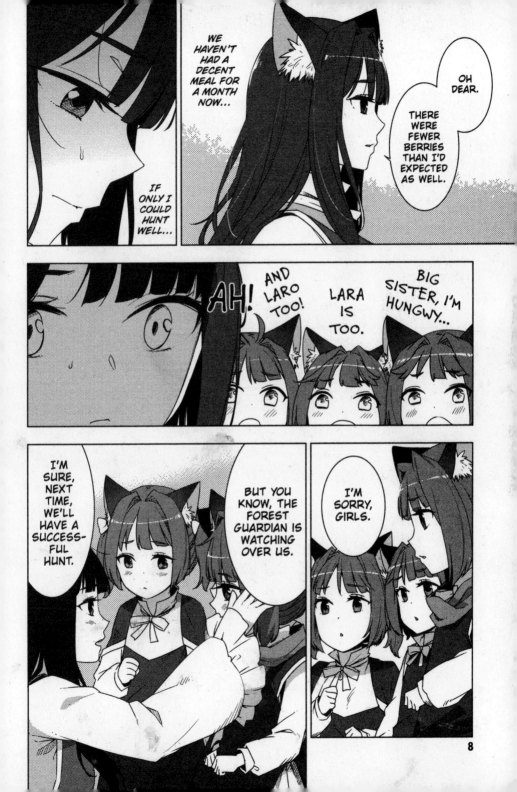

WE HAVEN'T HAD A DECENT MEAL FOR A MONTH NOW...

OH DEAR.

THERE WERE FEWER BERRIES THAN I'D EXPECTED AS WELL.

IF ONLY I COULD HUNT WELL...

AH!

AND LARO TOO!

LARA IS TOO.

BIG SISTER, I'M HUNGWY...

I'M SURE, NEXT TIME, WE'LL HAVE A SUCCESSFUL HUNT.

BUT YOU KNOW, THE FOREST GUARDIAN IS WATCHING OVER US.

I'M SORRY, GIRLS.

8

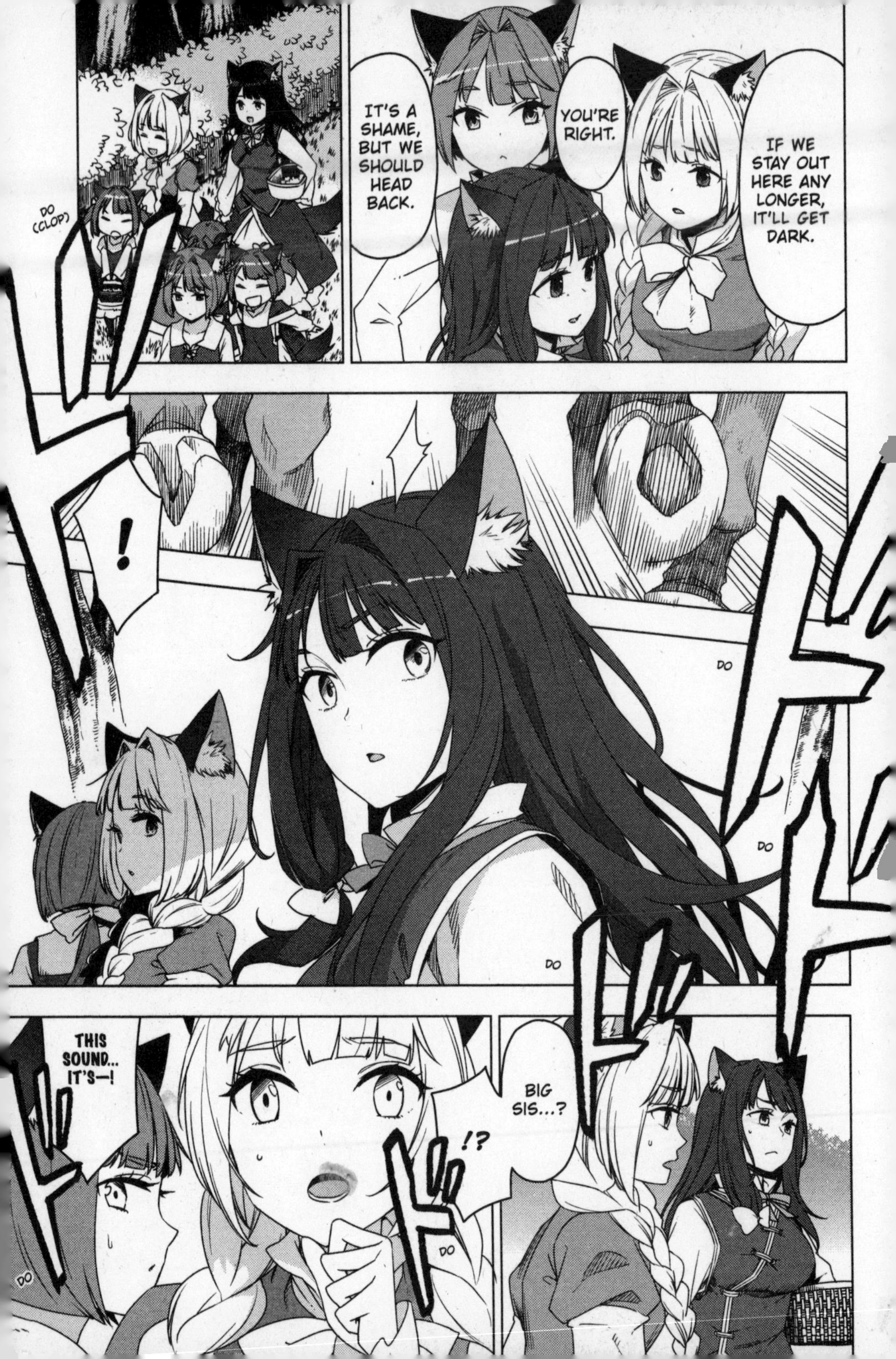

IF WE STAY OUT HERE ANY LONGER, IT'LL GET DARK.
YOU'RE RIGHT.
IT'S A SHAME, BUT WE SHOULD HEAD BACK.
DO (CLOP)
DO
DO
!
DO
BIG SIS...?
THIS SOUND... IT'S—!
!?
DO
DO

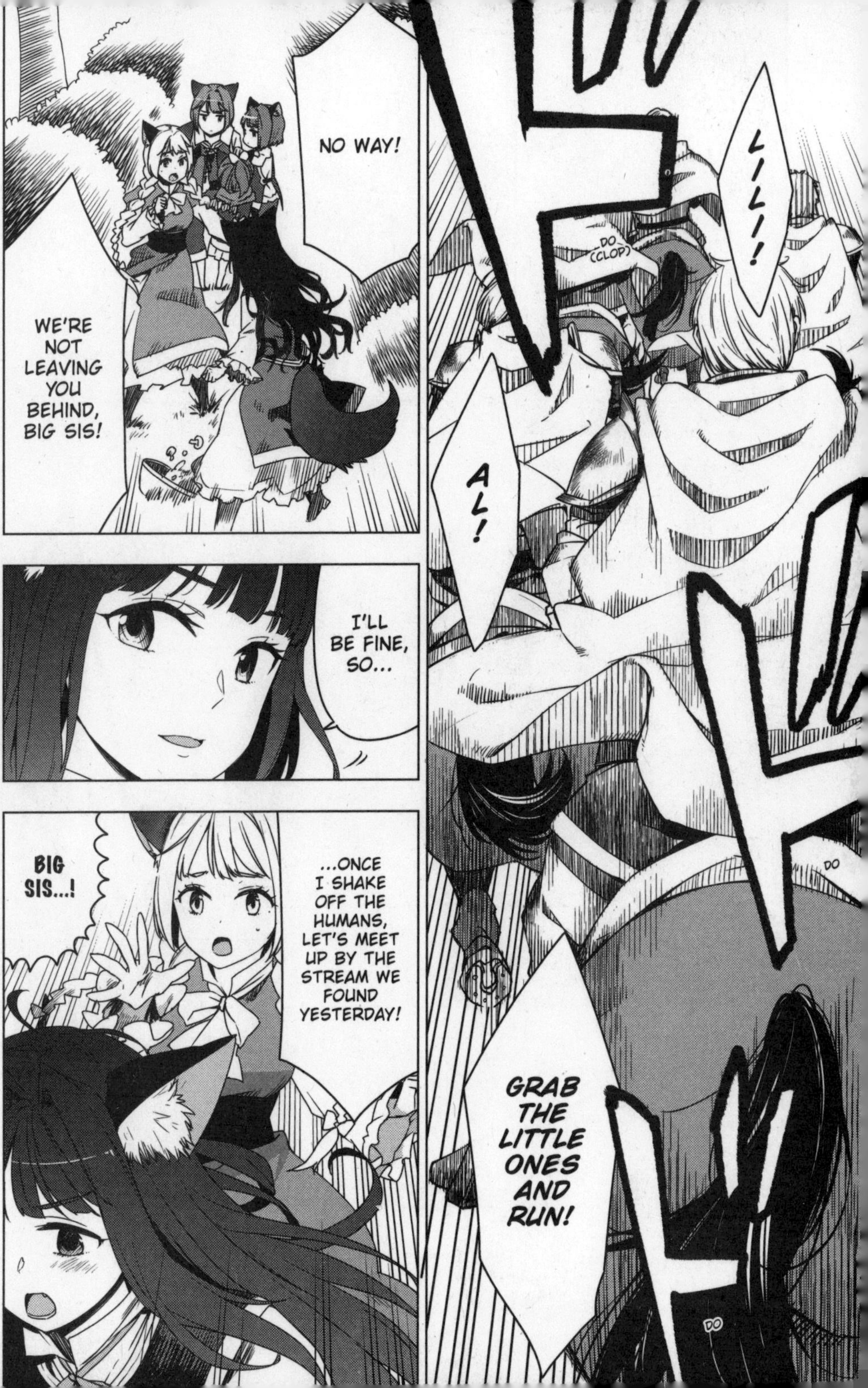
LILI!
DO (CLOP)
AL!
DO
GRAB THE LITTLE ONES AND RUN!
DO
NO WAY!
WE'RE NOT LEAVING YOU BEHIND, BIG SIS!
I'LL BE FINE, SO...
...ONCE I SHAKE OFF THE HUMANS, LET'S MEET UP BY THE STREAM WE FOUND YESTERDAY!
BIG SIS...!

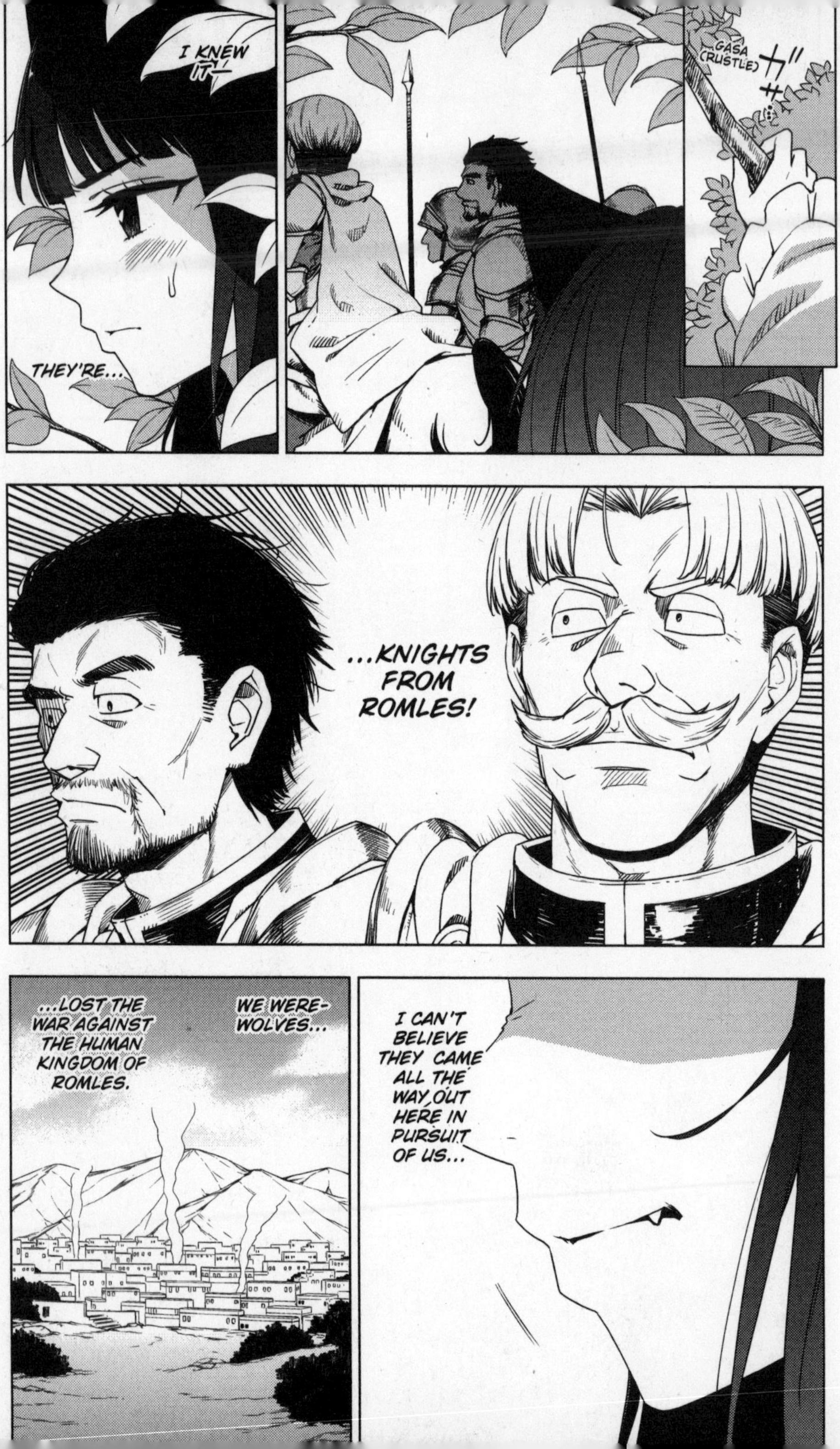
GASA (RUSTLE)
I KNEW IT—
THEY'RE...
...KNIGHTS FROM ROMLES!
I CAN'T BELIEVE THEY CAME ALL THE WAY OUT HERE IN PURSUIT OF US...
WE WERE-WOLVES...
...LOST THE WAR AGAINST THE HUMAN KINGDOM OF ROMLES.

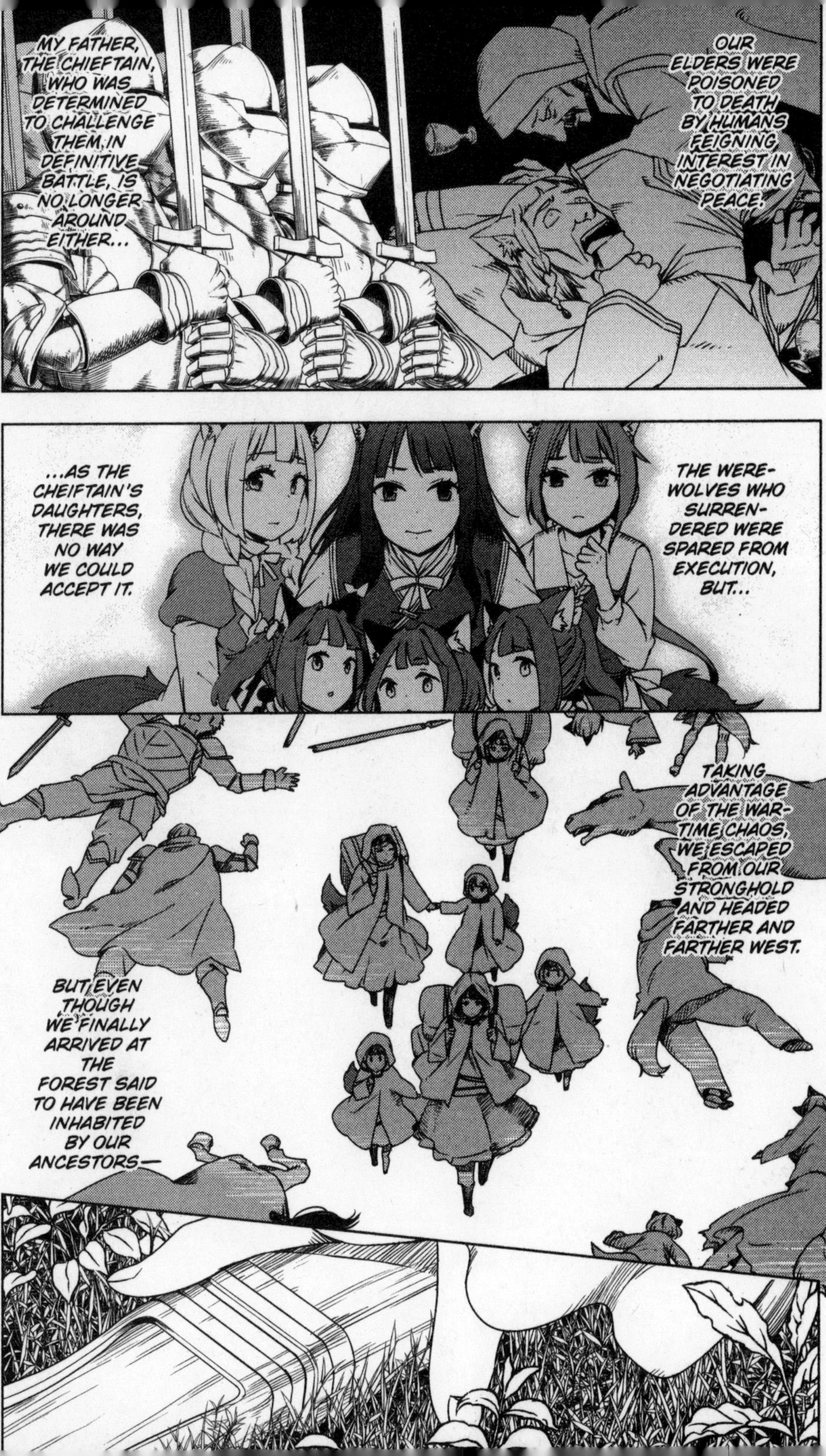
OUR ELDERS WERE POISONED TO DEATH BY HUMANS FEIGNING INTEREST IN NEGOTIATING PEACE.
MY FATHER, THE CHIEFTAIN, WHO WAS DETERMINED TO CHALLENGE THEM IN DEFINITIVE BATTLE, IS NO LONGER AROUND EITHER...
THE WERE-WOLVES WHO SURREN-DERED WERE SPARED FROM EXECUTION, BUT...
...AS THE CHEIFTAIN'S DAUGHTERS, THERE WAS NO WAY WE COULD ACCEPT IT.
TAKING ADVANTAGE OF THE WAR-TIME CHAOS, WE ESCAPED FROM OUR STRONGHOLD AND HEADED FARTHER AND FARTHER WEST.
BUT EVEN THOUGH WE FINALLY ARRIVED AT THE FOREST SAID TO HAVE BEEN INHABITED BY OUR ANCESTORS—

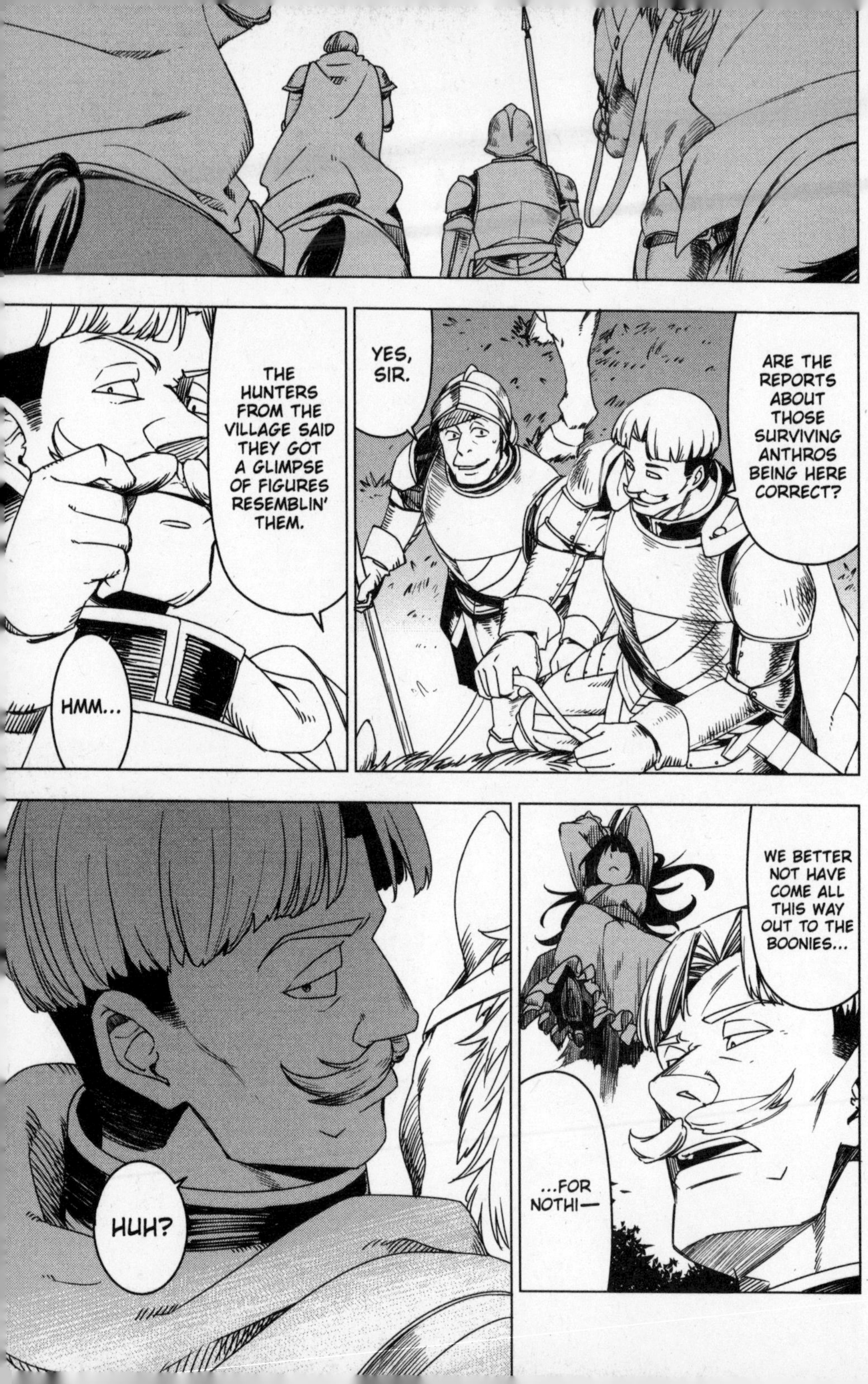
ARE THE REPORTS ABOUT THOSE SURVIVING ANTHROS BEING HERE CORRECT?
YES, SIR.
THE HUNTERS FROM THE VILLAGE SAID THEY GOT A GLIMPSE OF FIGURES RESEMBLIN' THEM.
HMM...
WE BETTER NOT HAVE COME ALL THIS WAY OUT TO THE BOONIES...
...FOR NOTHI—
HUH?

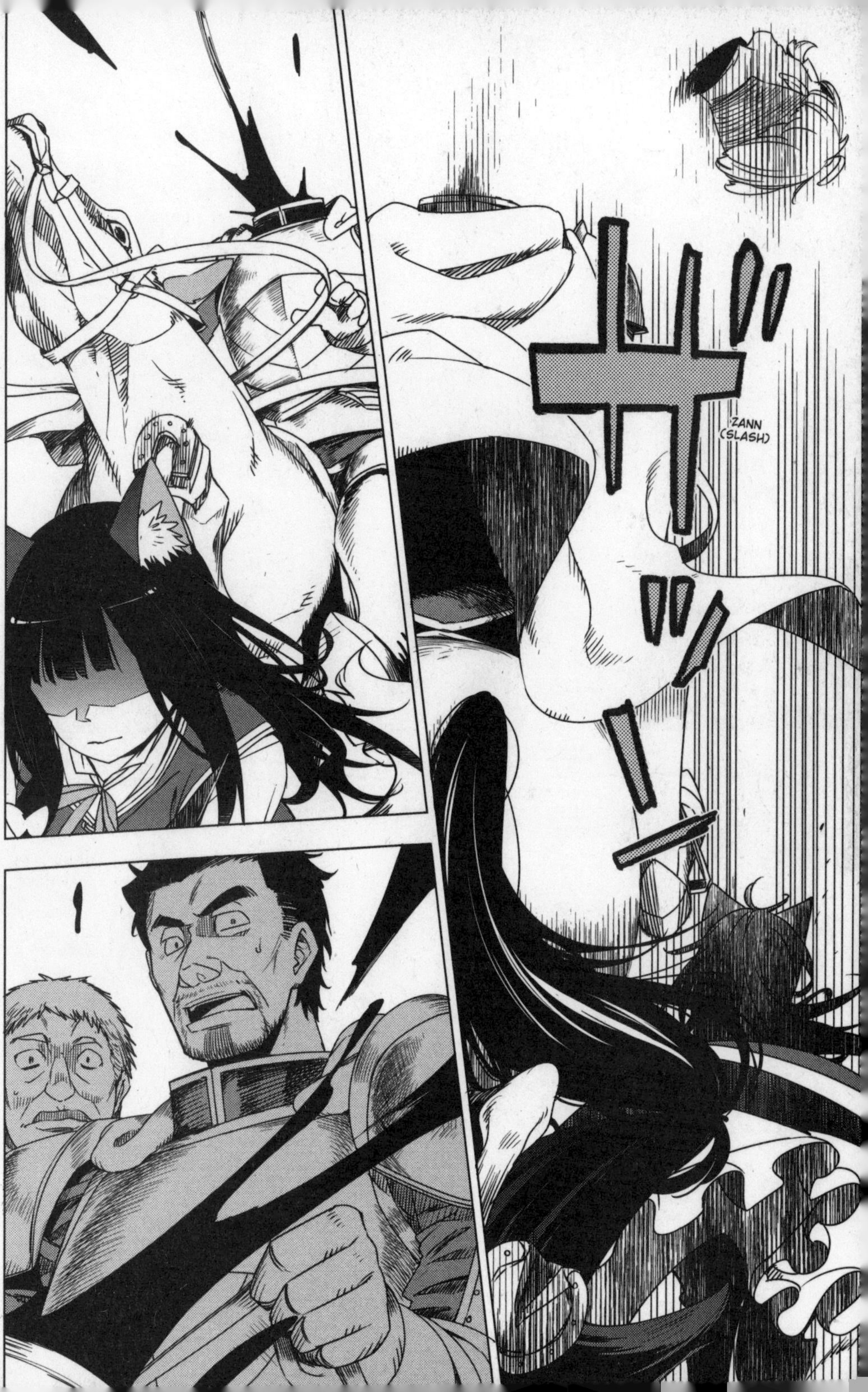
ZANN
(SLASH)

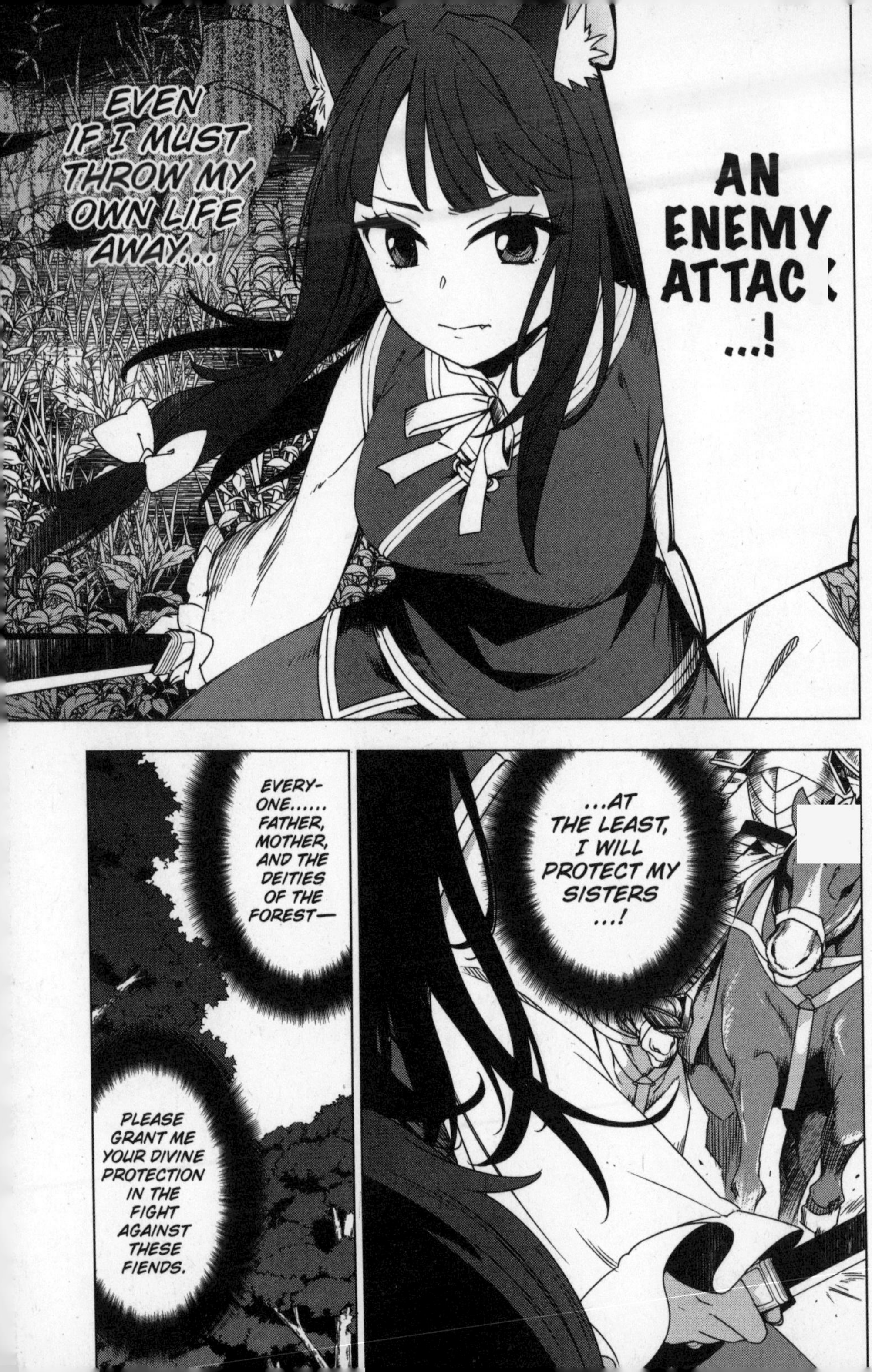
AN ENEMY ATTACK ...!
EVEN IF I MUST THROW MY OWN LIFE AWAY...
...AT THE LEAST, I WILL PROTECT MY SISTERS ...!
EVERY-ONE...... FATHER, MOTHER, AND THE DEITIES OF THE FOREST—
PLEASE GRANT ME YOUR DIVINE PROTECTION IN THE FIGHT AGAINST THESE FIENDS.

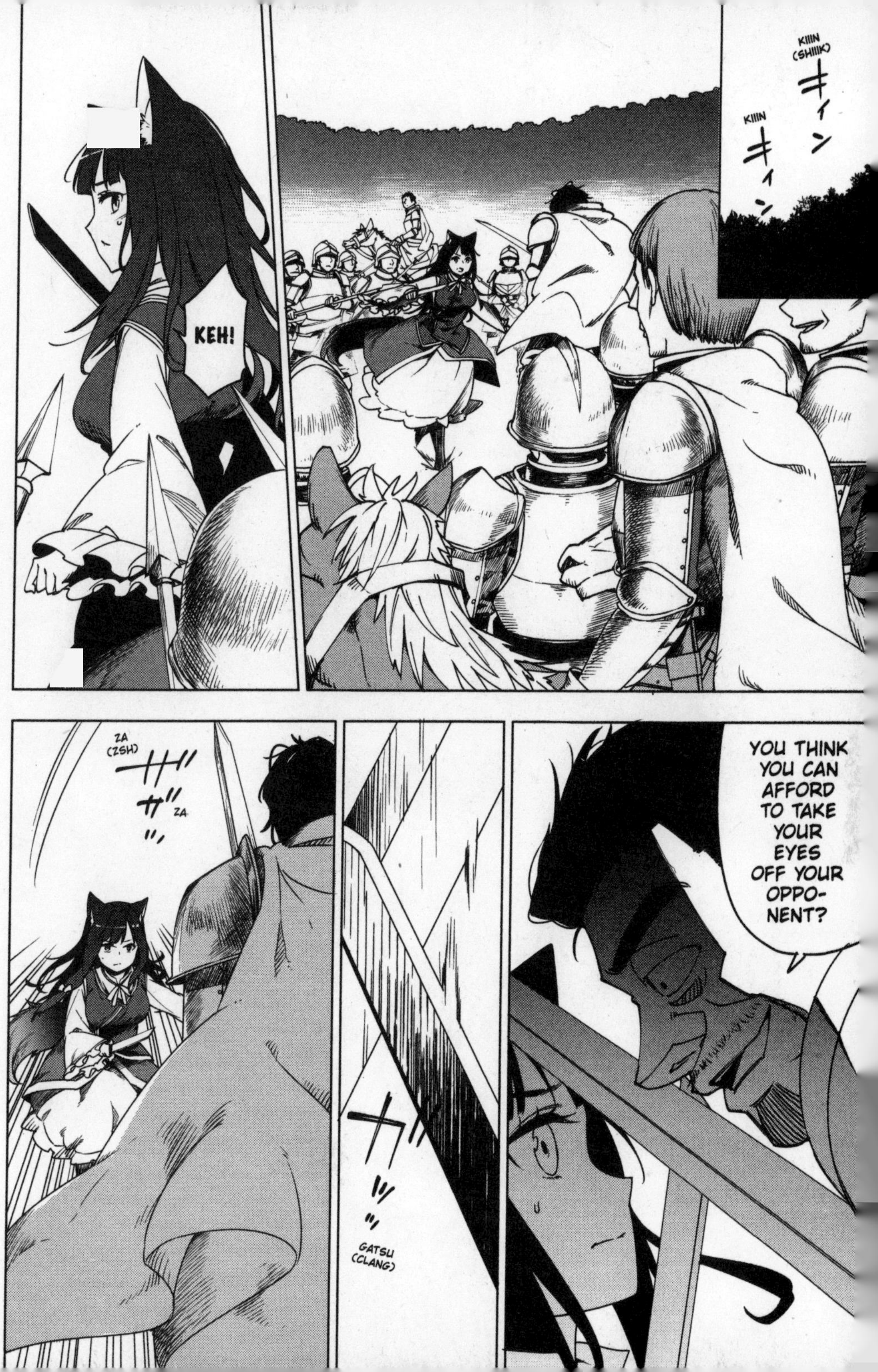
KIIIN (SHIIIK)
キィン
KIIIN
キィン
KEH!
YOU THINK YOU CAN AFFORD TO TAKE YOUR EYES OFF YOUR OPPO-NENT?
ガッ
GATSU (CLANG)
ZA (ZSH)
ザ
ザ
ZA

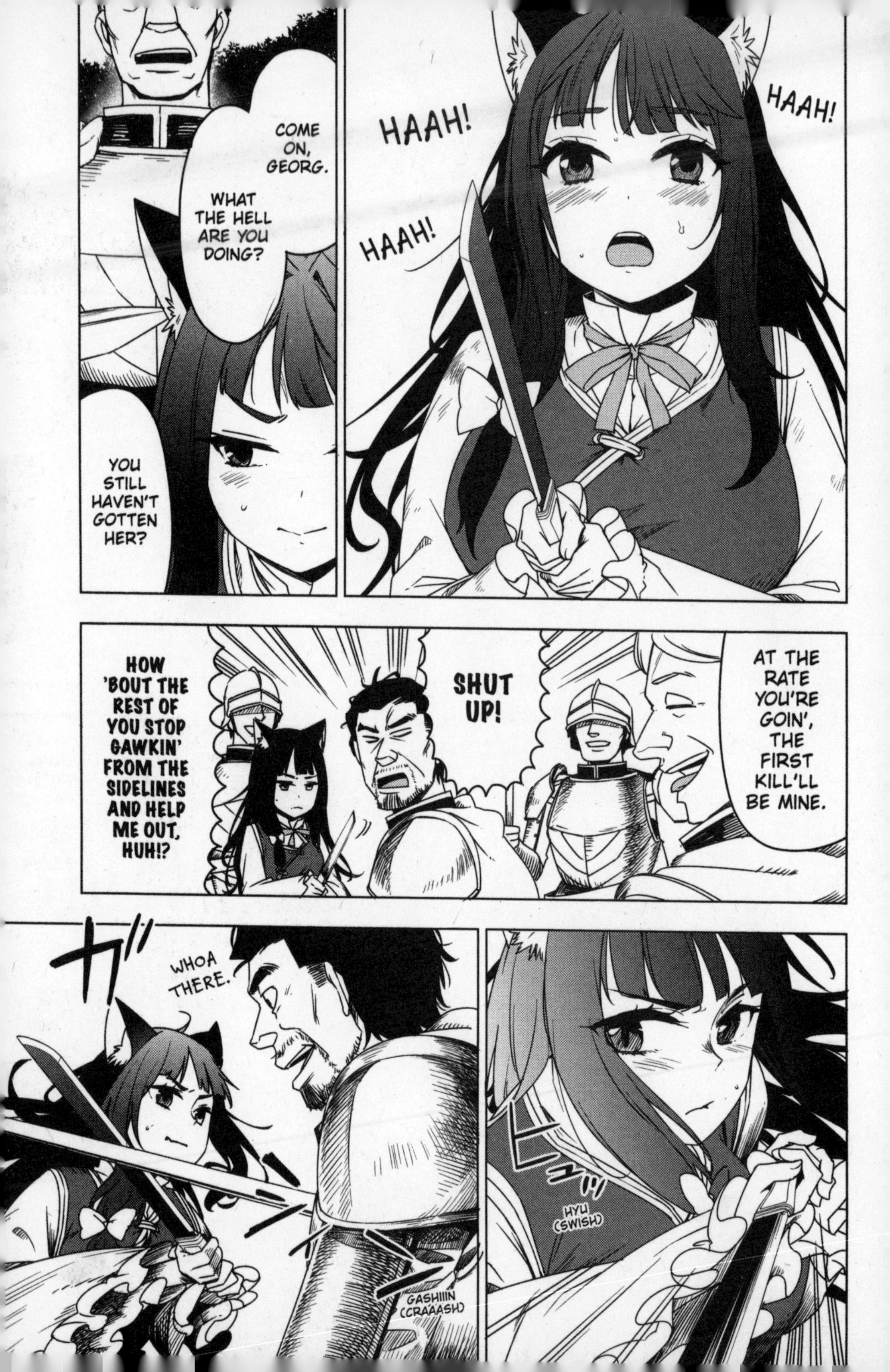
HAAH!
HAAH!
HAAH!
COME ON, GEORG.
WHAT THE HELL ARE YOU DOING?
YOU STILL HAVEN'T GOTTEN HER?
AT THE RATE YOU'RE GOIN', THE FIRST KILL'LL BE MINE.
SHUT UP!
HOW 'BOUT THE REST OF YOU STOP GAWKIN' FROM THE SIDELINES AND HELP ME OUT, HUH!?
HYU (SWISH)
WHOA THERE.
GASHIIIN (CRAAASH)

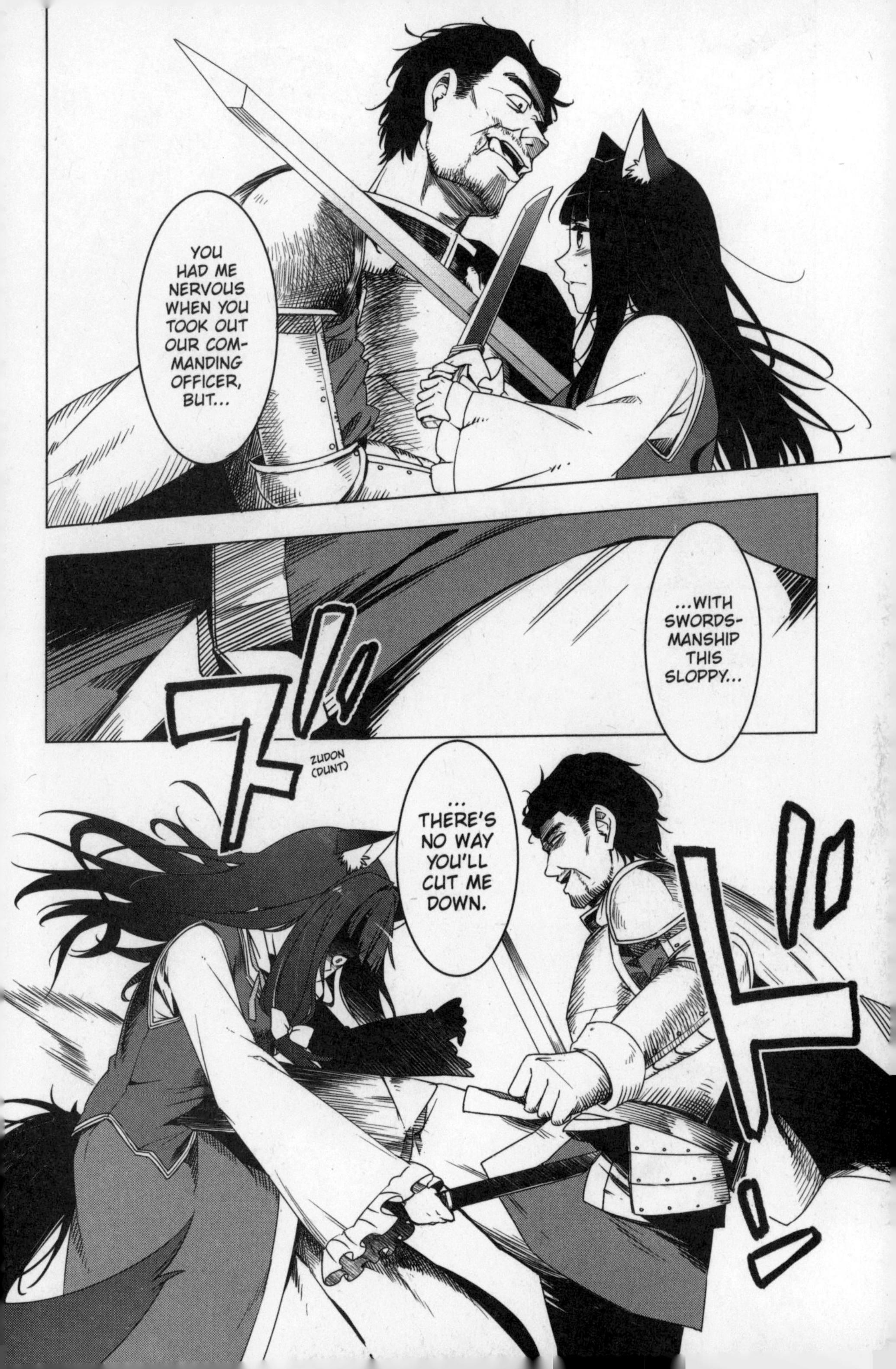
YOU HAD ME NERVOUS WHEN YOU TOOK OUT OUR COM-MANDING OFFICER, BUT...
...WITH SWORDS-MANSHIP THIS SLOPPY...
... THERE'S NO WAY YOU'LL CUT ME DOWN.
ZUDON (DUNT)

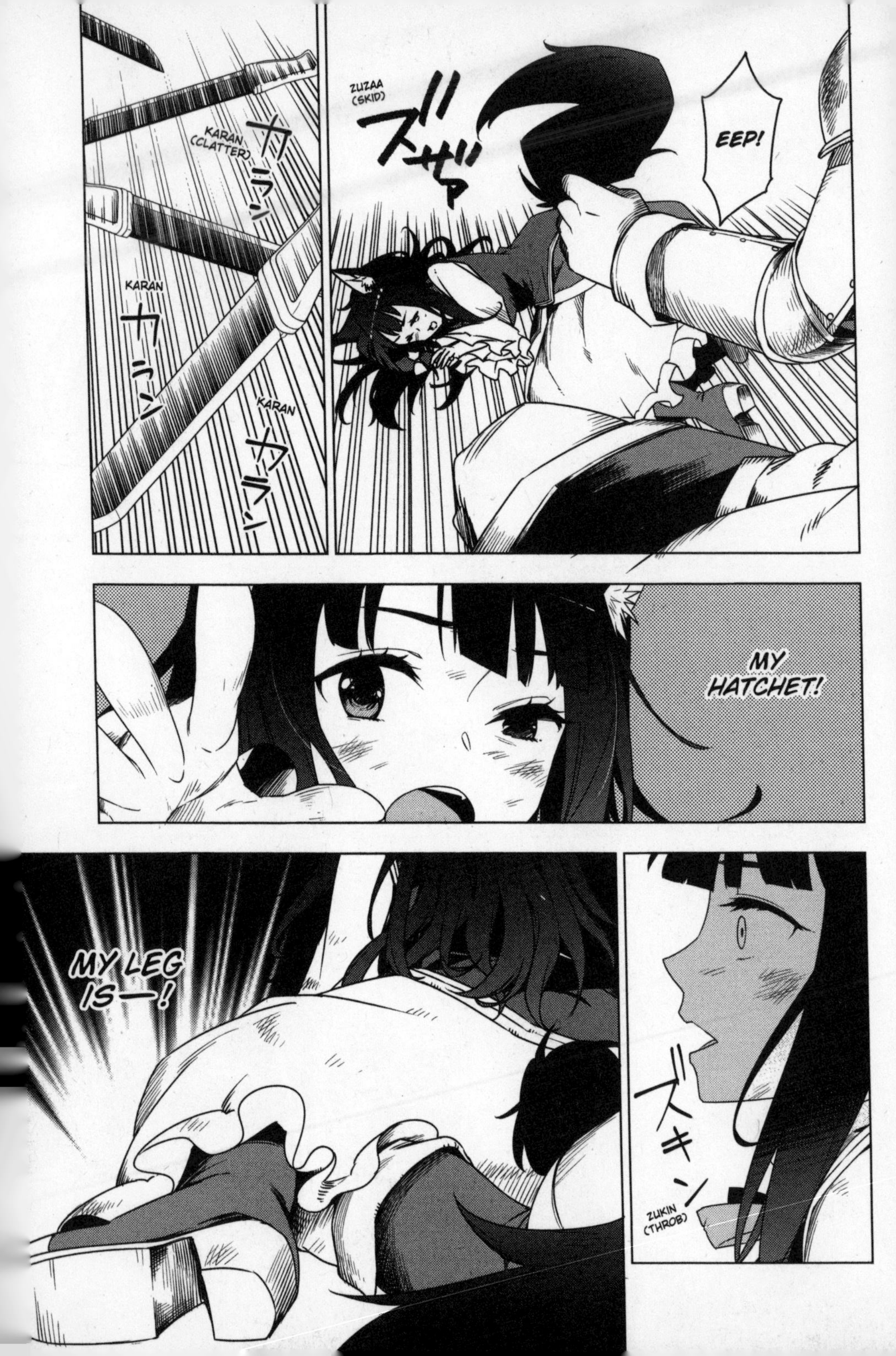
EEP!
ZUZAA (SKID)
ズザァ
KARAN (CLATTER)
カラン
KARAN
カラン
KARAN
カラン
MY HATCHET!
ズキン
ZUKIN (THROB)
MY LEG IS—!

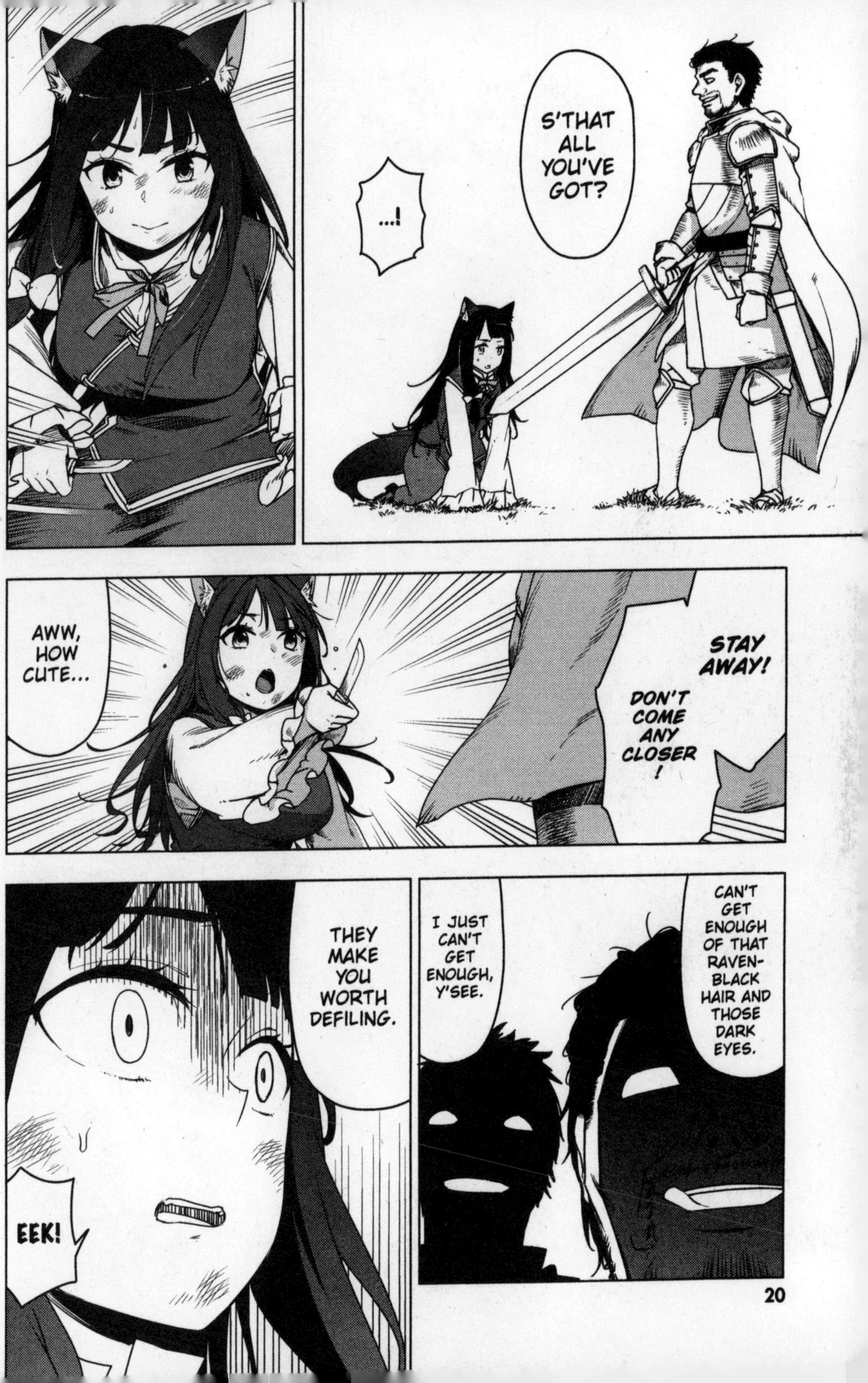
S'THAT ALL YOU'VE GOT?
...!
STAY AWAY!
DON'T COME ANY CLOSER!
AWW, HOW CUTE...
CAN'T GET ENOUGH OF THAT RAVEN-BLACK HAIR AND THOSE DARK EYES.
I JUST CAN'T GET ENOUGH, Y'SEE.
THEY MAKE YOU WORTH DEFILING.
EEK!

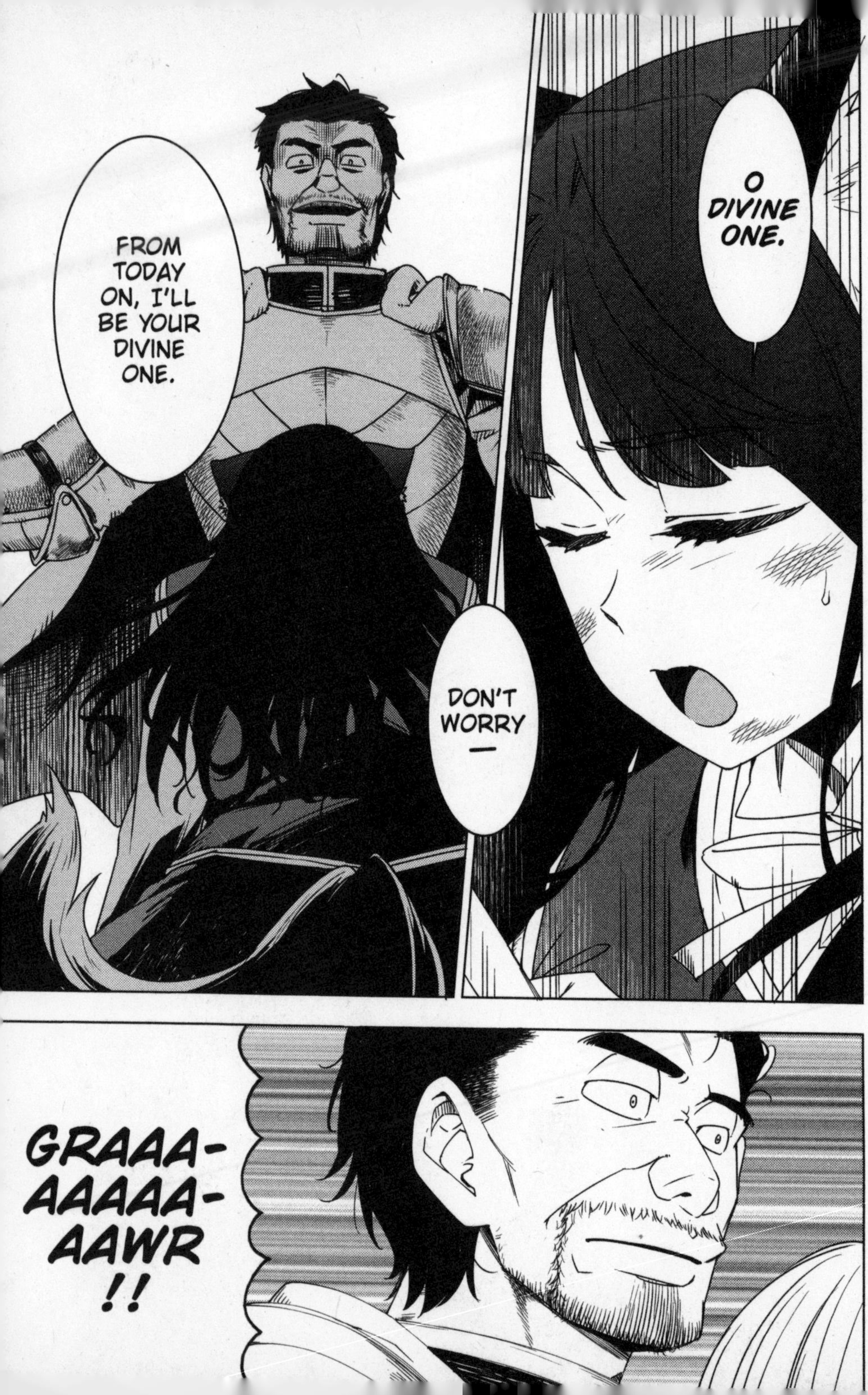
O DIVINE ONE.
DON'T WORRY —
FROM TODAY ON, I'LL BE YOUR DIVINE ONE.
GRAAA-AAAAA-AAWR!!

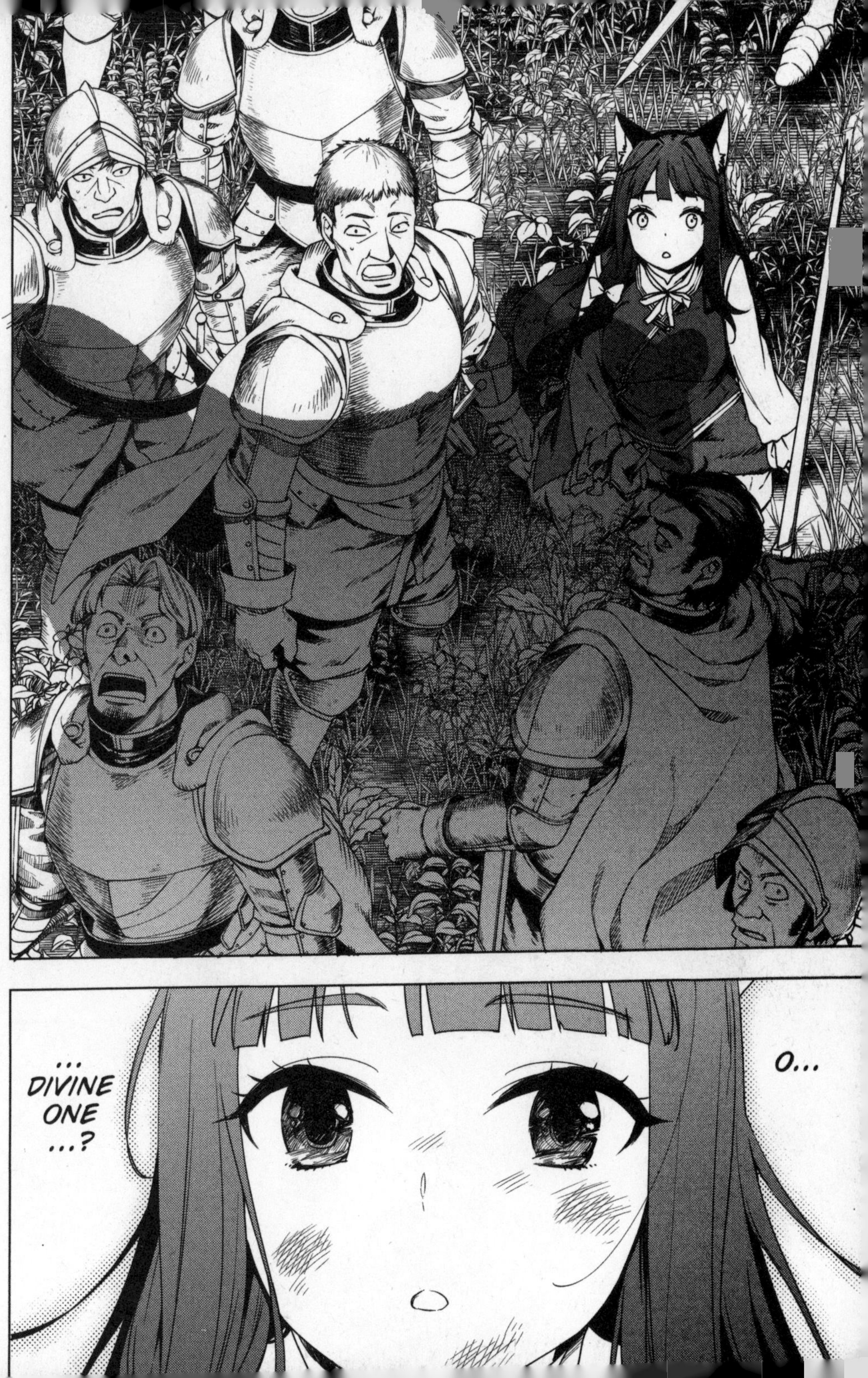
O...
...DIVINE ONE ...?

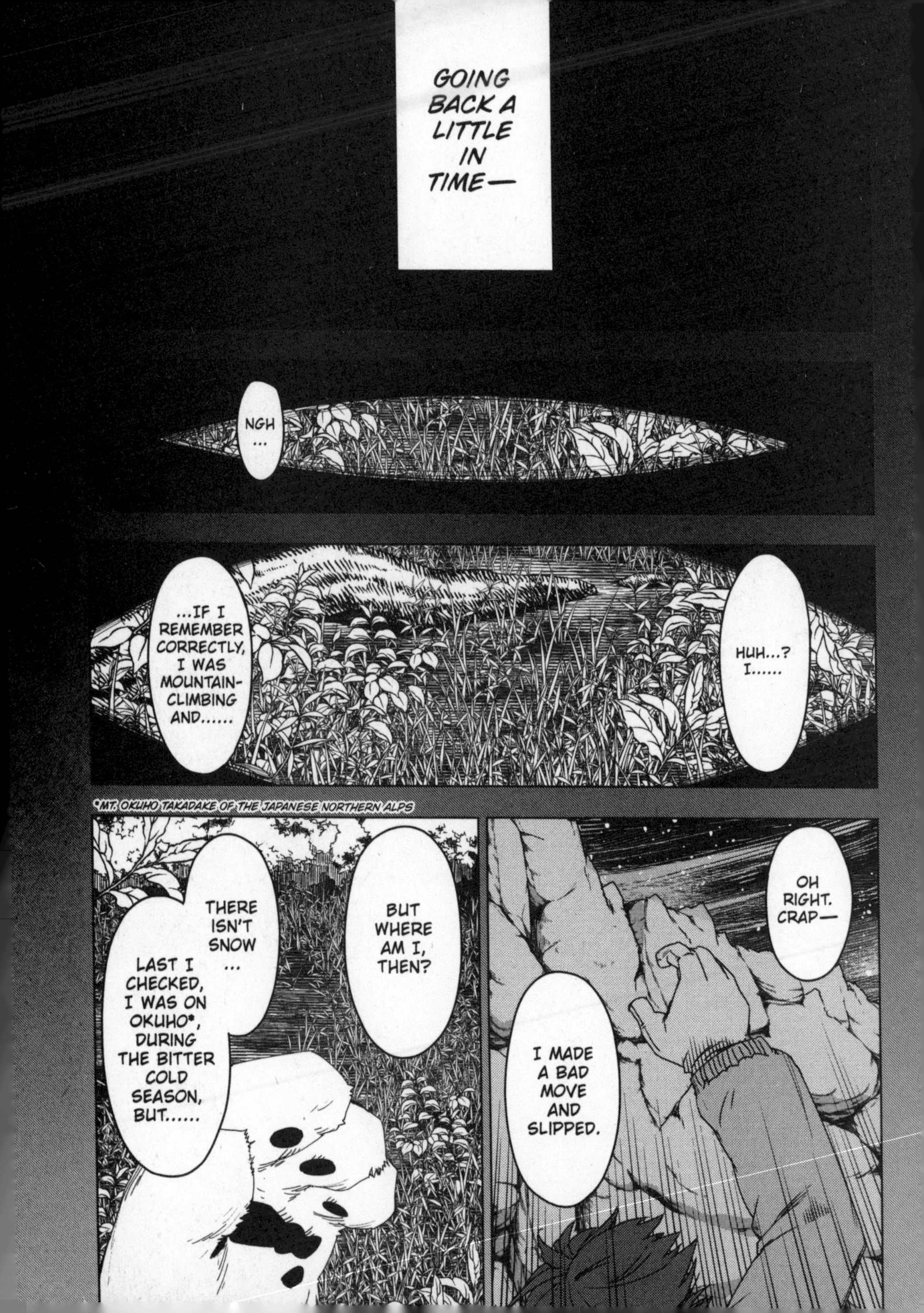
GOING BACK A LITTLE IN TIME—
NGH ...
HUH...? I......
...IF I REMEMBER CORRECTLY, I WAS MOUNTAIN-CLIMBING AND......
OH RIGHT. CRAP—
I MADE A BAD MOVE AND SLIPPED.
BUT WHERE AM I, THEN?
THERE ISN'T SNOW ...
LAST I CHECKED, I WAS ON OKUHO*, DURING THE BITTER COLD SEASON, BUT......
*MT. OKUHO TAKADAKE OF THE JAPANESE NORTHERN ALPS

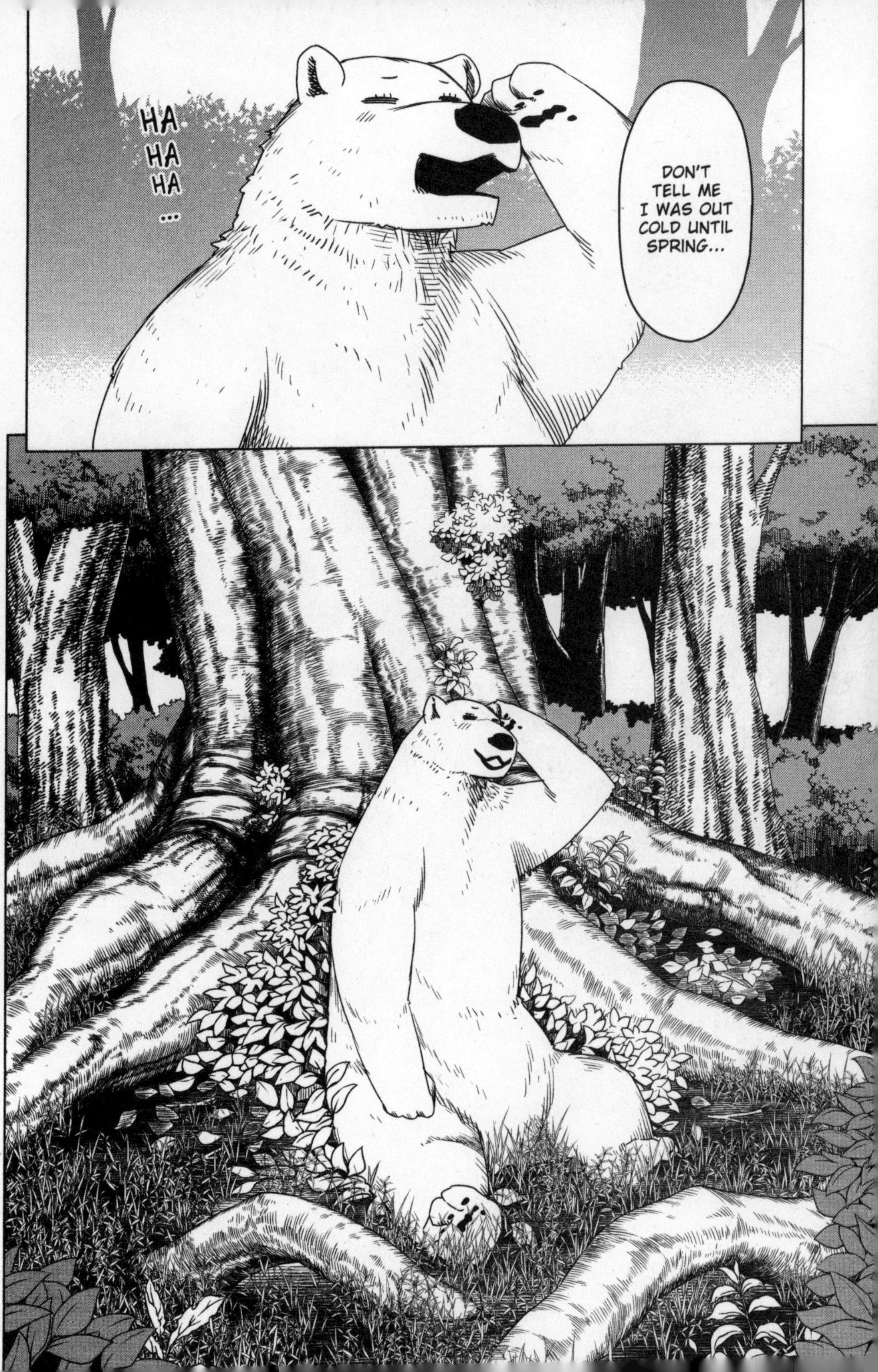
DON'T TELL ME I WAS OUT COLD UNTIL SPRING...
HA HA HA ...

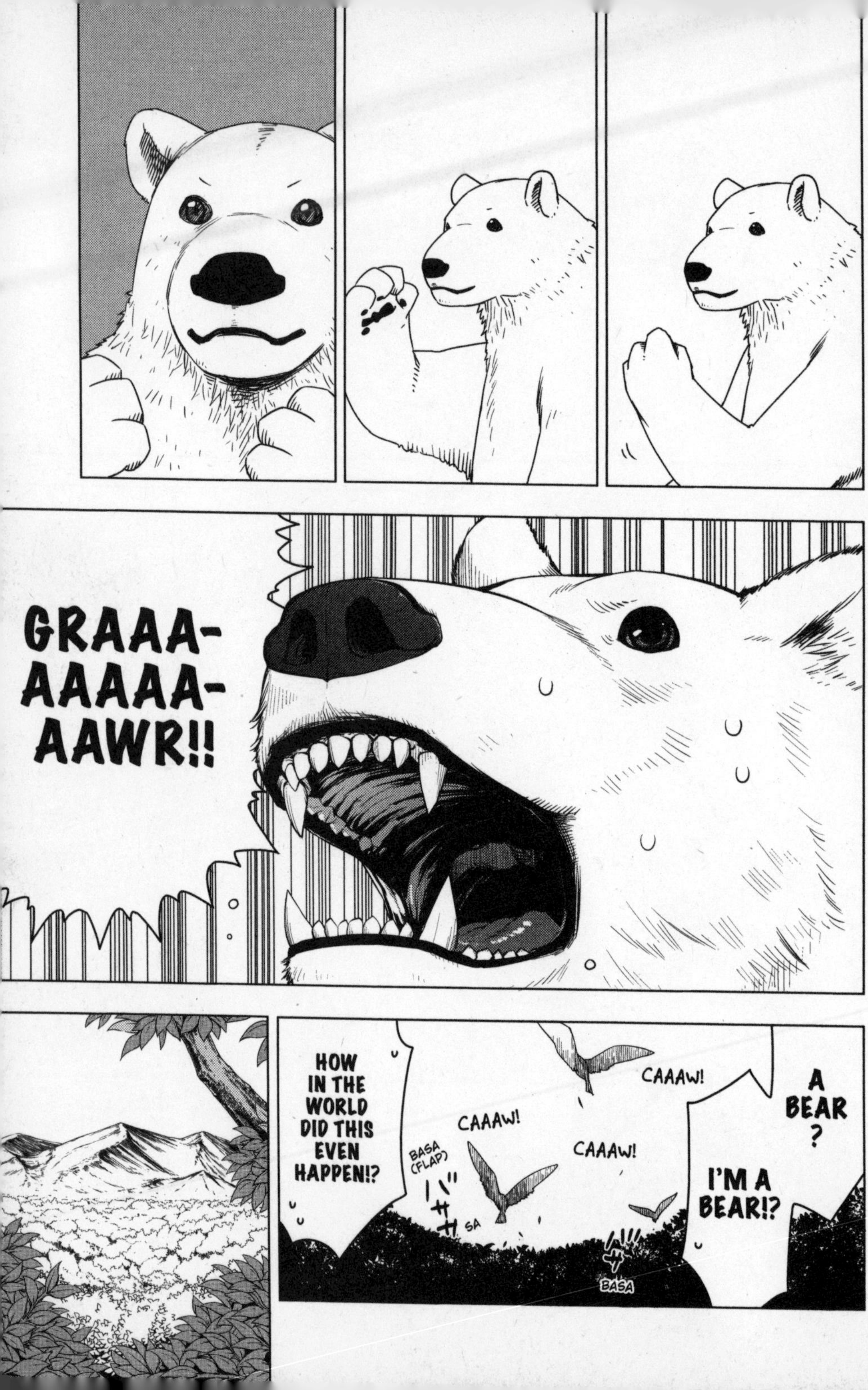
GRAAA-AAAAA-AAWR!!
A BEAR?
CAAAW!
I'M A BEAR!?
CAAAW!
CAAAW!
HOW IN THE WORLD DID THIS EVEN HAPPEN!?
BASA (FLAP)
SA
BASA

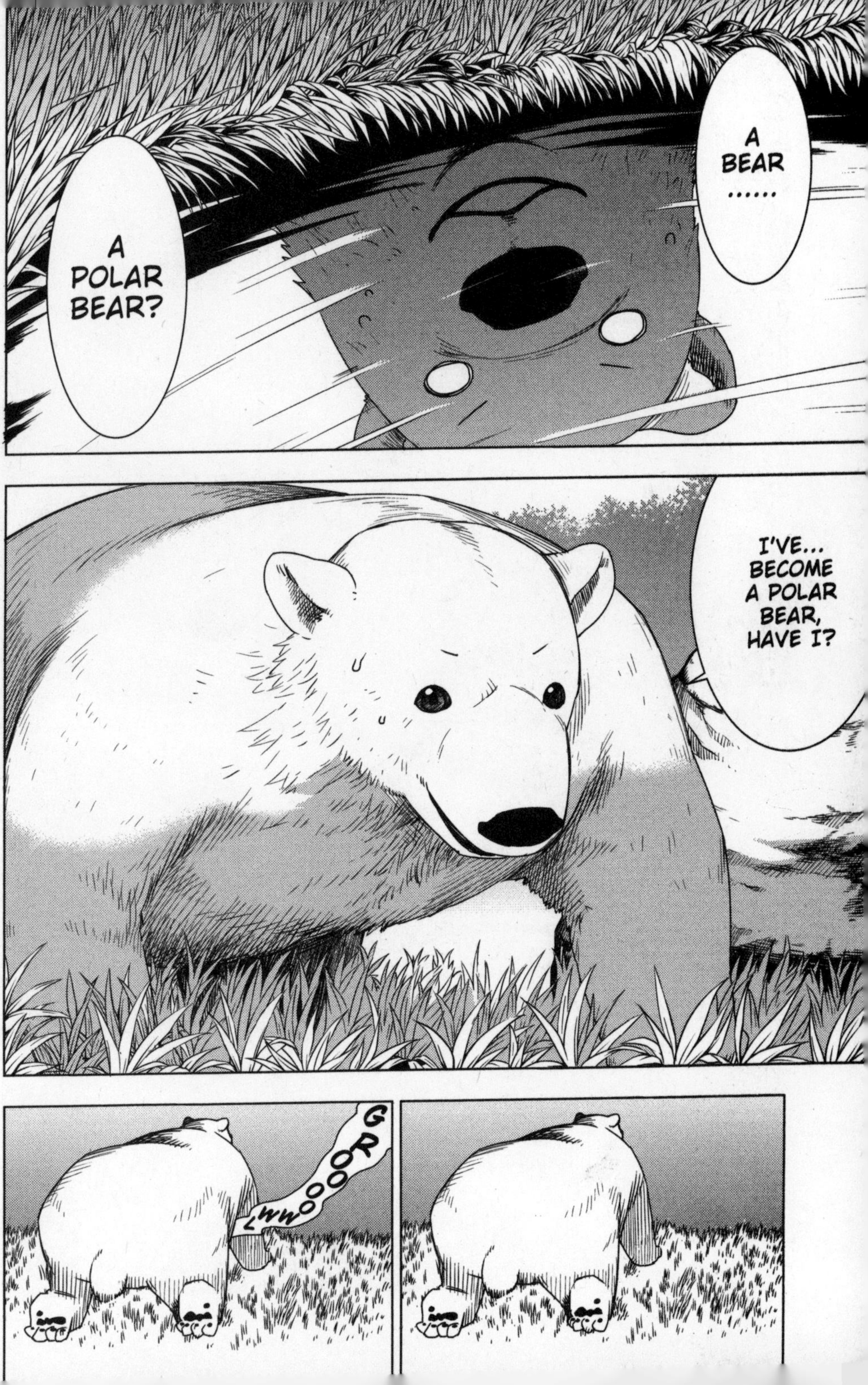
A BEAR ......
A POLAR BEAR?
I'VE... BECOME A POLAR BEAR, HAVE I?
GROOOOWW

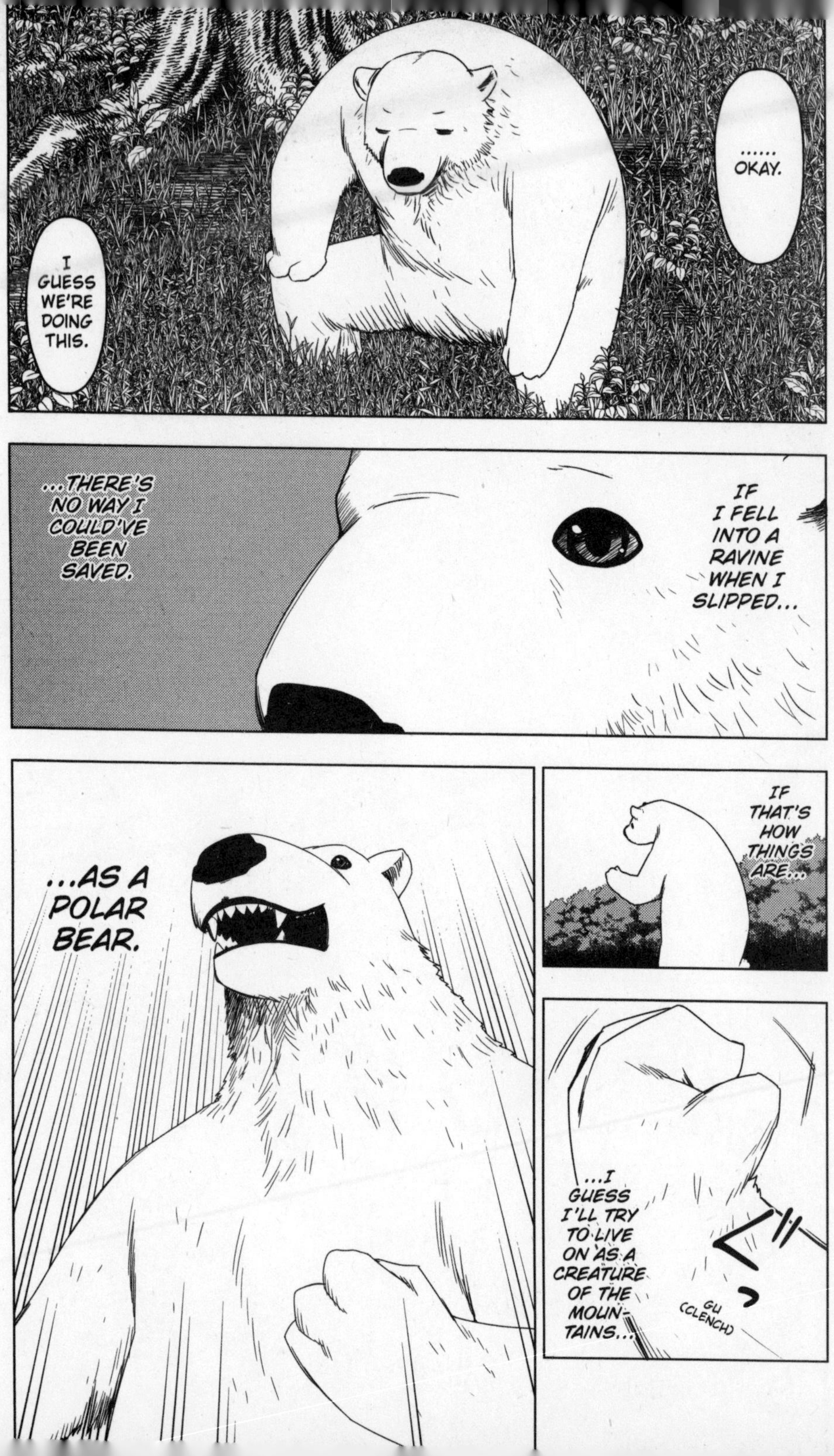
......OKAY.
I GUESS WE'RE DOING THIS.
IF I FELL INTO A RAVINE WHEN I SLIPPED...
...THERE'S NO WAY I COULD'VE BEEN SAVED.
IF THAT'S HOW THINGS ARE...
...I GUESS I'LL TRY TO LIVE ON AS A CREATURE OF THE MOUN-TAINS...
GU (CLENCH)
...AS A POLAR BEAR.

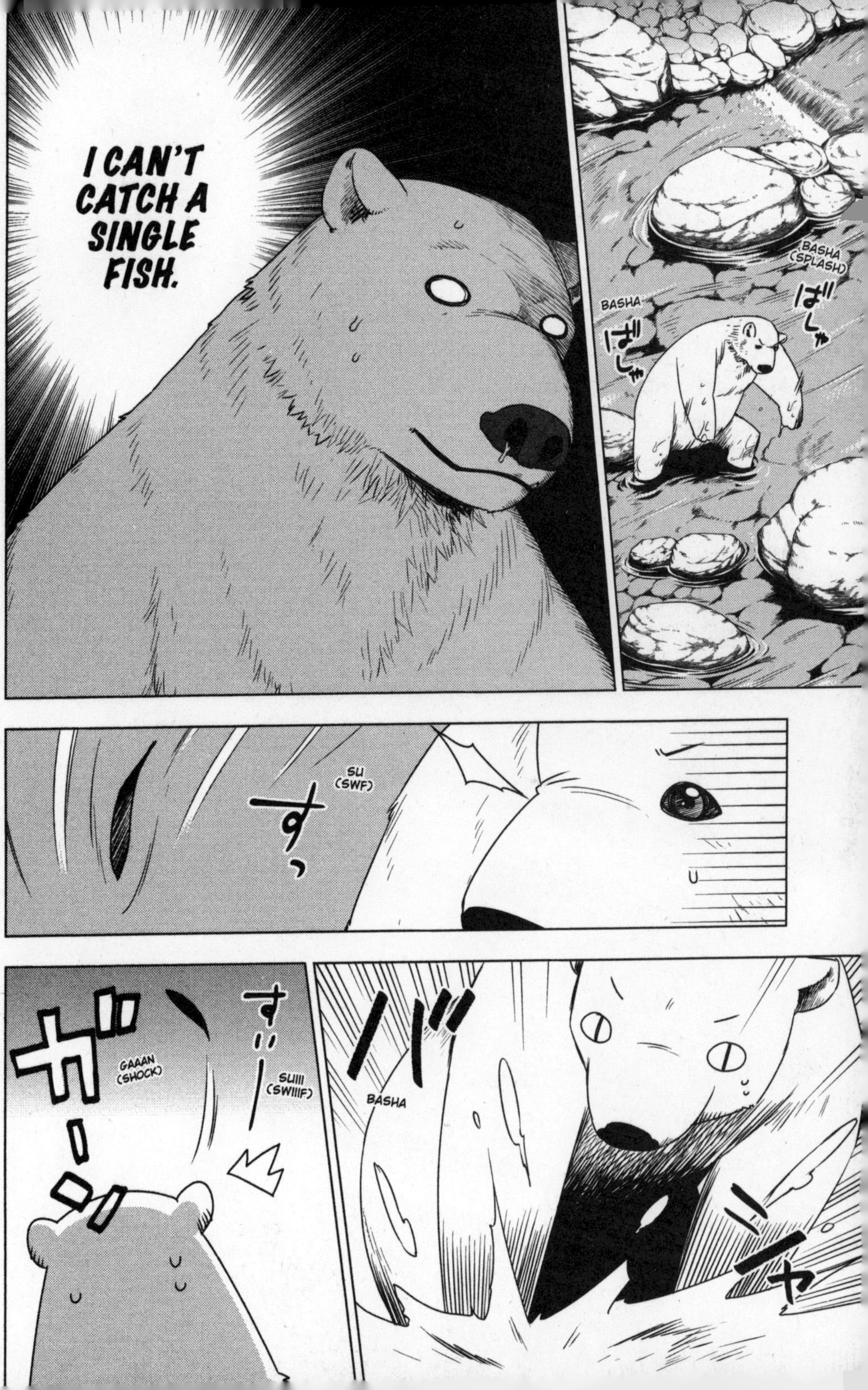
BASHA (SPLASH)
ばしゃ
BASHA
ばしゃ
I CAN'T CATCH A SINGLE FISH.
SU (SWF)
す
BASHA
バシャ
SUIII (SWIIIF)
すぃー
GAAAN (SHOCK)
ガーン

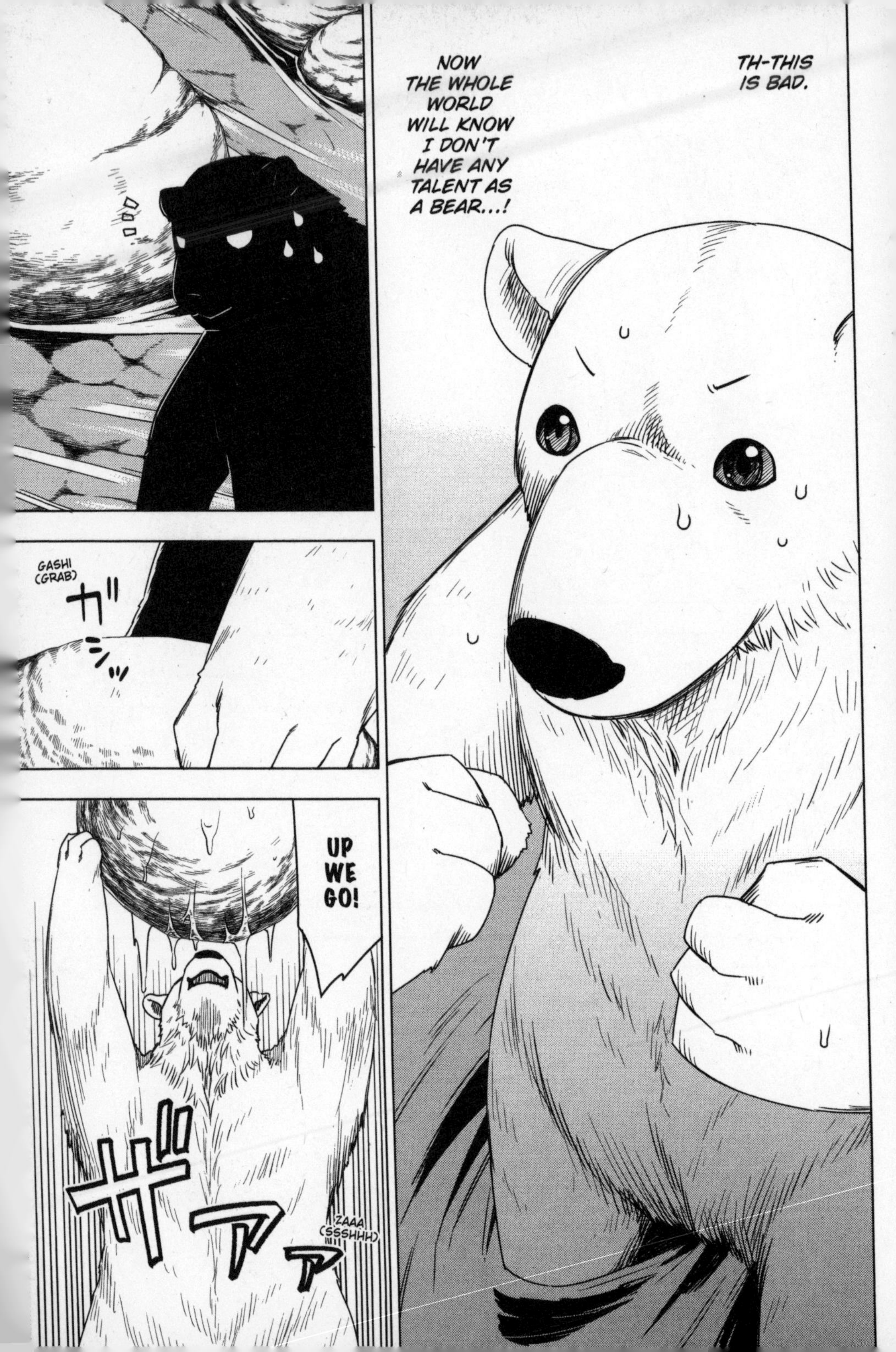
TH-THIS IS BAD.
NOW THE WHOLE WORLD WILL KNOW I DON'T HAVE ANY TALENT AS A BEAR...!
GASHI (GRAB)
ガシッ
UP WE GO!
ザァァ
ZAAA (SSSHHH)

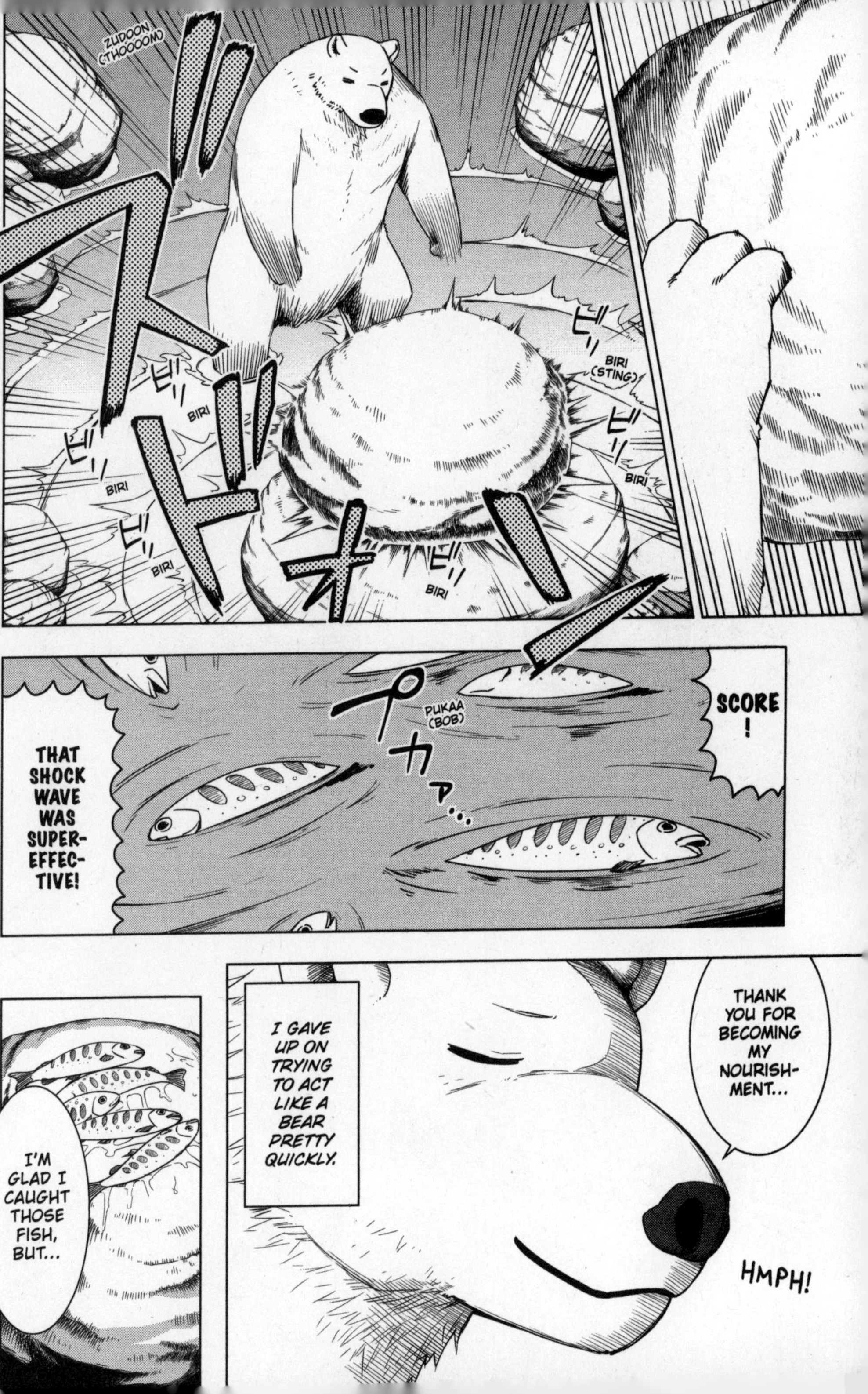
ZUDOON (THOOOOM)
BIRI (STING)
BIRI
BIRI
BIRI
BIRI
BIRI
SCORE!
PUKAA (BOB)
THAT SHOCK WAVE WAS SUPER-EFFECTIVE!
THANK YOU FOR BECOMING MY NOURISHMENT...
I GAVE UP ON TRYING TO ACT LIKE A BEAR PRETTY QUICKLY.
HMPH!
I'M GLAD I CAUGHT THOSE FISH, BUT...

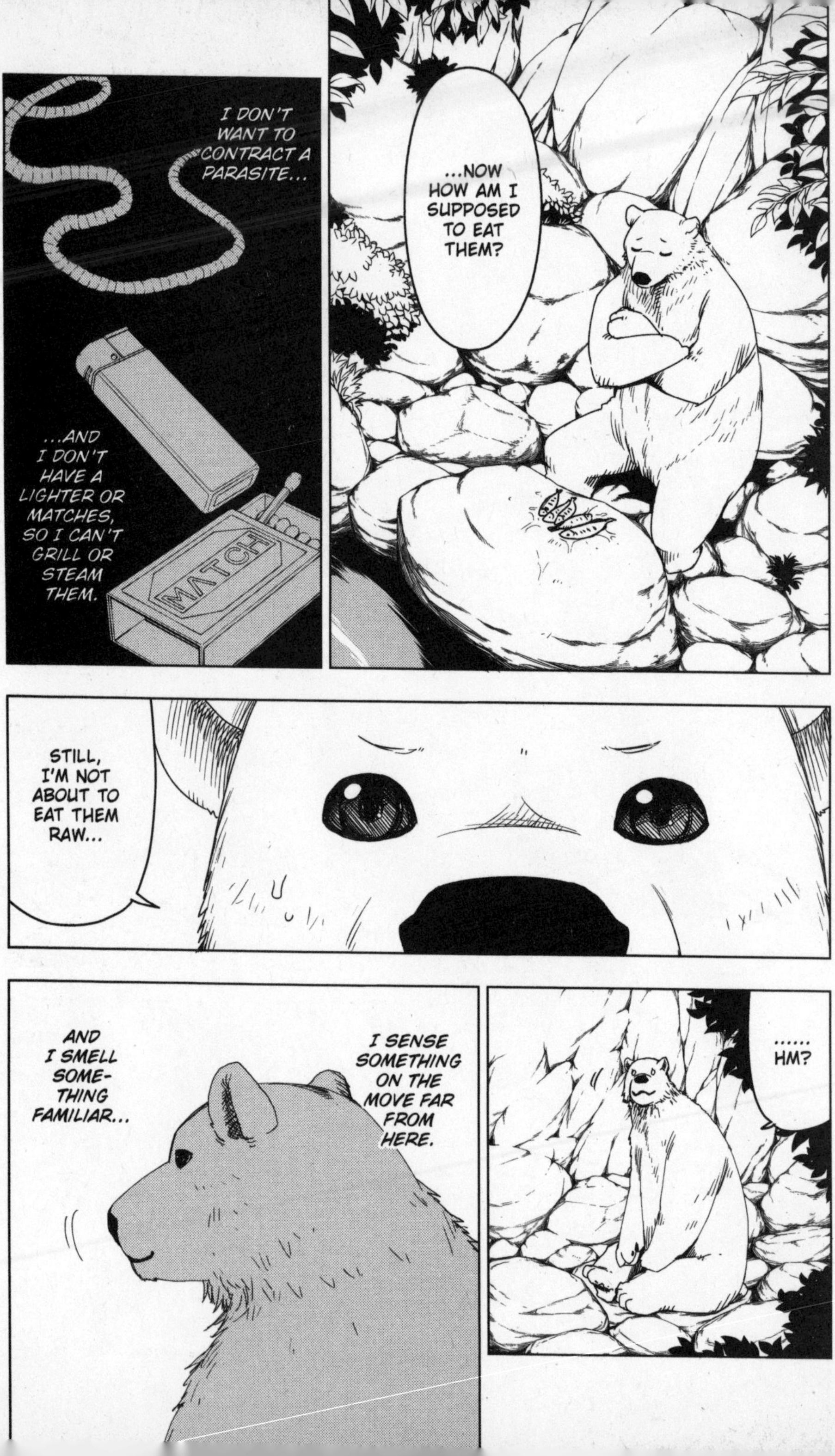
...NOW HOW AM I SUPPOSED TO EAT THEM?
I DON'T WANT TO CONTRACT A PARASITE...
...AND I DON'T HAVE A LIGHTER OR MATCHES, SO I CAN'T GRILL OR STEAM THEM.
MATCH
STILL, I'M NOT ABOUT TO EAT THEM RAW...
......HM?
I SENSE SOMETHING ON THE MOVE FAR FROM HERE.
AND I SMELL SOME-THING FAMILIAR...

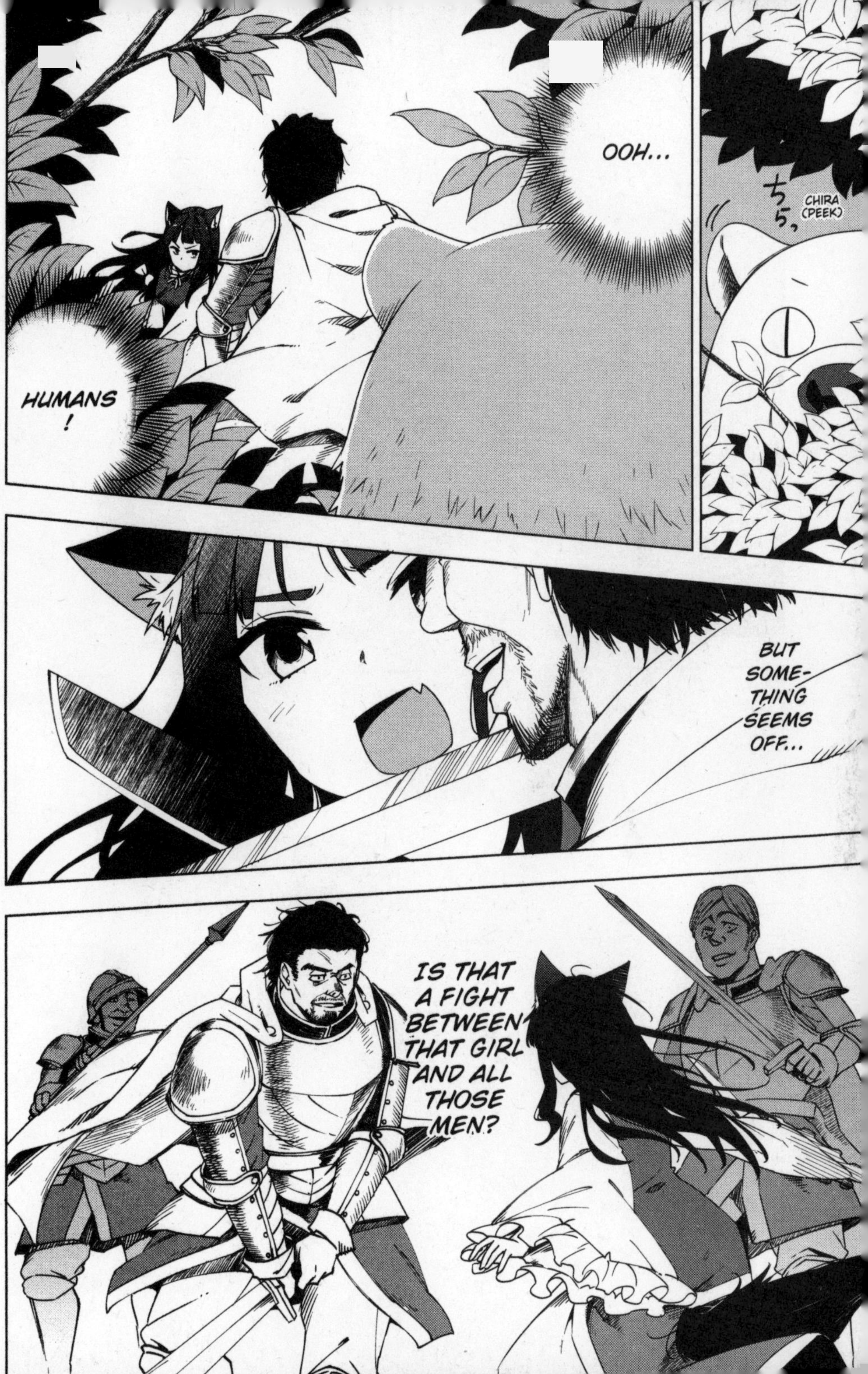
ちら
CHIRA (PEEK)
OOH...
HUMANS!
BUT SOMETHING SEEMS OFF...
IS THAT A FIGHT BETWEEN THAT GIRL AND ALL THOSE MEN?

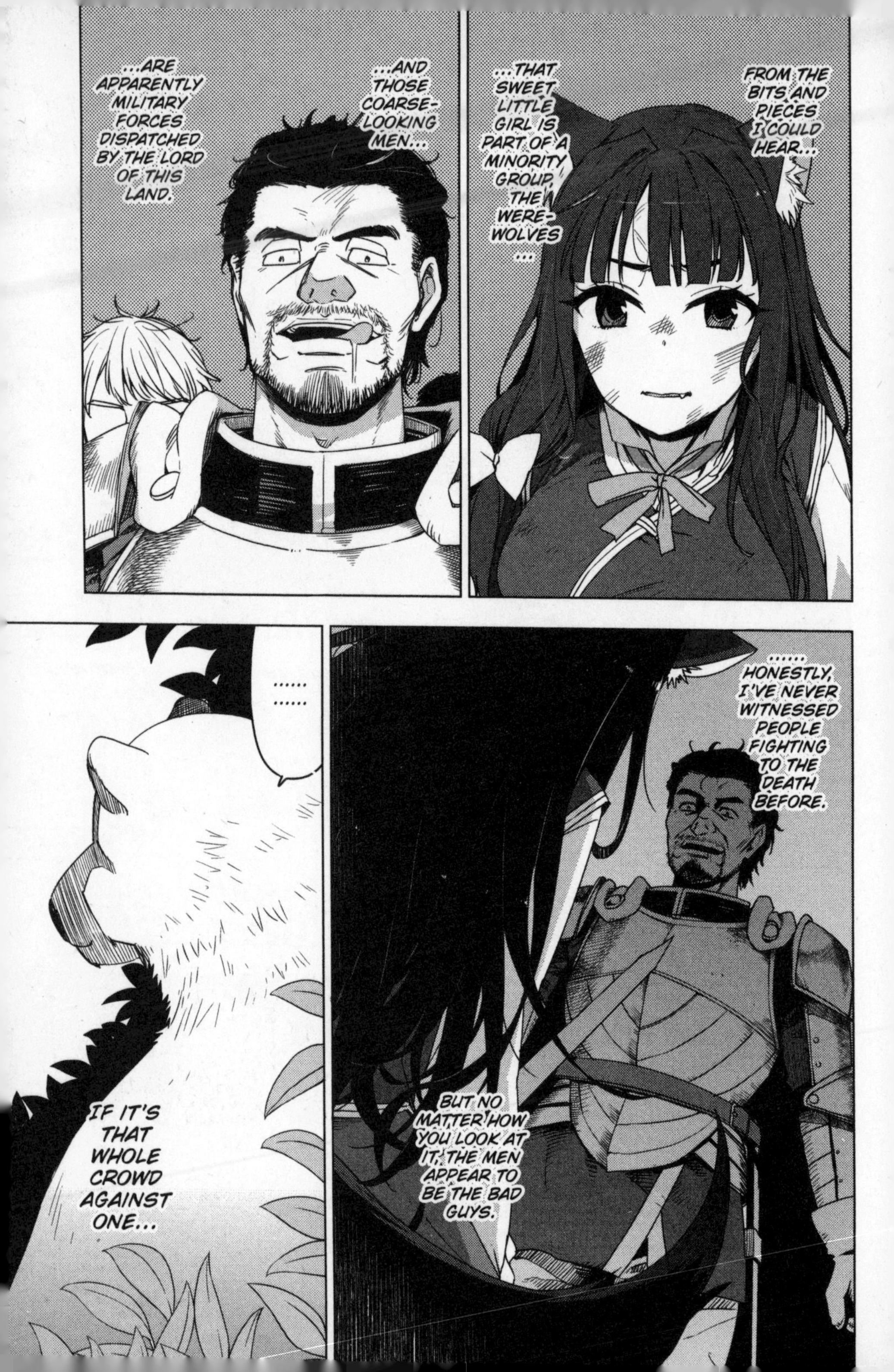
FROM THE BITS AND PIECES I COULD HEAR...
...THAT SWEET LITTLE GIRL IS PART OF A MINORITY GROUP, THE WEREWOLVES...
...AND THOSE COARSE-LOOKING MEN...
...ARE APPARENTLY MILITARY FORCES DISPATCHED BY THE LORD OF THIS LAND.
......
HONESTLY, I'VE NEVER WITNESSED PEOPLE FIGHTING TO THE DEATH BEFORE.
BUT NO MATTER HOW YOU LOOK AT IT, THE MEN APPEAR TO BE THE BAD GUYS.
......
......
IF IT'S THAT WHOLE CROWD AGAINST ONE...

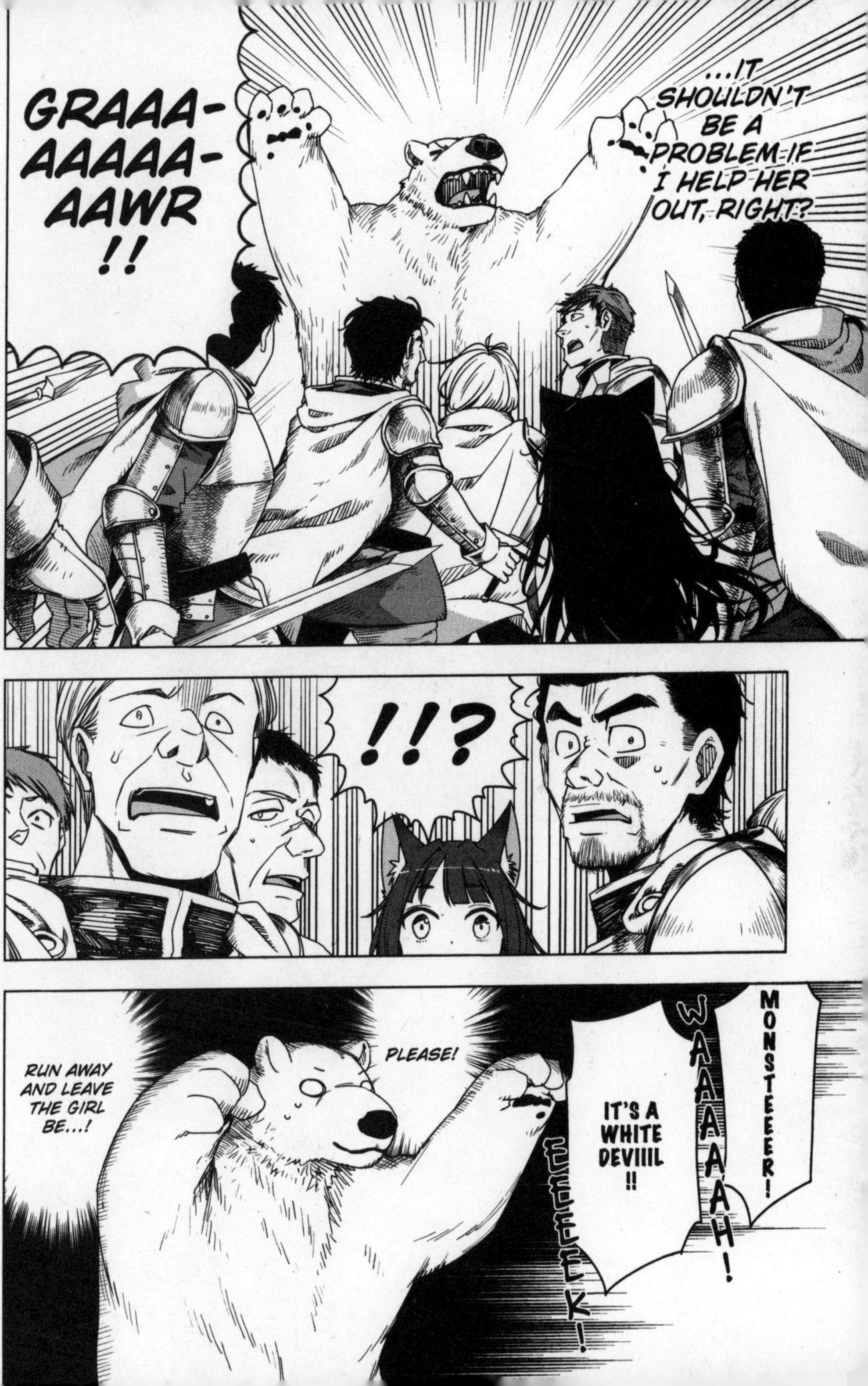
...IT SHOULDN'T BE A PROBLEM IF I HELP HER OUT, RIGHT?
GRAAA-AAAAA-AAWR!!
!!?
MONSTEEER!
WAAAAAAH!
IT'S A WHITE DEVIIIL!!
EEEEEK!
PLEASE!
RUN AWAY AND LEAVE THE GIRL BE...!

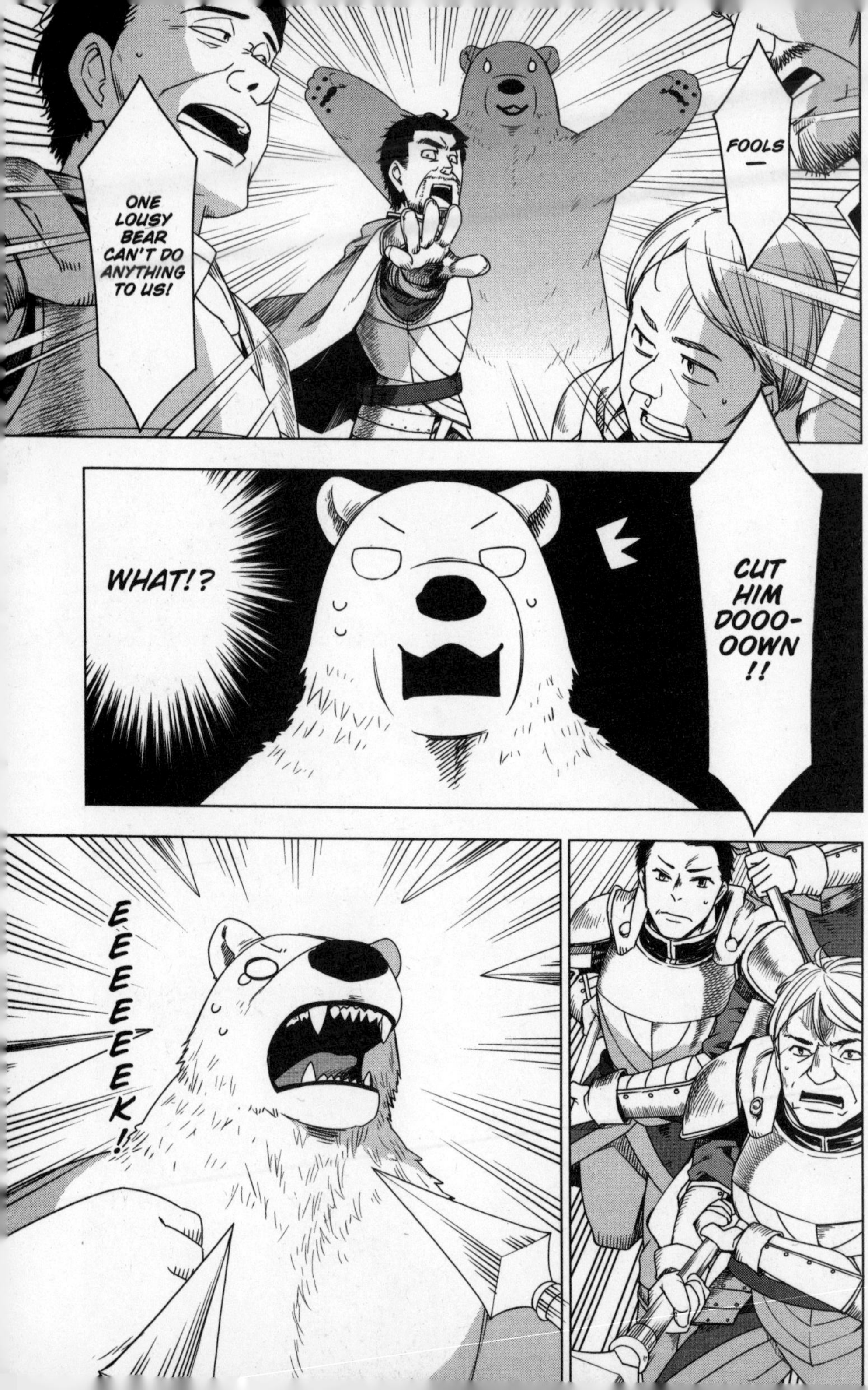
FOOLS —
ONE LOUSY BEAR CAN'T DO ANYTHING TO US!
CUT HIM DOOOOOWN!!
WHAT!?
EEEEEEK!

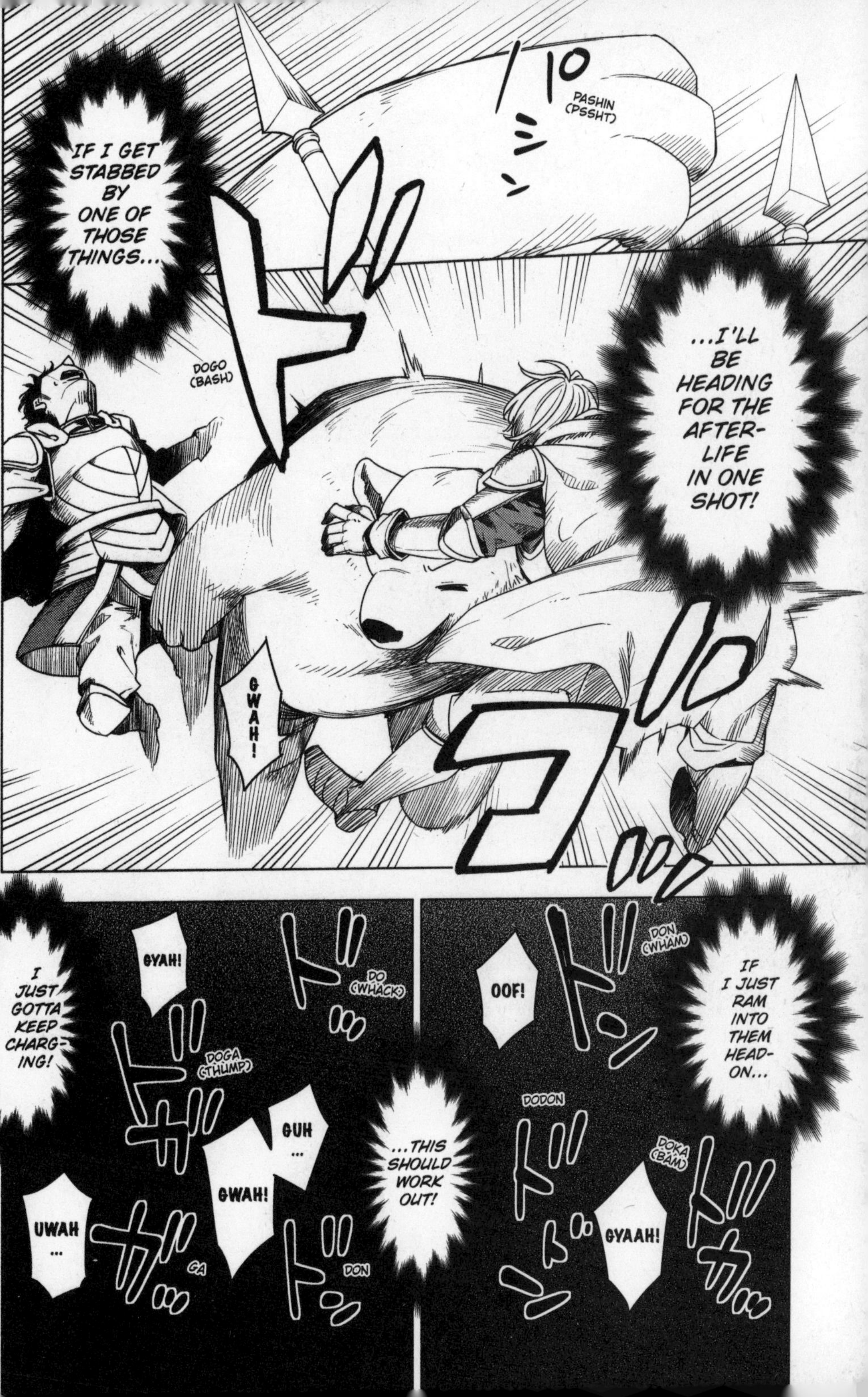
PASHIN (PSSHT)
IF I GET STABBED BY ONE OF THOSE THINGS...
...I'LL BE HEADING FOR THE AFTER-LIFE IN ONE SHOT!
DOGO (BASH)
GWAH!
DON (WHAM)
IF I JUST RAM INTO THEM HEAD-ON...
OOF!
DODON
DOKA (BAM)
GYAAH!
...THIS SHOULD WORK OUT!
DO (WHACK)
GYAH!
I JUST GOTTA KEEP CHARG-ING!
DOGA (THUMP)
GUH...
GWAH!
DON
UWAH...
GA

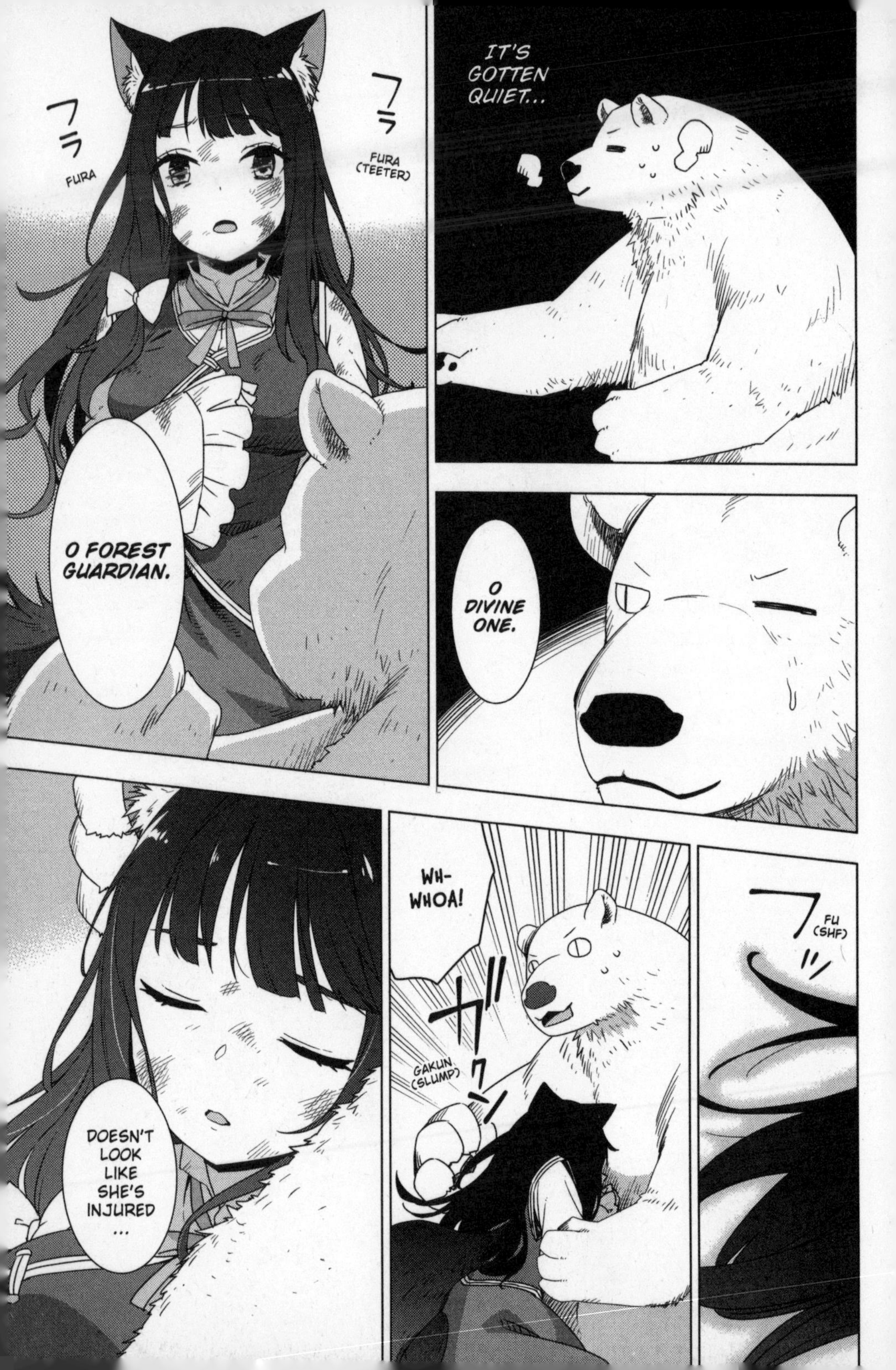

IT'S GOTTEN QUIET...
O DIVINE ONE.
フラ
FURA (TEETER)
フラ
FURA
O FOREST GUARDIAN.
フッ
FU (SHF)
WH- WHOA!
ガクン
GAKUN (SLUMP)
DOESN'T LOOK LIKE SHE'S INJURED ...

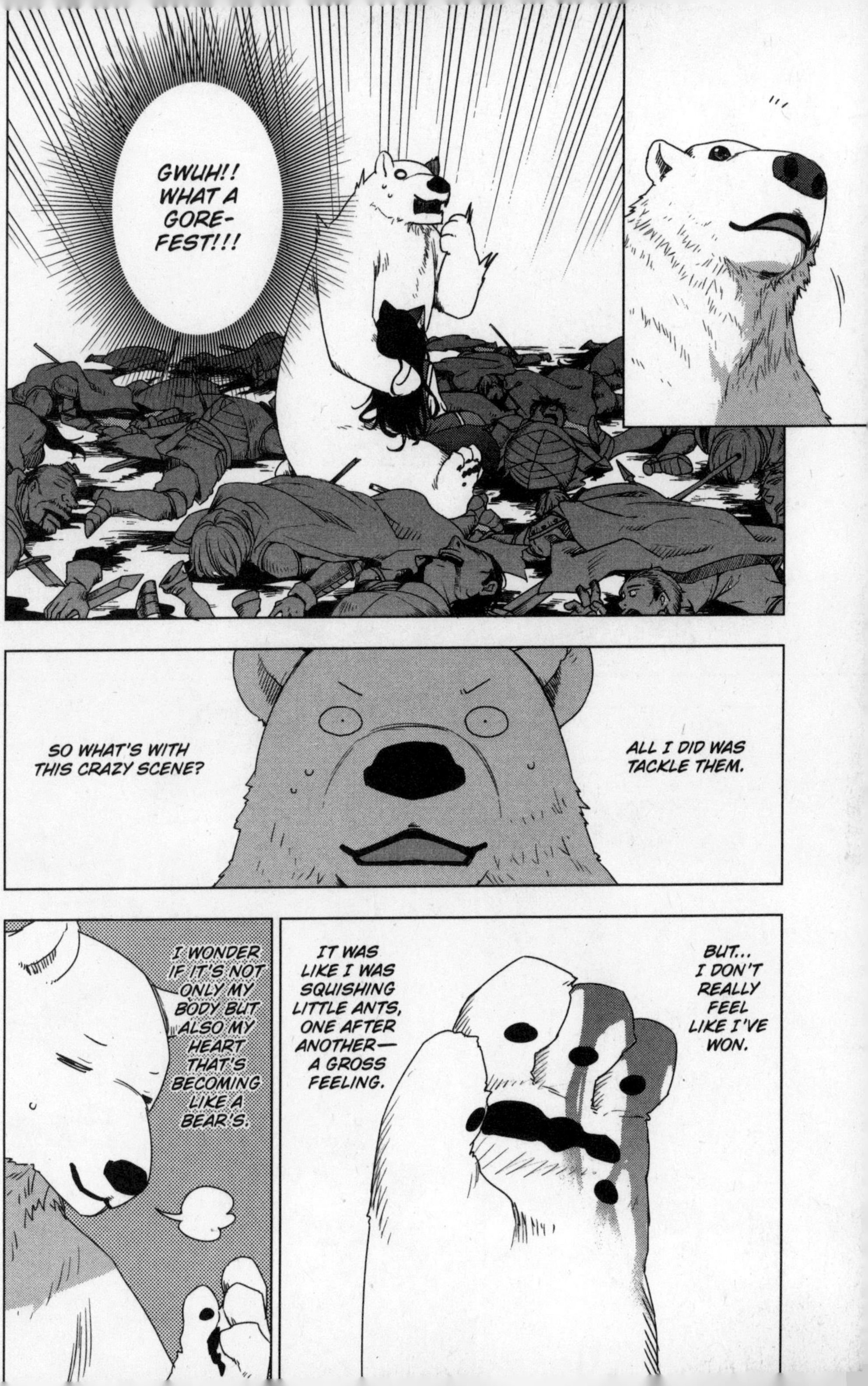
GWUH!! WHAT A GORE-FEST!!!
ALL I DID WAS TACKLE THEM.
SO WHAT'S WITH THIS CRAZY SCENE?
BUT... I DON'T REALLY FEEL LIKE I'VE WON.
IT WAS LIKE I WAS SQUISHING LITTLE ANTS, ONE AFTER ANOTHER— A GROSS FEELING.
I WONDER IF IT'S NOT ONLY MY BODY BUT ALSO MY HEART THAT'S BECOMING LIKE A BEAR'S.

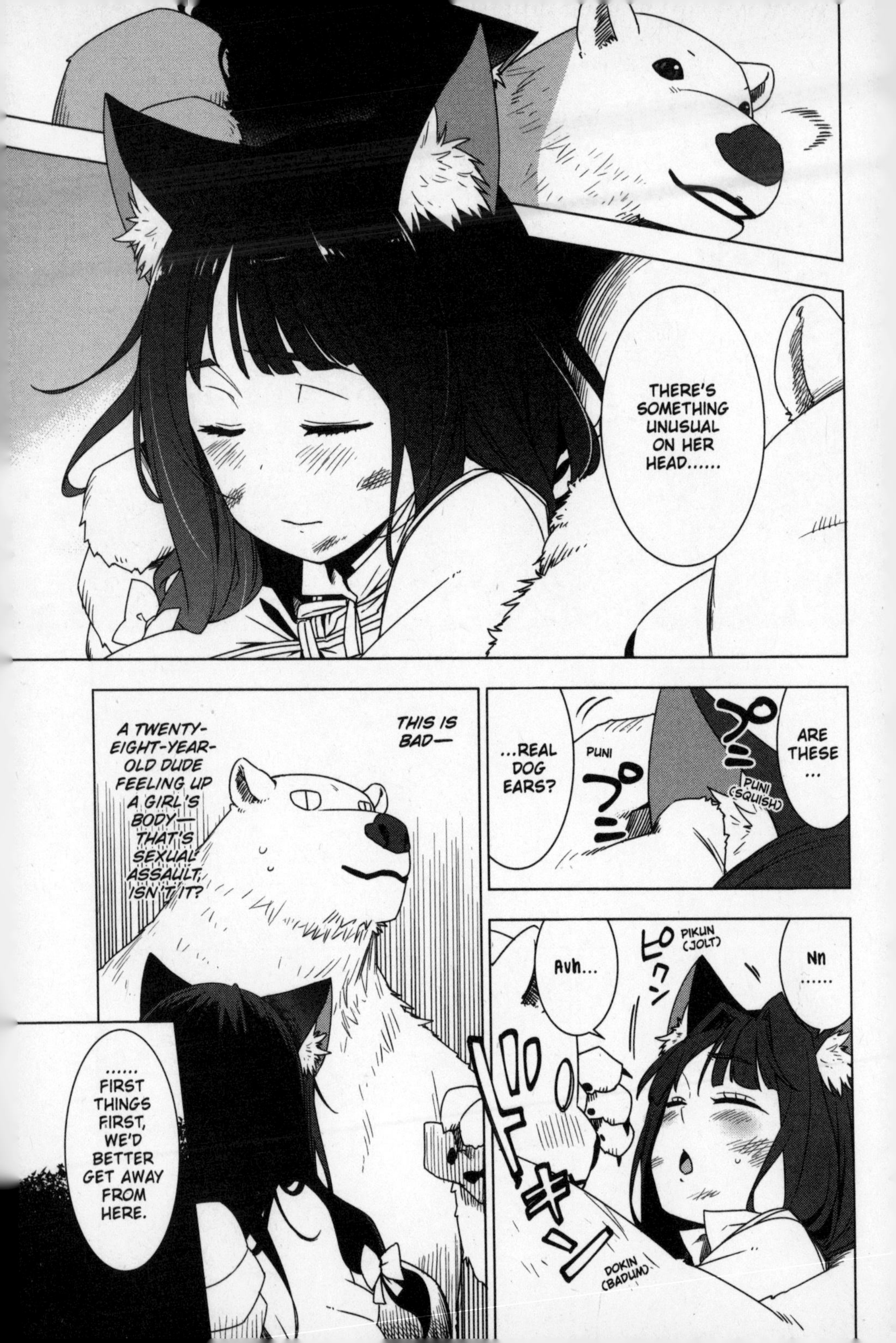
THERE'S SOMETHING UNUSUAL ON HER HEAD......
ARE THESE ...
プニ
PUNI (SQUISH)
PUNI
プニ
...REAL DOG EARS?
Nn ......
ピクン
PIKUN (JOLT)
Auh...
ドキン
DOKIN (BADUM)
THIS IS BAD—
A TWENTY-EIGHT-YEAR-OLD DUDE FEELING UP A GIRL'S BODY—THAT'S SEXUAL ASSAULT, ISN'T IT?
......FIRST THINGS FIRST, WE'D BETTER GET AWAY FROM HERE.

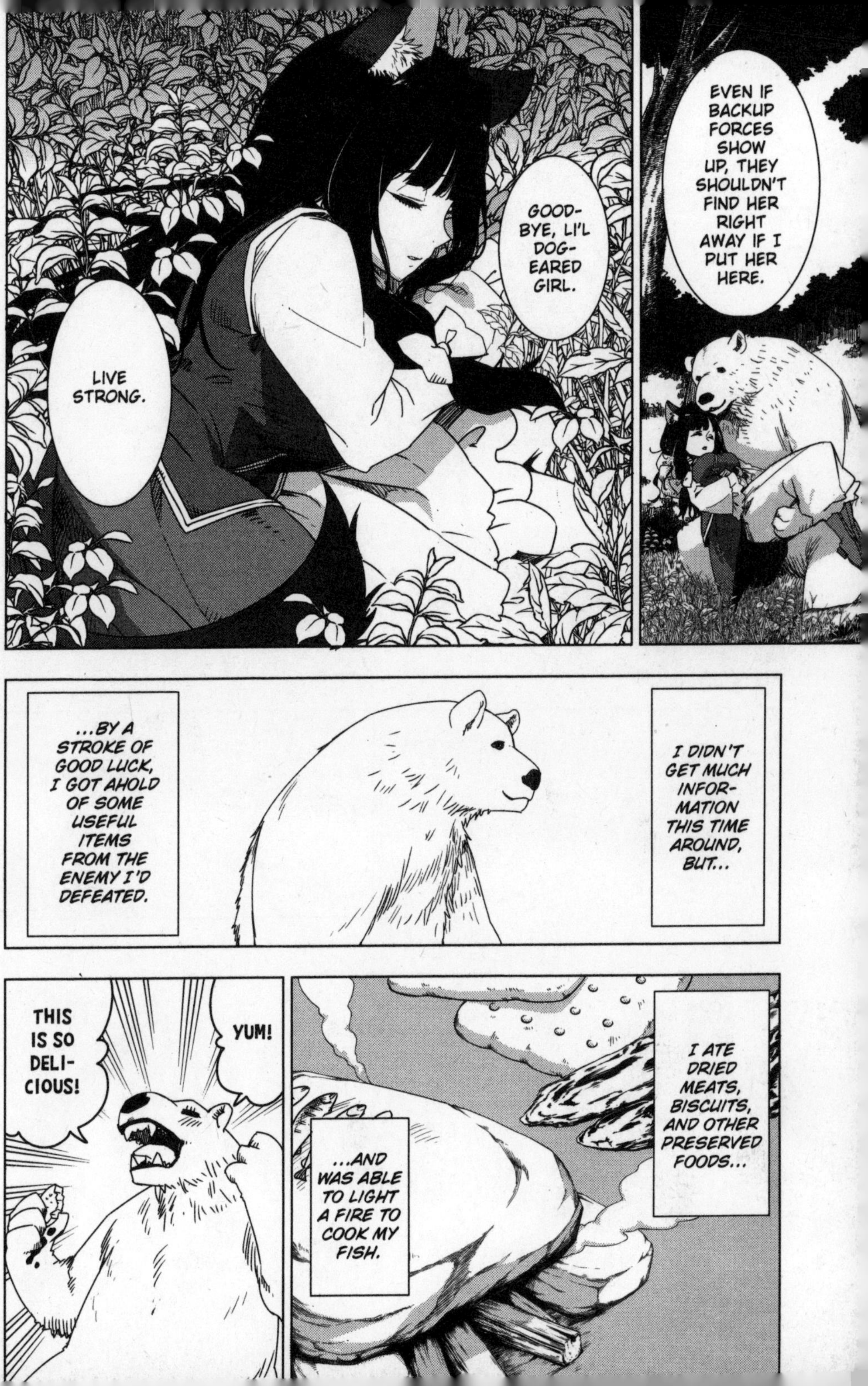
EVEN IF BACKUP FORCES SHOW UP, THEY SHOULDN'T FIND HER RIGHT AWAY IF I PUT HER HERE.
GOOD-BYE, LI'L DOG-EARED GIRL.
LIVE STRONG.
I DIDN'T GET MUCH INFORMATION THIS TIME AROUND, BUT...
...BY A STROKE OF GOOD LUCK, I GOT AHOLD OF SOME USEFUL ITEMS FROM THE ENEMY I'D DEFEATED.
I ATE DRIED MEATS, BISCUITS, AND OTHER PRESERVED FOODS...
...AND WAS ABLE TO LIGHT A FIRE TO COOK MY FISH.
YUM!
THIS IS SO DELICIOUS!

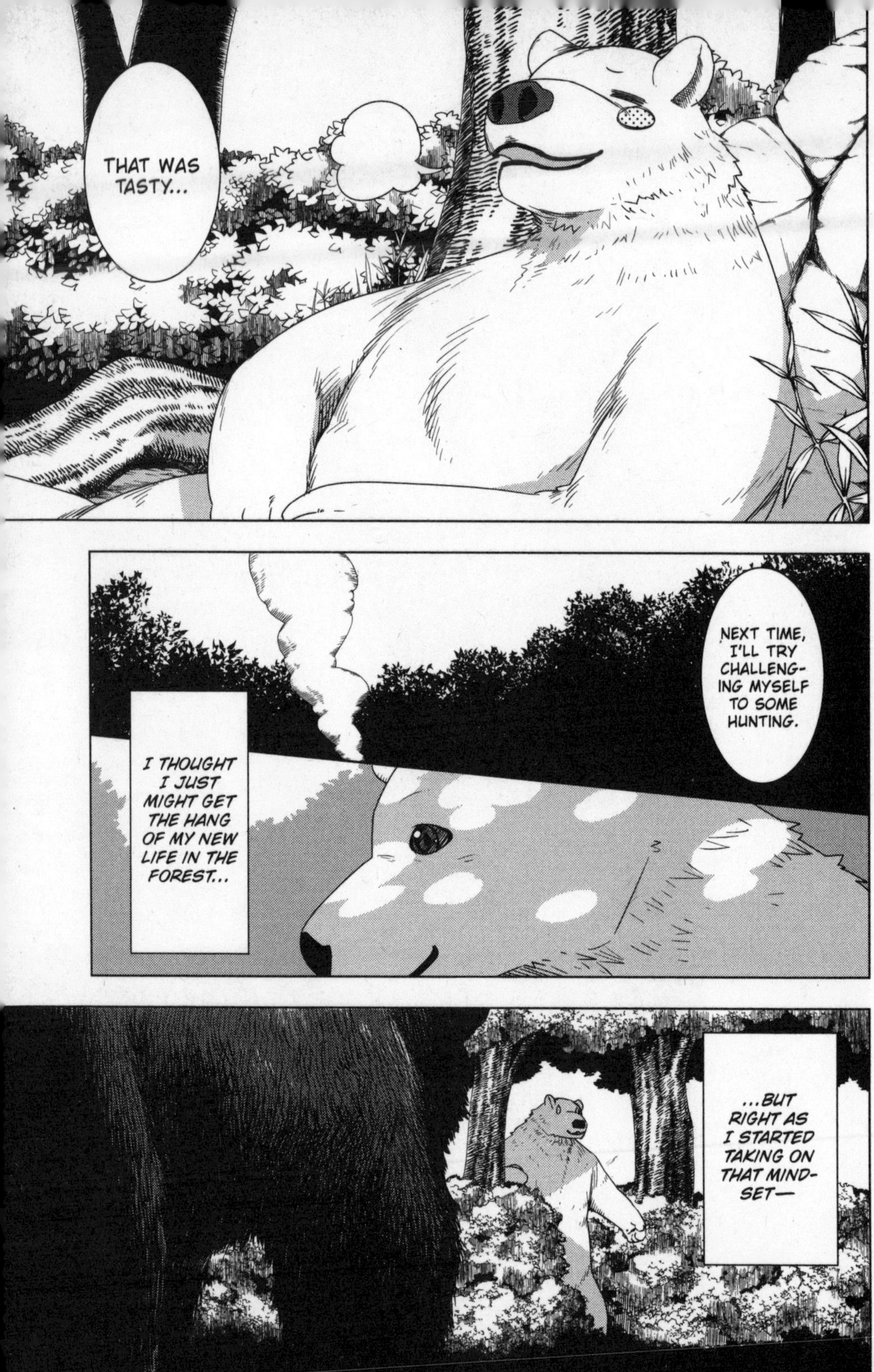
THAT WAS TASTY...
NEXT TIME, I'LL TRY CHALLENGING MYSELF TO SOME HUNTING.
I THOUGHT I JUST MIGHT GET THE HANG OF MY NEW LIFE IN THE FOREST...
...BUT RIGHT AS I STARTED TAKING ON THAT MINDSET—

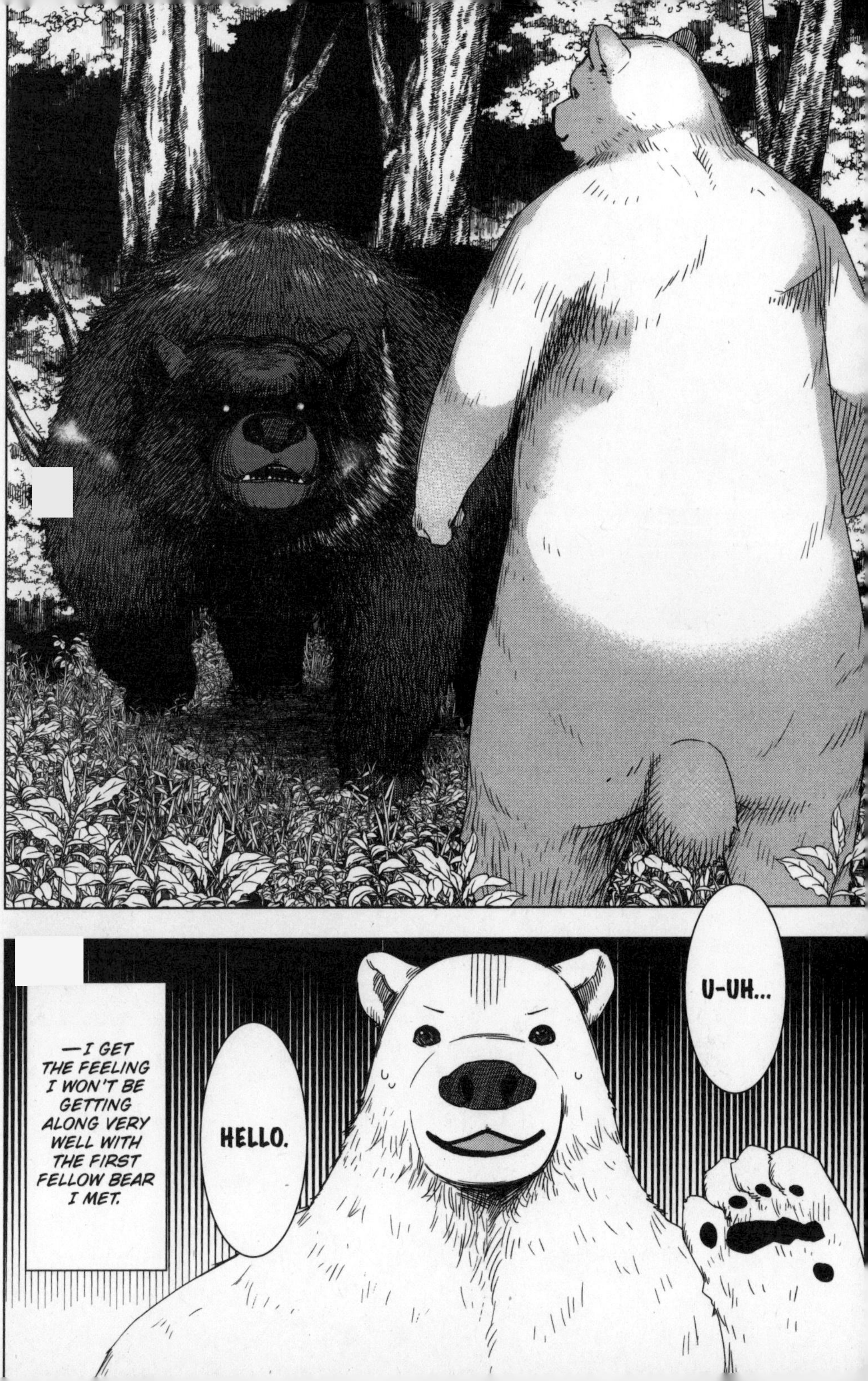
U-UH...
HELLO.
—I GET THE FEELING I WON'T BE GETTING ALONG VERY WELL WITH THE FIRST FELLOW BEAR I MET.

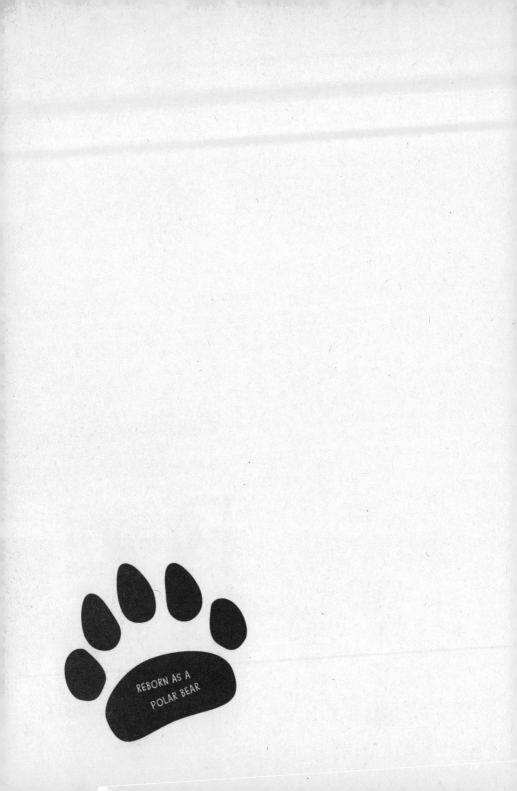

REBORN AS A
POLAR BEAR

Reborn as a Polar Bear

The Legend of How I Became a Forest Guardian

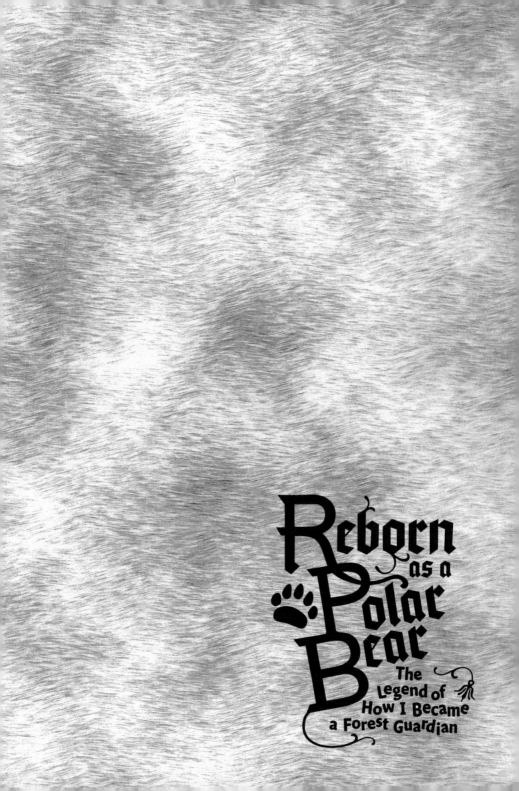

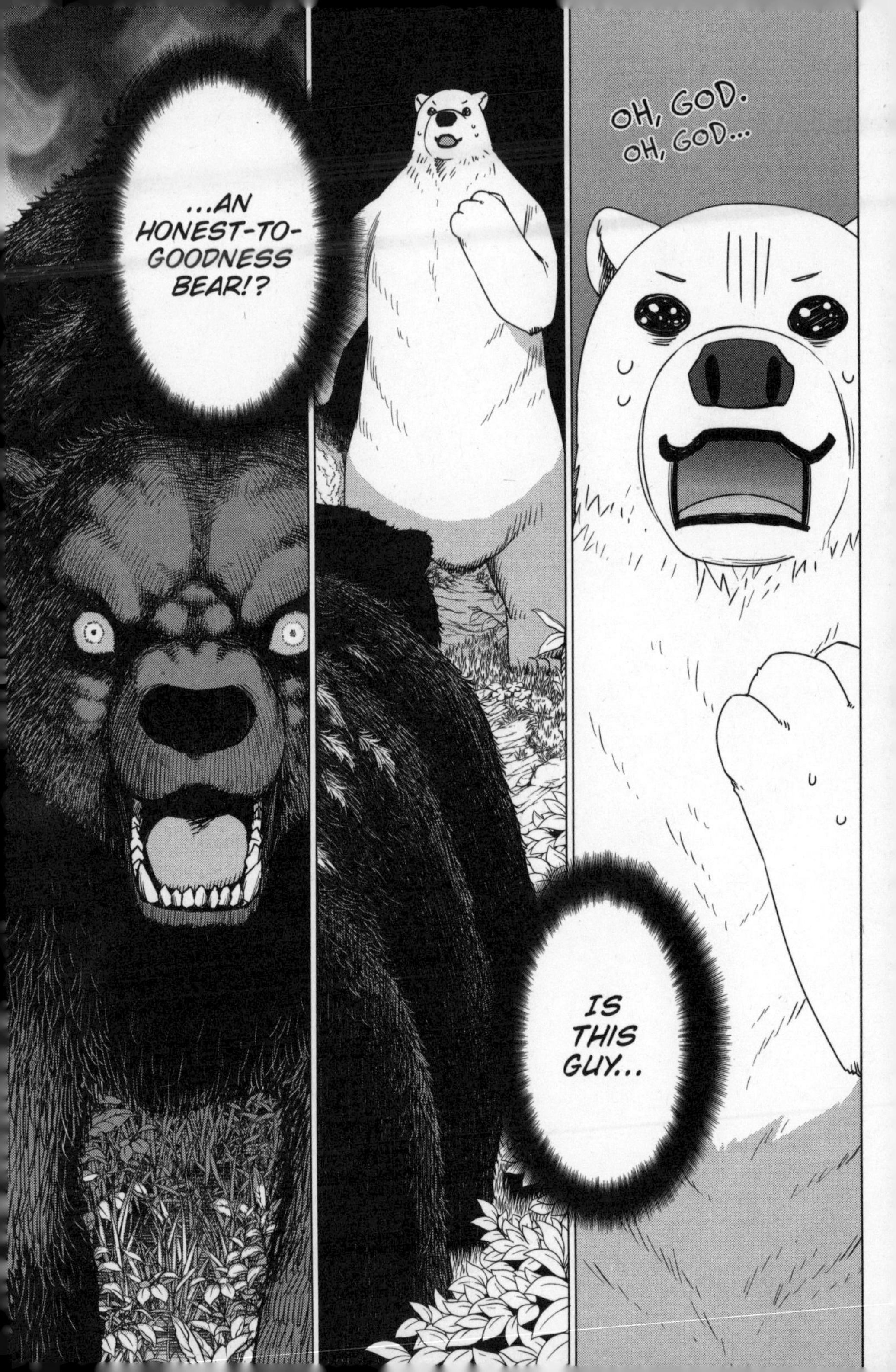
OH, GOD. OH, GOD...
IS THIS GUY...
...AN HONEST-TO-GOODNESS BEAR!?

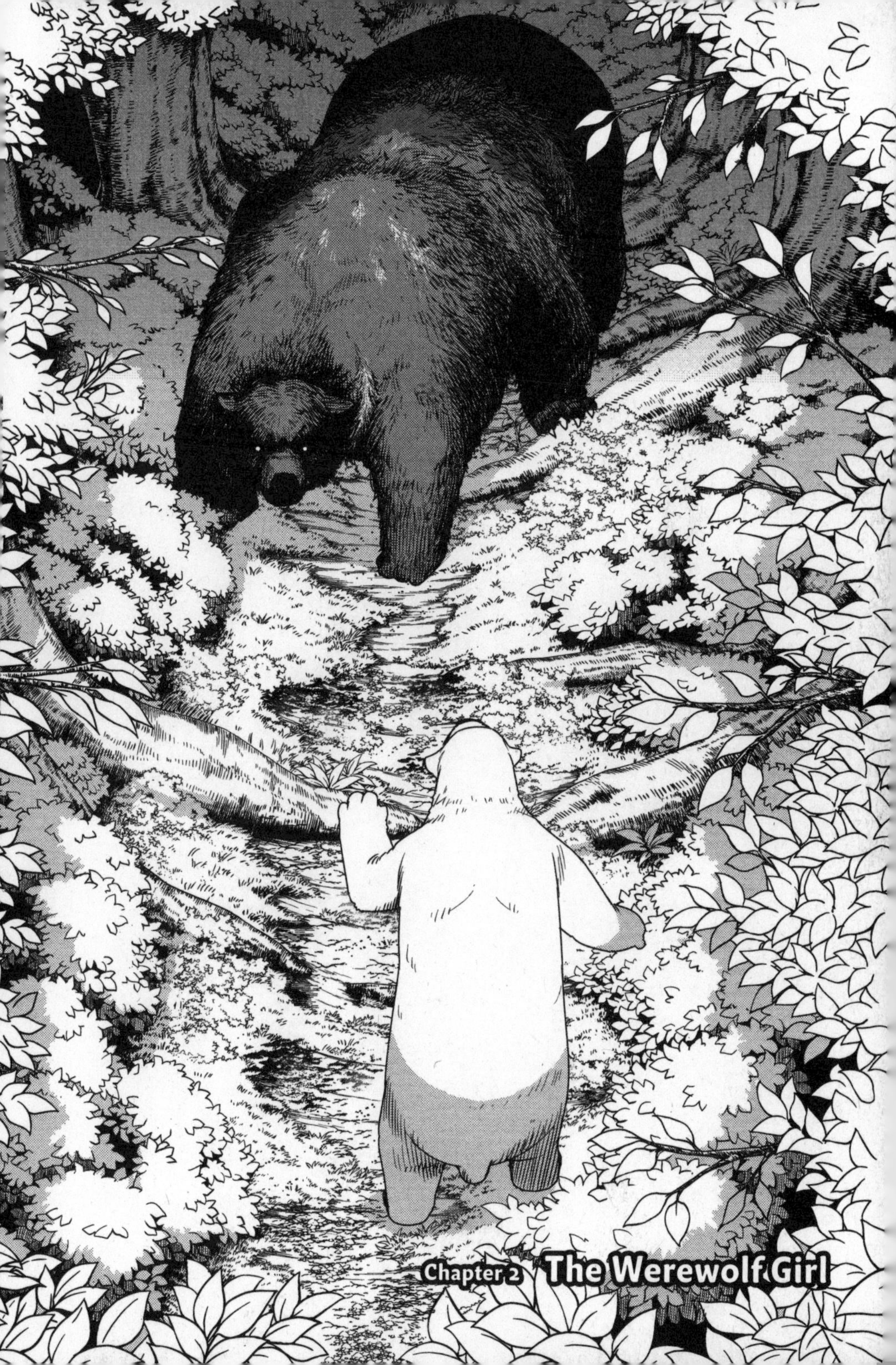
Chapter 2 The Werewolf Girl

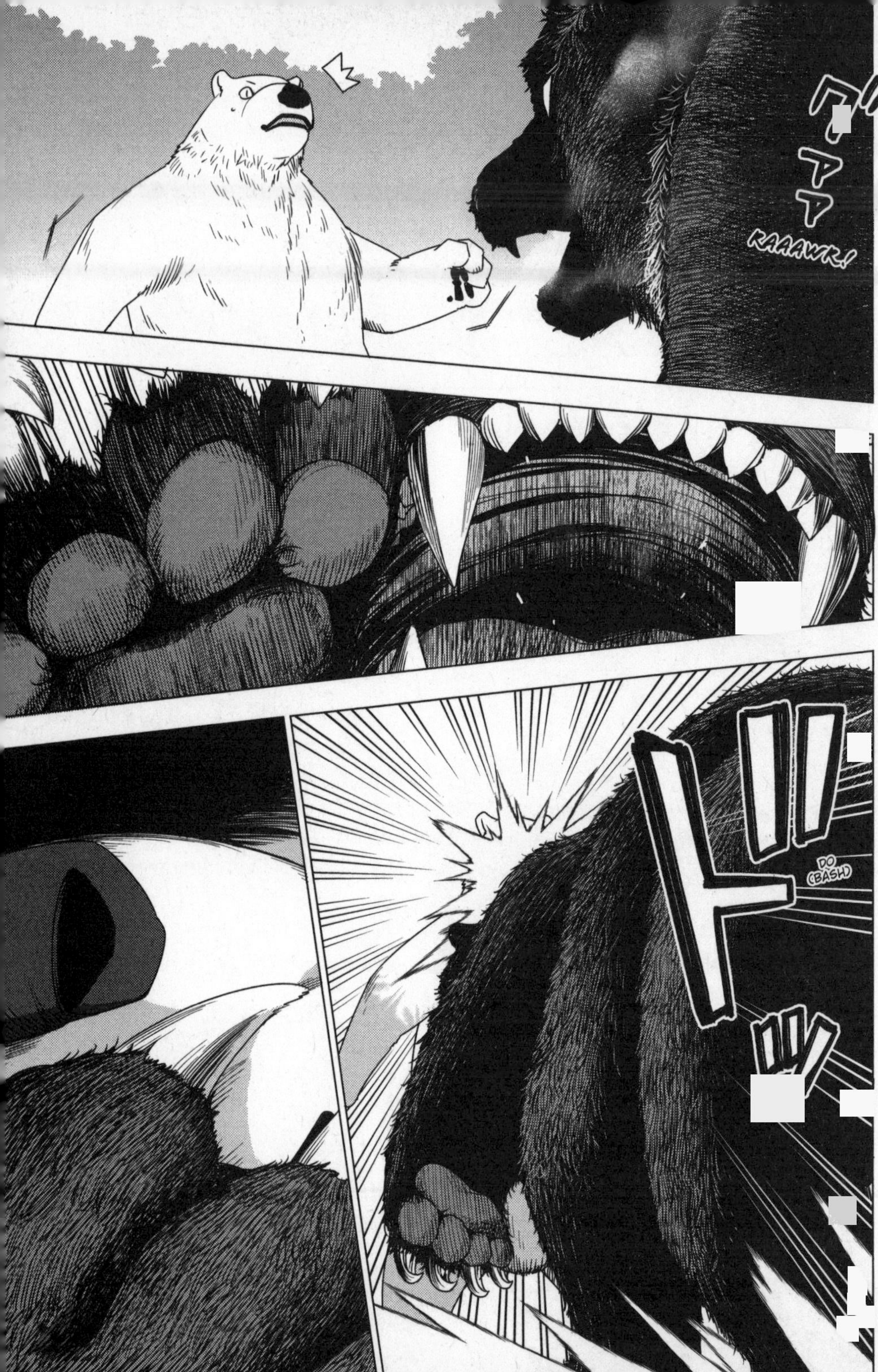
RAAAWR!
DO (BASH)

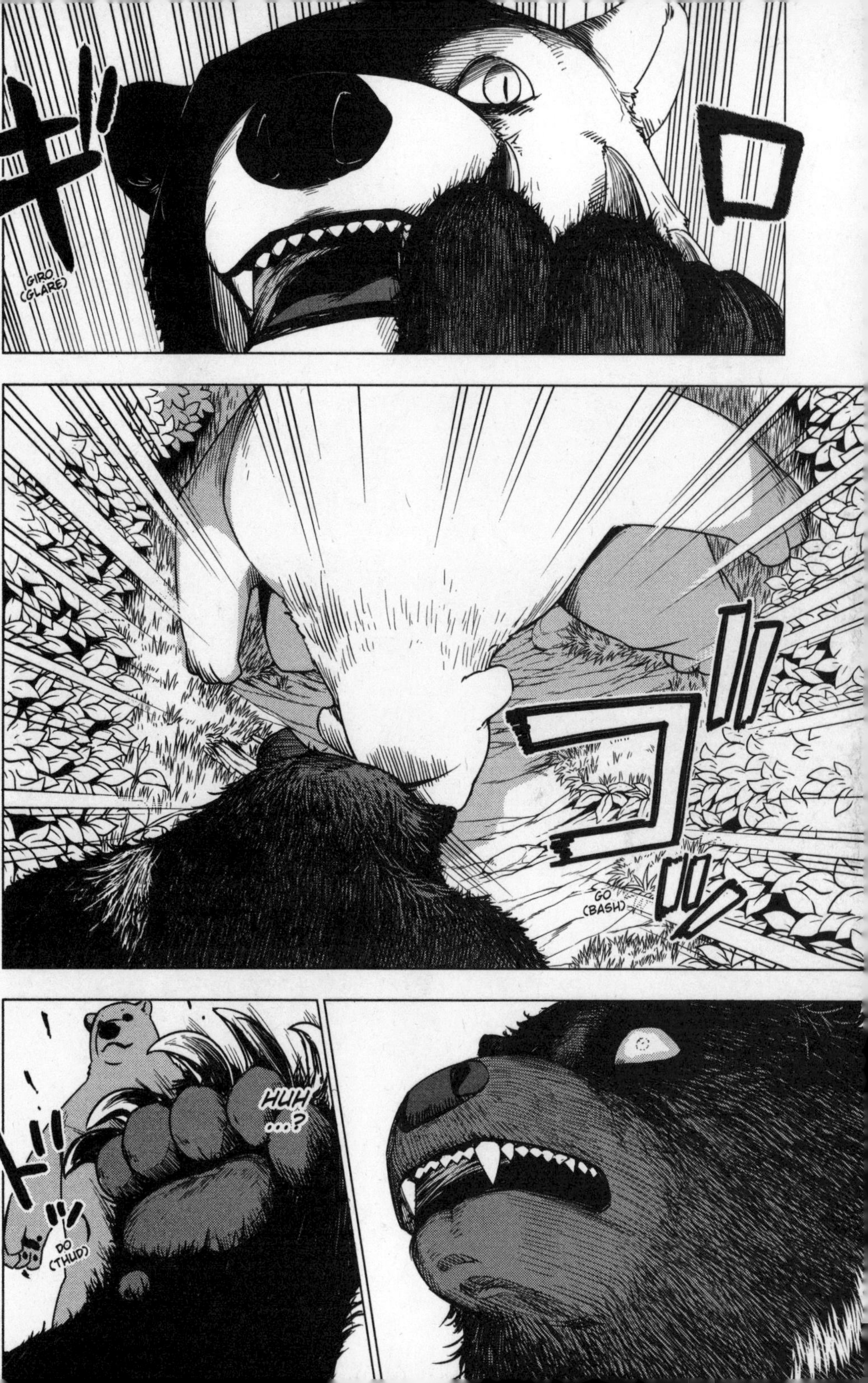

ギロ
GIRO (GLARE)
GO (BASH)
HUH ...?
DO (THUD)

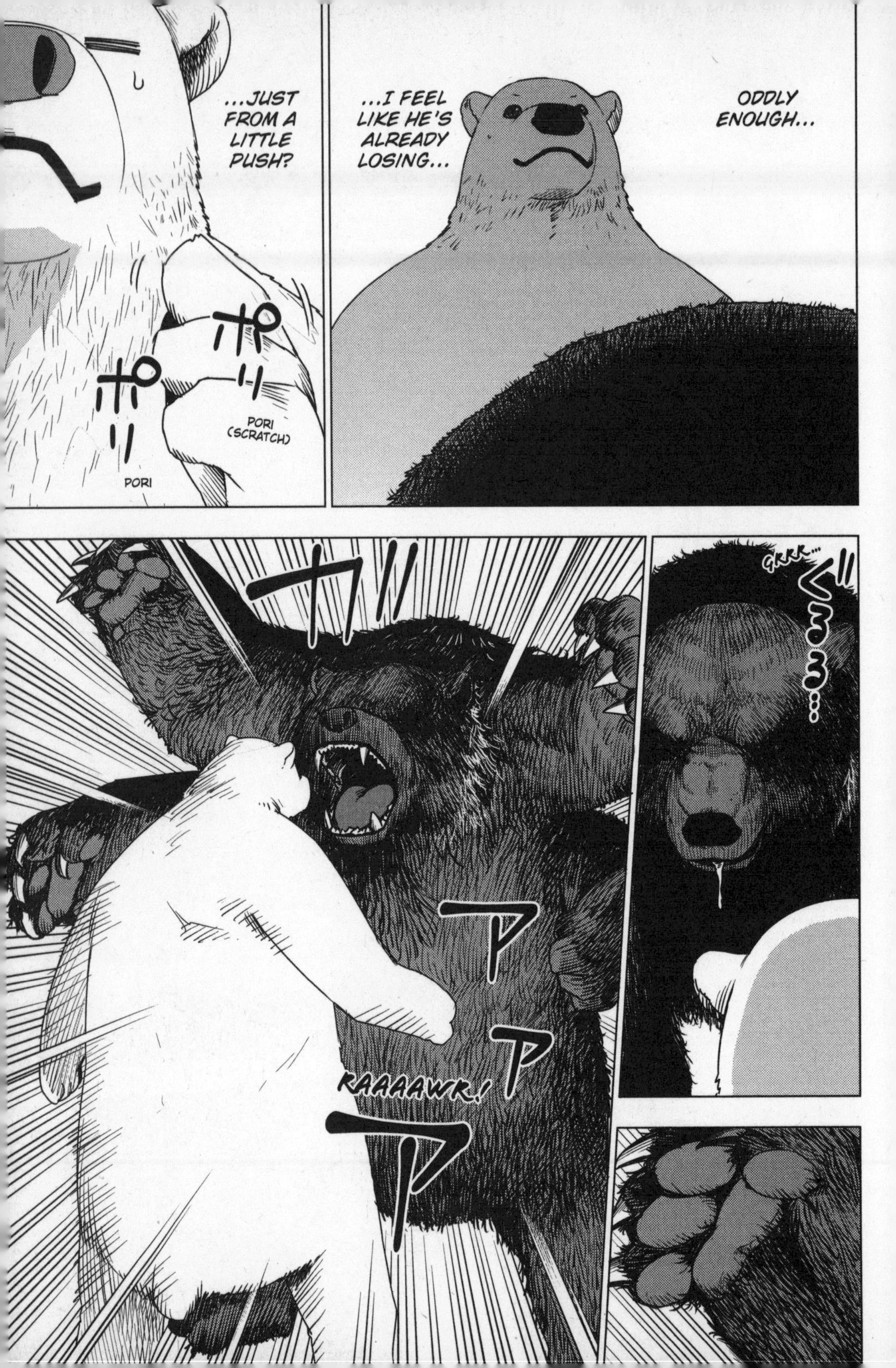
ODDLY ENOUGH...
...I FEEL LIKE HE'S ALREADY LOSING...
...JUST FROM A LITTLE PUSH?
PORI (SCRATCH)
PORI
GRRR...
RAAAAWR!

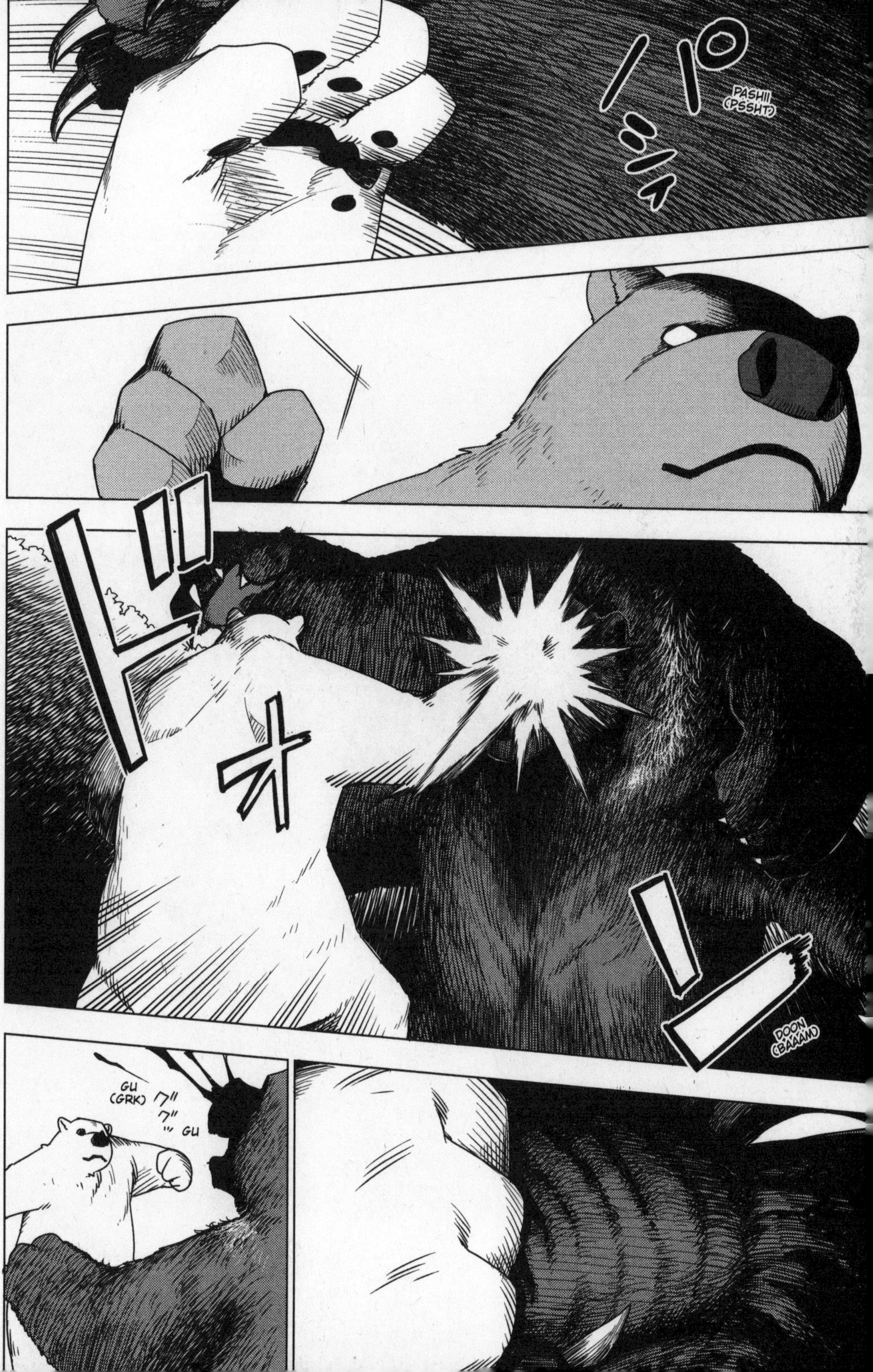
パシィ
PASHII
(PSSHT)
DOON
(BAAAM)
GU
(GRK)
GU

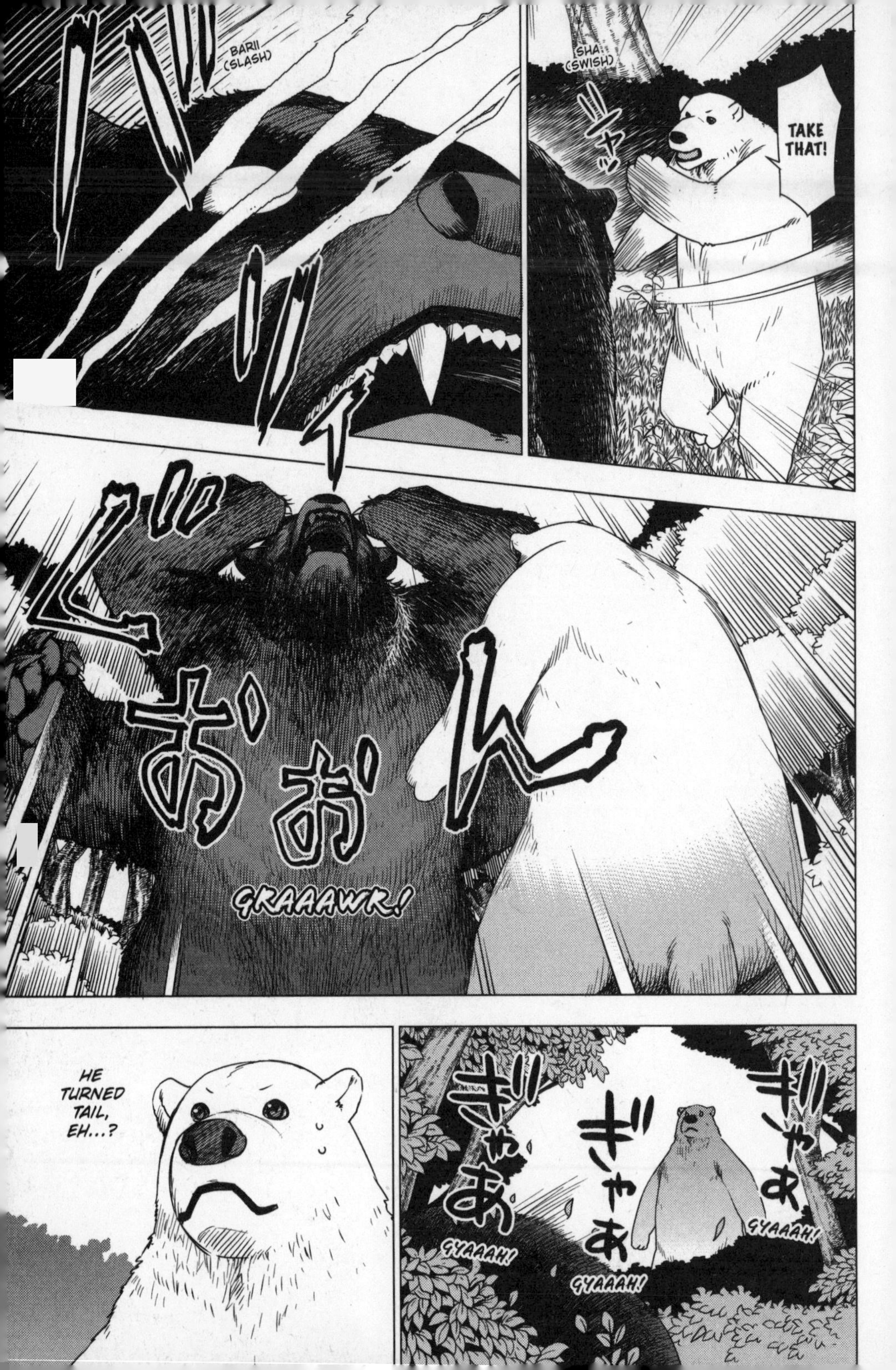
シャッ
SHA (SWISH)
TAKE THAT!
バリィ
BARII (SLASH)
ぐおおん
GRAAAWR!
ぎゃあ
GYAAAH!
ぎゃあ
GYAAAH!
ぎゃあ
GYAAAH!
HE TURNED TAIL, EH...?

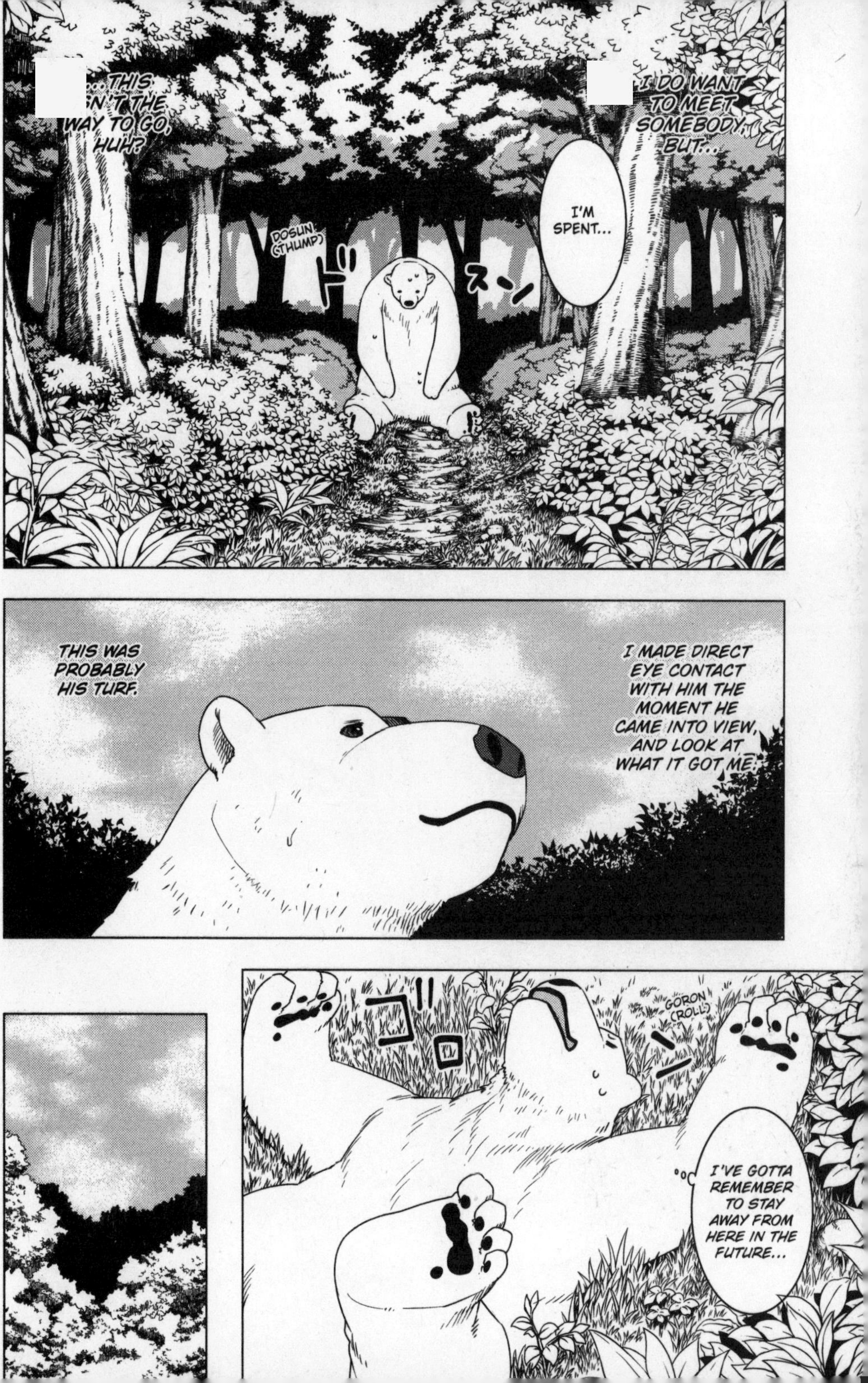
I DO WANT TO MEET SOMEBODY, BUT...
...THIS N'T THE WAY TO GO, HUH?
I'M SPENT...
DOSUN (THUMP)
I MADE DIRECT EYE CONTACT WITH HIM THE MOMENT HE CAME INTO VIEW, AND LOOK AT WHAT IT GOT ME.
THIS WAS PROBABLY HIS TURF.
GORON (ROLL)
I'VE GOTTA REMEMBER TO STAY AWAY FROM HERE IN THE FUTURE...

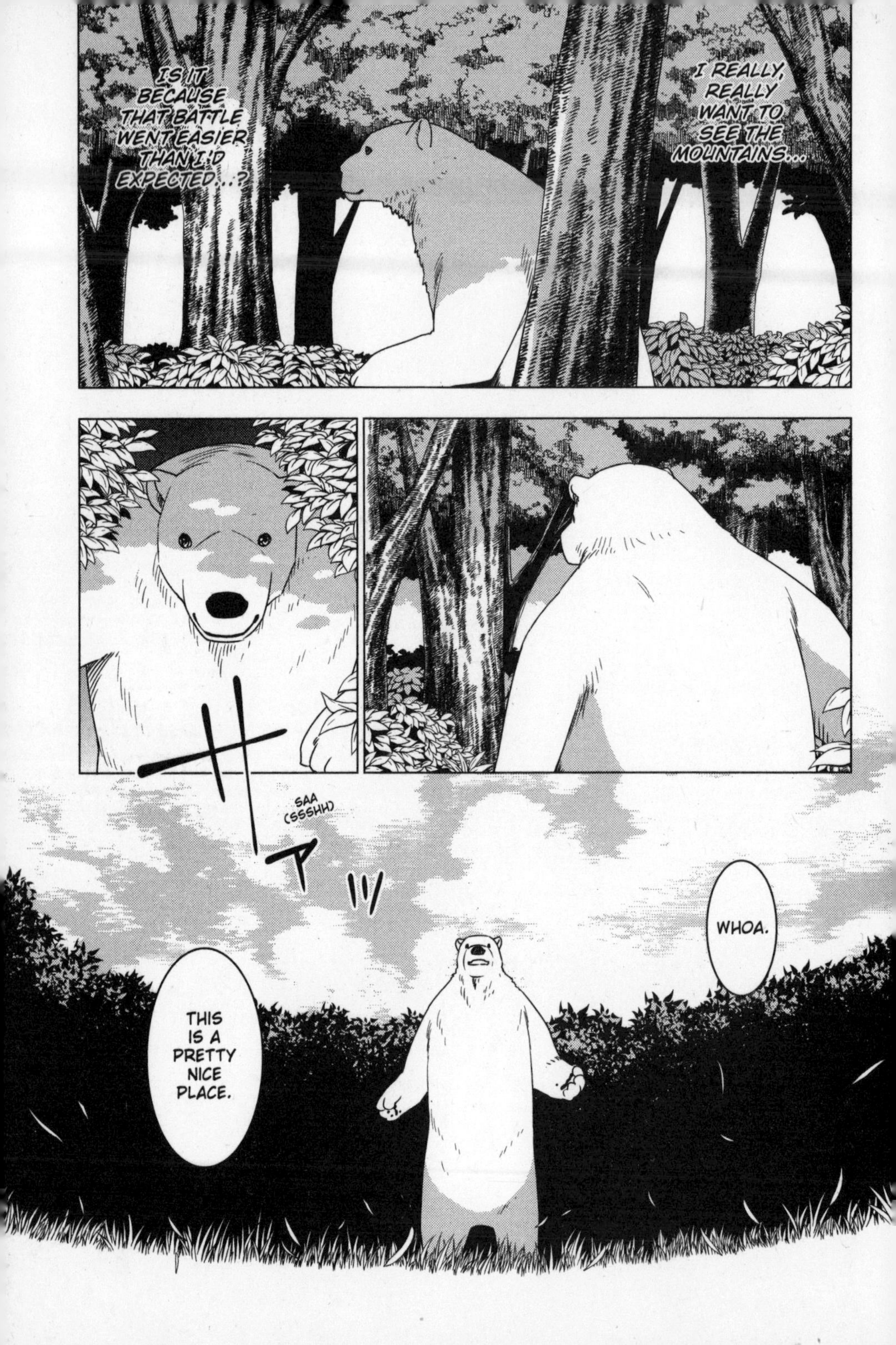
I REALLY, REALLY WANT TO SEE THE MOUNTAINS...
IS IT BECAUSE THAT BATTLE WENT EASIER THAN I'D EXPECTED...?
SAA (SSSHH)
WHOA.
THIS IS A PRETTY NICE PLACE.

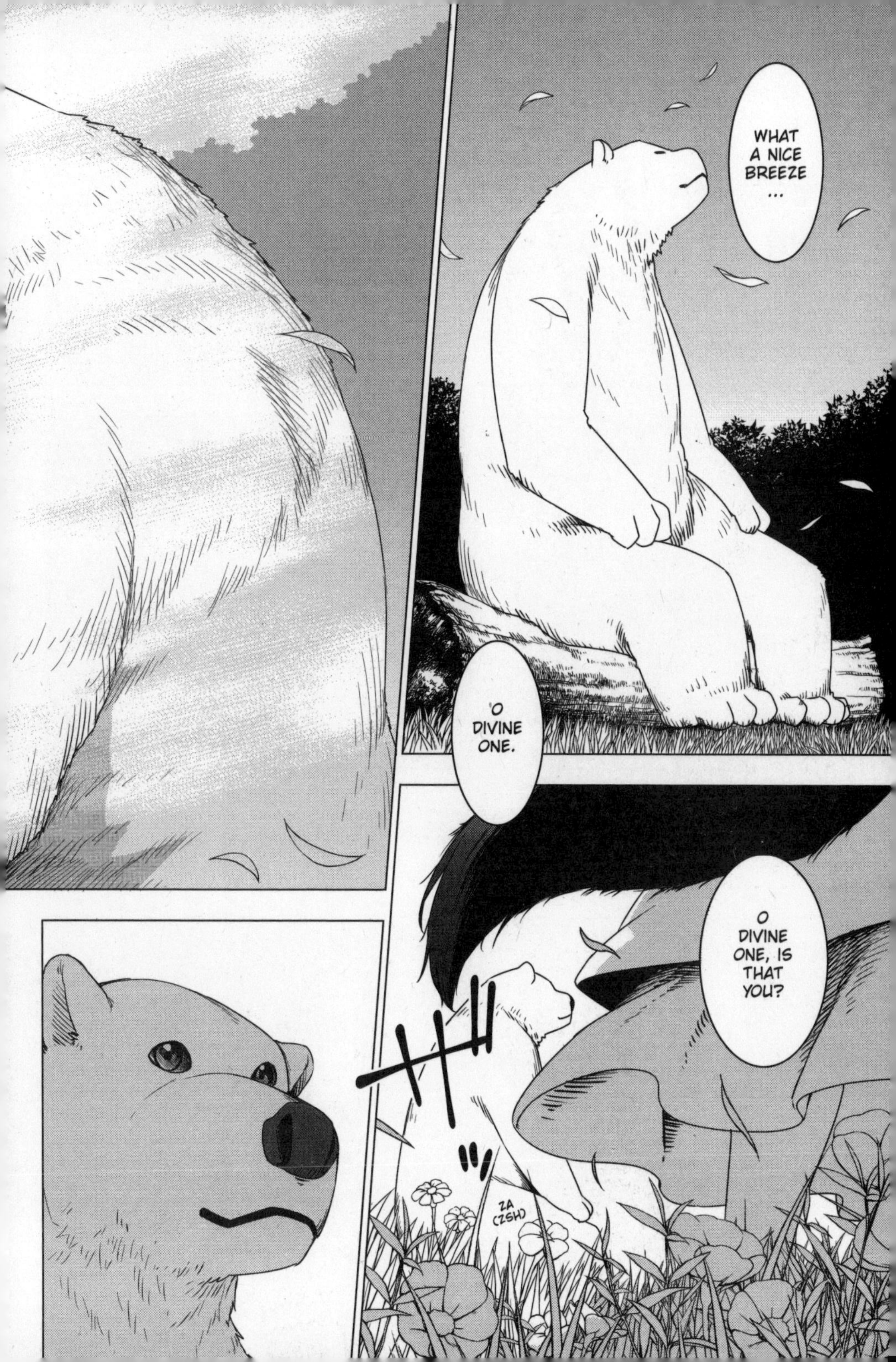
WHAT A NICE BREEZE ...
O DIVINE ONE.
O DIVINE ONE, IS THAT YOU?
ZA (ZSH)

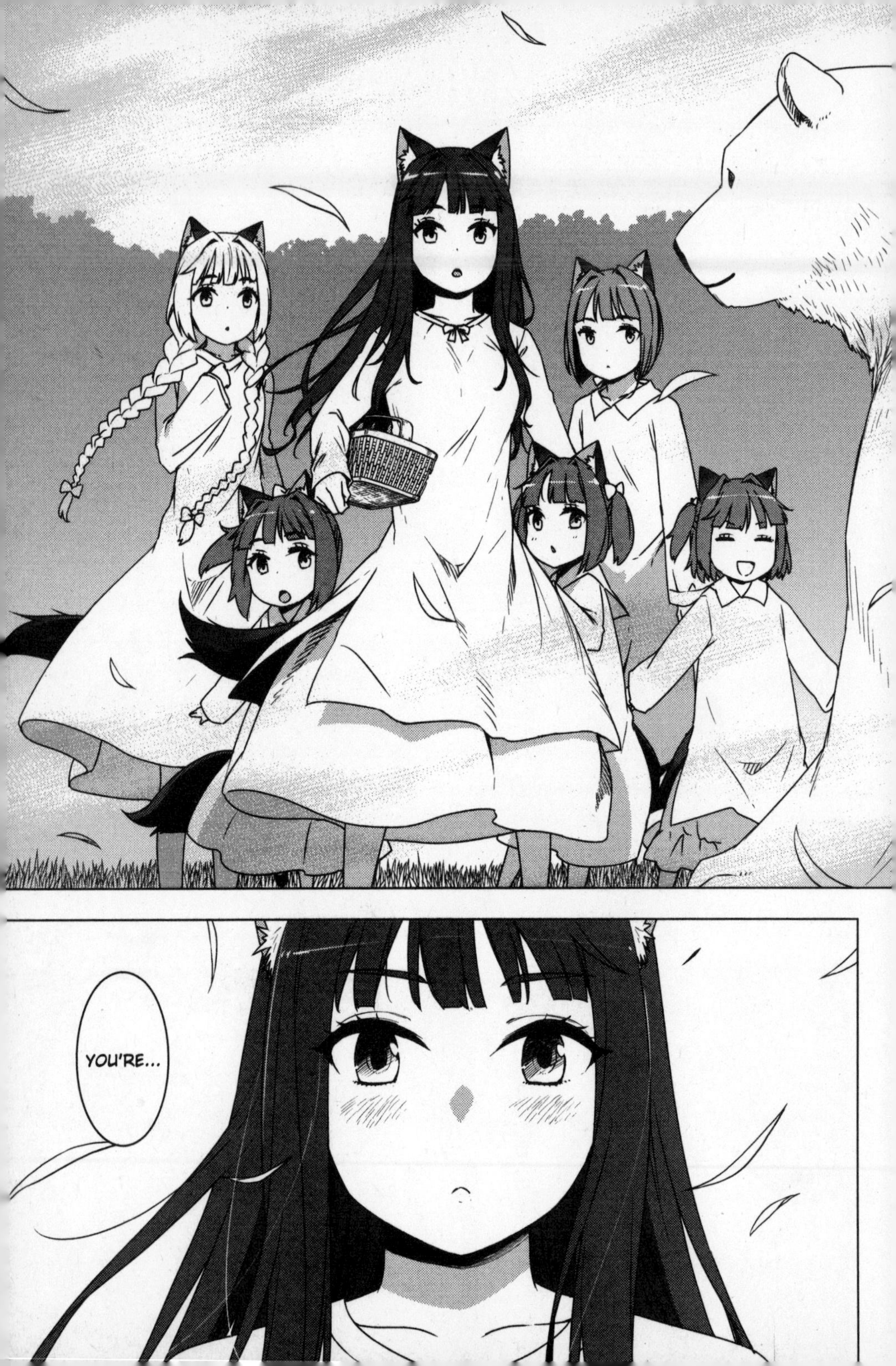
YOU'RE...

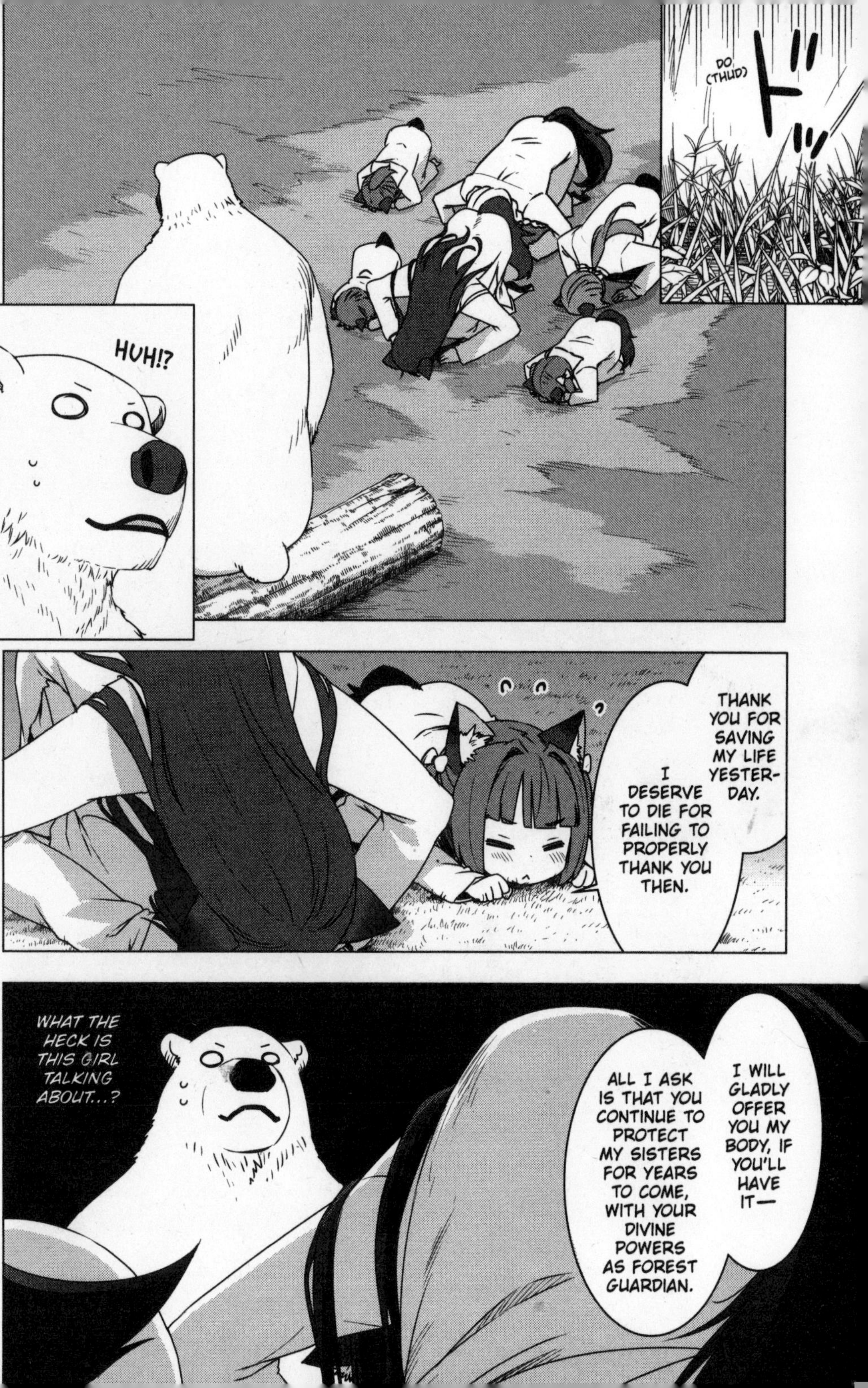
DO (THUD)
HUH!?
THANK YOU FOR SAVING MY LIFE YESTER-DAY.
I DESERVE TO DIE FOR FAILING TO PROPERLY THANK YOU THEN.
I WILL GLADLY OFFER YOU MY BODY, IF YOU'LL HAVE IT—
ALL I ASK IS THAT YOU CONTINUE TO PROTECT MY SISTERS FOR YEARS TO COME, WITH YOUR DIVINE POWERS AS FOREST GUARDIAN.
WHAT THE HECK IS THIS GIRL TALKING ABOUT...?

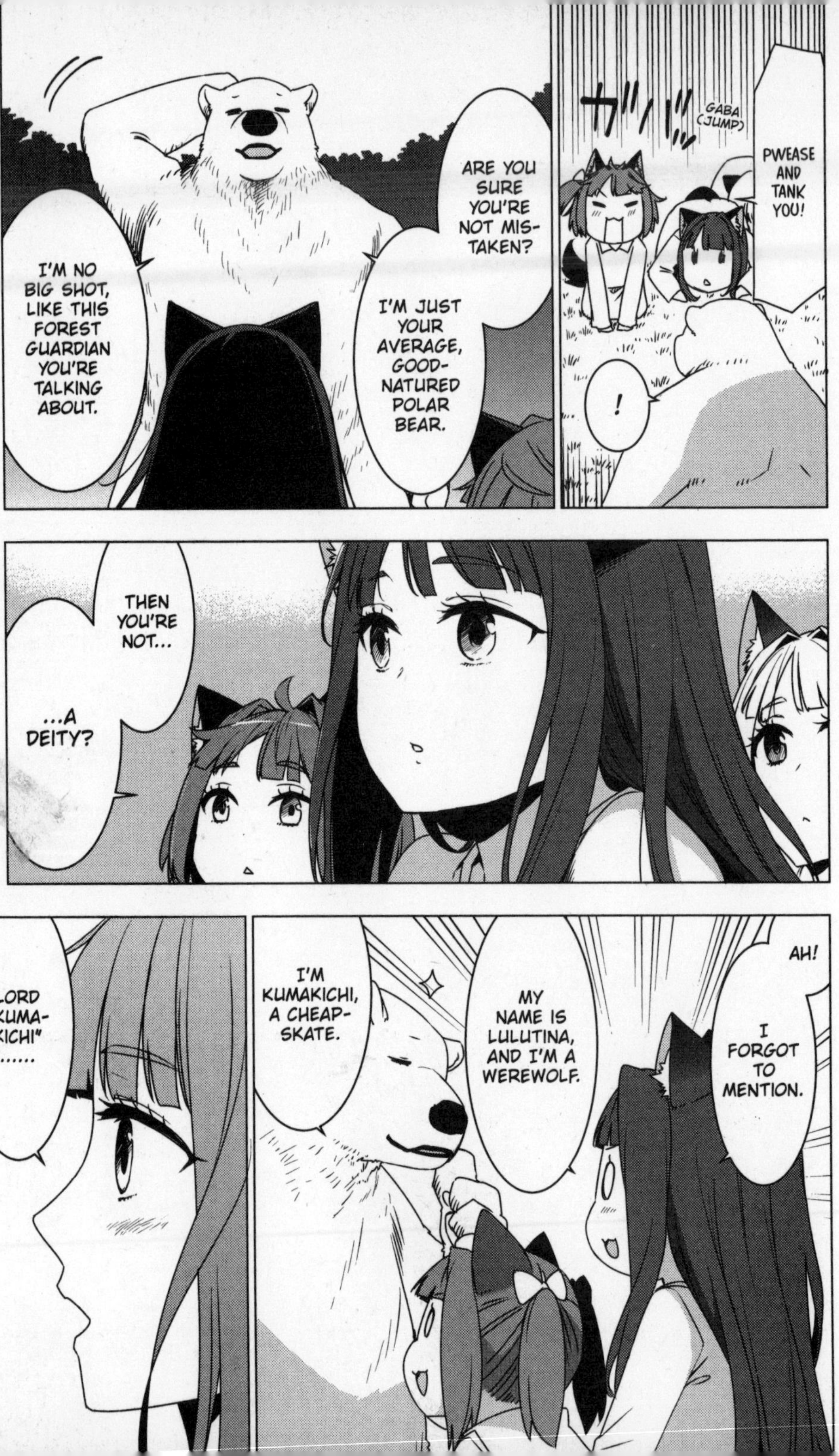
GABA (JUMP)
PWEASE AND TANK YOU!
!
ARE YOU SURE YOU'RE NOT MIS-TAKEN?
I'M JUST YOUR AVERAGE, GOOD-NATURED POLAR BEAR.
I'M NO BIG SHOT, LIKE THIS FOREST GUARDIAN YOU'RE TALKING ABOUT.
THEN YOU'RE NOT...
...A DEITY?
AH!
I FORGOT TO MENTION.
MY NAME IS LULUTINA, AND I'M A WEREWOLF.
I'M KUMAKICHI, A CHEAP-SKATE.
LORD "KUMA-KICHI" ......

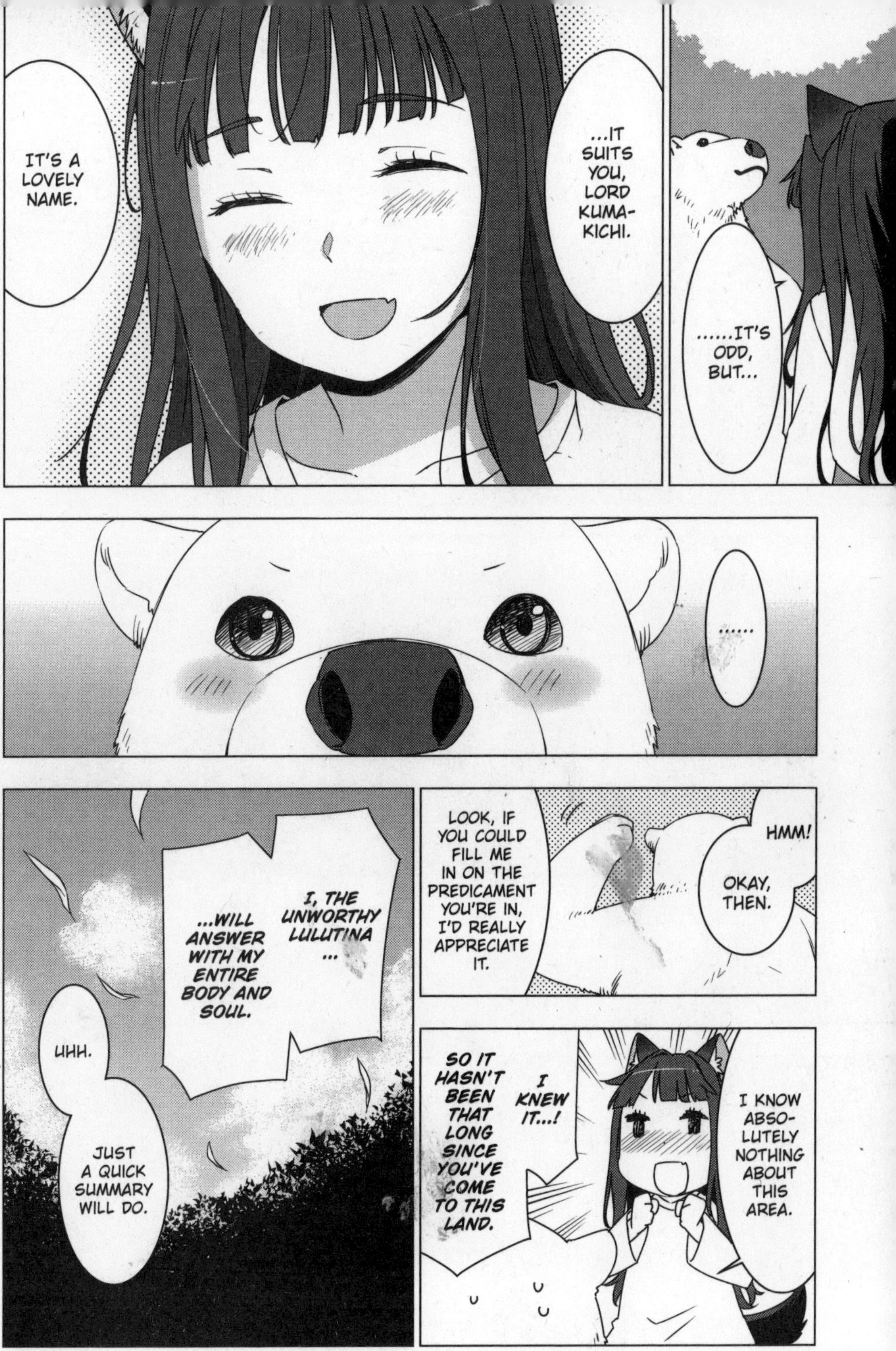
......IT'S ODD, BUT...
...IT SUITS YOU, LORD KUMA-KICHI.
IT'S A LOVELY NAME.
......
HMM!
OKAY, THEN.
LOOK, IF YOU COULD FILL ME IN ON THE PREDICAMENT YOU'RE IN, I'D REALLY APPRECIATE IT.
I KNOW ABSO-LUTELY NOTHING ABOUT THIS AREA.
I KNEW IT...!
SO IT HASN'T BEEN THAT LONG SINCE YOU'VE COME TO THIS LAND.
I, THE UNWORTHY LULUTINA...
...WILL ANSWER WITH MY ENTIRE BODY AND SOUL.
UHH.
JUST A QUICK SUMMARY WILL DO.

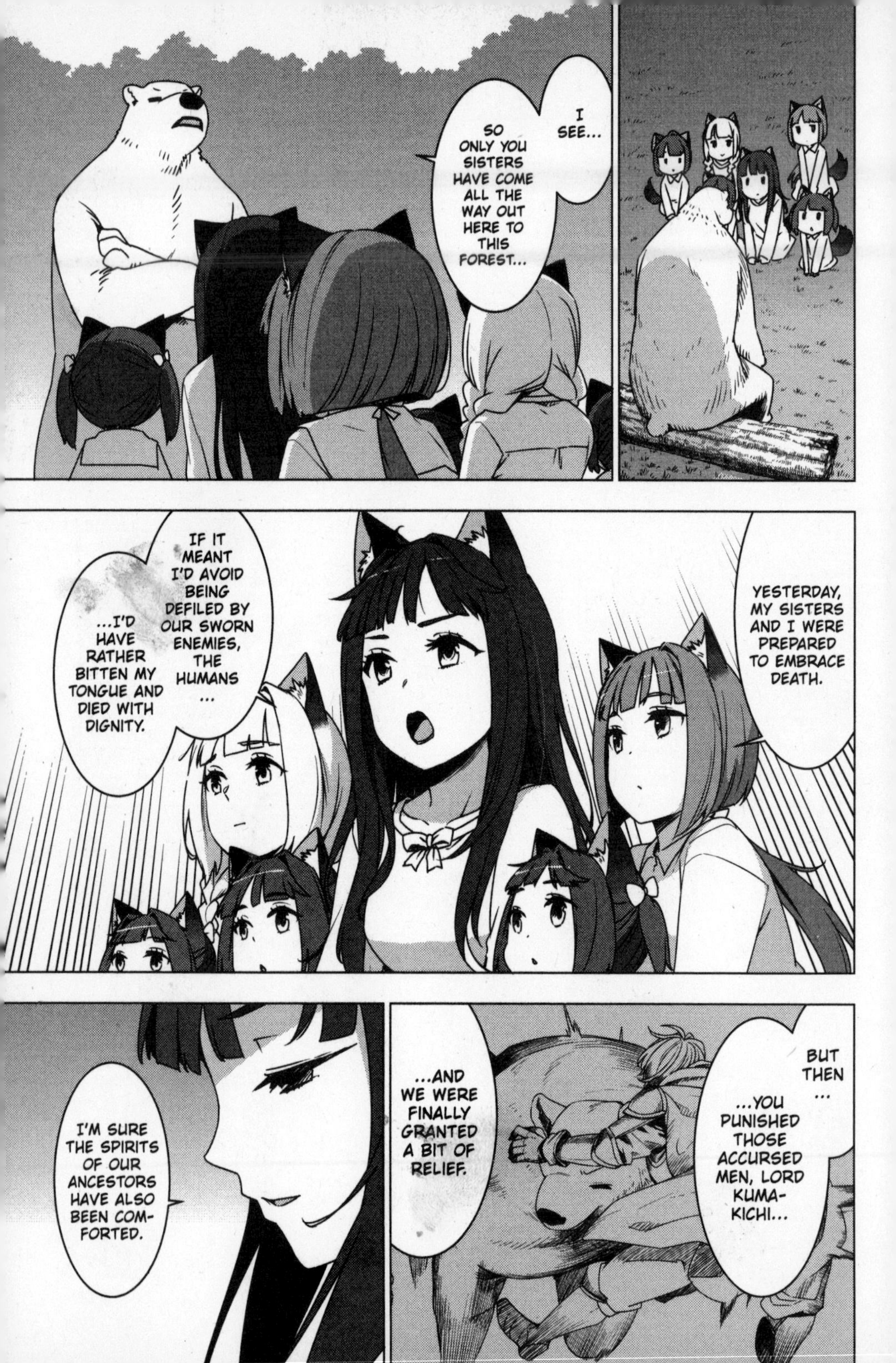
I SEE...
SO ONLY YOU SISTERS HAVE COME ALL THE WAY OUT HERE TO THIS FOREST...
YESTERDAY, MY SISTERS AND I WERE PREPARED TO EMBRACE DEATH.
IF IT MEANT I'D AVOID BEING DEFILED BY OUR SWORN ENEMIES, THE HUMANS...
...I'D HAVE RATHER BITTEN MY TONGUE AND DIED WITH DIGNITY.
BUT THEN...
...YOU PUNISHED THOSE ACCURSED MEN, LORD KUMA-KICHI...
...AND WE WERE FINALLY GRANTED A BIT OF RELIEF.
I'M SURE THE SPIRITS OF OUR ANCESTORS HAVE ALSO BEEN COM-FORTED.

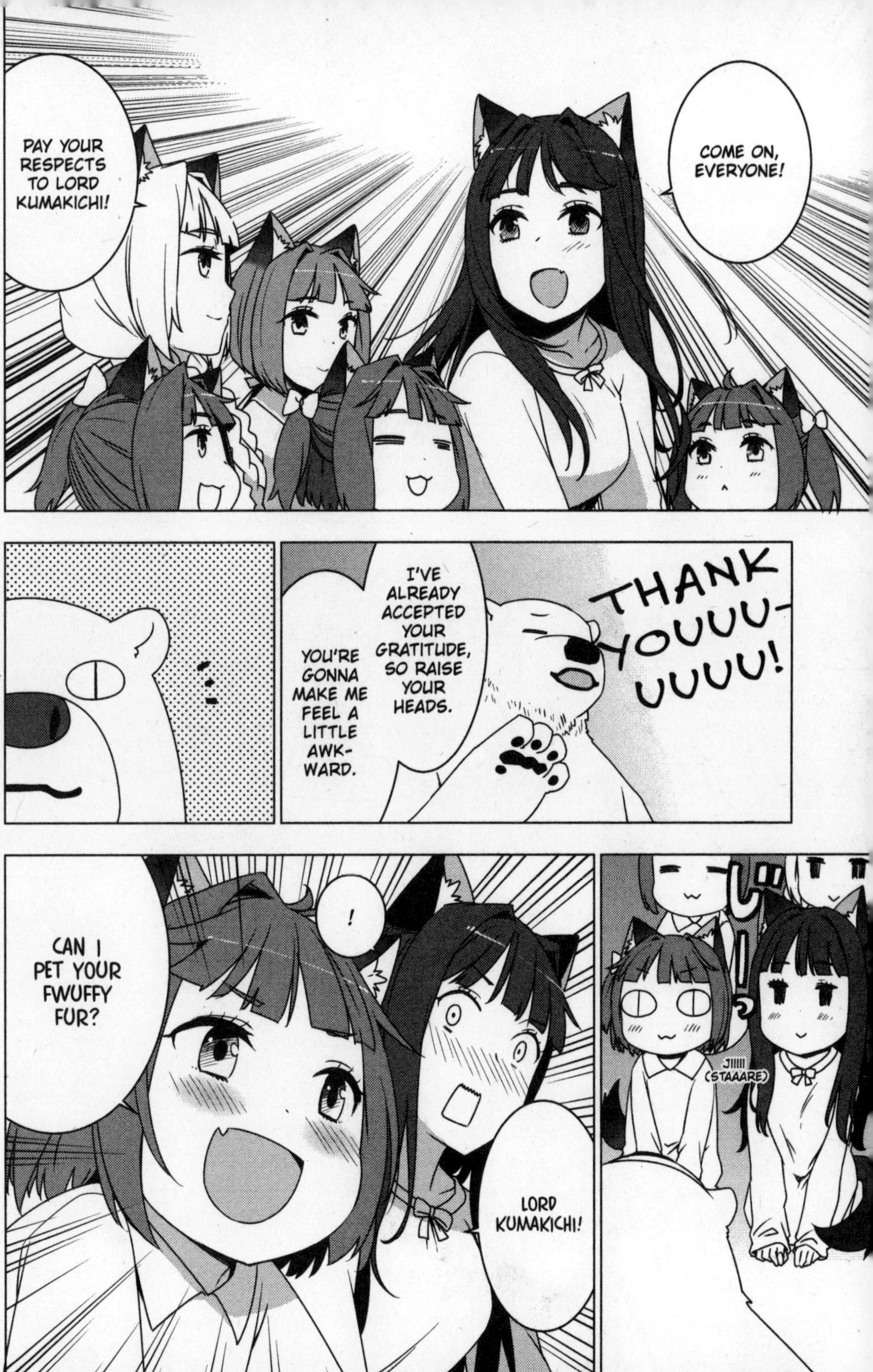

COME ON, EVERYONE!
PAY YOUR RESPECTS TO LORD KUMAKICHI!
THANK YOUUUU-UUUU!
I'VE ALREADY ACCEPTED YOUR GRATITUDE, SO RAISE YOUR HEADS.
YOU'RE GONNA MAKE ME FEEL A LITTLE AWK-WARD.
...
JI!!!! (STAAARE)
!
CAN I PET YOUR FWUFFY FUR?
LORD KUMAKICHI!

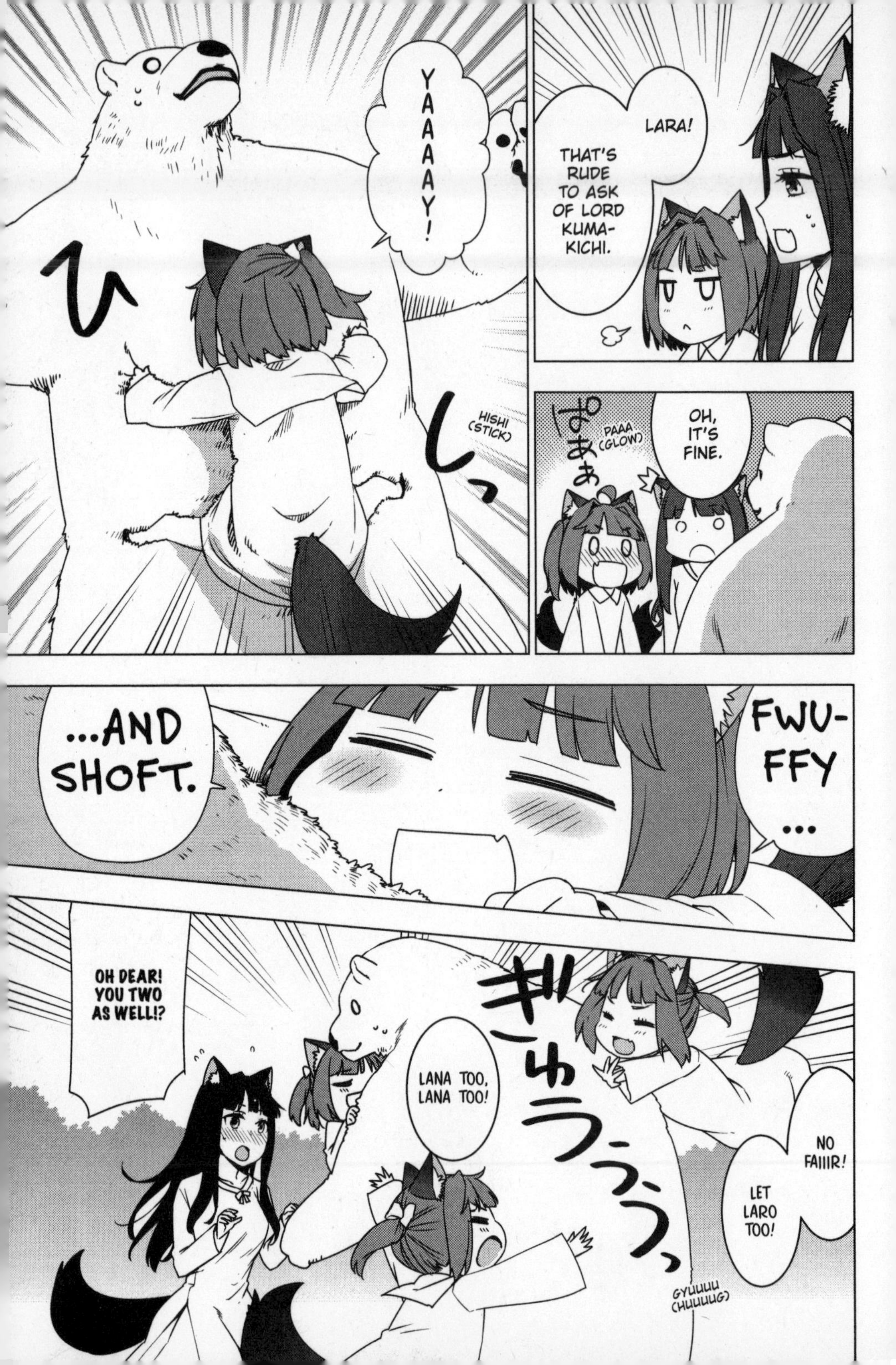
LARA!
THAT'S RUDE TO ASK OF LORD KUMA-KICHI.
OH, IT'S FINE.
PAAA (GLOW)
YAAAAAY!
HISHI (STICK)
FWU-FFY...
...AND SHOFT.
NO FAIIIR!
LET LARO TOO!
GYUUUU (HUUUUG)
LANA TOO, LANA TOO!
OH DEAR! YOU TWO AS WELL!?

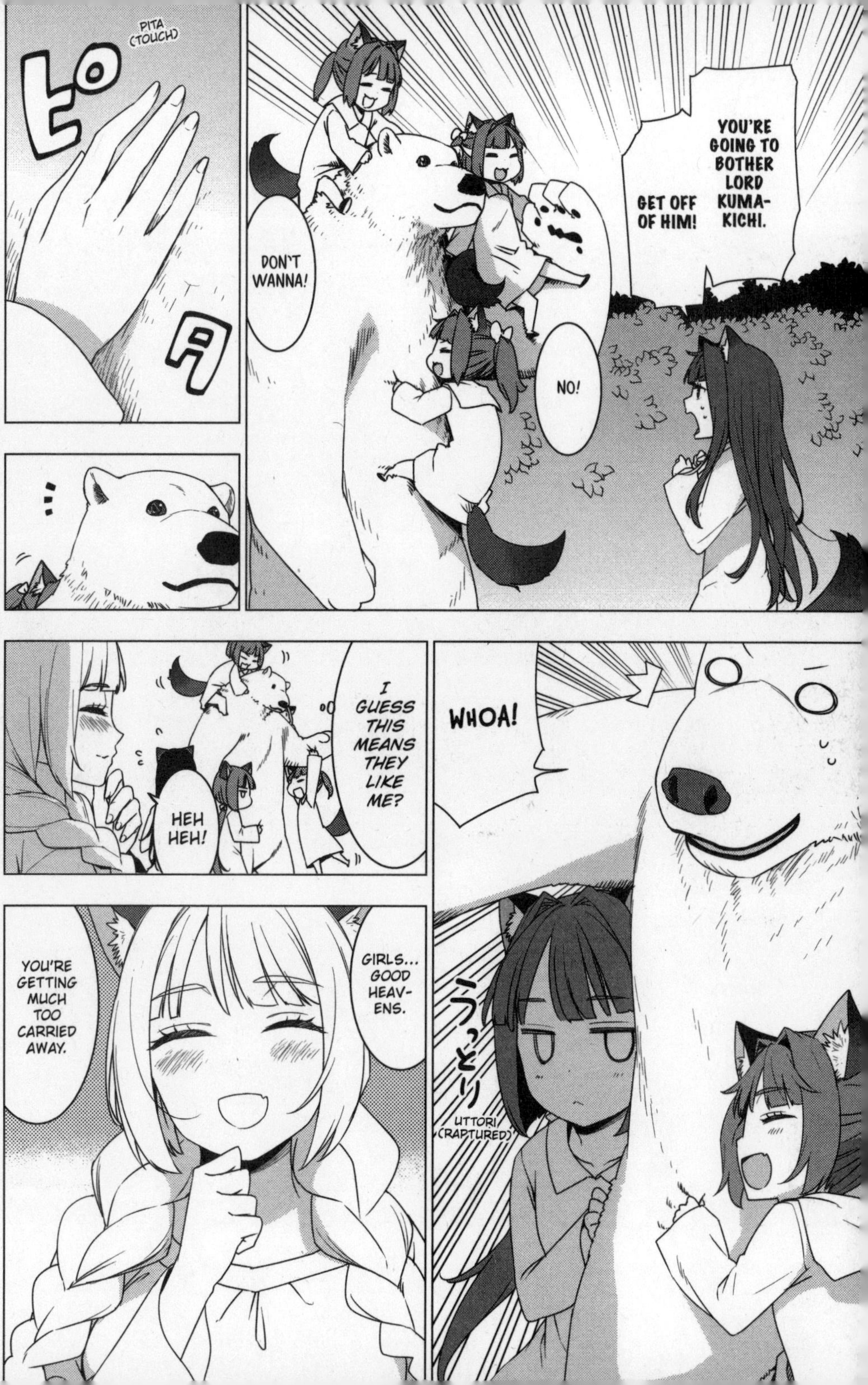
YOU'RE GOING TO BOTHER LORD KUMA-KICHI.
GET OFF OF HIM!
NO!
DON'T WANNA!
ピタ
PITA (TOUCH)
WHOA!
I GUESS THIS MEANS THEY LIKE ME?
HEH HEH!
うっとり
UTTORI (RAPTURED)
GIRLS... GOOD HEAVENS.
YOU'RE GETTING MUCH TOO CARRIED AWAY.

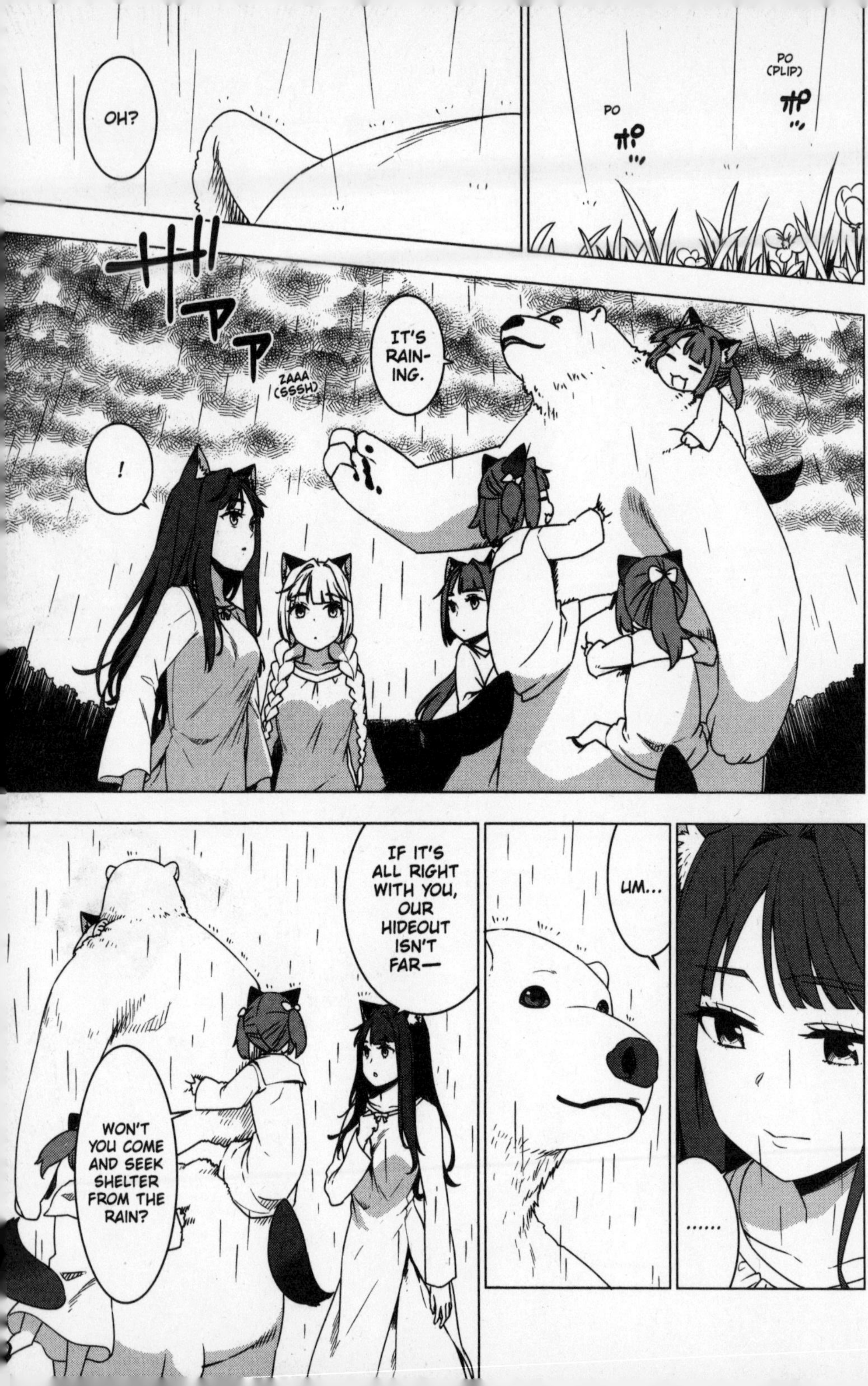
PO (PLIP)
PO
OH?
IT'S RAINING.
ZAAA (SSSH)
!
......
UM...
IF IT'S ALL RIGHT WITH YOU, OUR HIDEOUT ISN'T FAR—
WON'T YOU COME AND SEEK SHELTER FROM THE RAIN?

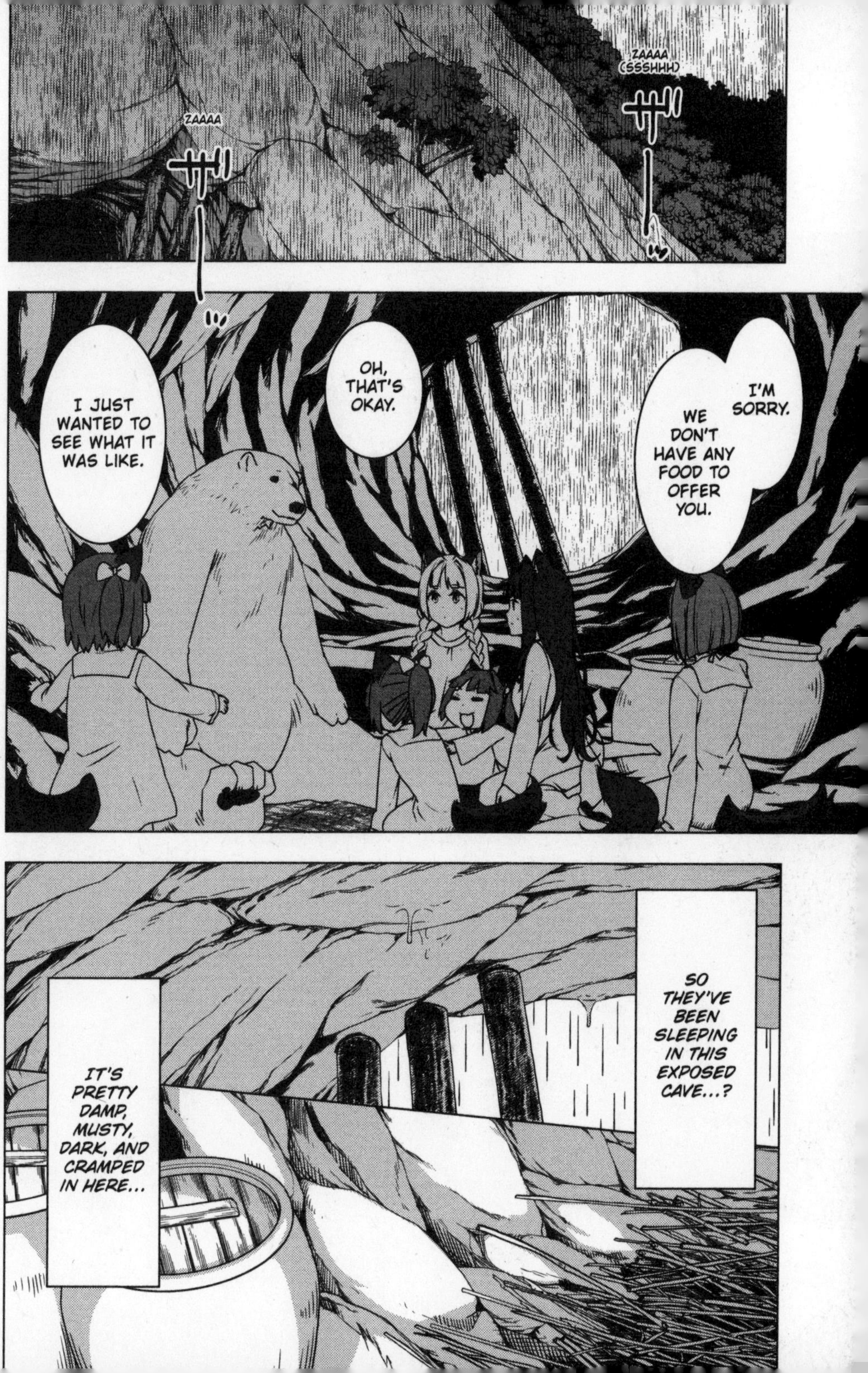
ZAAAA (SSSHHH)
ZAAAA
I'M SORRY.
WE DON'T HAVE ANY FOOD TO OFFER YOU.
OH, THAT'S OKAY.
I JUST WANTED TO SEE WHAT IT WAS LIKE.
SO THEY'VE BEEN SLEEPING IN THIS EXPOSED CAVE...?
IT'S PRETTY DAMP, MUSTY, DARK, AND CRAMPED IN HERE...

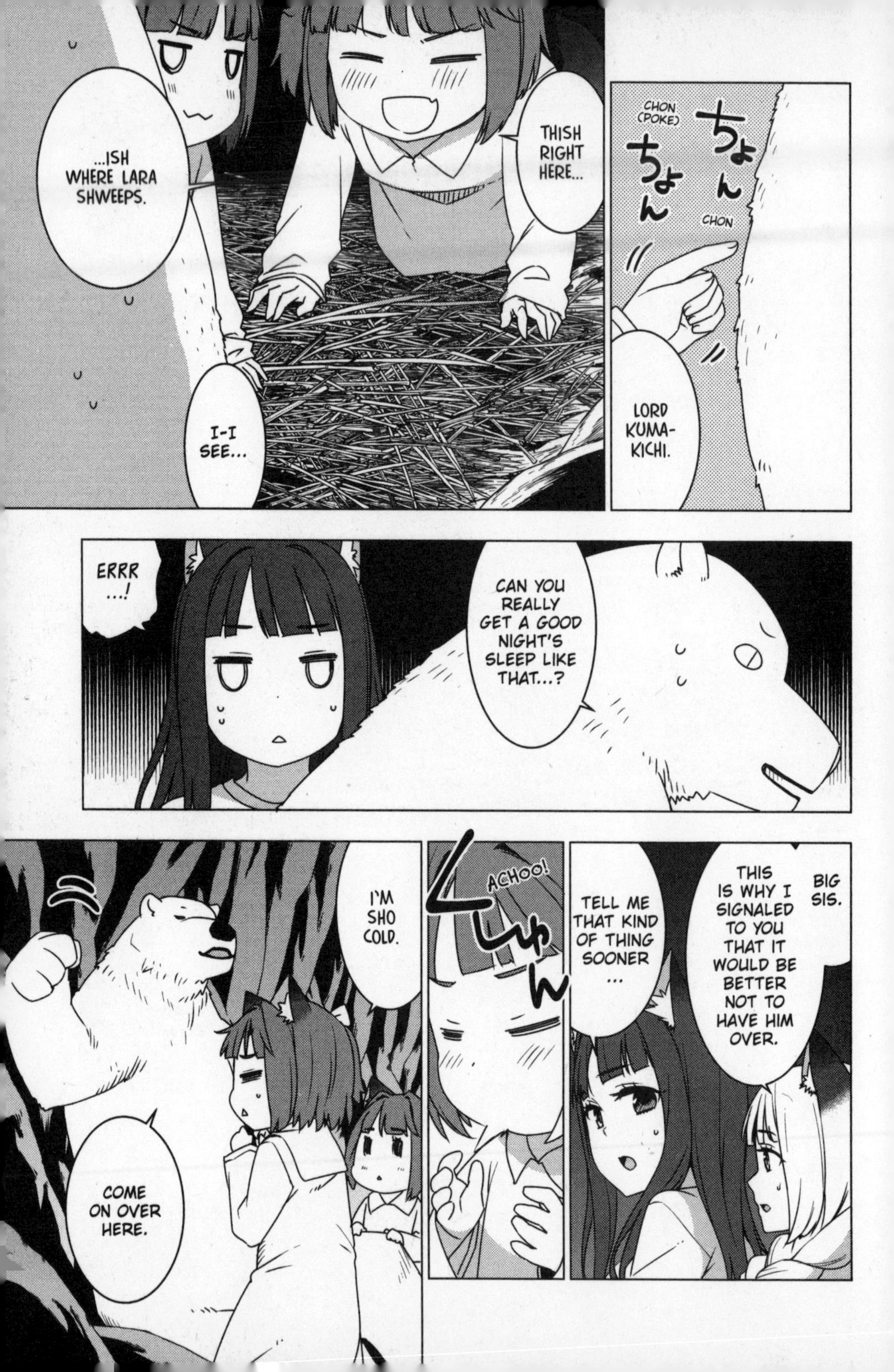
ちょんちょん
CHON (POKE)
CHON
LORD KUMA-KICHI.
THISH RIGHT HERE...
...ISH WHERE LARA SHWEEPS.
I-I SEE...
CAN YOU REALLY GET A GOOD NIGHT'S SLEEP LIKE THAT...?
ERRR...!
BIG SIS.
THIS IS WHY I SIGNALED TO YOU THAT IT WOULD BE BETTER NOT TO HAVE HIM OVER.
TELL ME THAT KIND OF THING SOONER...
くしゅん
ACHOO!
I'M SHO COLD.
COME ON OVER HERE.

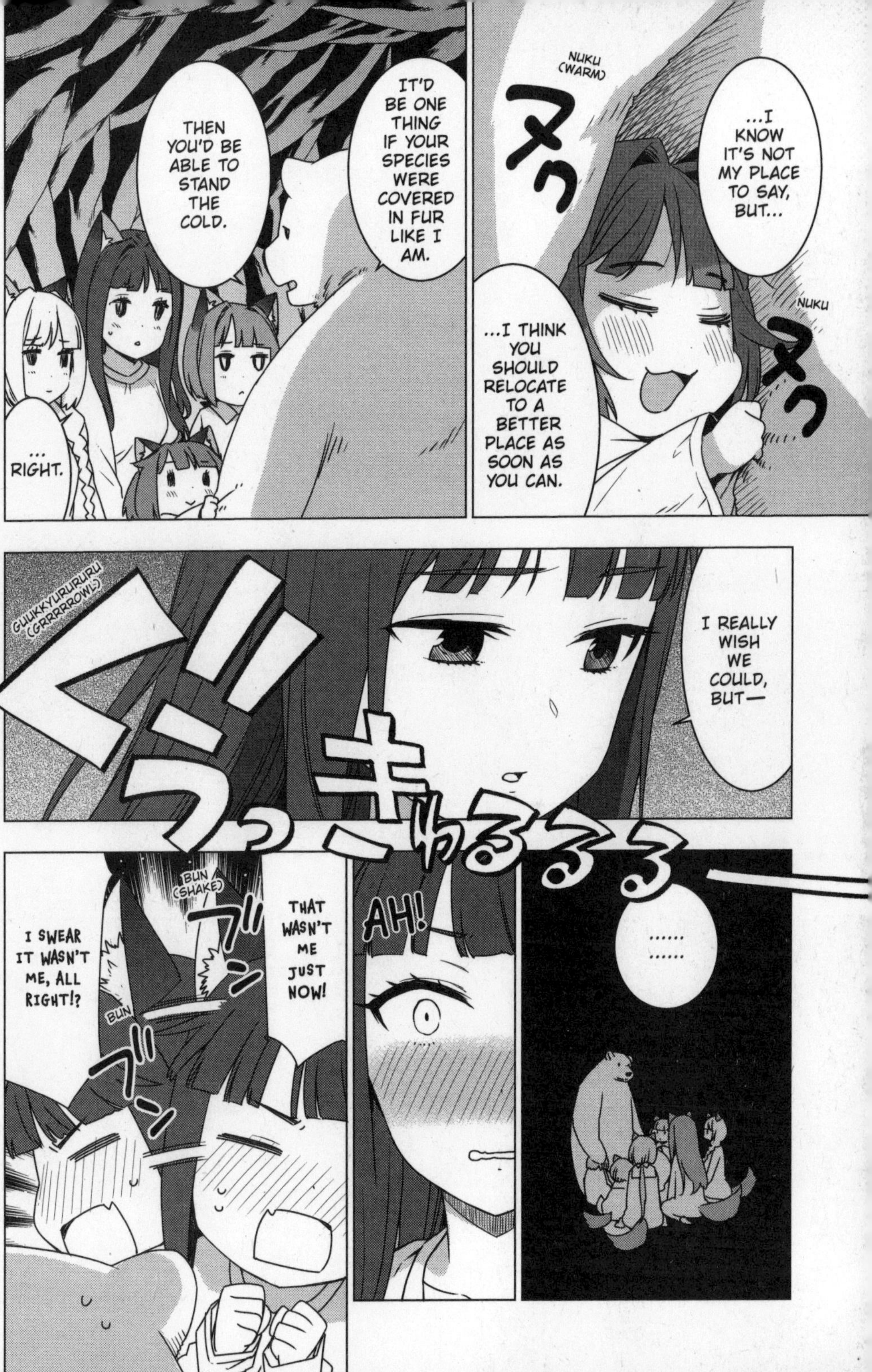
NUKU (WARM)
ヌク
...I KNOW IT'S NOT MY PLACE TO SAY, BUT...
...I THINK YOU SHOULD RELOCATE TO A BETTER PLACE AS SOON AS YOU CAN.
NUKU
ヌク
IT'D BE ONE THING IF YOUR SPECIES WERE COVERED IN FUR LIKE I AM.
THEN YOU'D BE ABLE TO STAND THE COLD.
... RIGHT.
I REALLY WISH WE COULD, BUT—
GUUKKYURURURU (GRRRRROWL)
ぐうっきゅるるる—
......
......
AH!
BUN (SHAKE)
ブン
THAT WASN'T ME JUST NOW!
I SWEAR IT WASN'T ME, ALL RIGHT!?
BUN
ブン

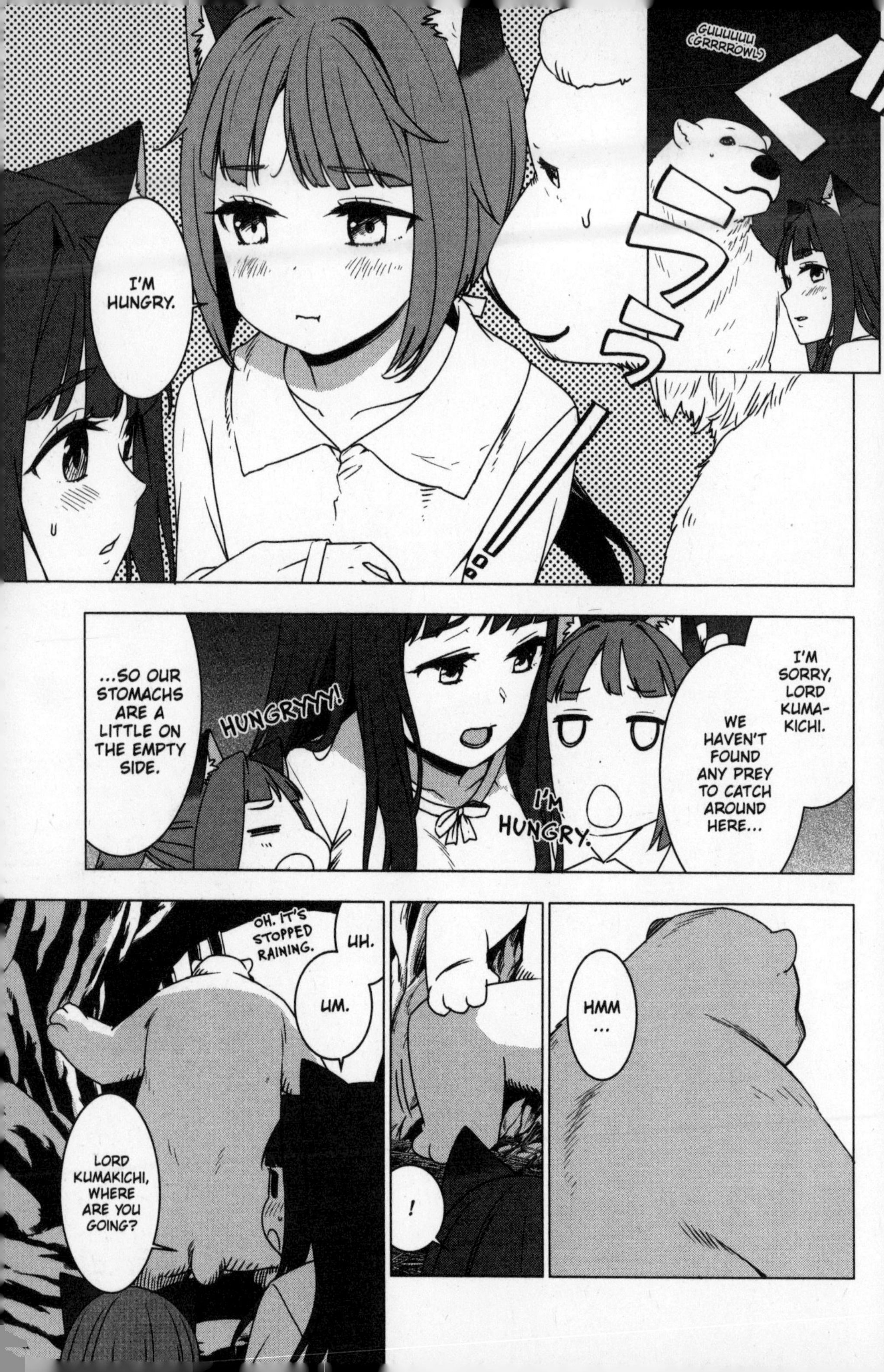
Guuuuuu
(GRRRROWL)
I'M HUNGRY.
I'M SORRY, LORD KUMA-KICHI.
WE HAVEN'T FOUND ANY PREY TO CATCH AROUND HERE...
I'M HUNGRY.
HUNGRYYY!
...SO OUR STOMACHS ARE A LITTLE ON THE EMPTY SIDE.
HMM ...
!
UH.
OH. IT'S STOPPED RAINING.
UM.
LORD KUMAKICHI, WHERE ARE YOU GOING?

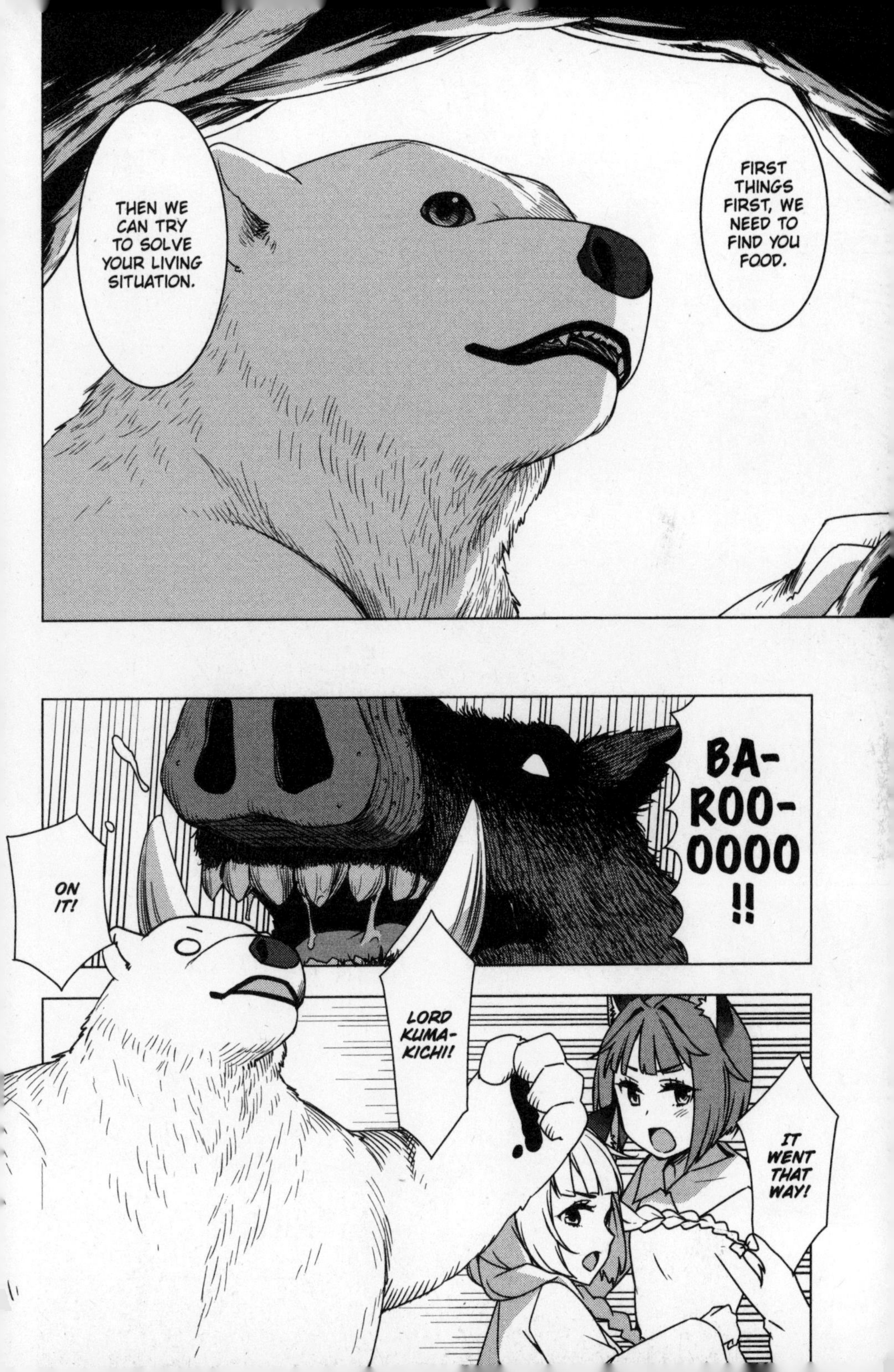
FIRST THINGS FIRST, WE NEED TO FIND YOU FOOD.
THEN WE CAN TRY TO SOLVE YOUR LIVING SITUATION.
BA-ROO-OOOO!!
IT WENT THAT WAY!
LORD KUMAKICHI!
ON IT!

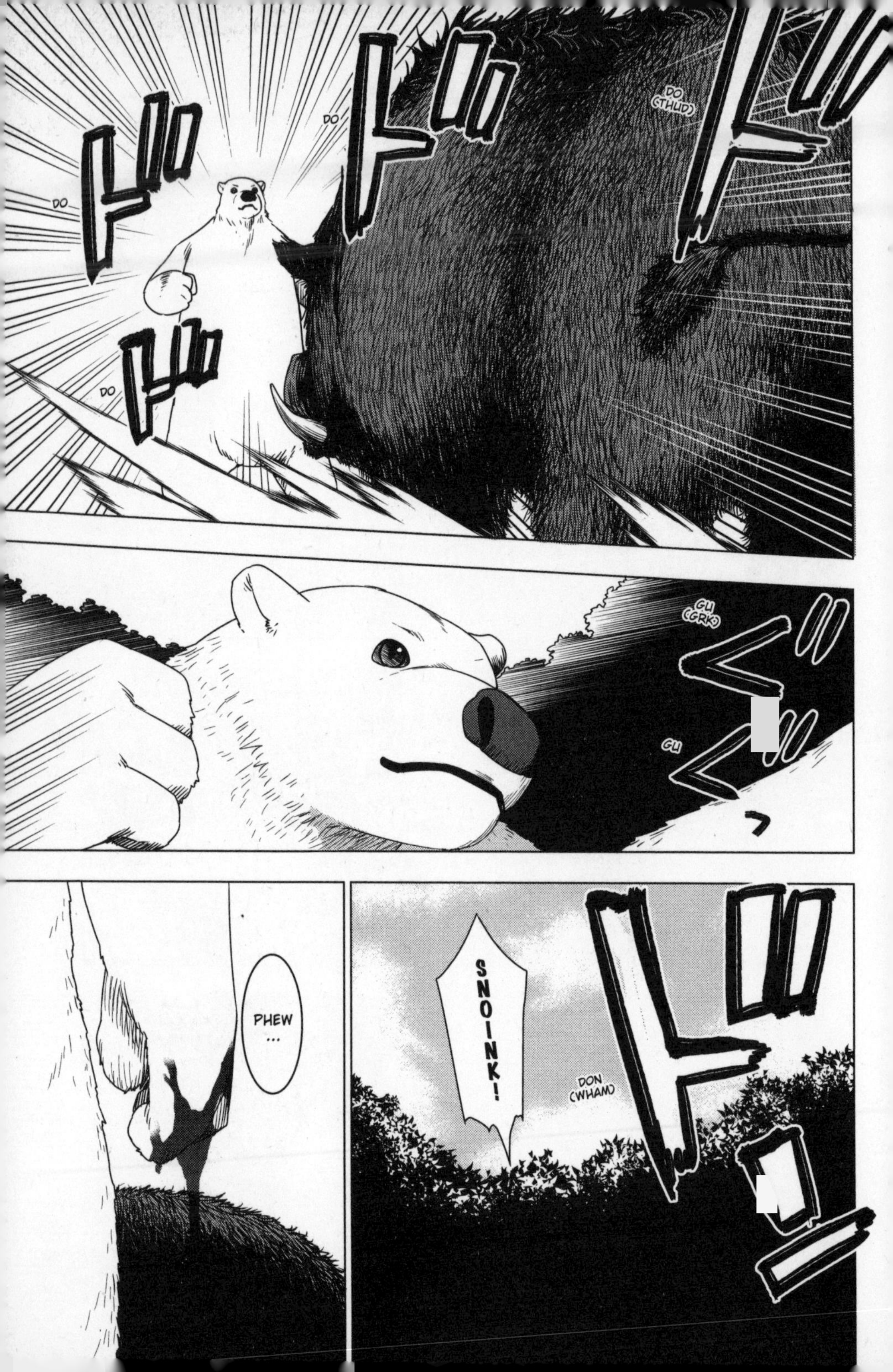
DO (THUD)
DO
DO
DO
GU (GRK)
GU
SNOINK!
DON (WHAM)
PHEW ...

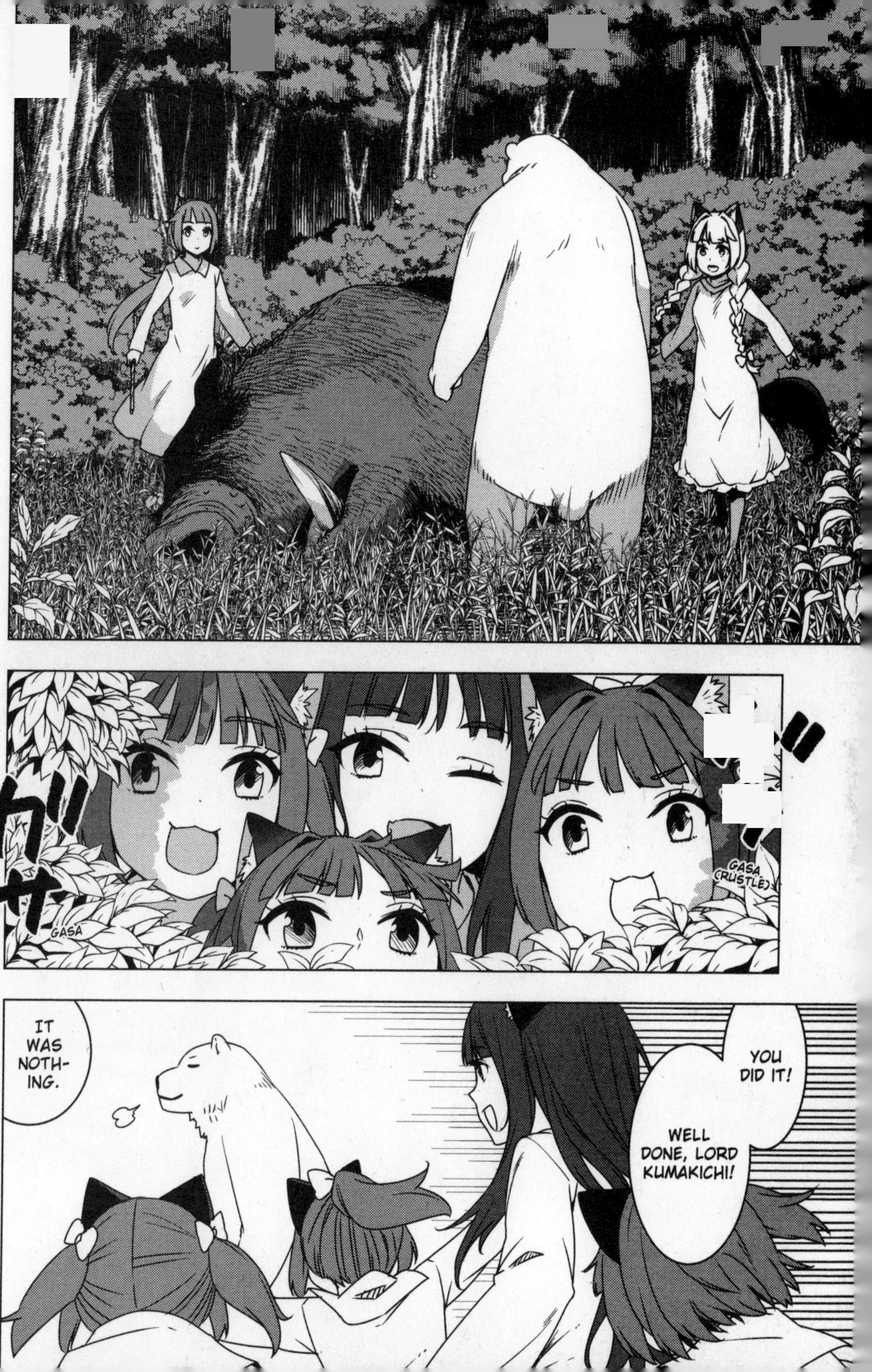
GASA (RUSTLE)
ガサ
GASA
YOU DID IT!
WELL DONE, LORD KUMAKICHI!
IT WAS NOTH-ING.

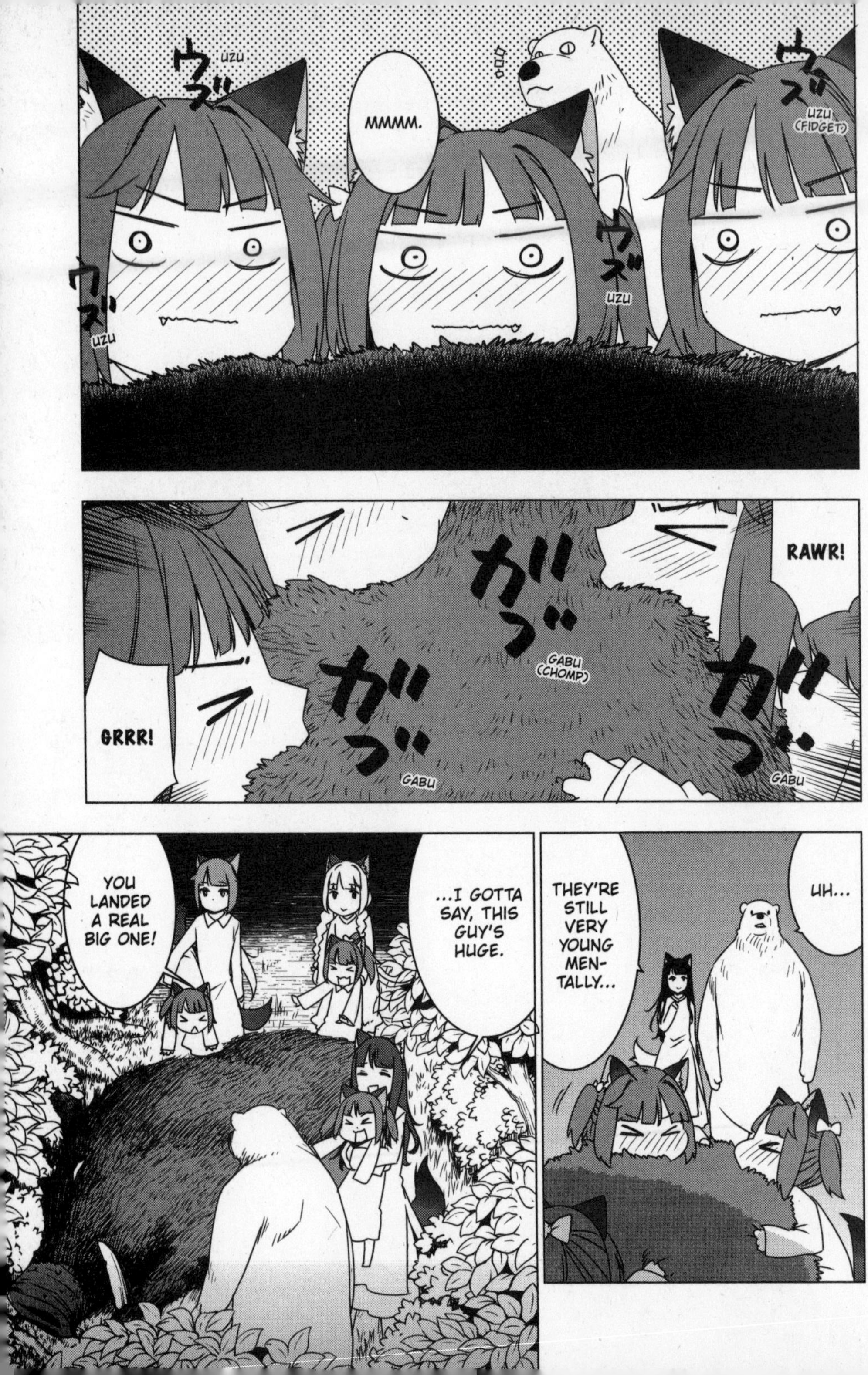
ウズ
UZU (FIDGET)
MMMM.
ウズ
UZU
ウズ
UZU
ウズ
UZU
RAWR!
GABU
GABU (CHOMP)
GABU
GRRR!
UH...
THEY'RE STILL VERY YOUNG MEN-TALLY...
...I GOTTA SAY, THIS GUY'S HUGE.
YOU LANDED A REAL BIG ONE!

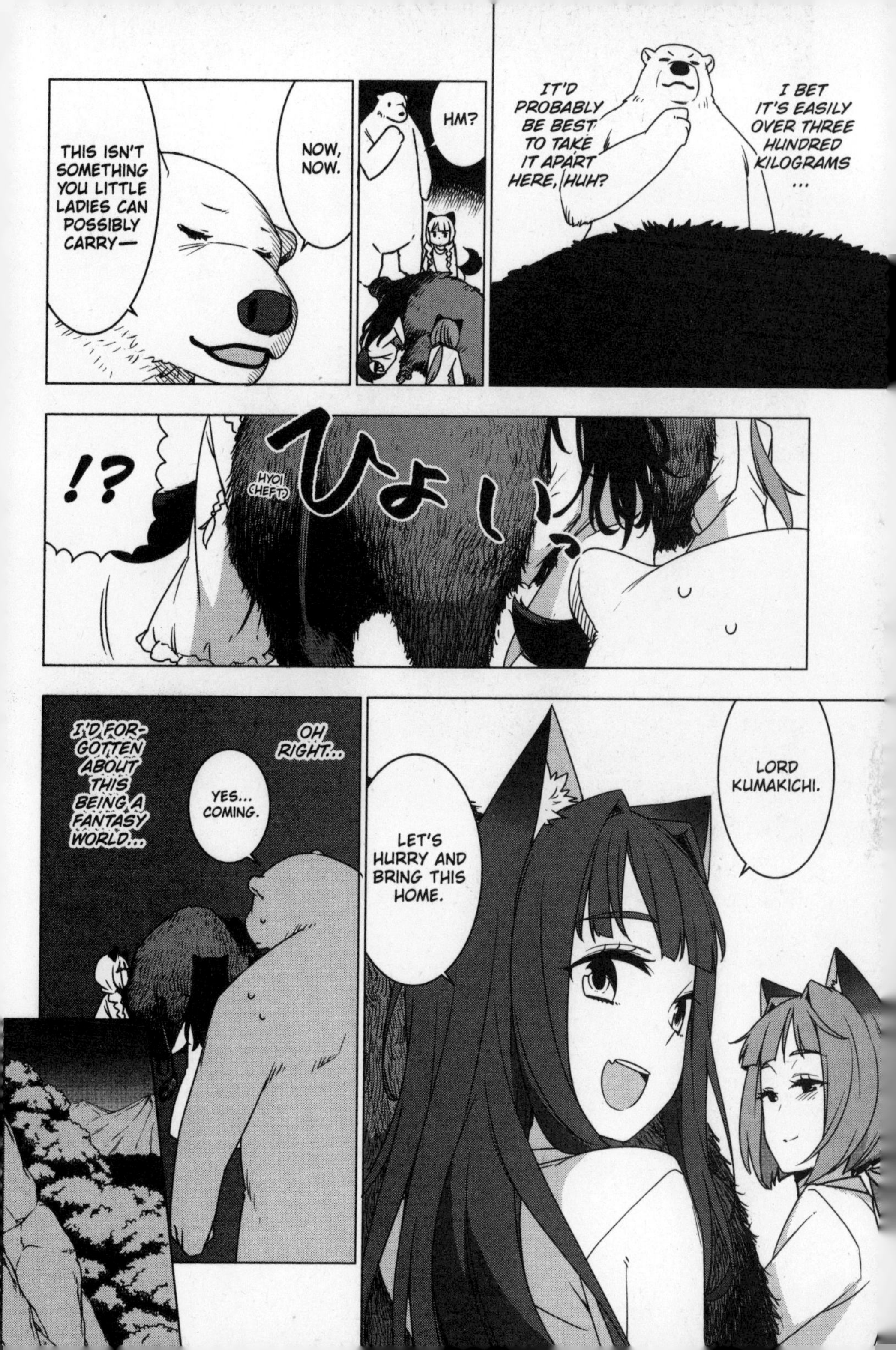
I BET IT'S EASILY OVER THREE HUNDRED KILOGRAMS...
IT'D PROBABLY BE BEST TO TAKE IT APART HERE, HUH?
HM?
NOW, NOW.
THIS ISN'T SOMETHING YOU LITTLE LADIES CAN POSSIBLY CARRY—
ひょいっ
HYOI (HEFT)
!?
LORD KUMAKICHI.
LET'S HURRY AND BRING THIS HOME.
OH RIGHT...
I'D FOR-GOTTEN ABOUT THIS BEING A FANTASY WORLD...
YES... COMING.

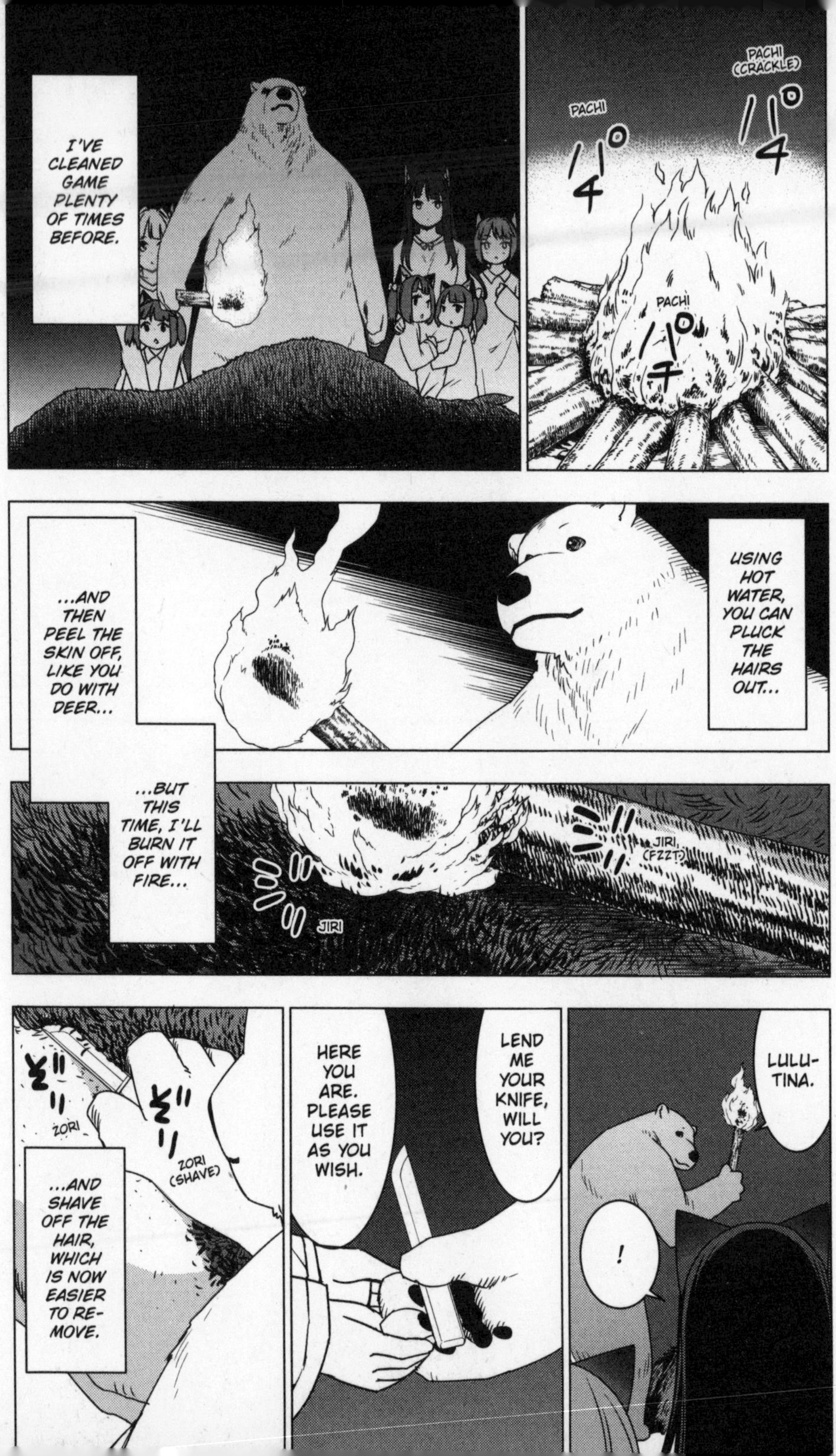
PACHI (CRACKLE)
PACHI
PACHI
I'VE CLEANED GAME PLENTY OF TIMES BEFORE.
USING HOT WATER, YOU CAN PLUCK THE HAIRS OUT...
...AND THEN PEEL THE SKIN OFF, LIKE YOU DO WITH DEER...
...BUT THIS TIME, I'LL BURN IT OFF WITH FIRE...
JIRI (FZZT)
JIRI
LULU-TINA.
!
LEND ME YOUR KNIFE, WILL YOU?
HERE YOU ARE. PLEASE USE IT AS YOU WISH.
ZORI (SHAVE)
ZORI
...AND SHAVE OFF THE HAIR, WHICH IS NOW EASIER TO RE-MOVE.

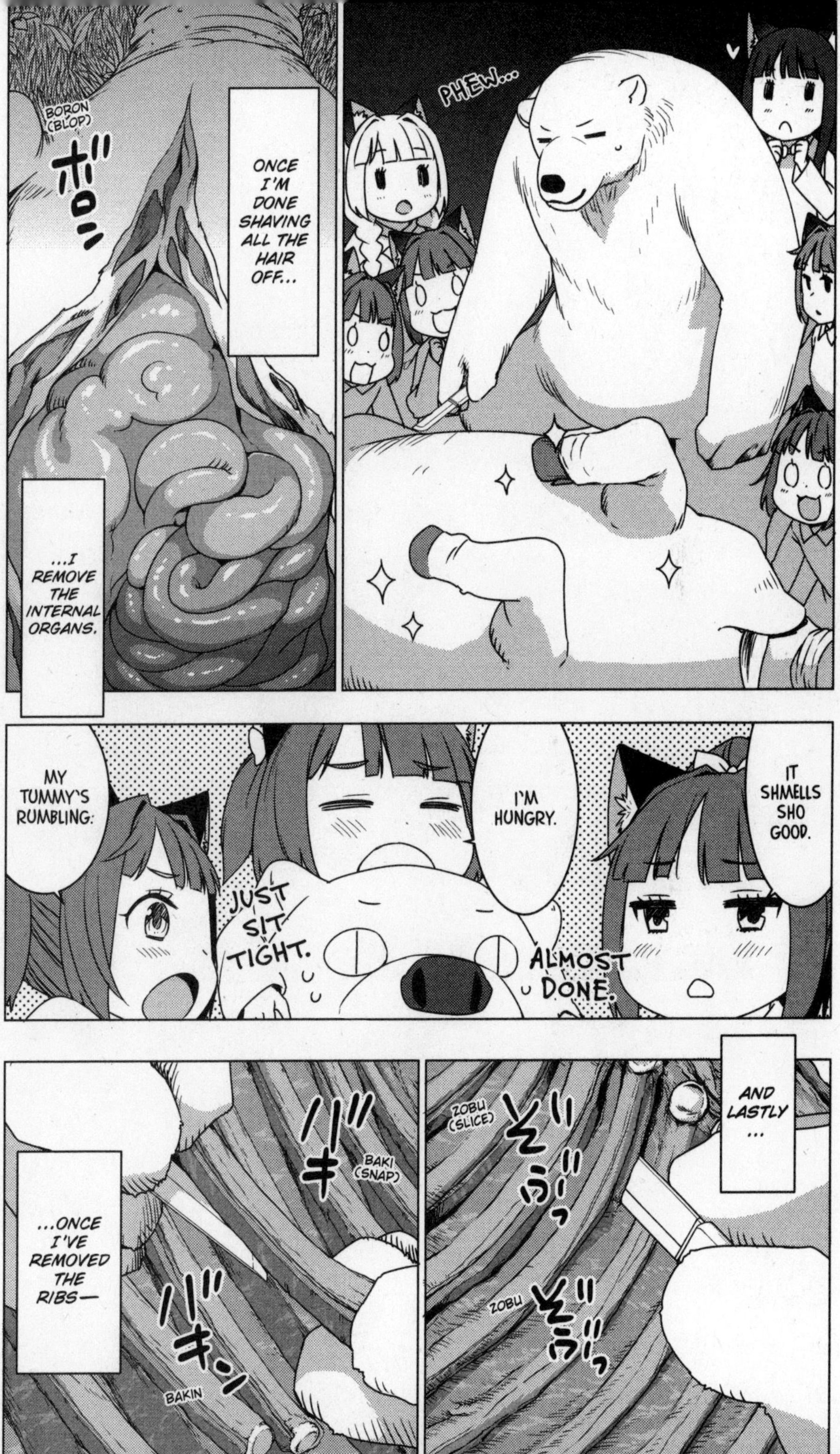
PHEW...
ONCE I'M DONE SHAVING ALL THE HAIR OFF...
BORON (BLOP)
ボロン
...I REMOVE THE INTERNAL ORGANS.
IT SHMELLS SHO GOOD.
I'M HUNGRY.
MY TUMMY'S RUMBLING.
ALMOST DONE.
JUST SIT TIGHT.
AND LASTLY...
ZOBU (SLICE)
ぞぶっ
ZOBU
ぞぶっ
BAKI (SNAP)
バキ
...ONCE I'VE REMOVED THE RIBS—
バキン
BAKIN

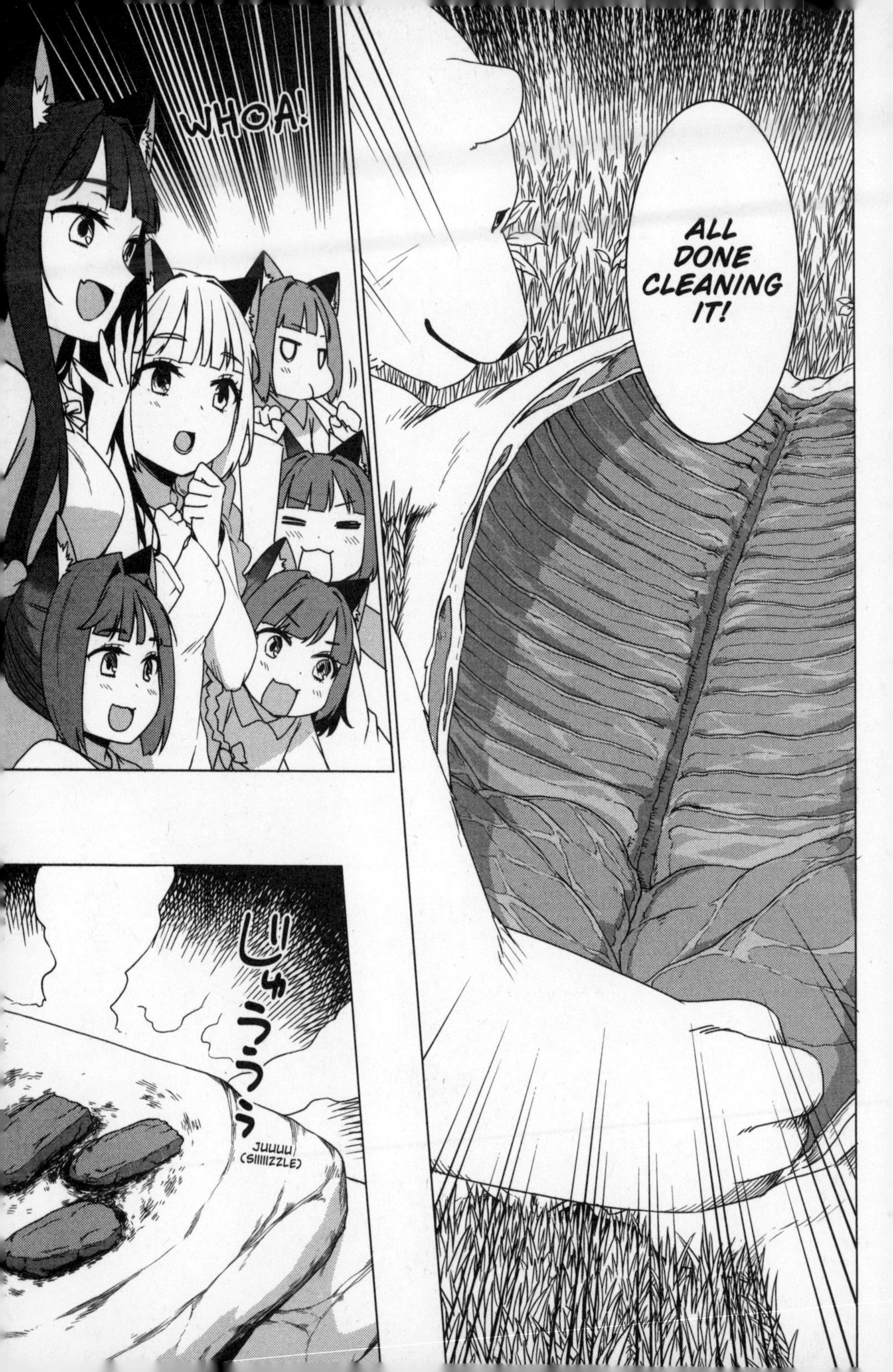
ALL DONE CLEANING IT!
WHOA!
じゅううう
JUUUU (SIIIIIZZLE)

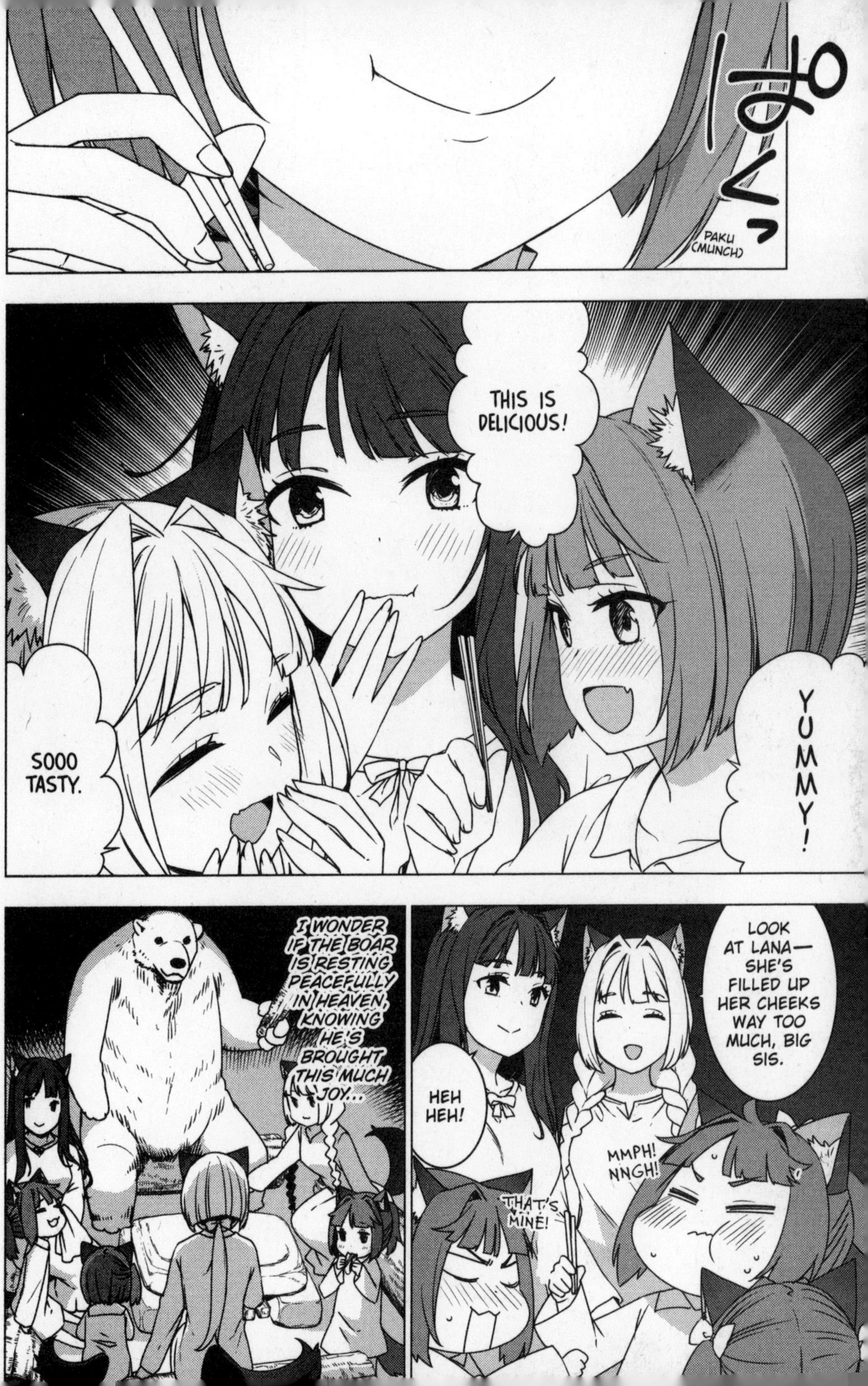
ぱくっ
PAKU (MUNCH)
THIS IS DELICIOUS!
YUMMY!
SOOO TASTY.
LOOK AT LANA— SHE'S FILLED UP HER CHEEKS WAY TOO MUCH, BIG SIS.
HEH HEH!
MMPH! NNGH!
THAT'S MINE!
I WONDER IF THE BOAR IS RESTING PEACEFULLY IN HEAVEN, KNOWING HE'S BROUGHT THIS MUCH JOY...

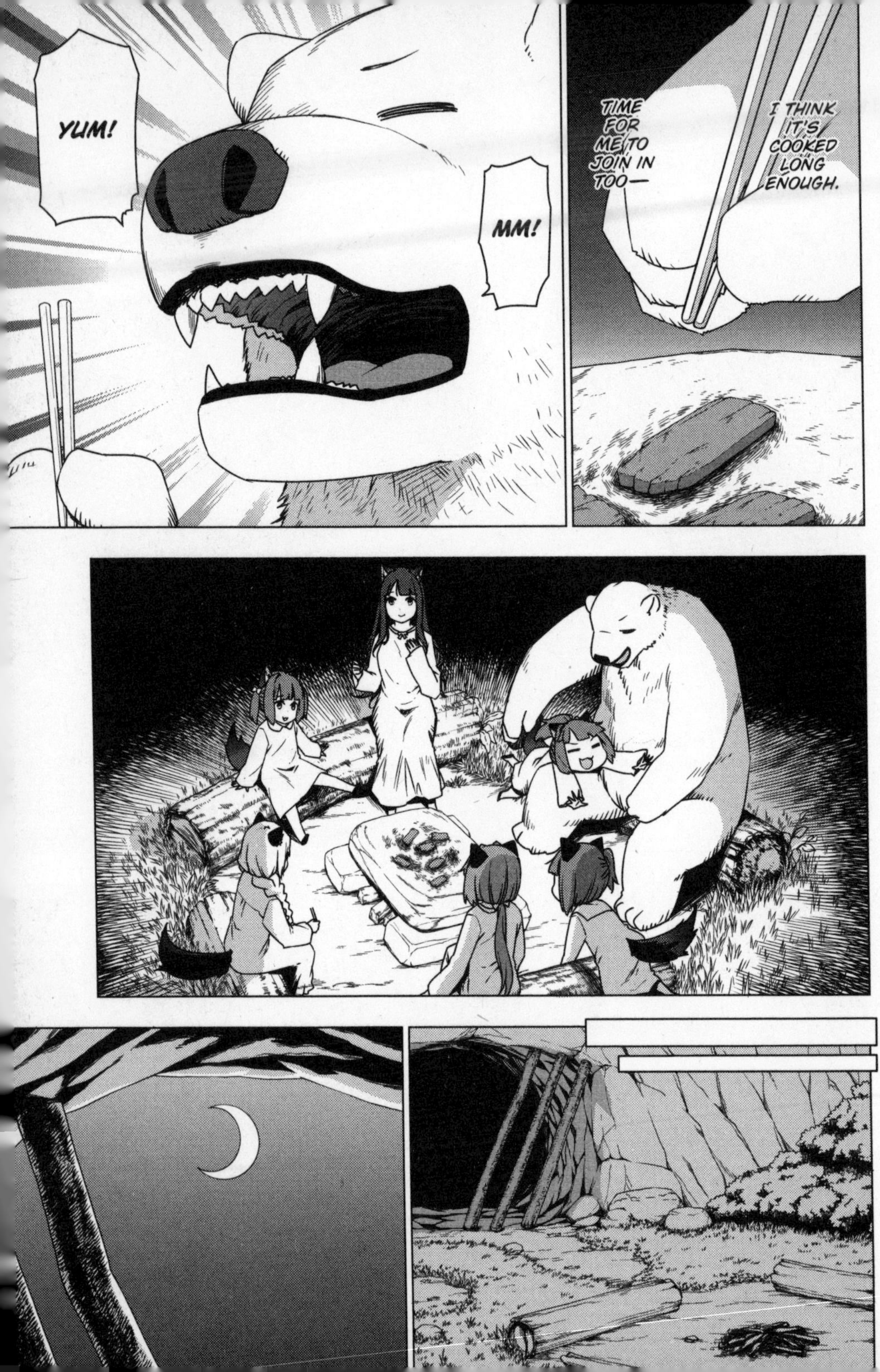
I THINK IT'S COOKED LONG ENOUGH.
TIME FOR ME TO JOIN IN TOO—
MM!
YUM!

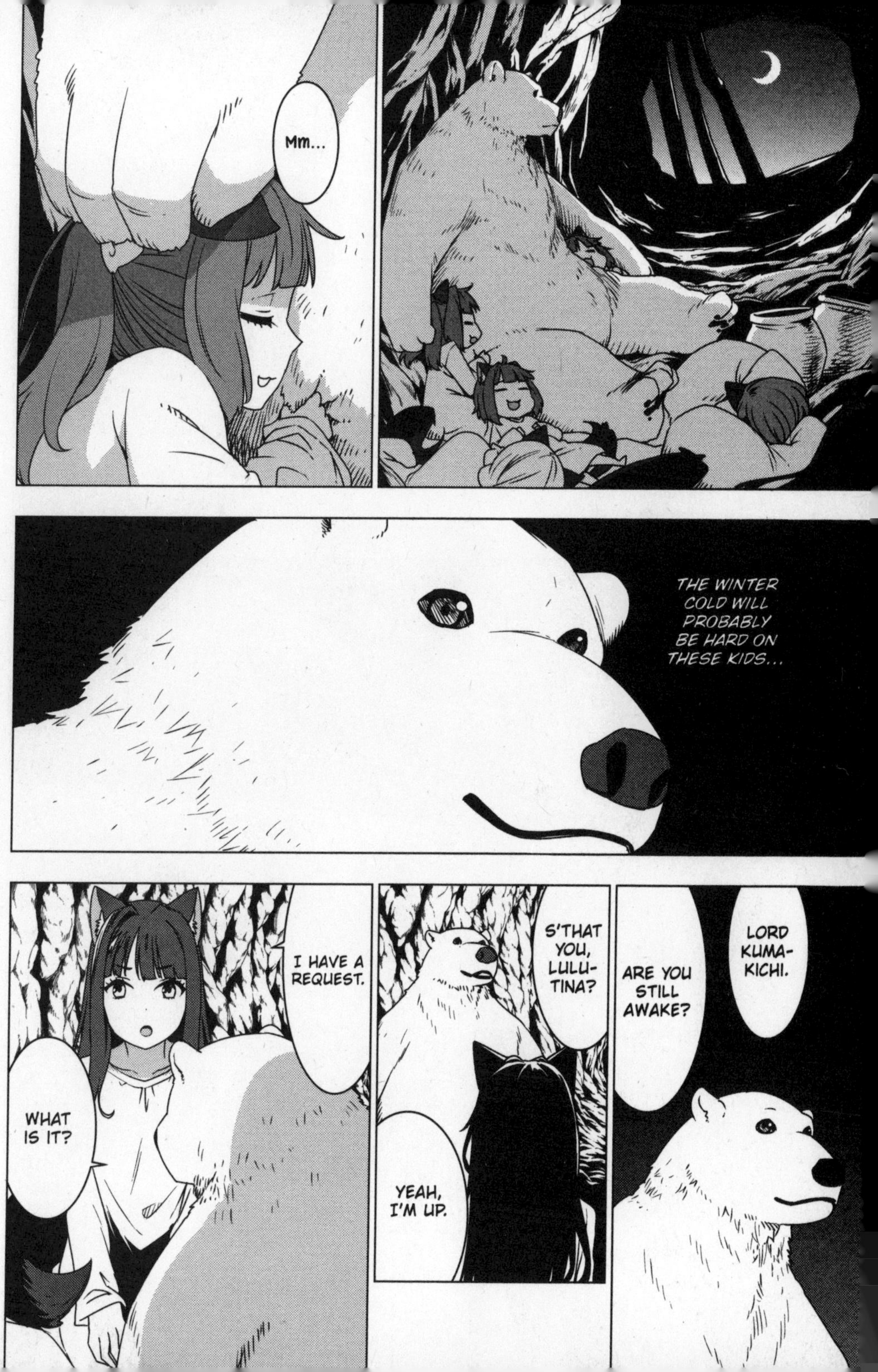
Mm...
THE WINTER COLD WILL PROBABLY BE HARD ON THESE KIDS...
LORD KUMA-KICHI.
ARE YOU STILL AWAKE?
S'THAT YOU, LULU-TINA?
YEAH, I'M UP.
I HAVE A REQUEST.
WHAT IS IT?

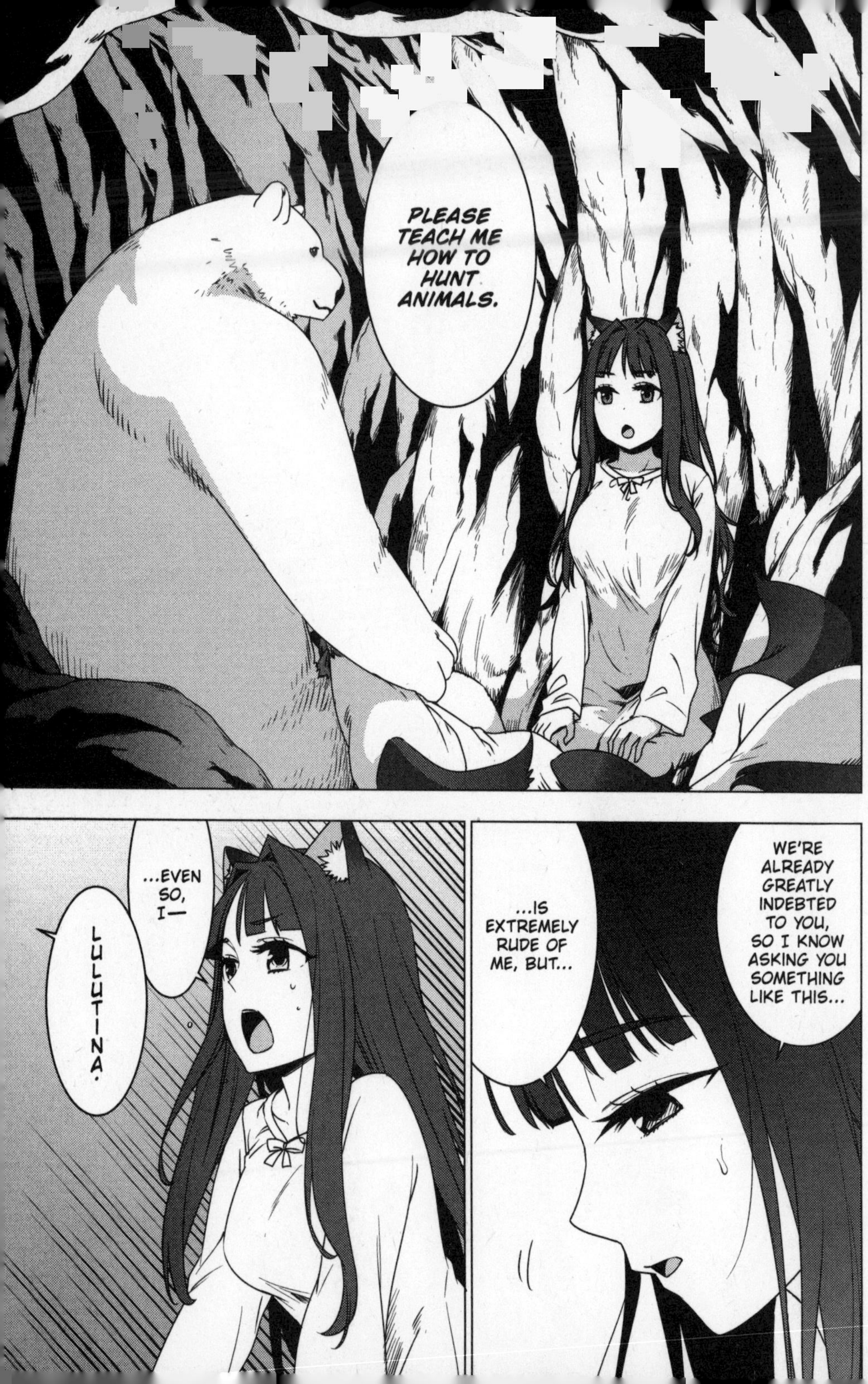
PLEASE TEACH ME HOW TO HUNT ANIMALS.
WE'RE ALREADY GREATLY INDEBTED TO YOU, SO I KNOW ASKING YOU SOMETHING LIKE THIS...
...IS EXTREMELY RUDE OF ME, BUT...
...EVEN SO, I—
LULUTINA.

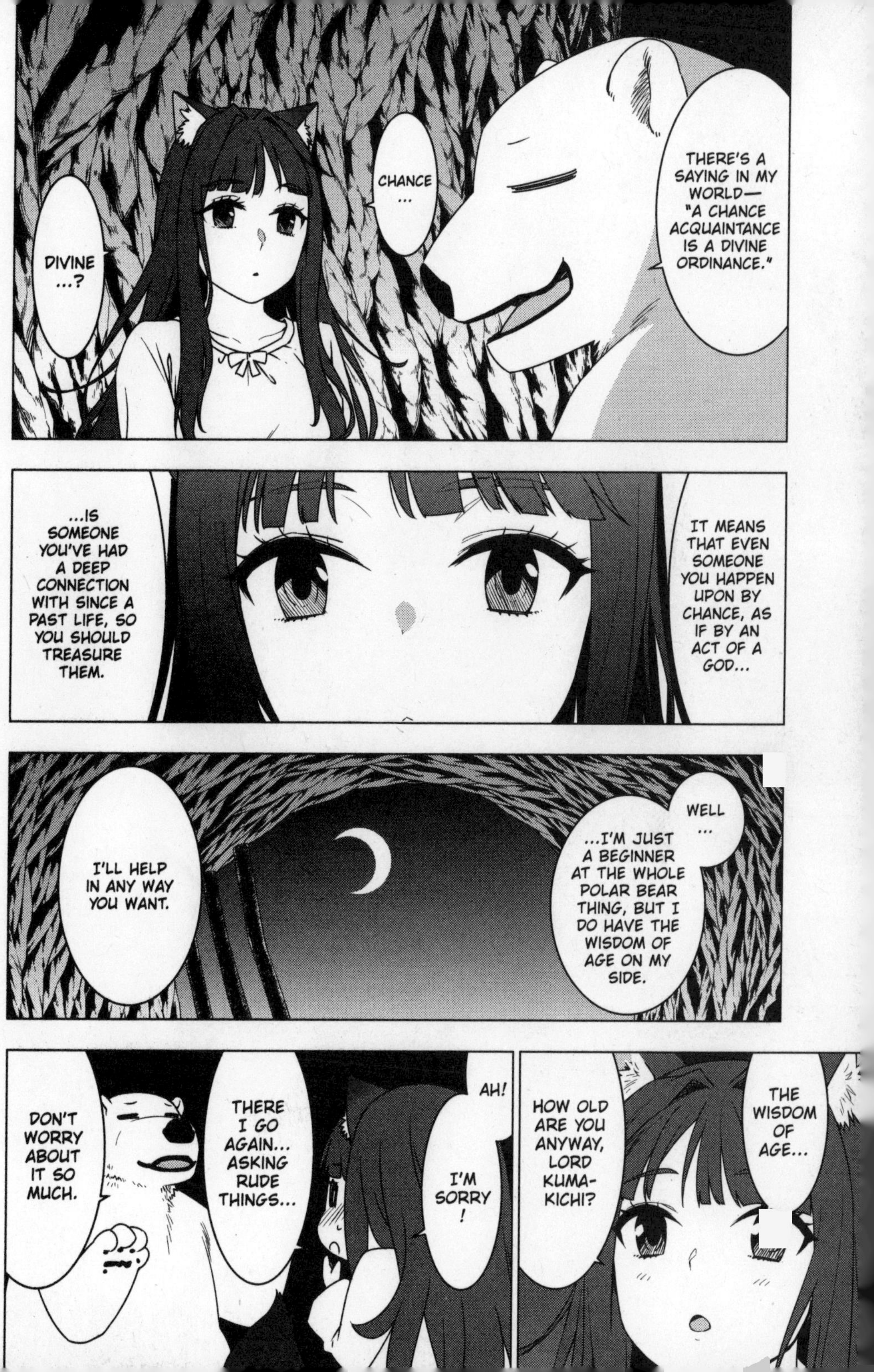
THERE'S A SAYING IN MY WORLD— "A CHANCE ACQUAINTANCE IS A DIVINE ORDINANCE."
CHANCE ...
DIVINE ...?
IT MEANS THAT EVEN SOMEONE YOU HAPPEN UPON BY CHANCE, AS IF BY AN ACT OF A GOD...
...IS SOMEONE YOU'VE HAD A DEEP CONNECTION WITH SINCE A PAST LIFE, SO YOU SHOULD TREASURE THEM.
WELL ...
...I'M JUST A BEGINNER AT THE WHOLE POLAR BEAR THING, BUT I DO HAVE THE WISDOM OF AGE ON MY SIDE.
I'LL HELP IN ANY WAY YOU WANT.
THE WISDOM OF AGE...
HOW OLD ARE YOU ANYWAY, LORD KUMA-KICHI?
AH!
I'M SORRY!
THERE I GO AGAIN... ASKING RUDE THINGS...
DON'T WORRY ABOUT IT SO MUCH.

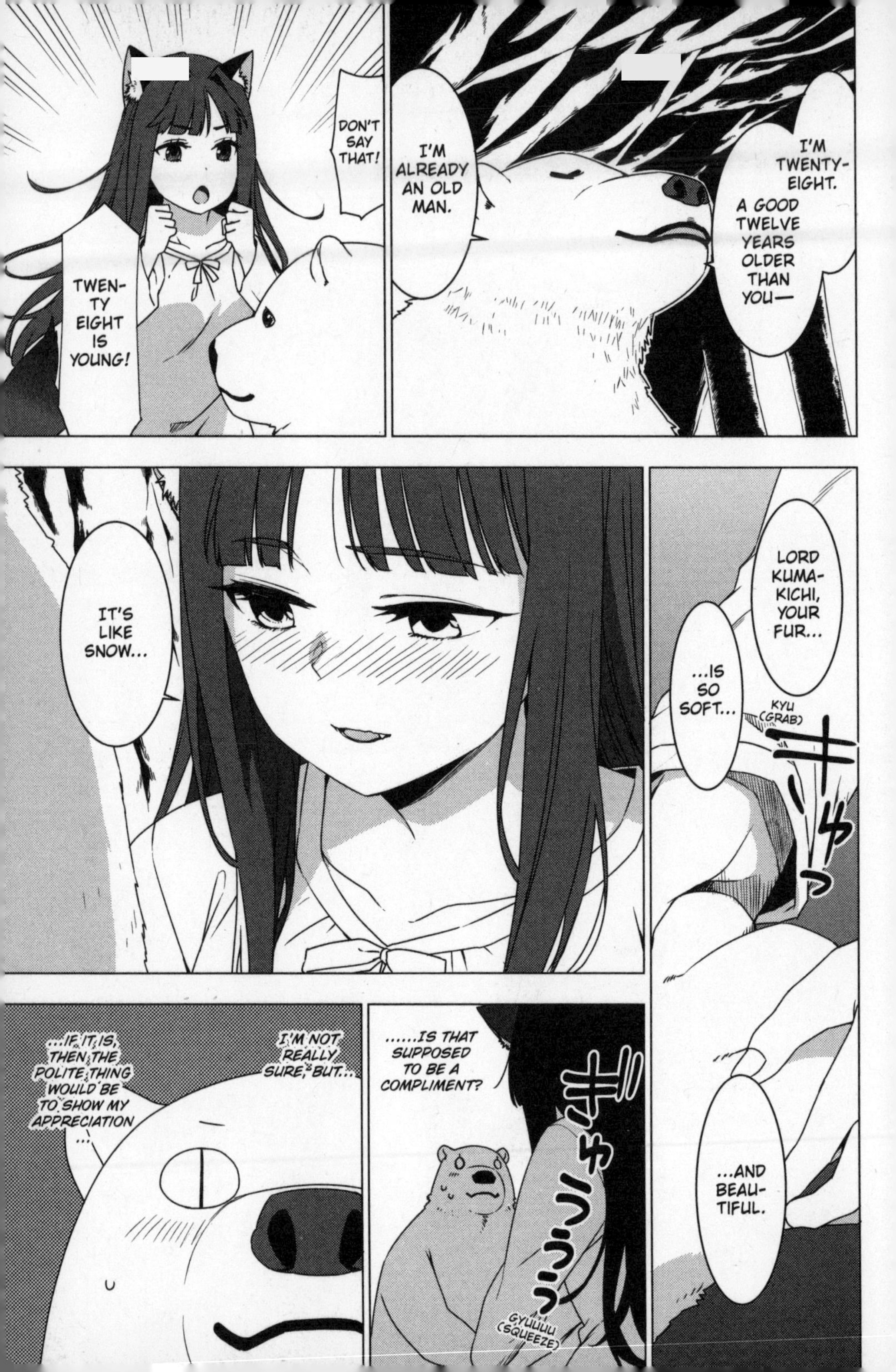
I'M TWENTY-EIGHT.
A GOOD TWELVE YEARS OLDER THAN YOU—
I'M ALREADY AN OLD MAN.
DON'T SAY THAT!
TWENTY EIGHT IS YOUNG!
LORD KUMAKICHI, YOUR FUR...
...IS SO SOFT...
KYU (GRAB)
IT'S LIKE SNOW...
...AND BEAUTIFUL.
......IS THAT SUPPOSED TO BE A COMPLIMENT?
GYUUUU (SQUEEZE)
I'M NOT REALLY SURE, BUT...
...IF IT IS, THEN THE POLITE THING WOULD BE TO SHOW MY APPRECIATION...

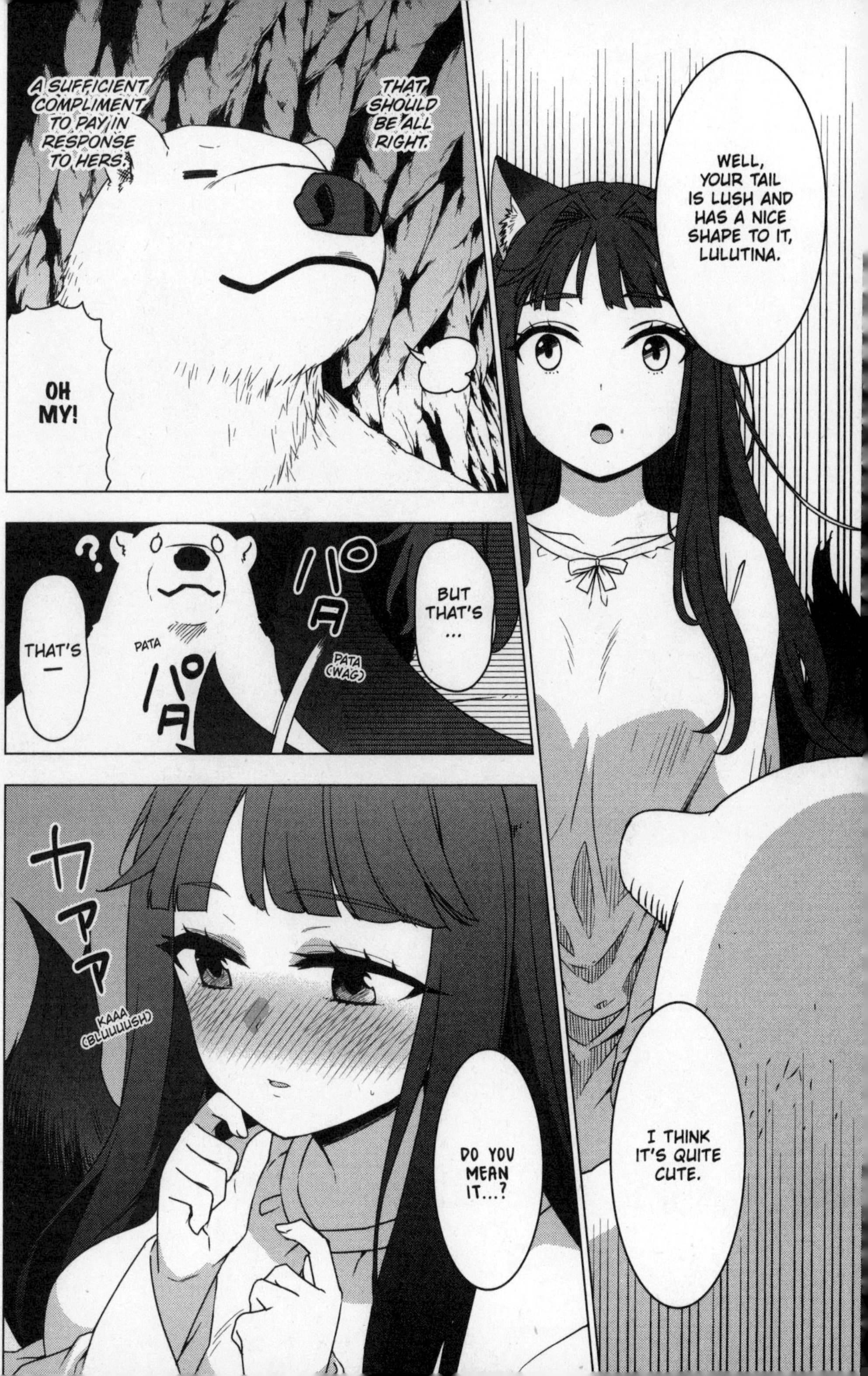
WELL, YOUR TAIL IS LUSH AND HAS A NICE SHAPE TO IT, LULUTINA.
I THINK IT'S QUITE CUTE.
THAT SHOULD BE ALL RIGHT.
A SUFFICIENT COMPLIMENT TO PAY IN RESPONSE TO HERS.
OH MY!
BUT THAT'S ...
PATA (WAG)
PATA
THAT'S —
KAAA (BLUUUUSH)
DO YOU MEAN IT...?

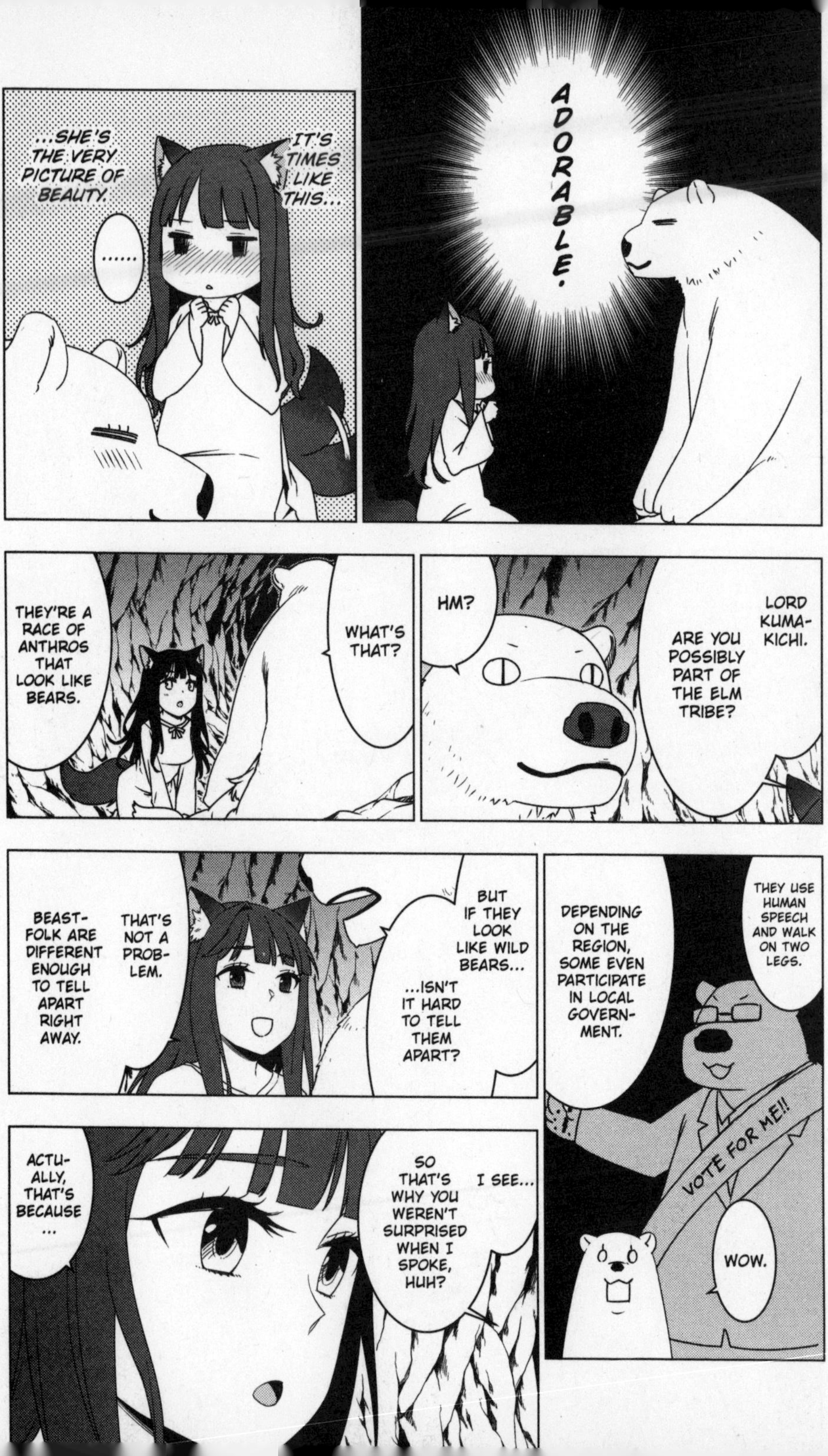
ADORABLE.
IT'S TIMES LIKE THIS...
...SHE'S THE VERY PICTURE OF BEAUTY.
......
LORD KUMAKICHI.
ARE YOU POSSIBLY PART OF THE ELM TRIBE?
HM?
WHAT'S THAT?
THEY'RE A RACE OF ANTHROS THAT LOOK LIKE BEARS.
THEY USE HUMAN SPEECH AND WALK ON TWO LEGS.
DEPENDING ON THE REGION, SOME EVEN PARTICIPATE IN LOCAL GOVERNMENT.
VOTE FOR ME!!
WOW.
BUT IF THEY LOOK LIKE WILD BEARS...
...ISN'T IT HARD TO TELL THEM APART?
THAT'S NOT A PROBLEM.
BEASTFOLK ARE DIFFERENT ENOUGH TO TELL APART RIGHT AWAY.
I SEE...
SO THAT'S WHY YOU WEREN'T SURPRISED WHEN I SPOKE, HUH?
ACTUALLY, THAT'S BECAUSE...

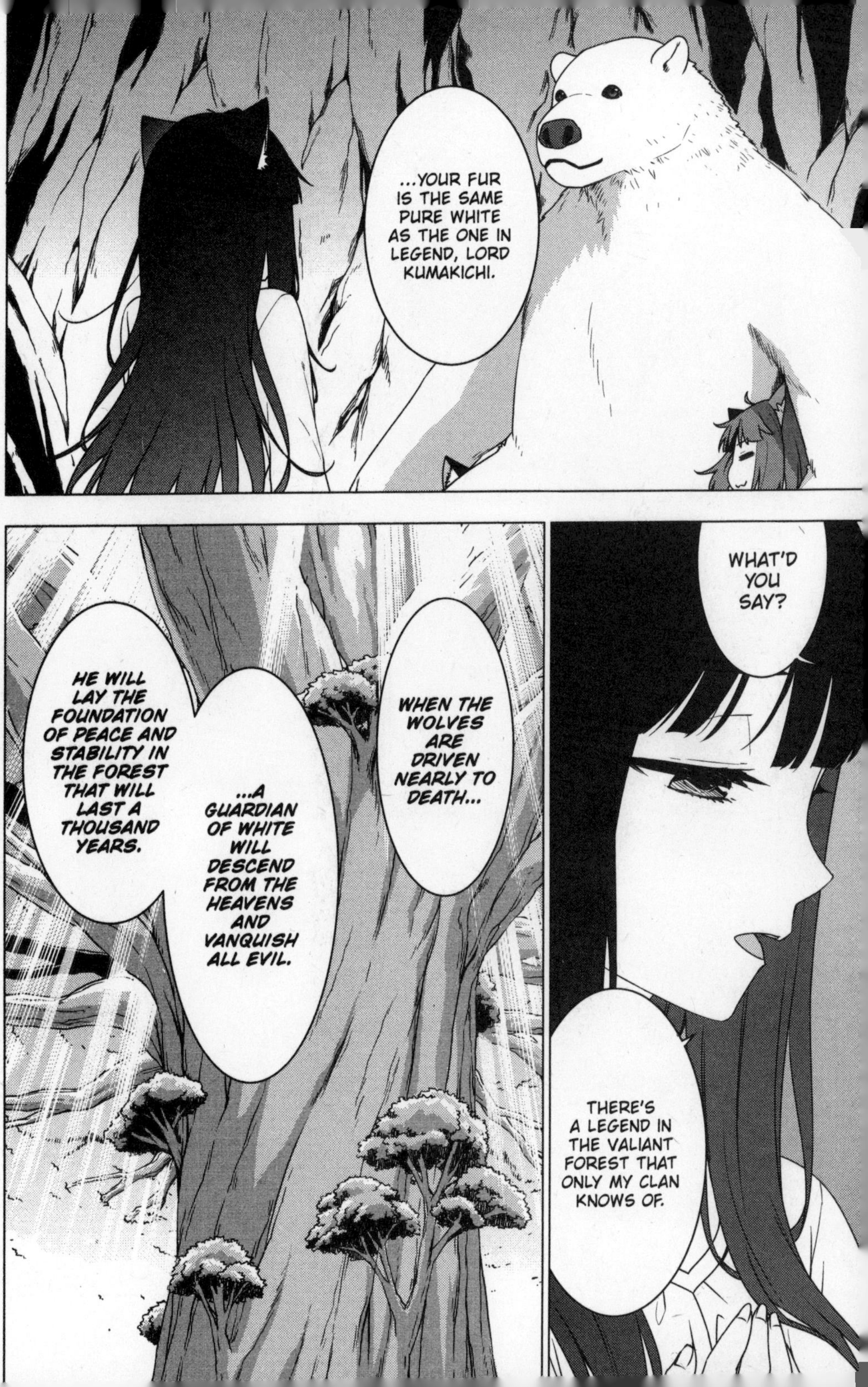
...YOUR FUR IS THE SAME PURE WHITE AS THE ONE IN LEGEND, LORD KUMAKICHI.
WHAT'D YOU SAY?
THERE'S A LEGEND IN THE VALIANT FOREST THAT ONLY MY CLAN KNOWS OF.
WHEN THE WOLVES ARE DRIVEN NEARLY TO DEATH...
...A GUARDIAN OF WHITE WILL DESCEND FROM THE HEAVENS AND VANQUISH ALL EVIL.
HE WILL LAY THE FOUNDATION OF PEACE AND STABILITY IN THE FOREST THAT WILL LAST A THOUSAND YEARS.

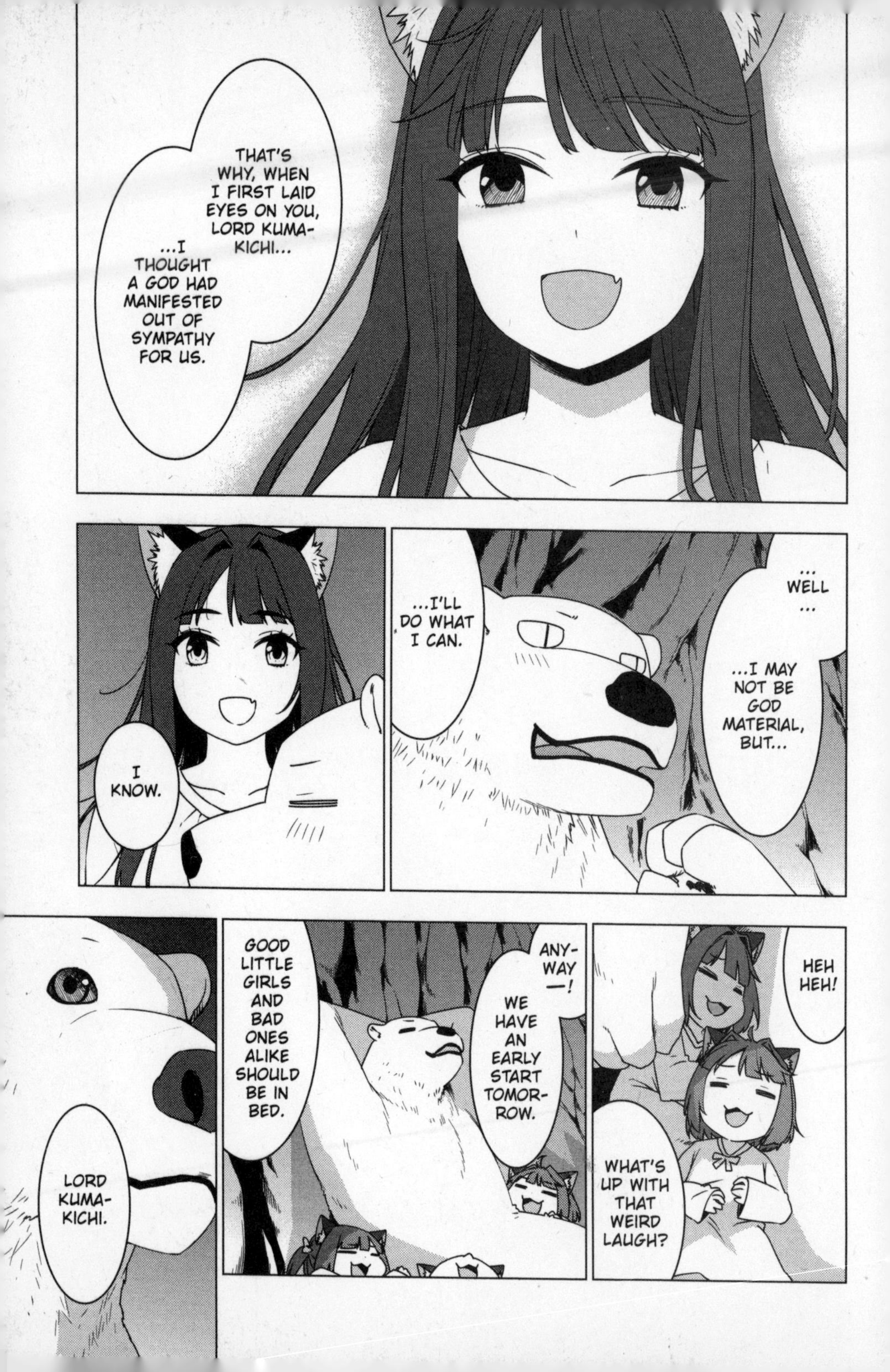
THAT'S WHY, WHEN I FIRST LAID EYES ON YOU, LORD KUMA-KICHI...
...I THOUGHT A GOD HAD MANIFESTED OUT OF SYMPATHY FOR US.
... WELL ...
...I MAY NOT BE GOD MATERIAL, BUT...
...I'LL DO WHAT I CAN.
I KNOW.
HEH HEH!
WHAT'S UP WITH THAT WEIRD LAUGH?
ANY-WAY—!
WE HAVE AN EARLY START TOMORROW.
GOOD LITTLE GIRLS AND BAD ONES ALIKE SHOULD BE IN BED.
LORD KUMA-KICHI.

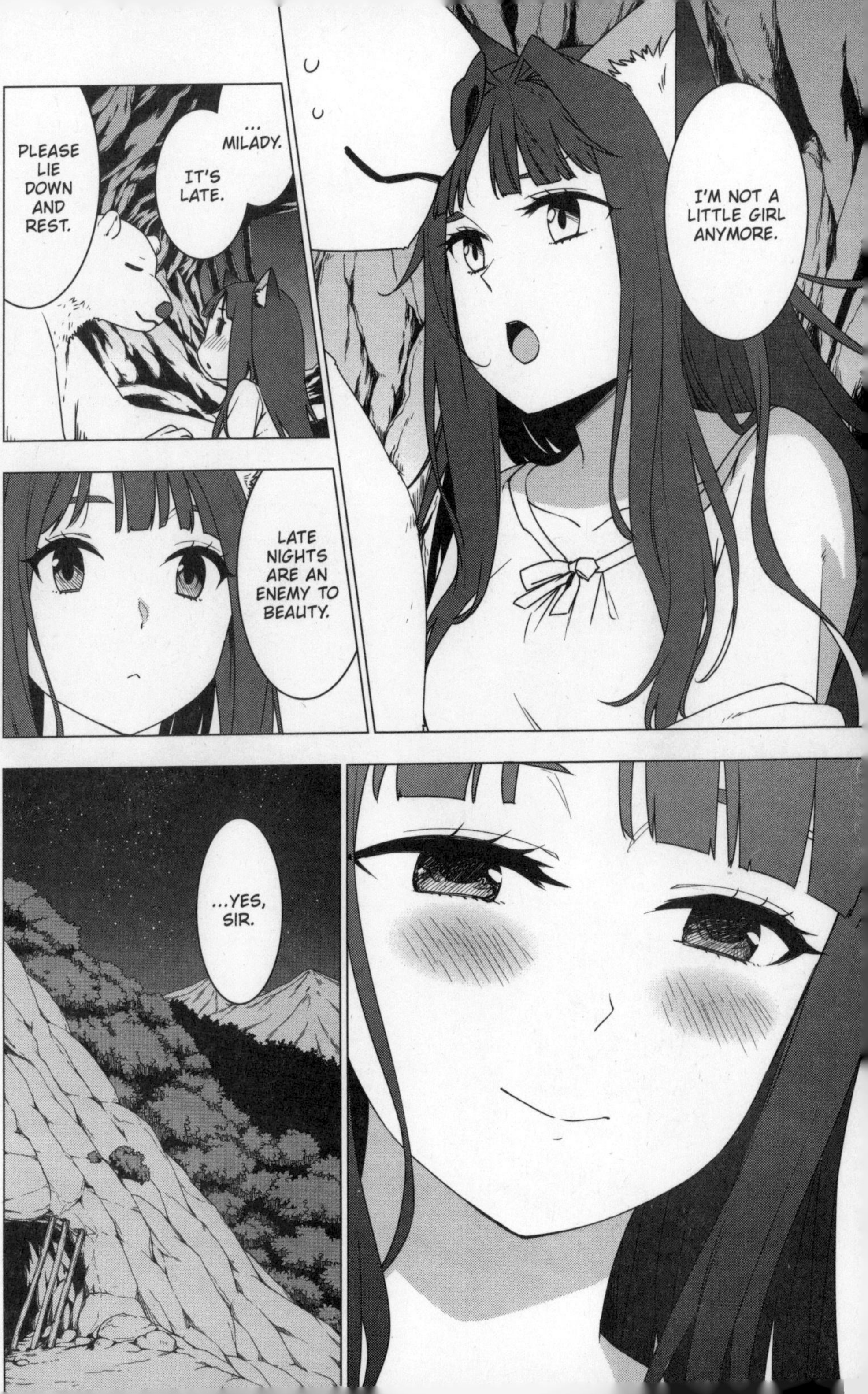
I'M NOT A LITTLE GIRL ANYMORE.
...MILADY.
IT'S LATE.
PLEASE LIE DOWN AND REST.
LATE NIGHTS ARE AN ENEMY TO BEAUTY.
...YES, SIR.

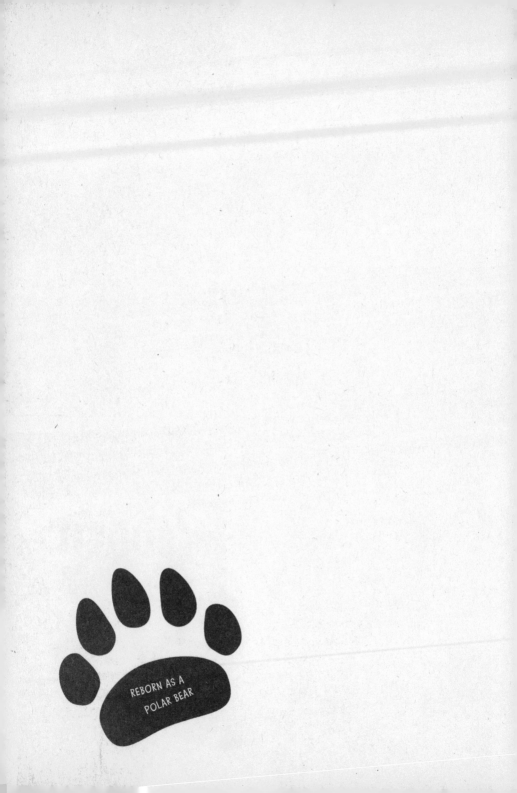

REBORN AS A
POLAR BEAR

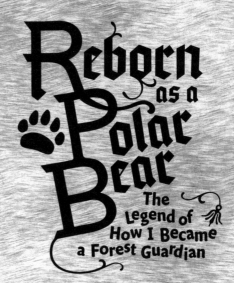

Reborn
as a
Polar
Bear

The
Legend of
How I Became
a Forest Guardian

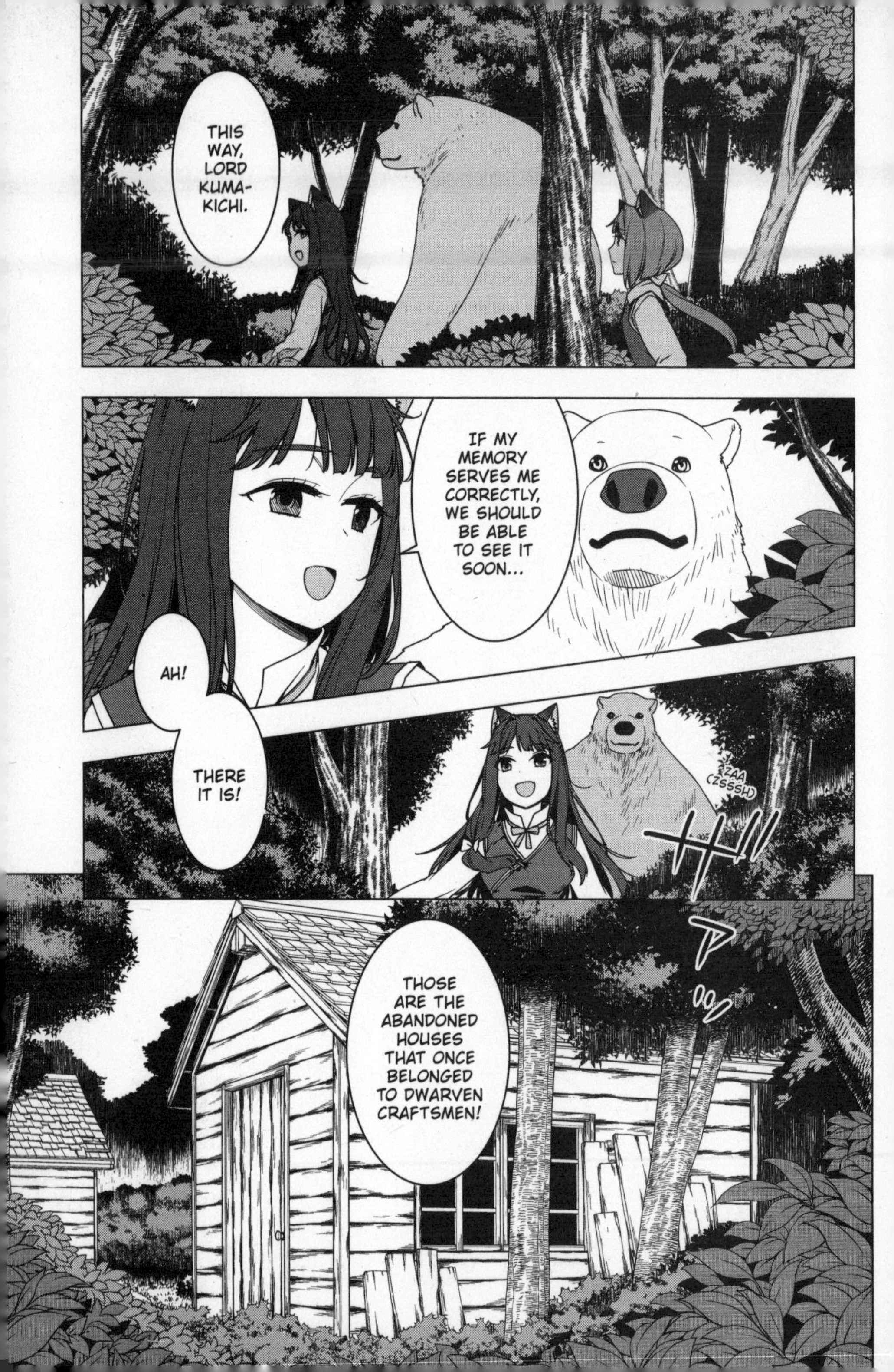
THIS WAY, LORD KUMA-KICHI.
IF MY MEMORY SERVES ME CORRECTLY, WE SHOULD BE ABLE TO SEE IT SOON...
AH!
THERE IT IS!
ZAA (ZSSSH)
THOSE ARE THE ABANDONED HOUSES THAT ONCE BELONGED TO DWARVEN CRAFTSMEN!

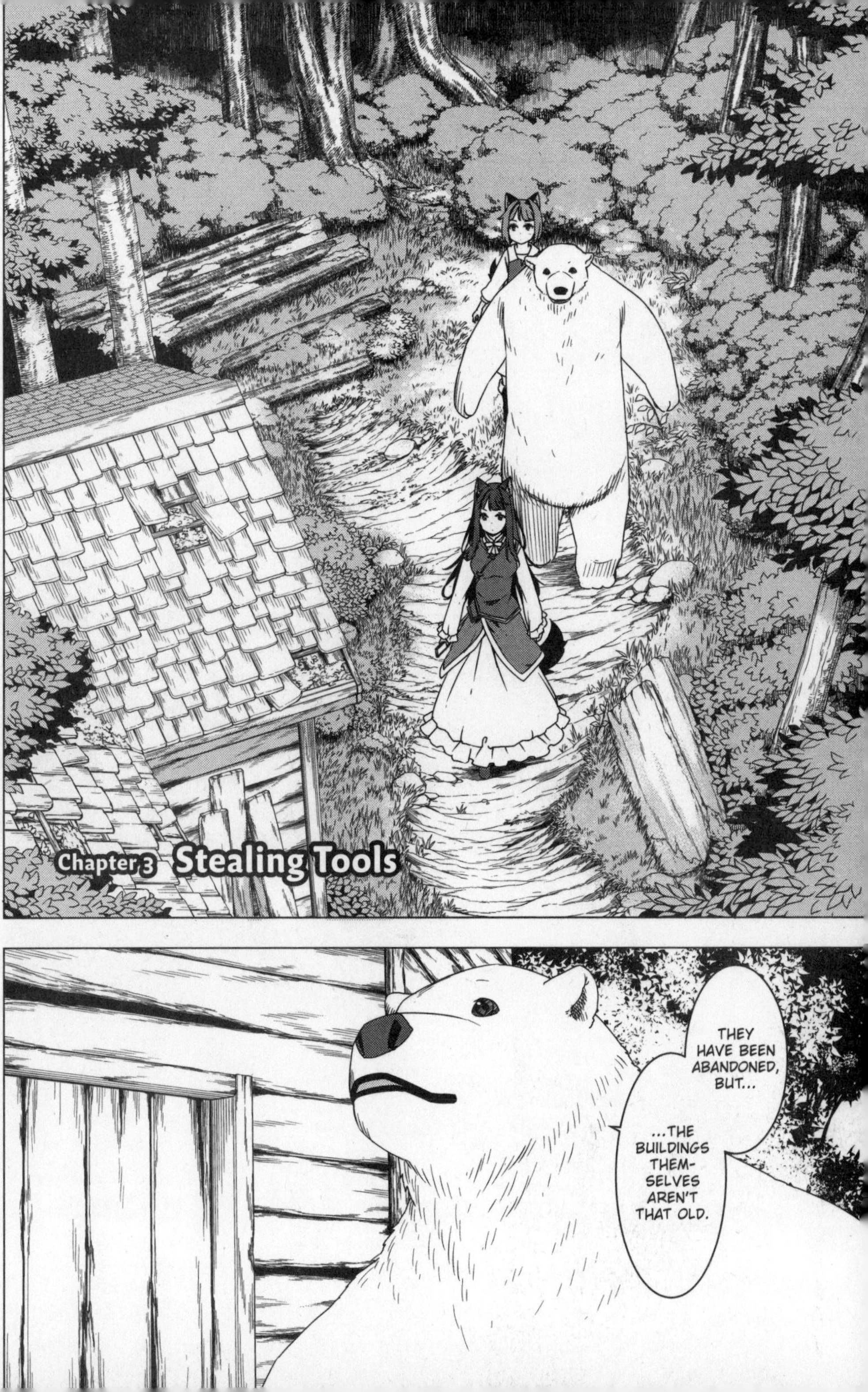
Chapter 3 Stealing Tools
THEY HAVE BEEN ABANDONED, BUT...
...THE BUILDINGS THEM-SELVES AREN'T THAT OLD.

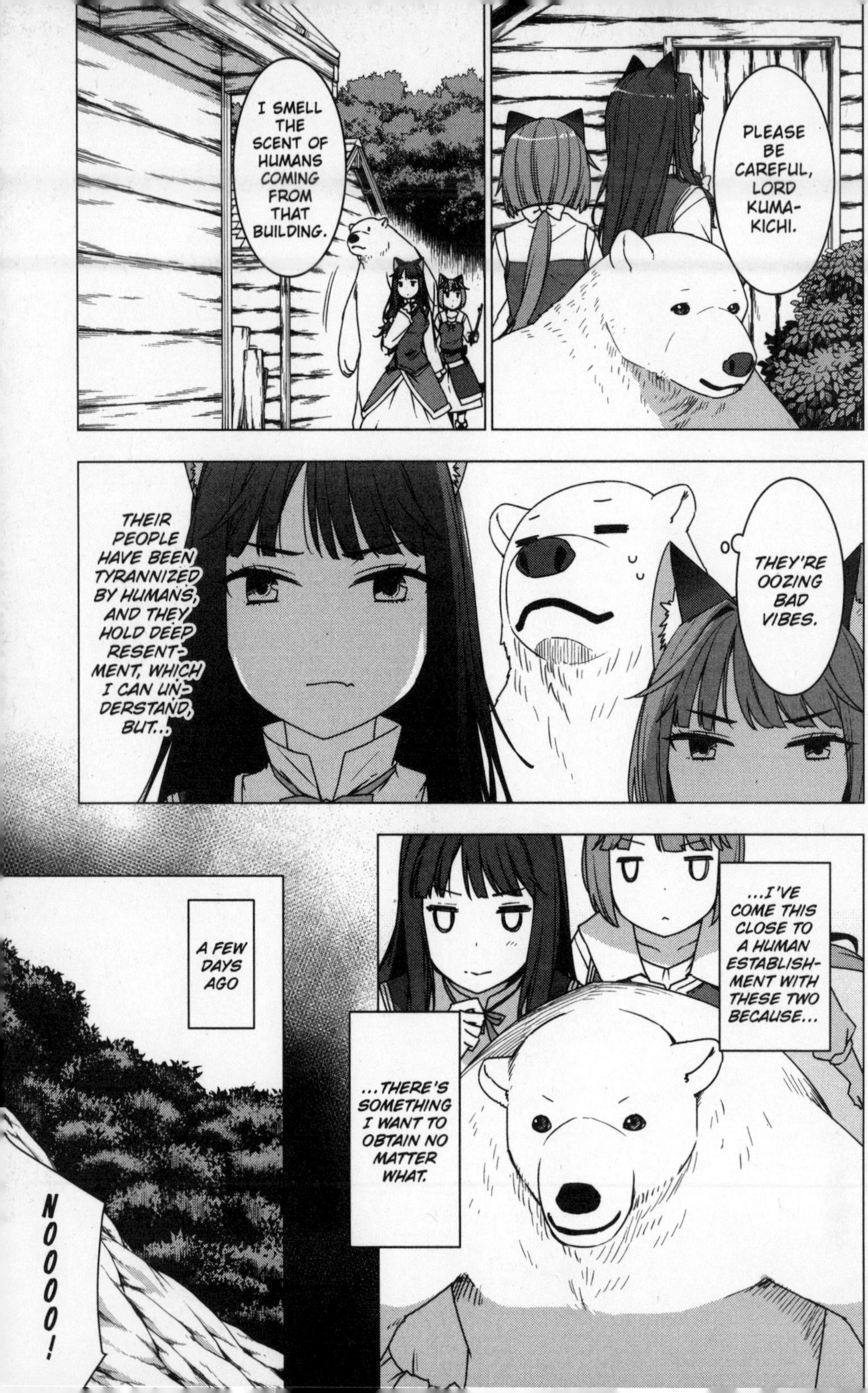
PLEASE BE CAREFUL, LORD KUMA-KICHI.
I SMELL THE SCENT OF HUMANS COMING FROM THAT BUILDING.
THEY'RE OOZING BAD VIBES.
THEIR PEOPLE HAVE BEEN TYRANNIZED BY HUMANS, AND THEY HOLD DEEP RESENT-MENT, WHICH I CAN UN-DERSTAND, BUT...
...I'VE COME THIS CLOSE TO A HUMAN ESTABLISH-MENT WITH THESE TWO BECAUSE...
...THERE'S SOMETHING I WANT TO OBTAIN NO MATTER WHAT.
A FEW DAYS AGO
NOOOOO!

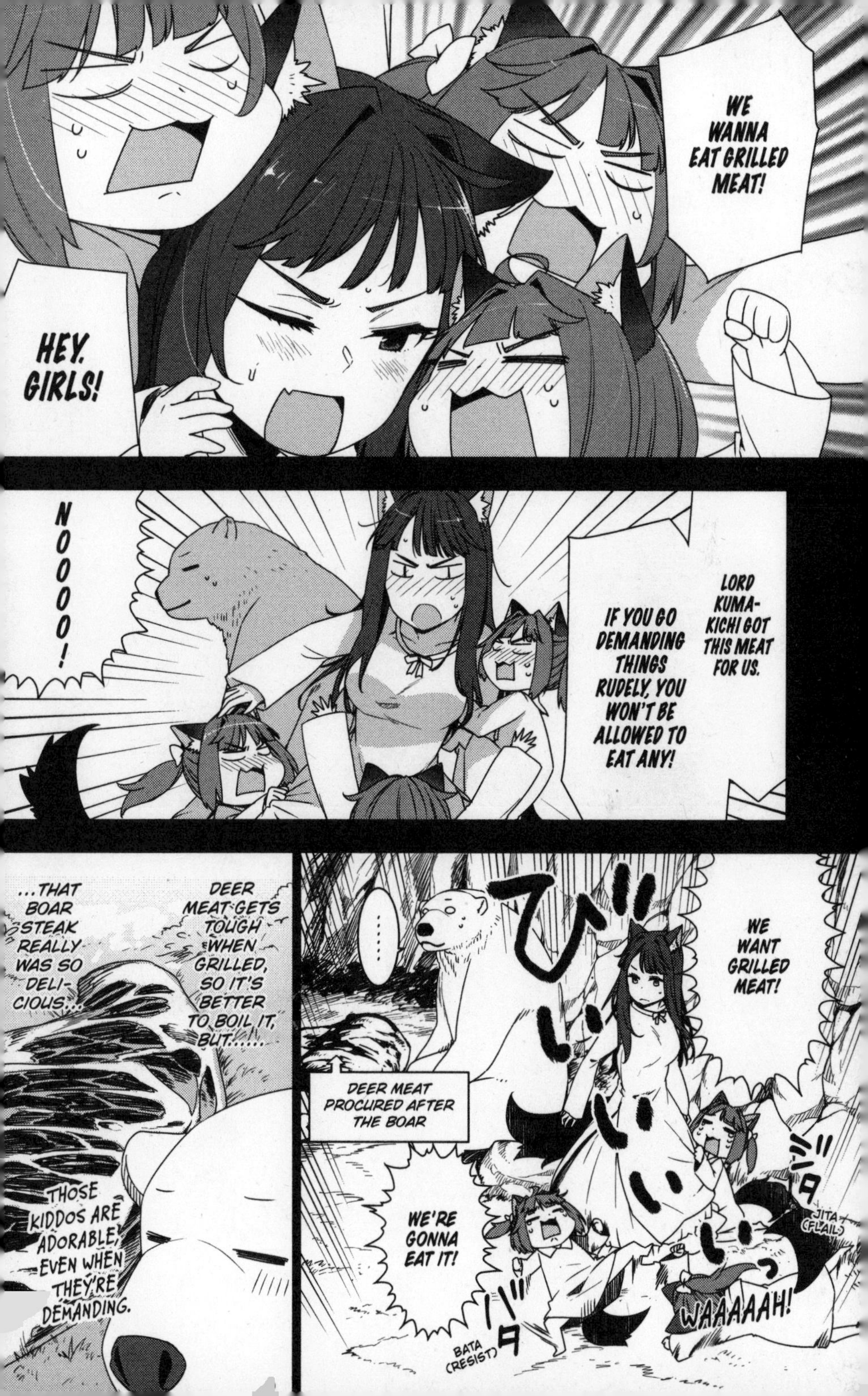
WE WANNA EAT GRILLED MEAT!
HEY. GIRLS!
LORD KUMA-KICHI GOT THIS MEAT FOR US.
IF YOU GO DEMANDING THINGS RUDELY, YOU WON'T BE ALLOWED TO EAT ANY!
NOOOOO!
WE WANT GRILLED MEAT!
......
DEER MEAT PROCURED AFTER THE BOAR
JITA (FLAIL)
WE'RE GONNA EAT IT!
WAAAAAH!
BATA (RESIST)
DEER MEAT GETS TOUGH WHEN GRILLED, SO IT'S BETTER TO BOIL IT, BUT......
...THAT BOAR STEAK REALLY WAS SO DELI-CIOUS...
THOSE KIDDOS ARE ADORABLE, EVEN WHEN THEY'RE DEMANDING.

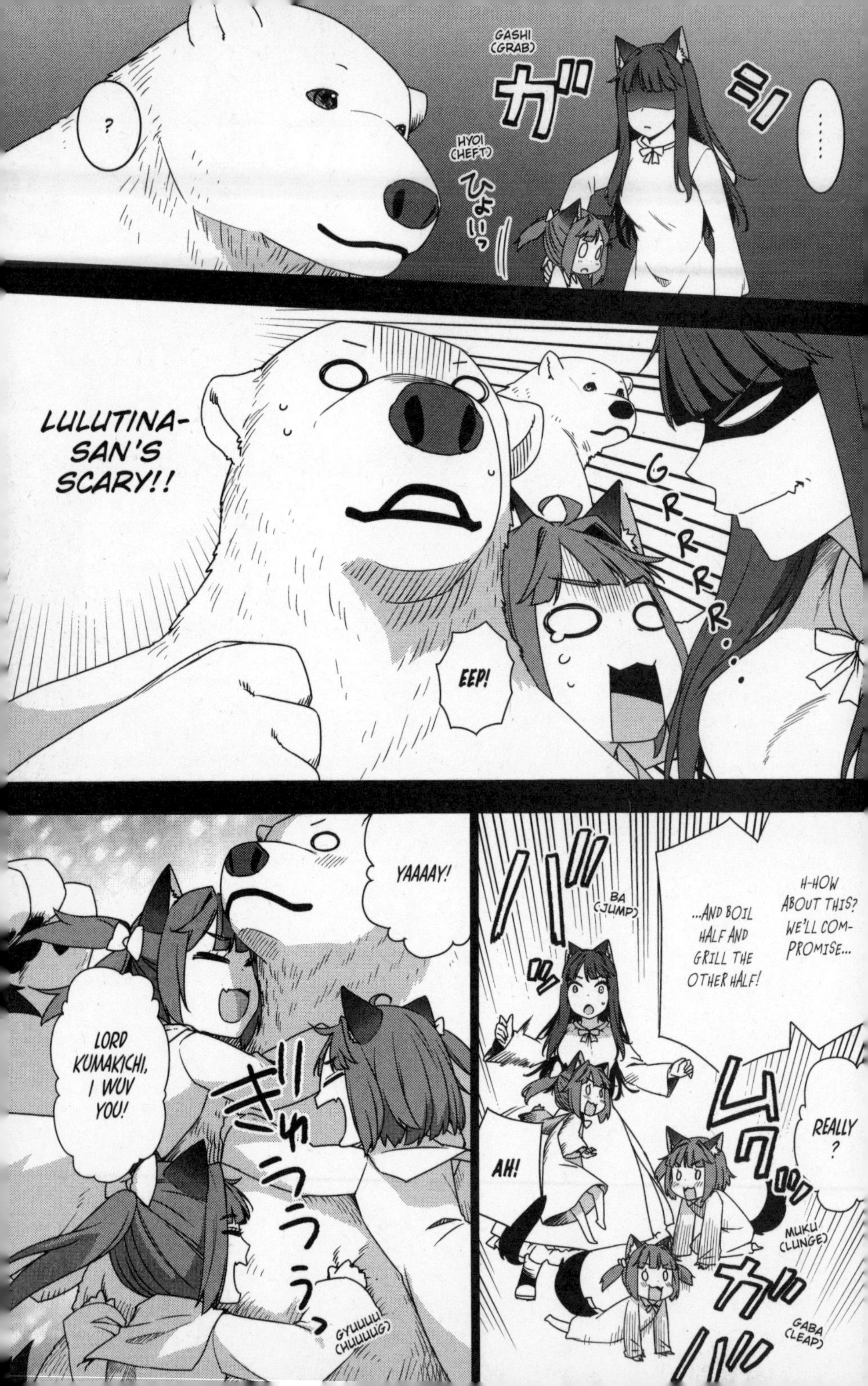
......
GASHI (GRAB)
HYOI (HEFT)
?
LULUTINA-SAN'S SCARY!!
GRRRRR...
EEP!
H-HOW ABOUT THIS? WE'LL COMPROMISE...
...AND BOIL HALF AND GRILL THE OTHER HALF!
BA (JUMP)
REALLY?
AH!
MUKU (LUNGE)
GABA (LEAP)
YAAAAY!
LORD KUMAKICHI, I WUV YOU!
GYUUUU (HUUUUG)

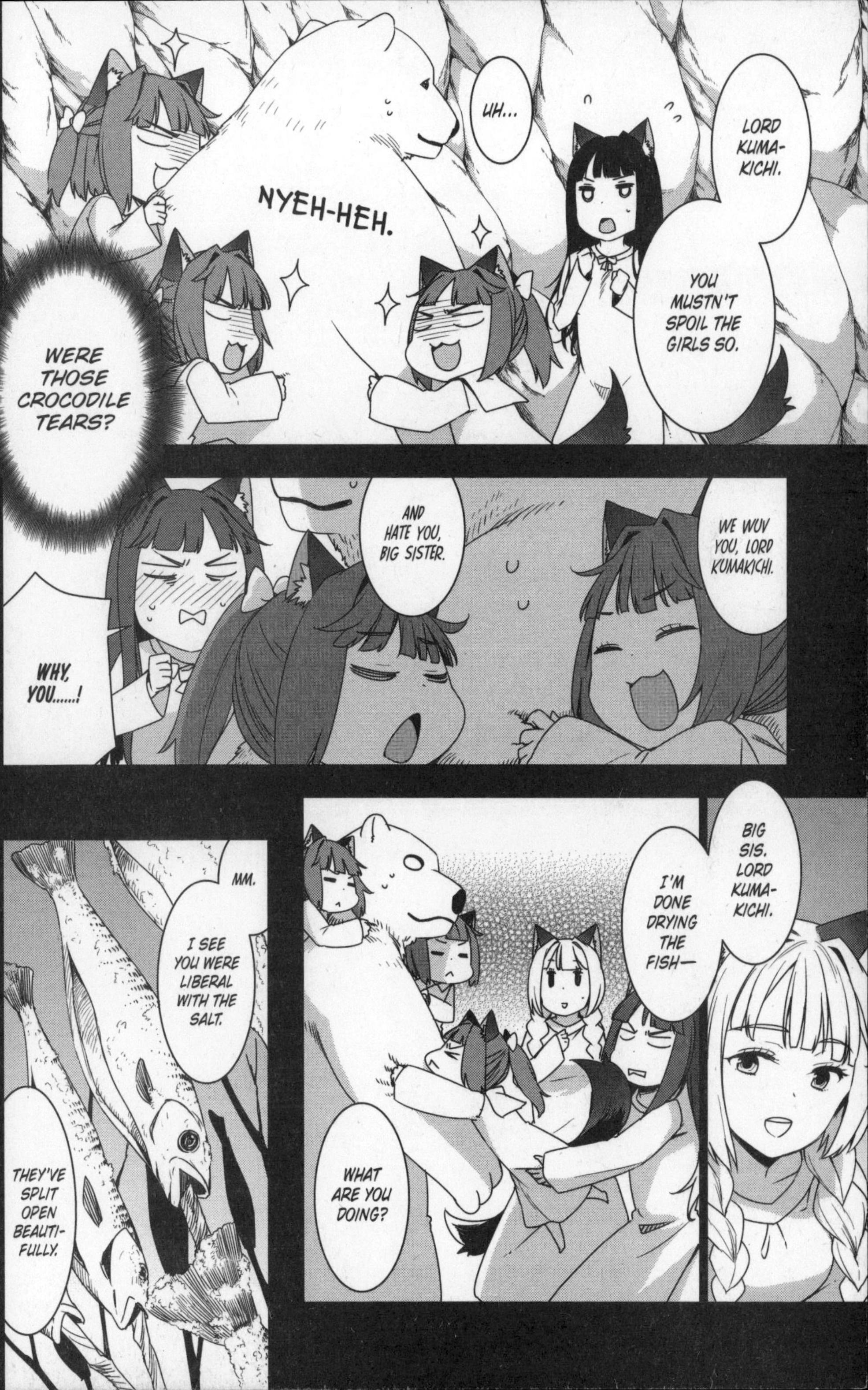

LORD KUMA-KICHI.
YOU MUSTN'T SPOIL THE GIRLS SO.
UH...
NYEH-HEH.
WERE THOSE CROCODILE TEARS?
WE WUV YOU, LORD KUMAKICHI.
AND HATE YOU, BIG SISTER.
WHY, YOU......!
BIG SIS. LORD KUMA-KICHI.
I'M DONE DRYING THE FISH—
WHAT ARE YOU DOING?
MM.
I SEE YOU WERE LIBERAL WITH THE SALT.
THEY'VE SPLIT OPEN BEAUTI-FULLY.

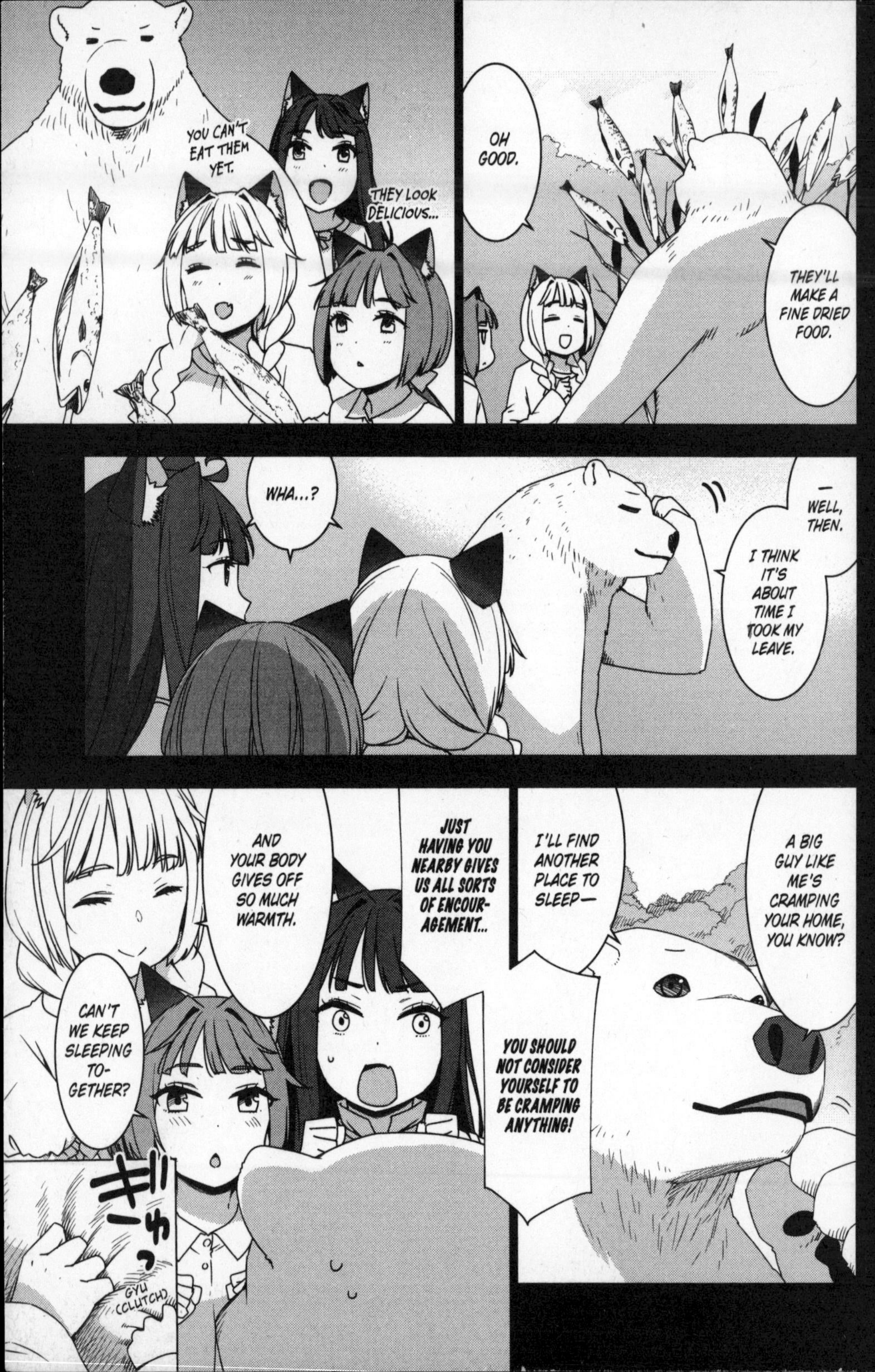
THEY'LL MAKE A FINE DRIED FOOD.
OH GOOD.
THEY LOOK DELICIOUS...
YOU CAN'T EAT THEM YET.
—WELL, THEN.
I THINK IT'S ABOUT TIME I TOOK MY LEAVE.
WHA...?
A BIG GUY LIKE ME'S CRAMPING YOUR HOME, YOU KNOW?
I'LL FIND ANOTHER PLACE TO SLEEP—
YOU SHOULD NOT CONSIDER YOURSELF TO BE CRAMPING ANYTHING!
JUST HAVING YOU NEARBY GIVES US ALL SORTS OF ENCOURAGEMENT...
AND YOUR BODY GIVES OFF SO MUCH WARMTH.
CAN'T WE KEEP SLEEPING TOGETHER?
ぎゅっ
GYU (CLUTCH)

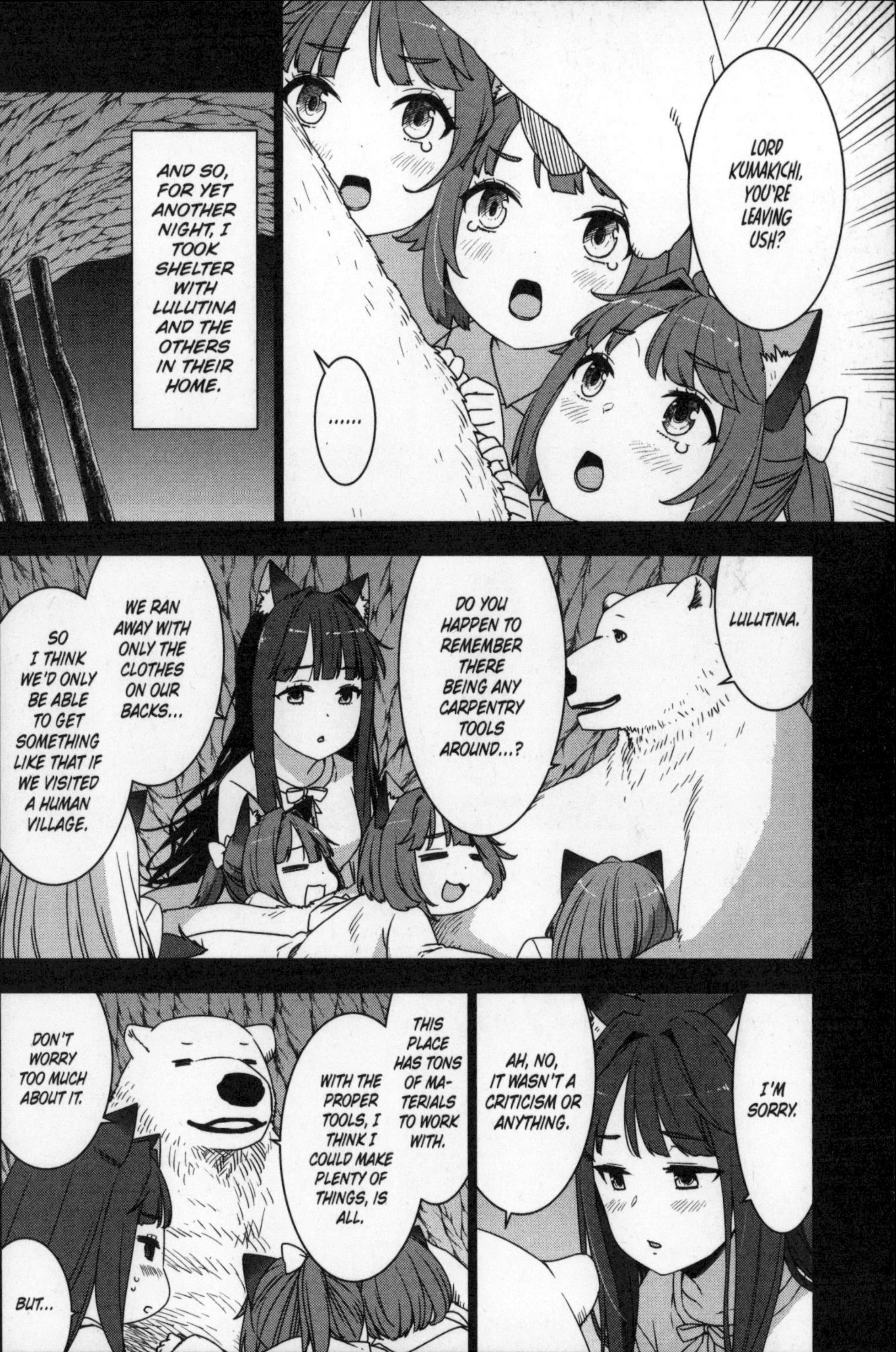
LORD KUMAKICHI, YOU'RE LEAVING USH?
......
AND SO, FOR YET ANOTHER NIGHT, I TOOK SHELTER WITH LULUTINA AND THE OTHERS IN THEIR HOME.
LULUTINA.
DO YOU HAPPEN TO REMEMBER THERE BEING ANY CARPENTRY TOOLS AROUND...?
WE RAN AWAY WITH ONLY THE CLOTHES ON OUR BACKS...
SO I THINK WE'D ONLY BE ABLE TO GET SOMETHING LIKE THAT IF WE VISITED A HUMAN VILLAGE.
I'M SORRY.
AH, NO, IT WASN'T A CRITICISM OR ANYTHING.
THIS PLACE HAS TONS OF MA-TERIALS TO WORK WITH.
WITH THE PROPER TOOLS, I THINK I COULD MAKE PLENTY OF THINGS, IS ALL.
DON'T WORRY TOO MUCH ABOUT IT.
BUT...

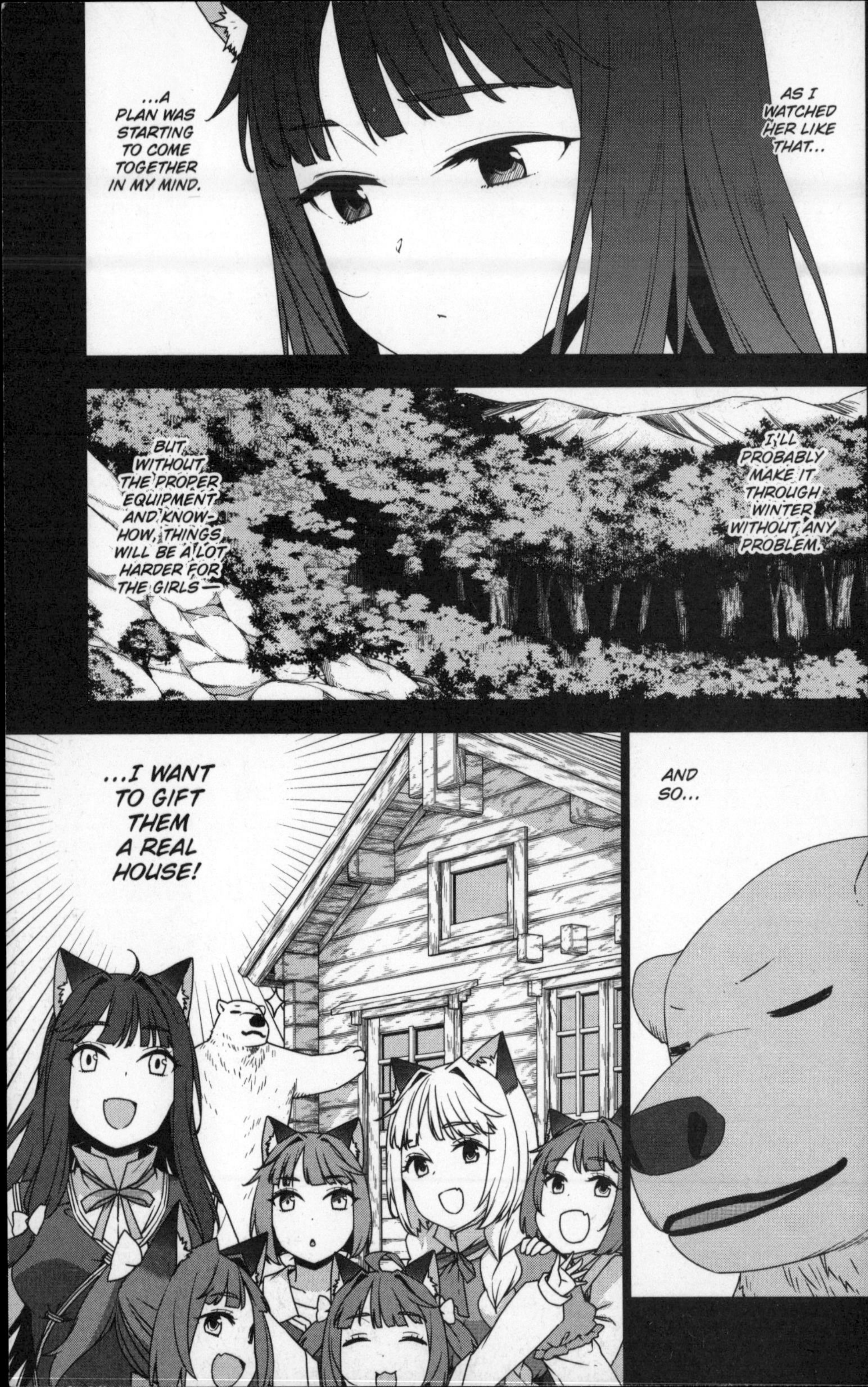
AS I WATCHED HER LIKE THAT...
...A PLAN WAS STARTING TO COME TOGETHER IN MY MIND.
I'LL PROBABLY MAKE IT THROUGH WINTER WITHOUT ANY PROBLEM.
BUT, WITHOUT THE PROPER EQUIPMENT AND KNOW-HOW, THINGS WILL BE A LOT HARDER FOR THE GIRLS—
AND SO...
...I WANT TO GIFT THEM A REAL HOUSE!

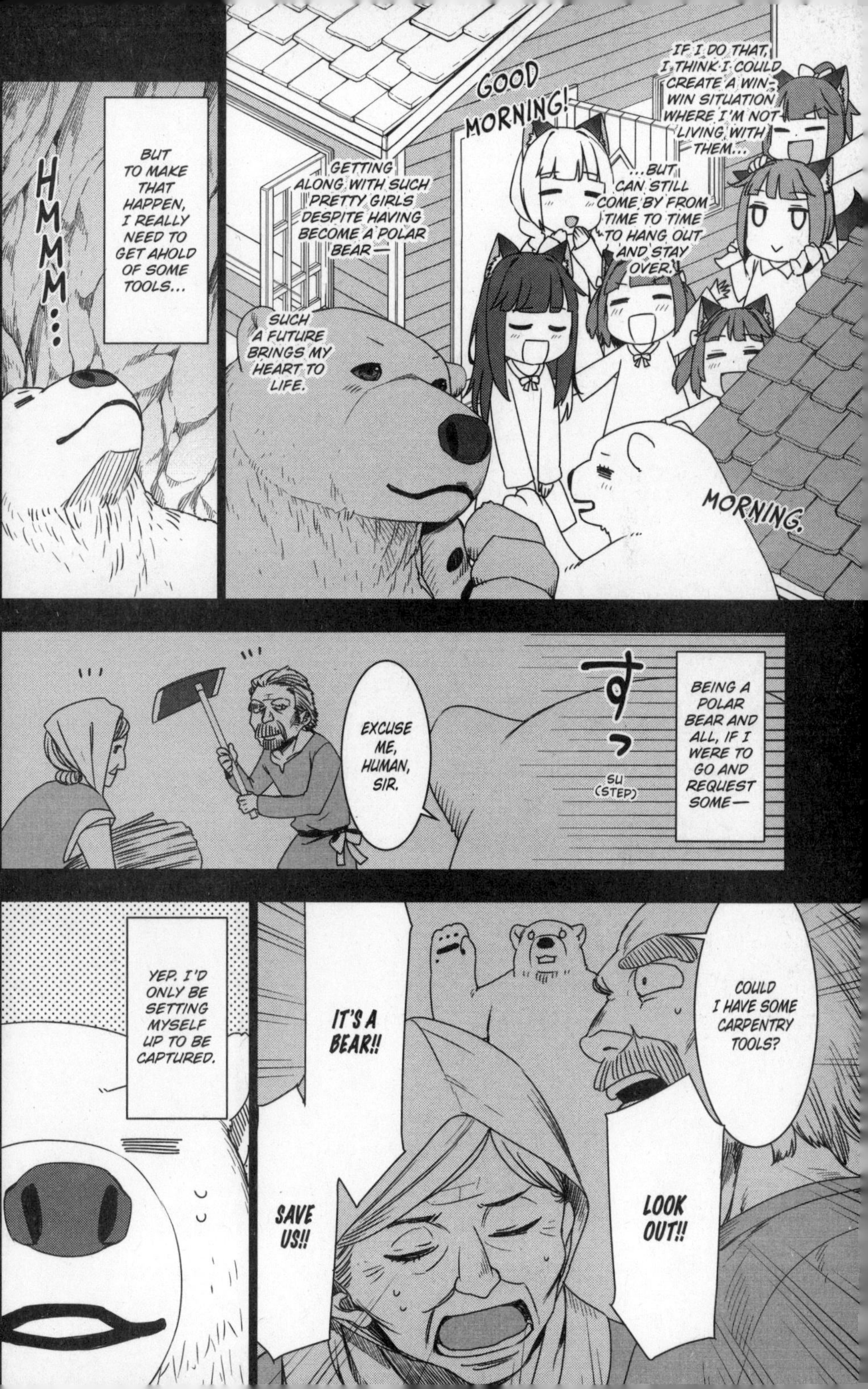
IF I DO THAT, I THINK I COULD CREATE A WIN-WIN SITUATION WHERE I'M NOT LIVING WITH THEM...
...BUT CAN STILL COME BY FROM TIME TO TIME TO HANG OUT AND STAY OVER.
GOOD MORNING!
GETTING ALONG WITH SUCH PRETTY GIRLS DESPITE HAVING BECOME A POLAR BEAR—
SUCH A FUTURE BRINGS MY HEART TO LIFE.
MORNING.
BUT TO MAKE THAT HAPPEN, I REALLY NEED TO GET AHOLD OF SOME TOOLS...
HMMM...
BEING A POLAR BEAR AND ALL, IF I WERE TO GO AND REQUEST SOME—
すっ
SU (STEP)
EXCUSE ME, HUMAN, SIR.
COULD I HAVE SOME CARPENTRY TOOLS?
IT'S A BEAR!!
LOOK OUT!!
SAVE US!!
YEP. I'D ONLY BE SETTING MYSELF UP TO BE CAPTURED.

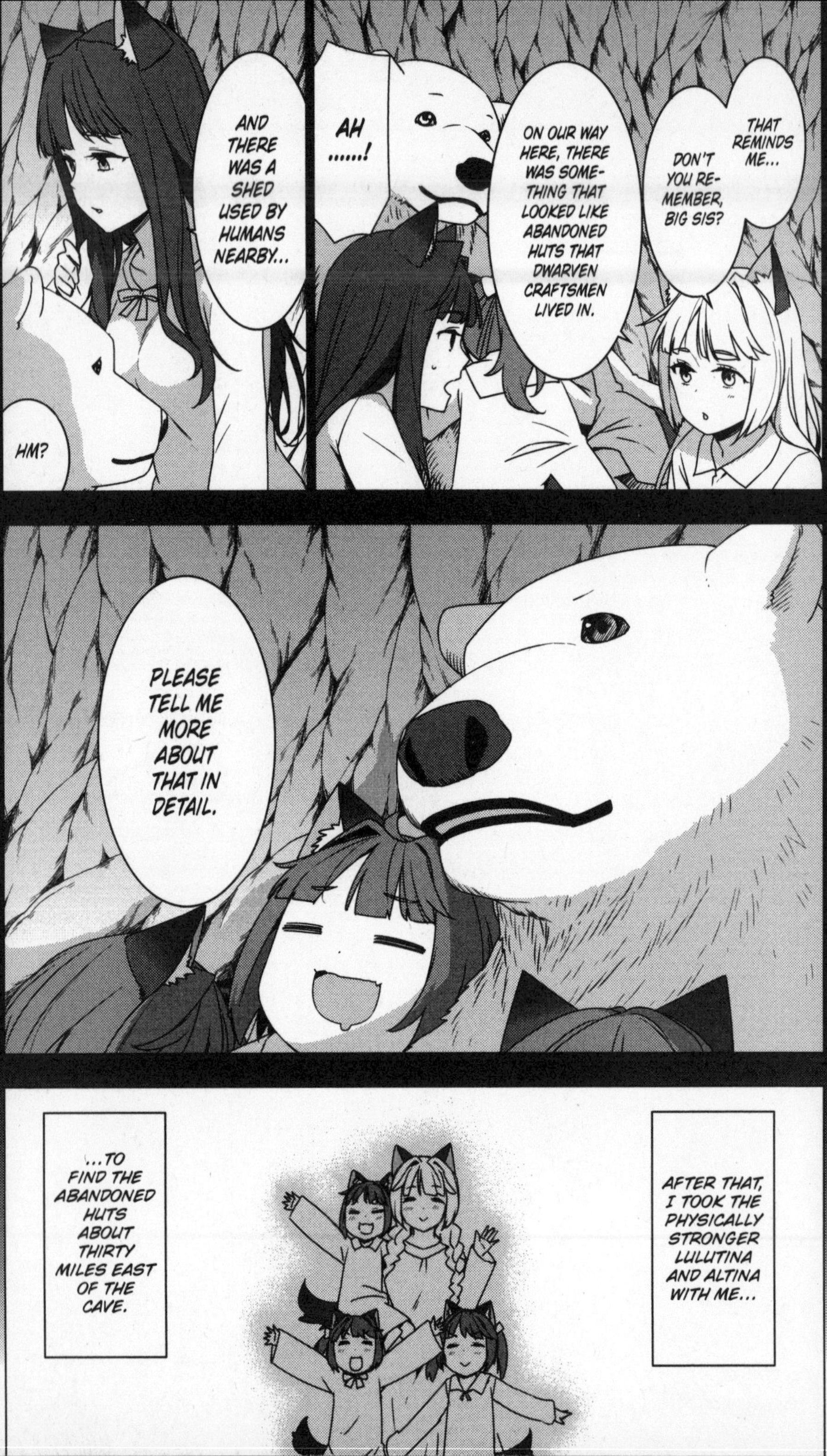
THAT REMINDS ME...
DON'T YOU RE-MEMBER, BIG SIS?
ON OUR WAY HERE, THERE WAS SOME-THING THAT LOOKED LIKE ABANDONED HUTS THAT DWARVEN CRAFTSMEN LIVED IN.
AH ......!
AND THERE WAS A SHED USED BY HUMANS NEARBY...
HM?
PLEASE TELL ME MORE ABOUT THAT IN DETAIL.
AFTER THAT, I TOOK THE PHYSICALLY STRONGER LULUTINA AND ALTINA WITH ME...
...TO FIND THE ABANDONED HUTS ABOUT THIRTY MILES EAST OF THE CAVE.

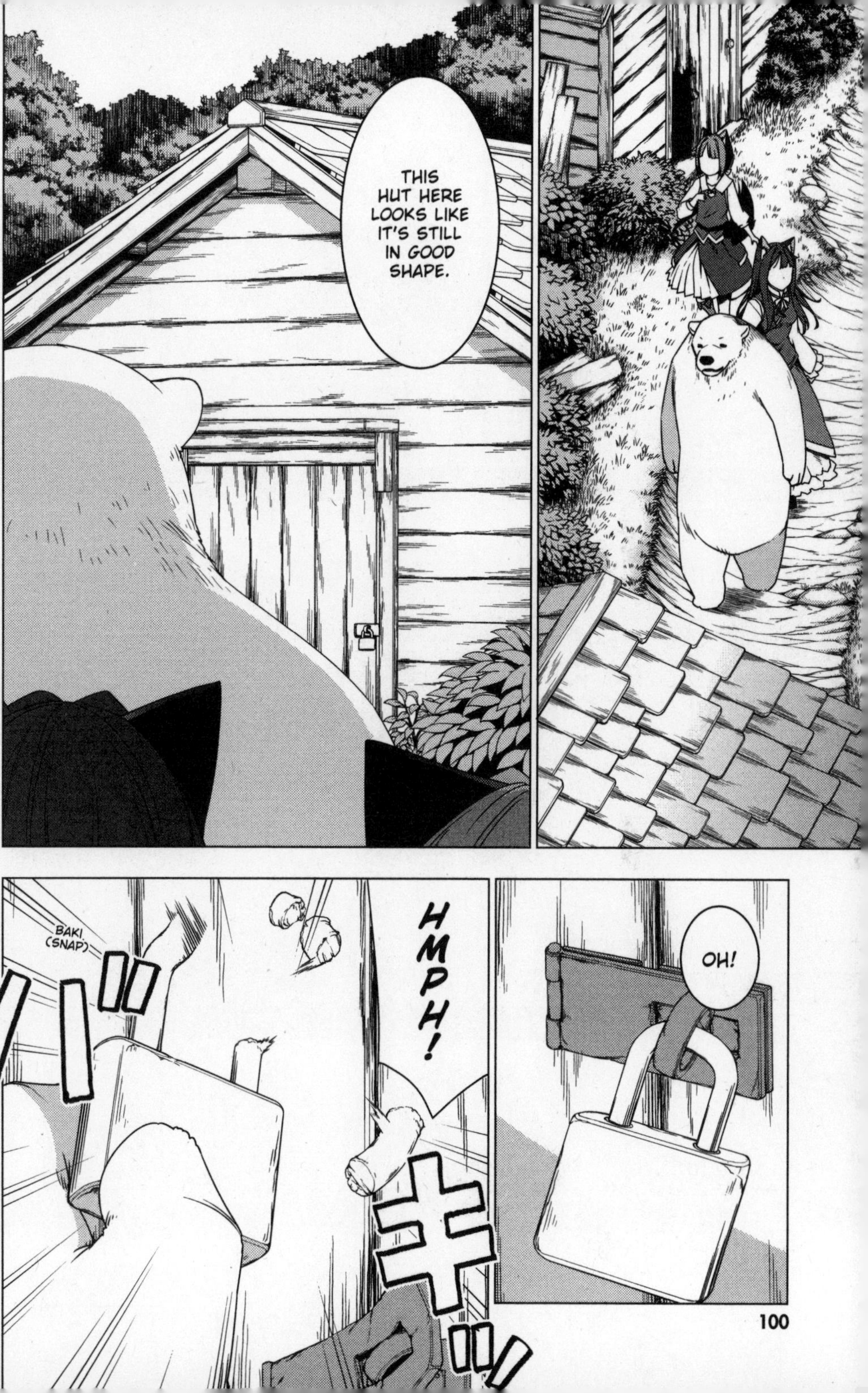
THIS HUT HERE LOOKS LIKE IT'S STILL IN GOOD SHAPE.
OH!
HMPH!
BAKI (SNAP)

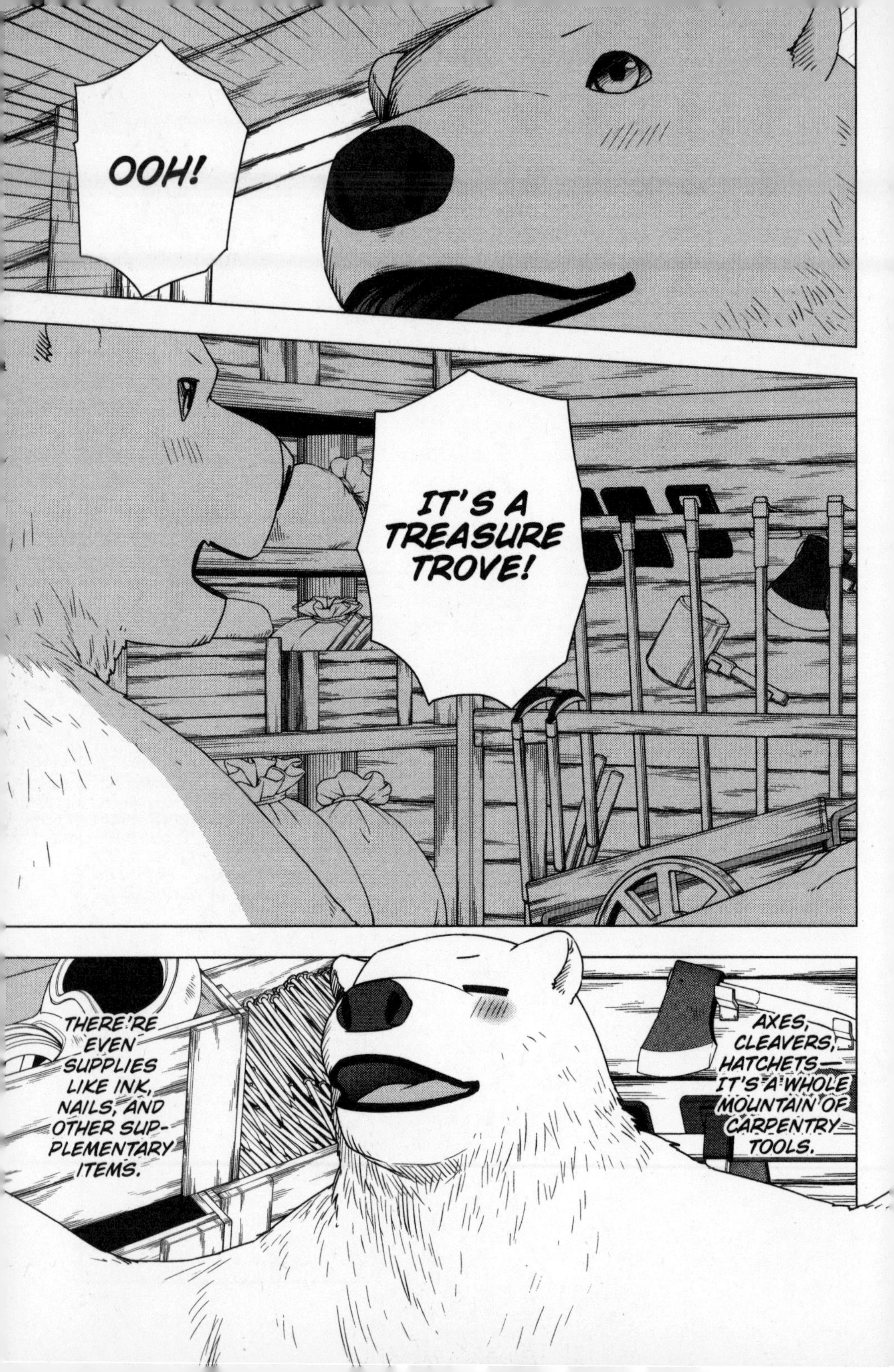
OOH!
IT'S A TREASURE TROVE!
AXES, CLEAVERS, HATCHETS— IT'S A WHOLE MOUNTAIN OF CARPENTRY TOOLS.
THERE'RE EVEN SUPPLIES LIKE INK, NAILS, AND OTHER SUP-PLEMENTARY ITEMS.

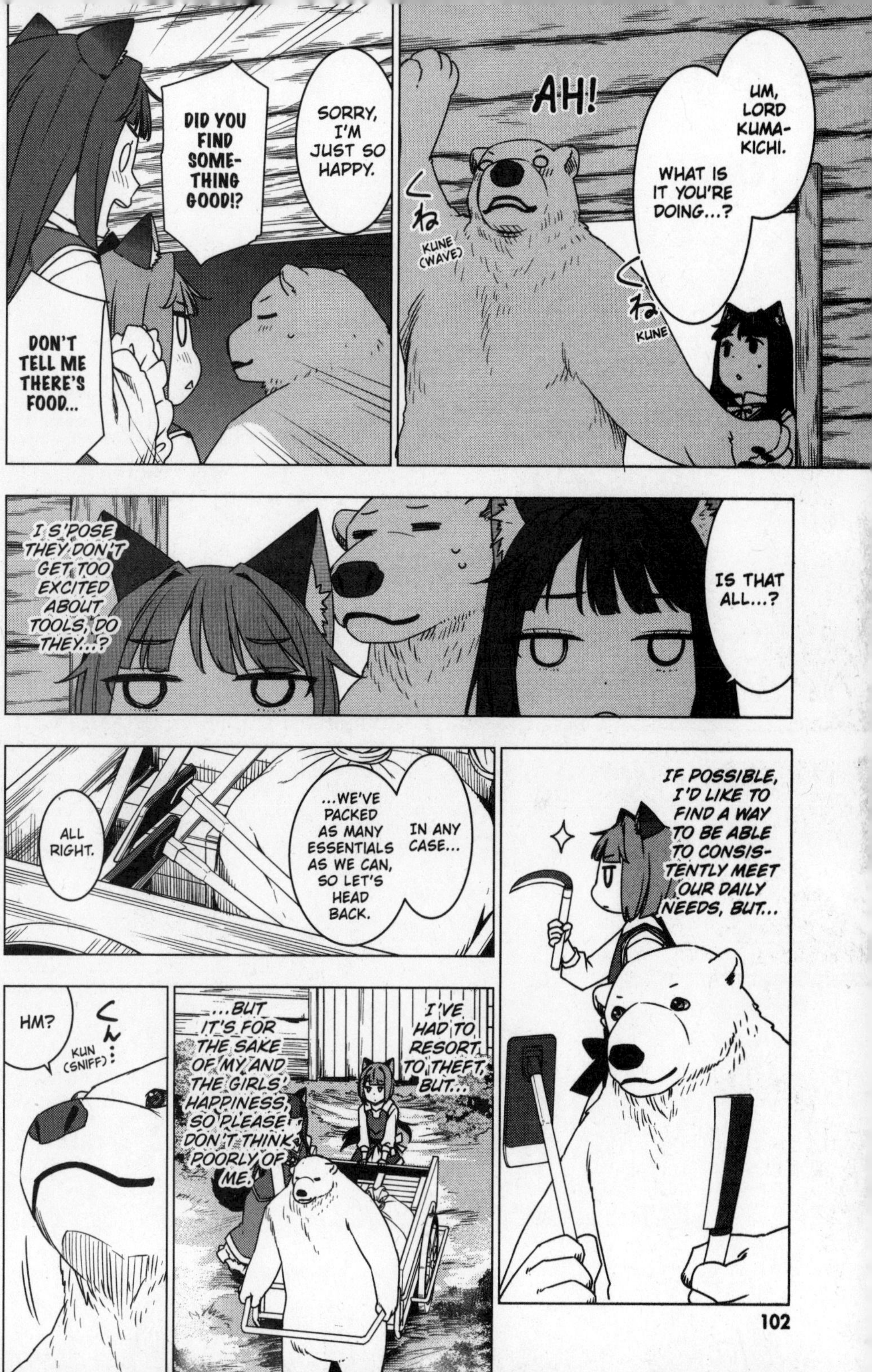
UM, LORD KUMA-KICHI.
WHAT IS IT YOU'RE DOING...?
AH!
くね KUNE (WAVE)
くね KUNE
SORRY, I'M JUST SO HAPPY.
DID YOU FIND SOME-THING GOOD!?
DON'T TELL ME THERE'S FOOD...
IS THAT ALL...?
I S'POSE THEY DON'T GET TOO EXCITED ABOUT TOOLS, DO THEY...?
IF POSSIBLE, I'D LIKE TO FIND A WAY TO BE ABLE TO CONSIS-TENTLY MEET OUR DAILY NEEDS, BUT...
IN ANY CASE...
...WE'VE PACKED AS MANY ESSENTIALS AS WE CAN, SO LET'S HEAD BACK.
ALL RIGHT.
I'VE HAD TO RESORT TO THEFT, BUT...
...BUT IT'S FOR THE SAKE OF MY AND THE GIRLS' HAPPINESS, SO PLEASE DON'T THINK POORLY OF ME.
くん KUN (SNIFF)
HM?

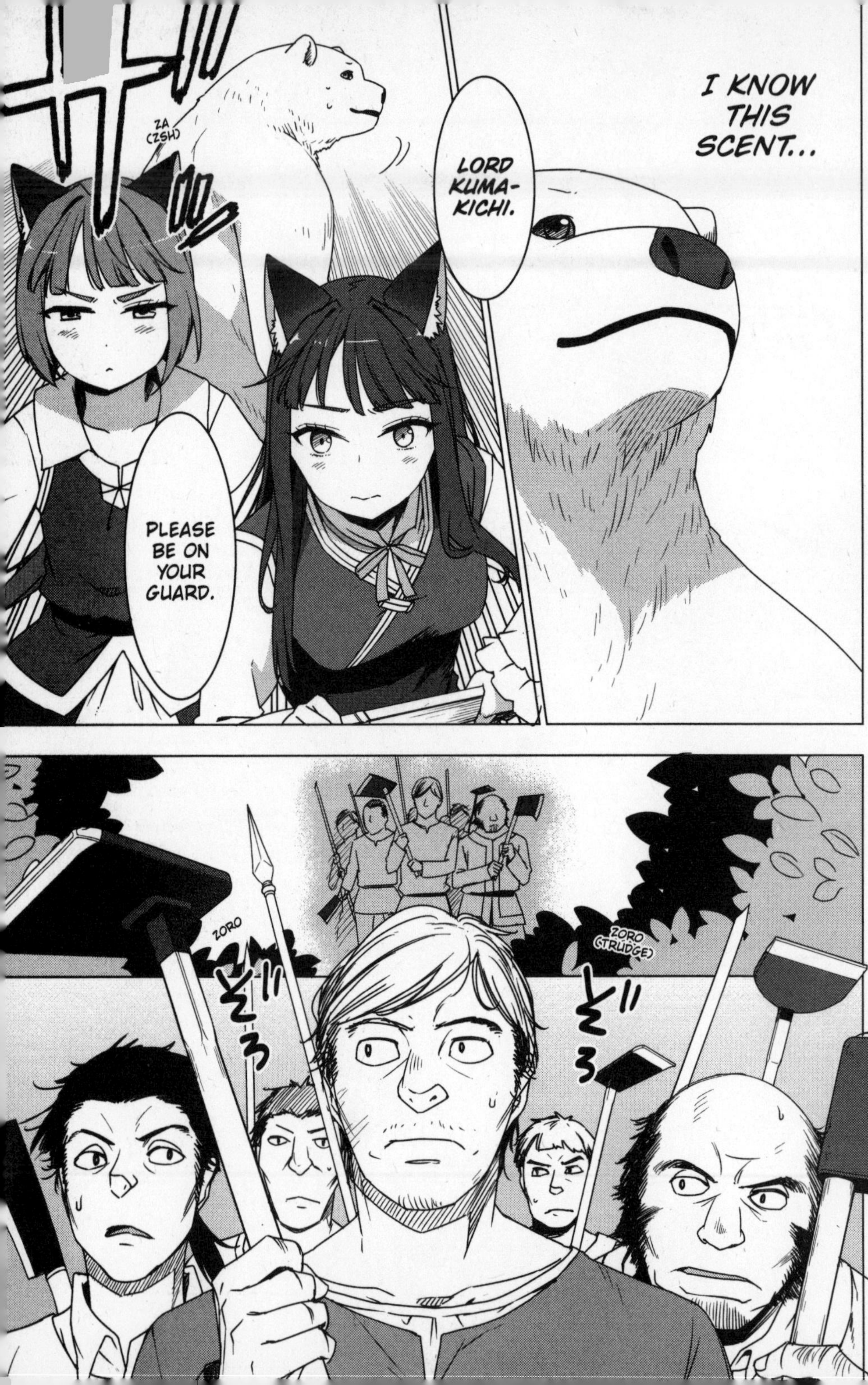
I KNOW THIS SCENT...
LORD KUMA-KICHI.
ZA (ZSH)
PLEASE BE ON YOUR GUARD.
ZORO (TRUDGE)
ZORO

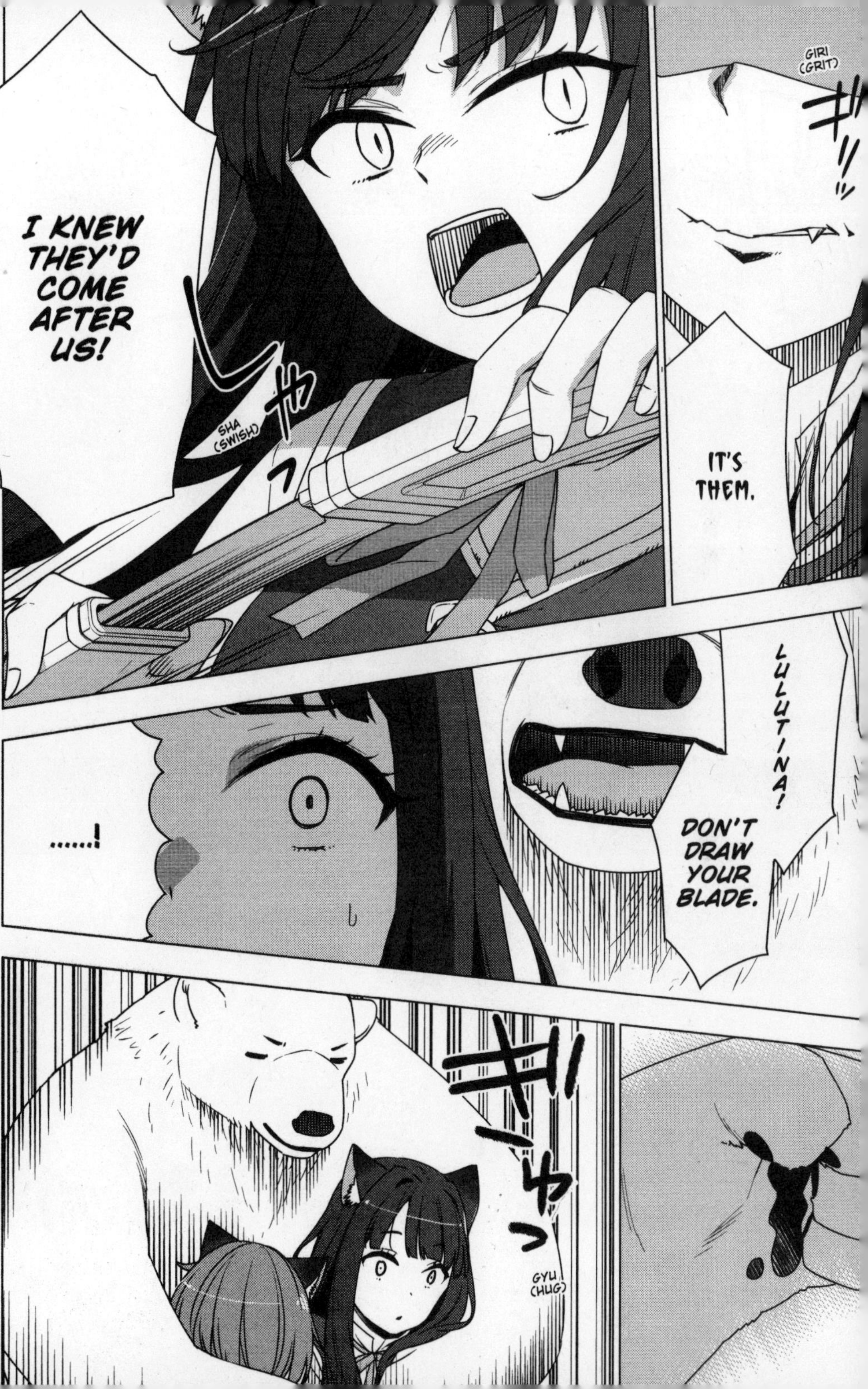
GIRI (GRIT)
IT'S THEM.
I KNEW THEY'D COME AFTER US!
SHA (SWISH)
LULUTINA!
DON'T DRAW YOUR BLADE.
......!
GYU (HUG)

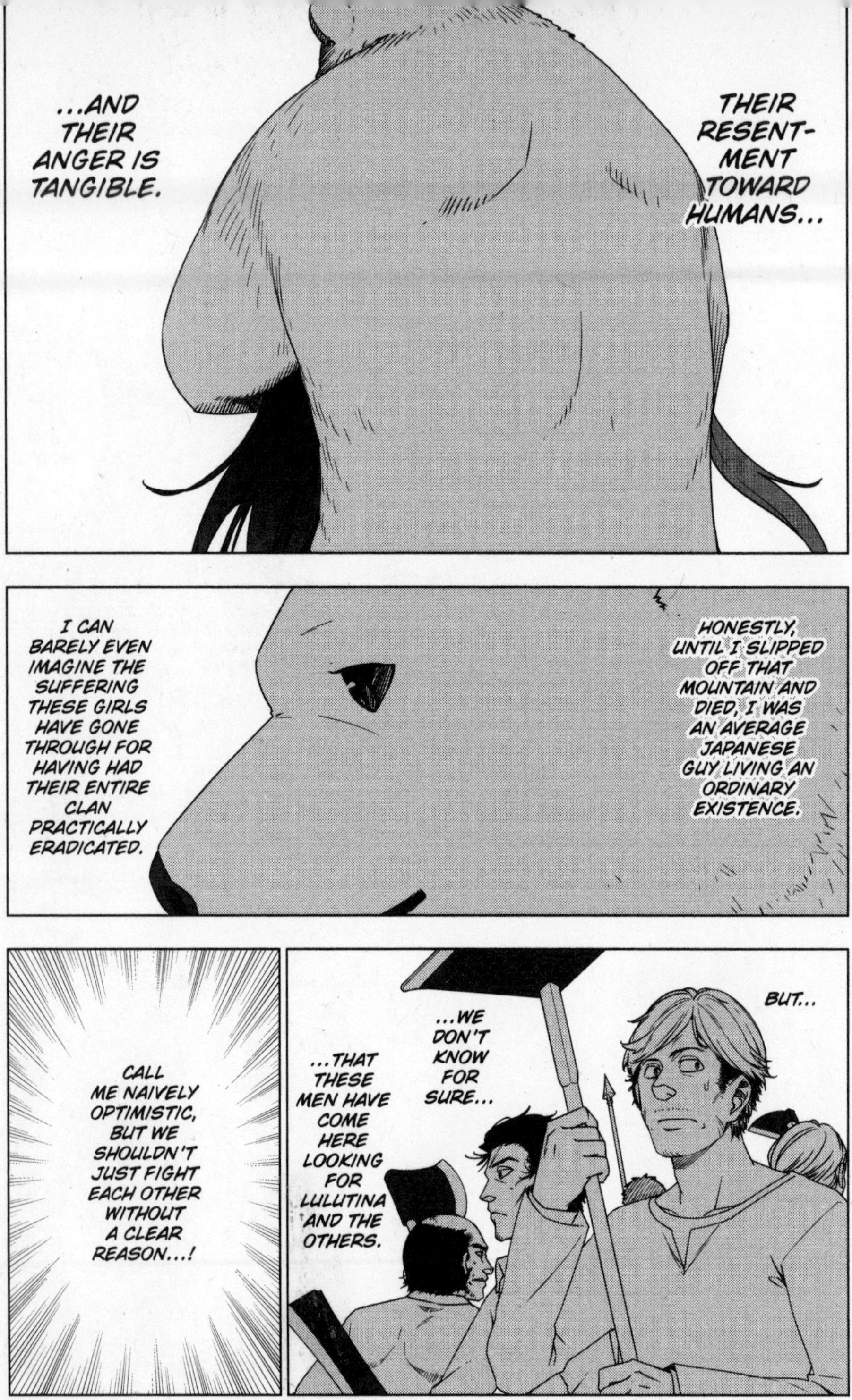
THEIR RESENTMENT TOWARD HUMANS...
...AND THEIR ANGER IS TANGIBLE.
HONESTLY, UNTIL I SLIPPED OFF THAT MOUNTAIN AND DIED, I WAS AN AVERAGE JAPANESE GUY LIVING AN ORDINARY EXISTENCE.
I CAN BARELY EVEN IMAGINE THE SUFFERING THESE GIRLS HAVE GONE THROUGH FOR HAVING HAD THEIR ENTIRE CLAN PRACTICALLY ERADICATED.
BUT...
...WE DON'T KNOW FOR SURE...
...THAT THESE MEN HAVE COME HERE LOOKING FOR LULUTINA AND THE OTHERS.
CALL ME NAIVELY OPTIMISTIC, BUT WE SHOULDN'T JUST FIGHT EACH OTHER WITHOUT A CLEAR REASON...!

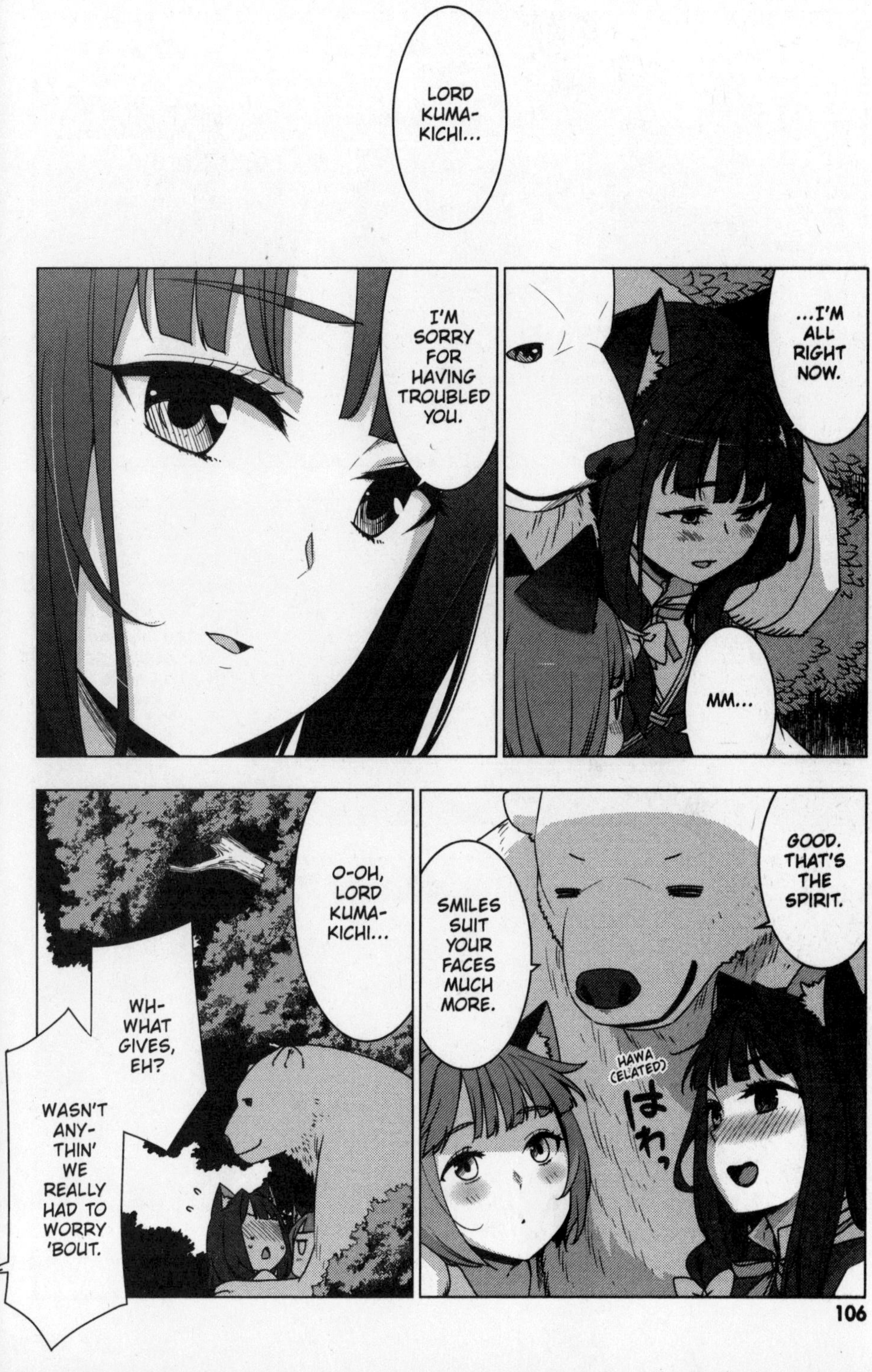
LORD KUMA-KICHI...
...I'M ALL RIGHT NOW.
MM...
I'M SORRY FOR HAVING TROUBLED YOU.
GOOD. THAT'S THE SPIRIT.
SMILES SUIT YOUR FACES MUCH MORE.
HAWA (ELATED)
はわ、
O-OH, LORD KUMA-KICHI...
WH-WHAT GIVES, EH?
WASN'T ANY-THIN' WE REALLY HAD TO WORRY 'BOUT.

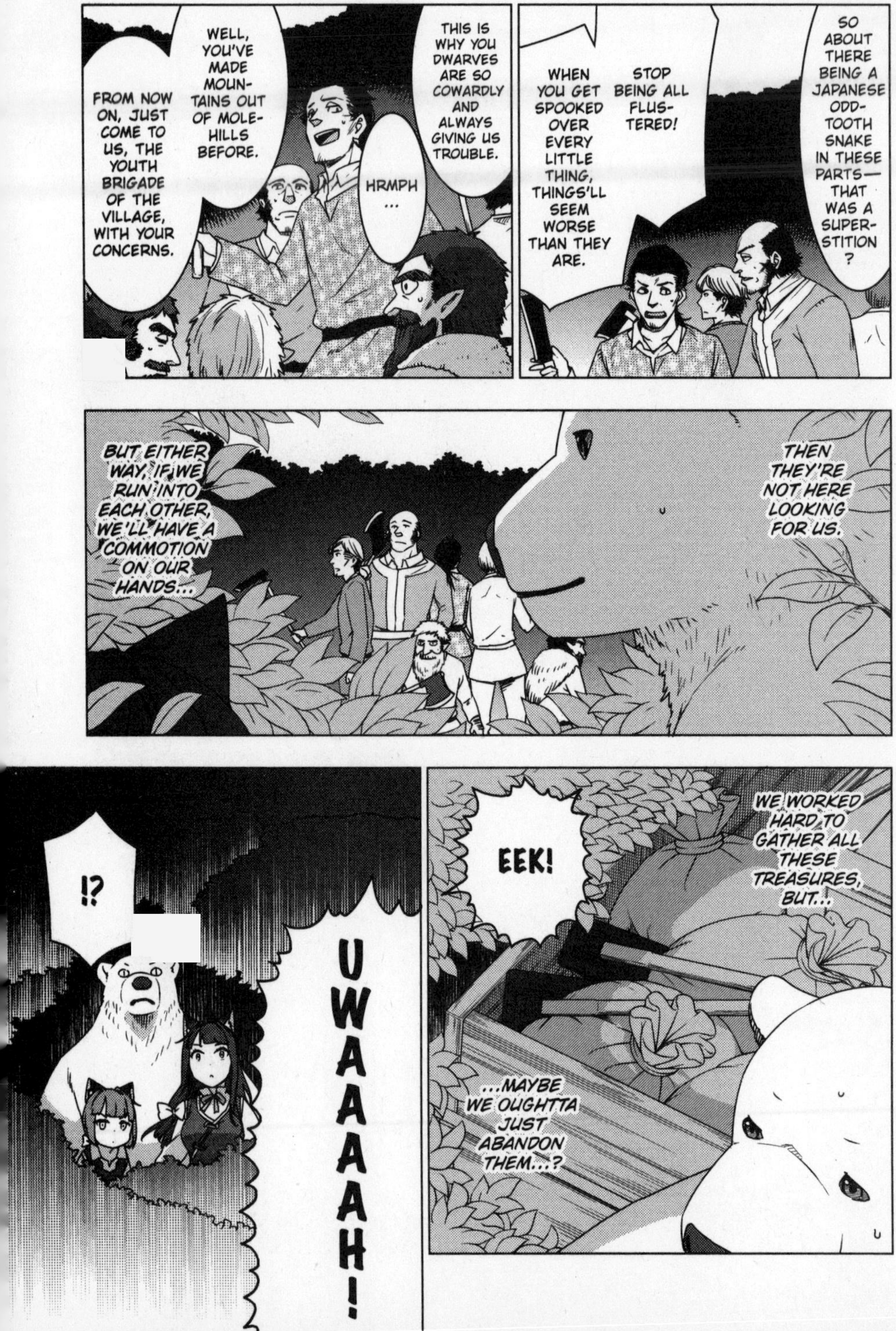

SO ABOUT THERE BEING A JAPANESE ODD-TOOTH SNAKE IN THESE PARTS— THAT WAS A SUPERSTITION?
STOP BEING ALL FLUSTERED!
WHEN YOU GET SPOOKED OVER EVERY LITTLE THING, THINGS'LL SEEM WORSE THAN THEY ARE.
THIS IS WHY YOU DWARVES ARE SO COWARDLY AND ALWAYS GIVING US TROUBLE.
HRMPH...
WELL, YOU'VE MADE MOUN-TAINS OUT OF MOLE-HILLS BEFORE.
FROM NOW ON, JUST COME TO US, THE YOUTH BRIGADE OF THE VILLAGE, WITH YOUR CONCERNS.
THEN THEY'RE NOT HERE LOOKING FOR US.
BUT EITHER WAY, IF WE RUN INTO EACH OTHER, WE'LL HAVE A COMMOTION ON OUR HANDS...
WE WORKED HARD TO GATHER ALL THESE TREASURES, BUT...
EEK!
...MAYBE WE OUGHTTA JUST ABANDON THEM...?
!?
UWAAAAAH!

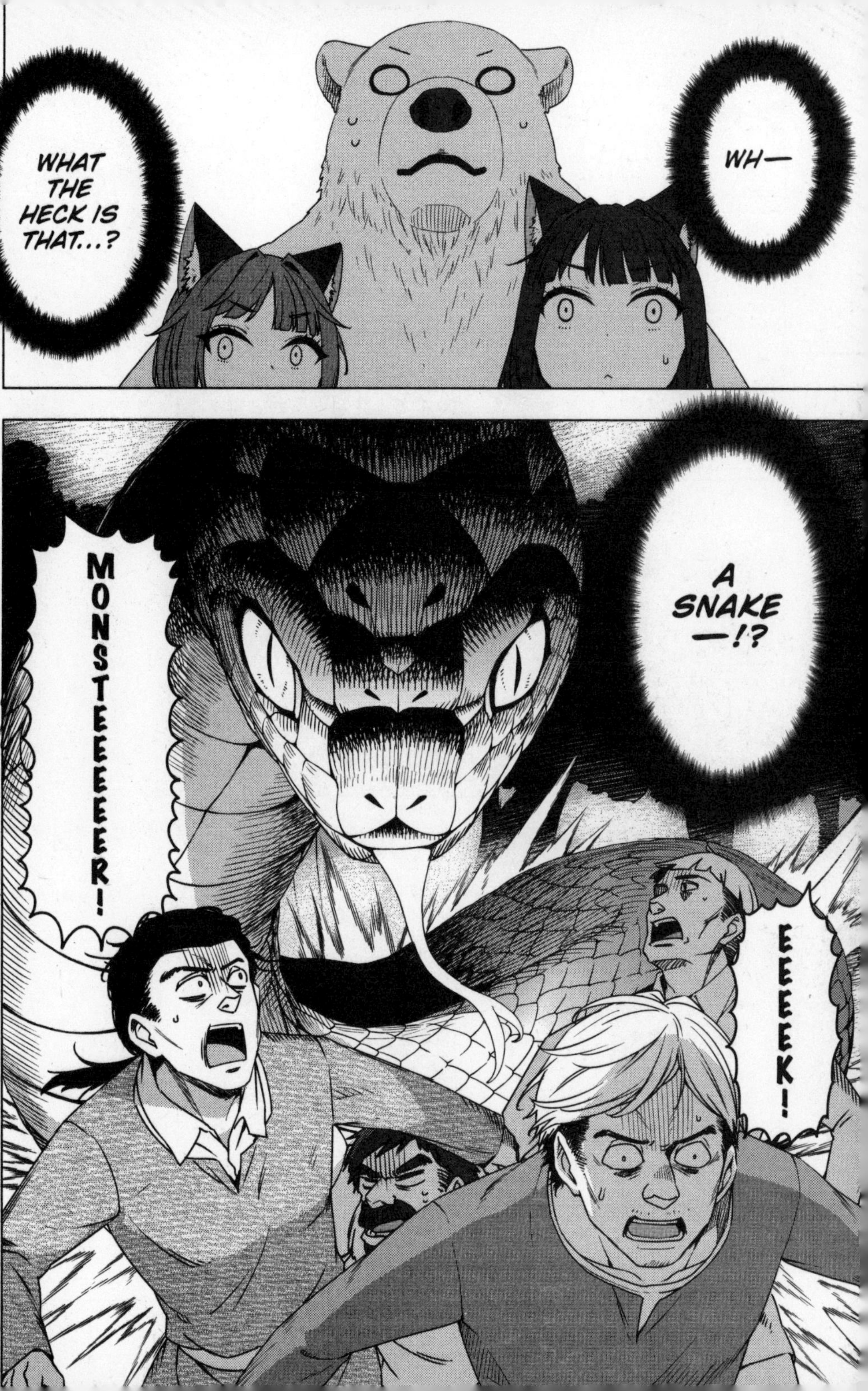
WH—
WHAT THE HECK IS THAT...?
A SNAKE—!?
MONSTEEEEER!
EEEEEK!

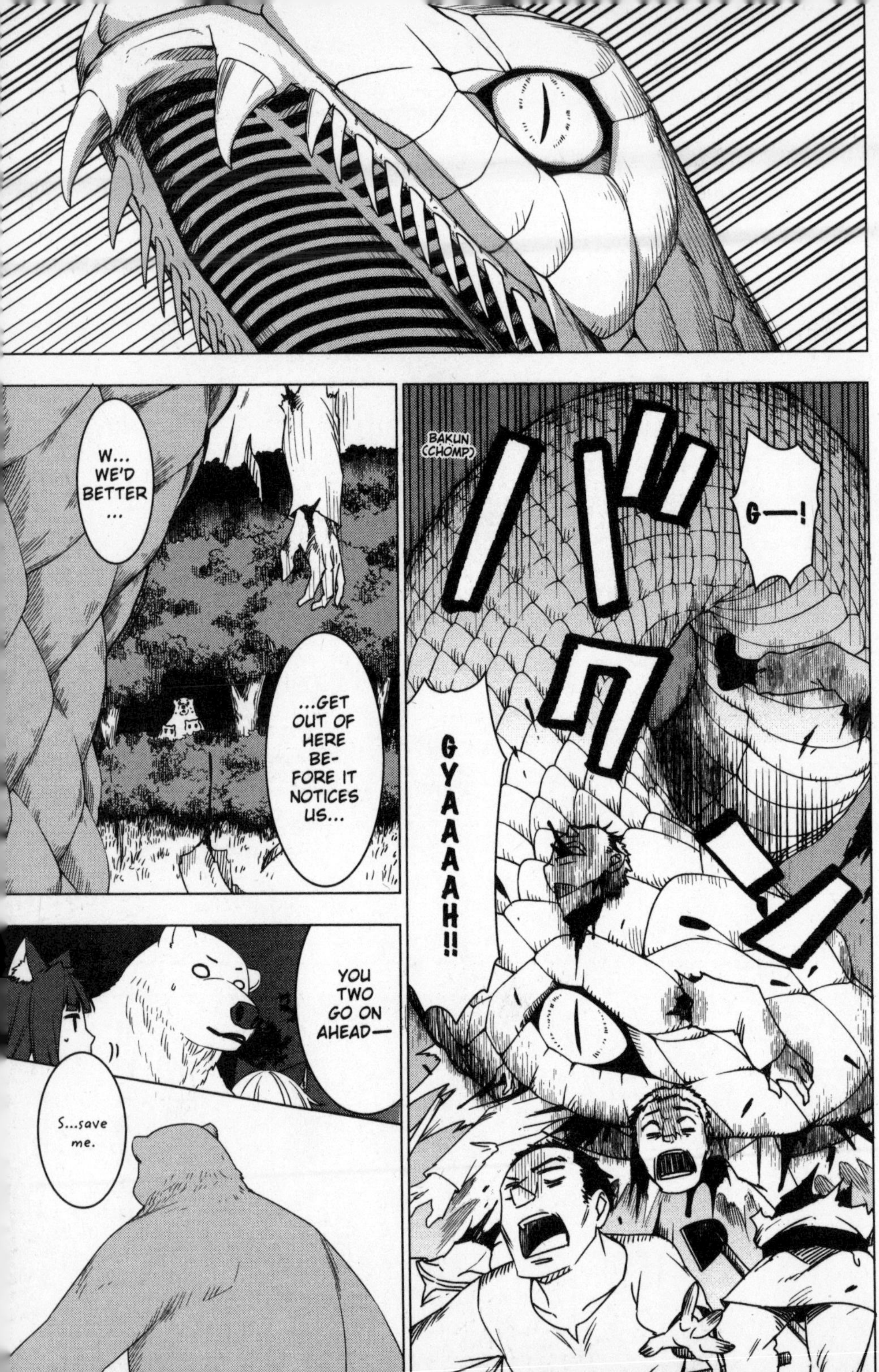
G—!
BAKUN (CHOMP)
GYAAAAAH!!
W... WE'D BETTER ...
...GET OUT OF HERE BE-FORE IT NOTICES US...
YOU TWO GO ON AHEAD—
S...save me.

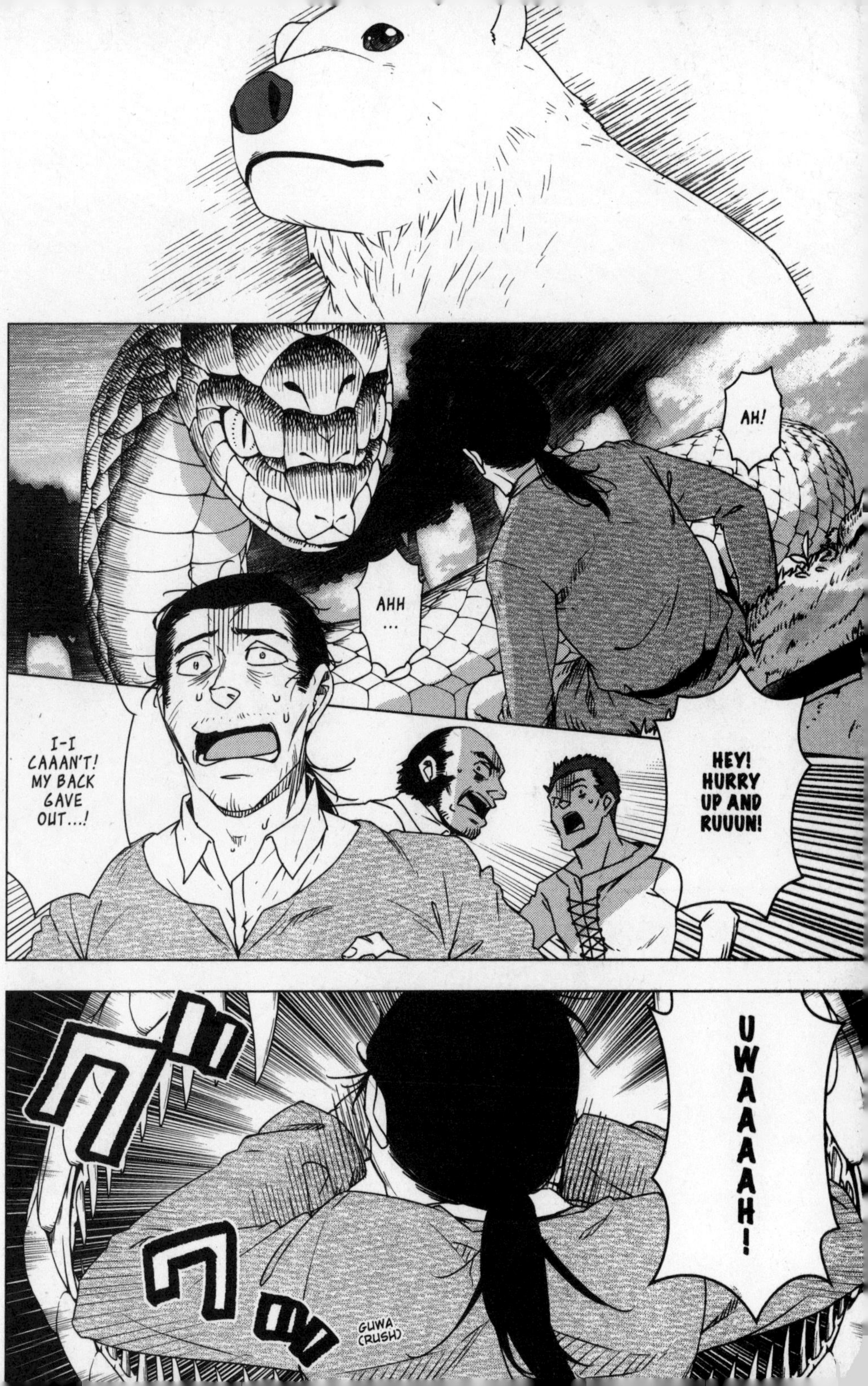
AH!
AHH
...
HEY! HURRY UP AND RUUUN!
I-I CAAAN'T! MY BACK GAVE OUT...!
UWAAAAAH!
GUWA (RUSH)

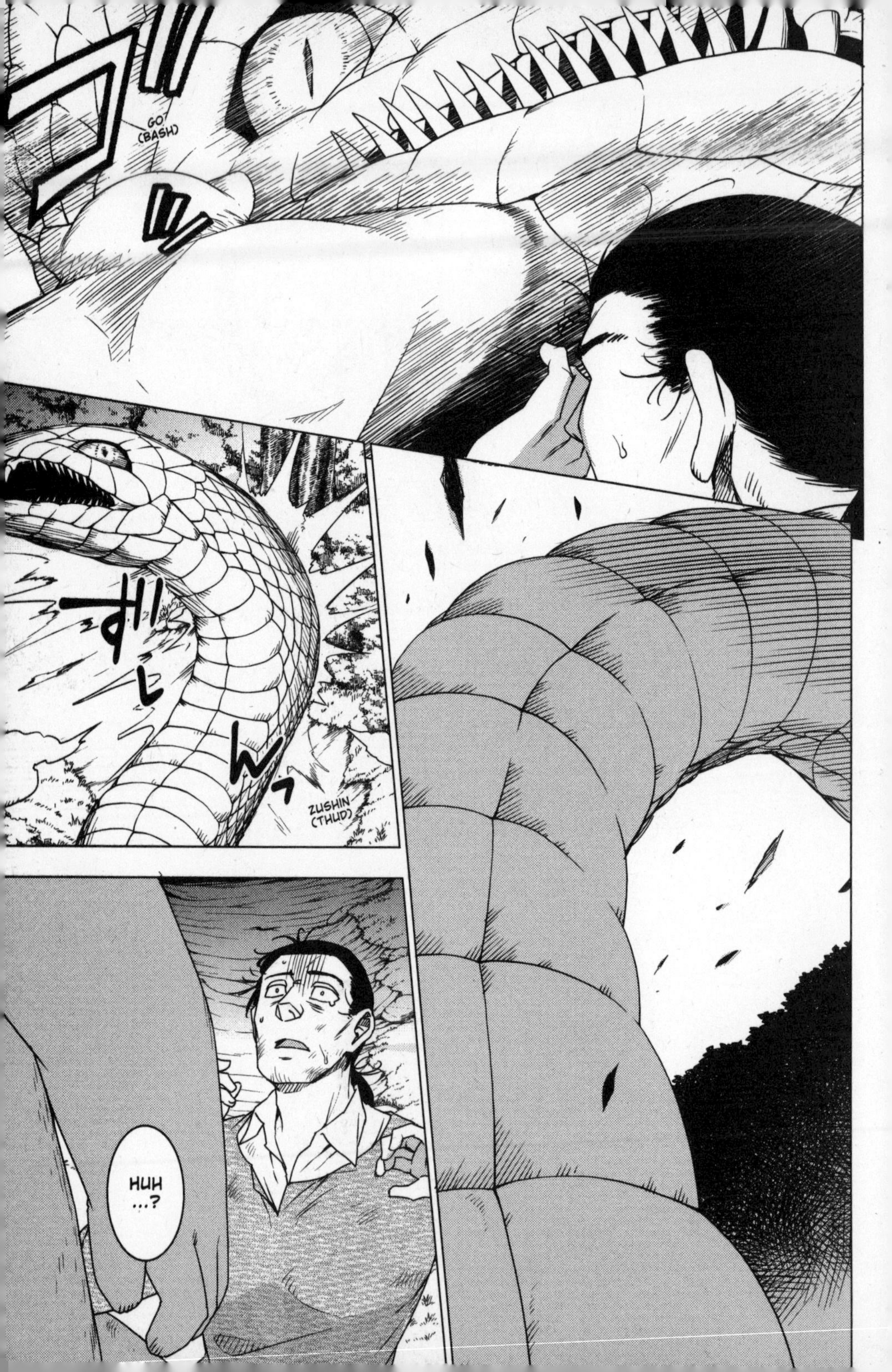
GO (BASH)
ZUSHIN (THUD)
HUH ...?

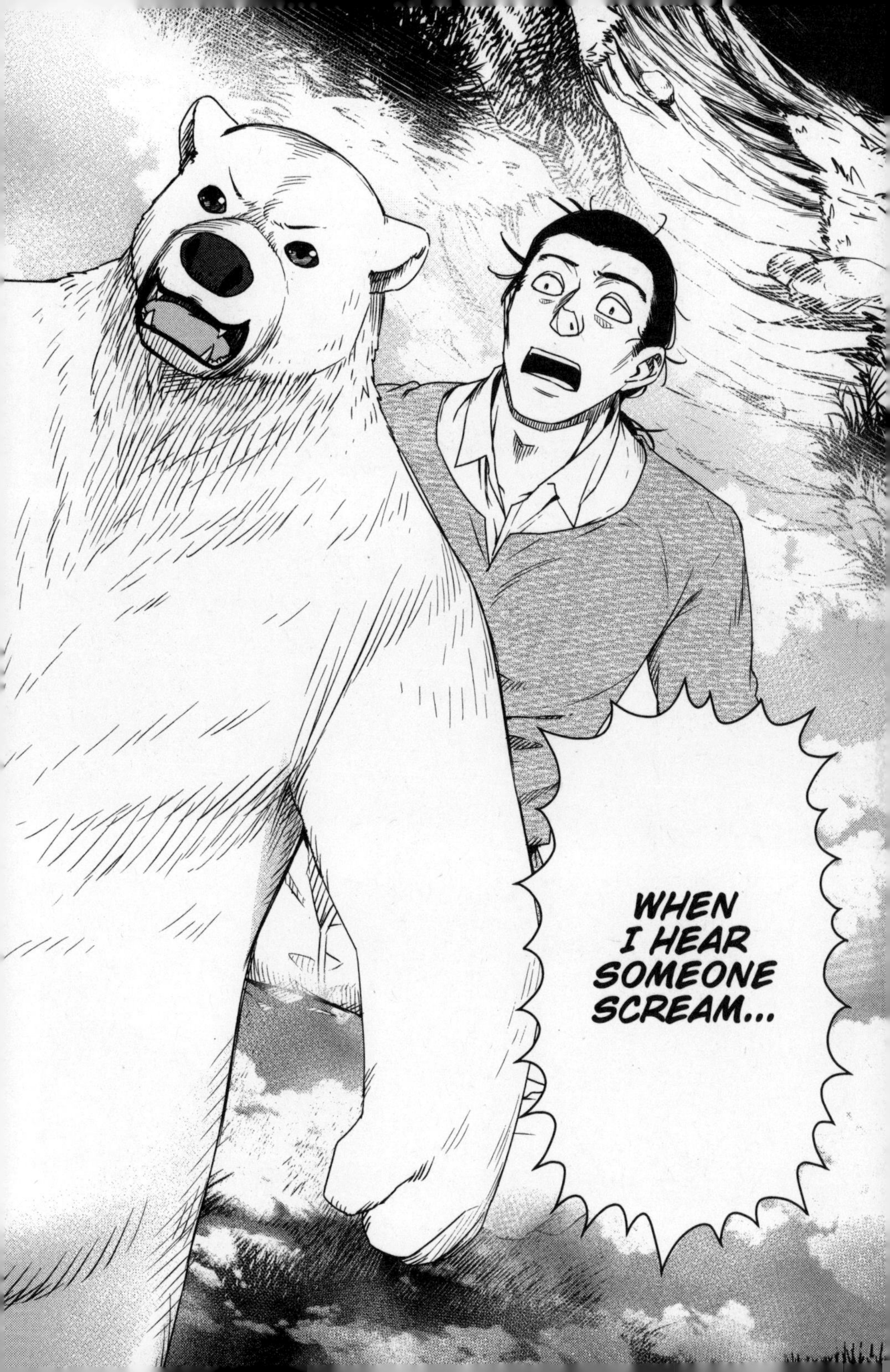
WHEN I HEAR SOMEONE SCREAM...

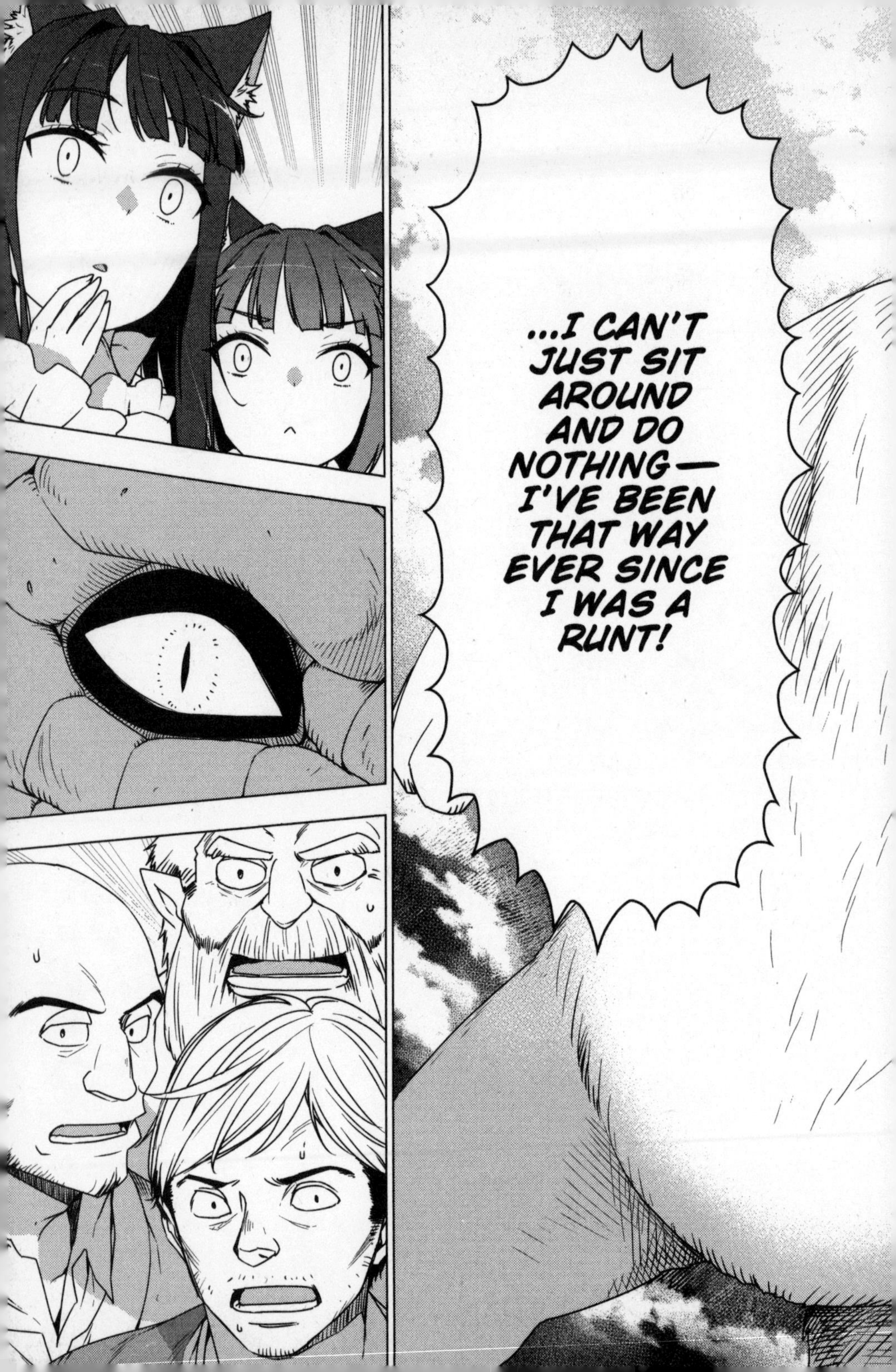
...I CAN'T JUST SIT AROUND AND DO NOTHING— I'VE BEEN THAT WAY EVER SINCE I WAS A RUNT!

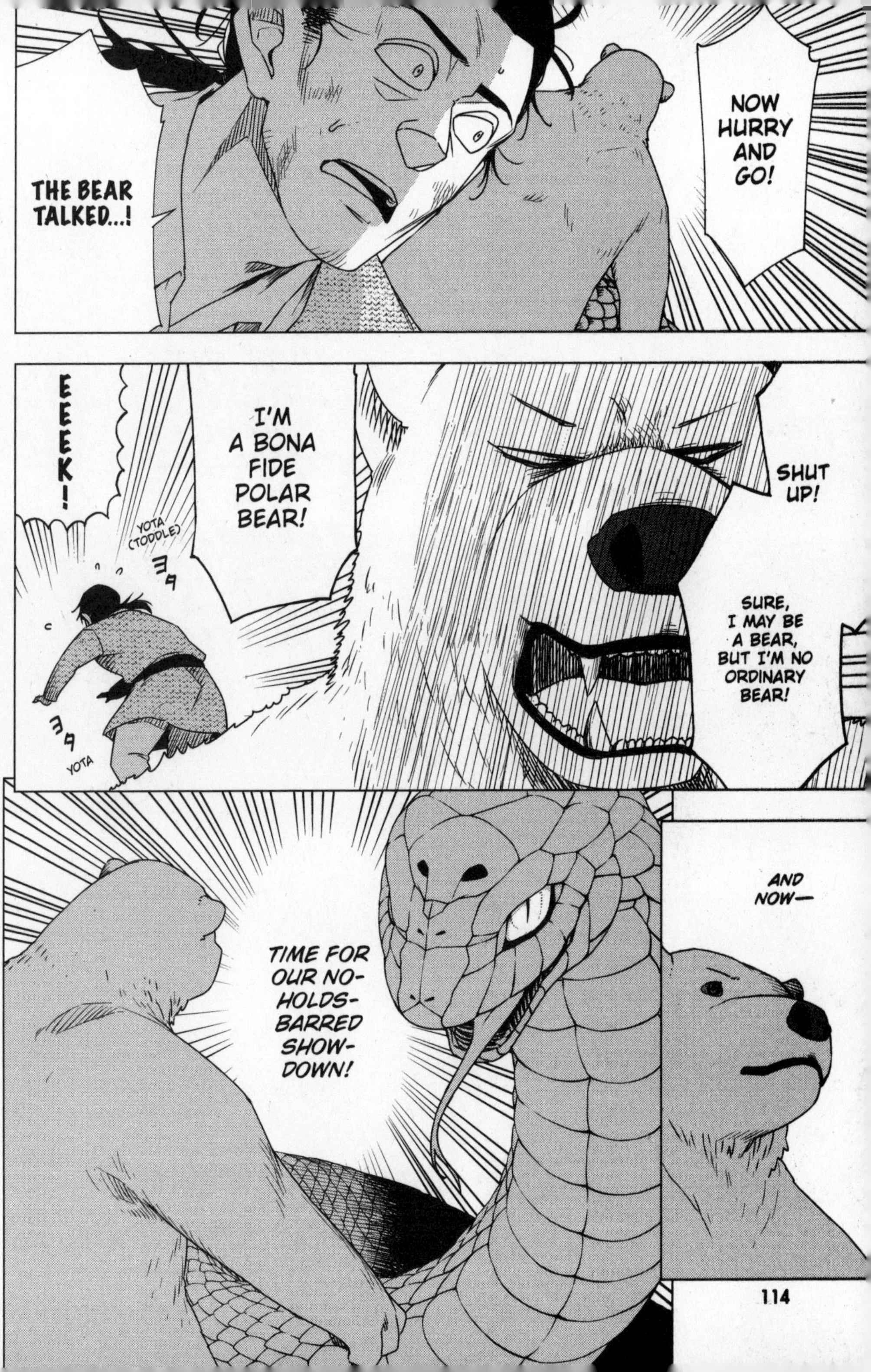
NOW HURRY AND GO!
THE BEAR TALKED...!
SHUT UP!
SURE, I MAY BE A BEAR, BUT I'M NO ORDINARY BEAR!
I'M A BONA FIDE POLAR BEAR!
EEEEK!
ヨタ
YOTA (TODDLE)
ヨタ
YOTA
AND NOW—
TIME FOR OUR NO-HOLDS-BARRED SHOWDOWN!

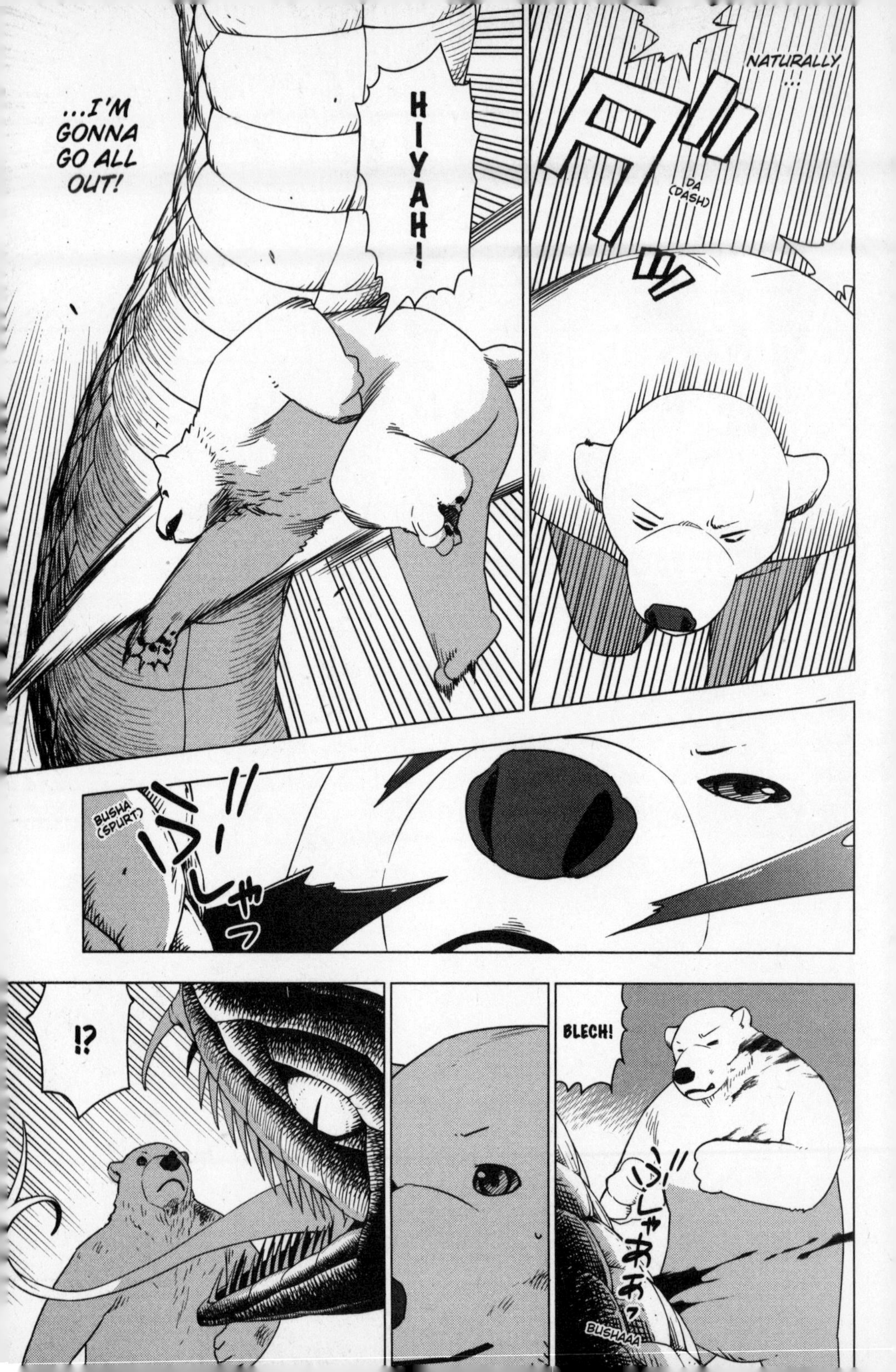

NATURALLY ...!!
ダッ
DA (DASH)
HIYAH!
...I'M GONNA GO ALL OUT!
ぶしゃっ
BUSHA (SPURT)
BLECH!
ぶしゃあああっ
BUSHAAA
!?

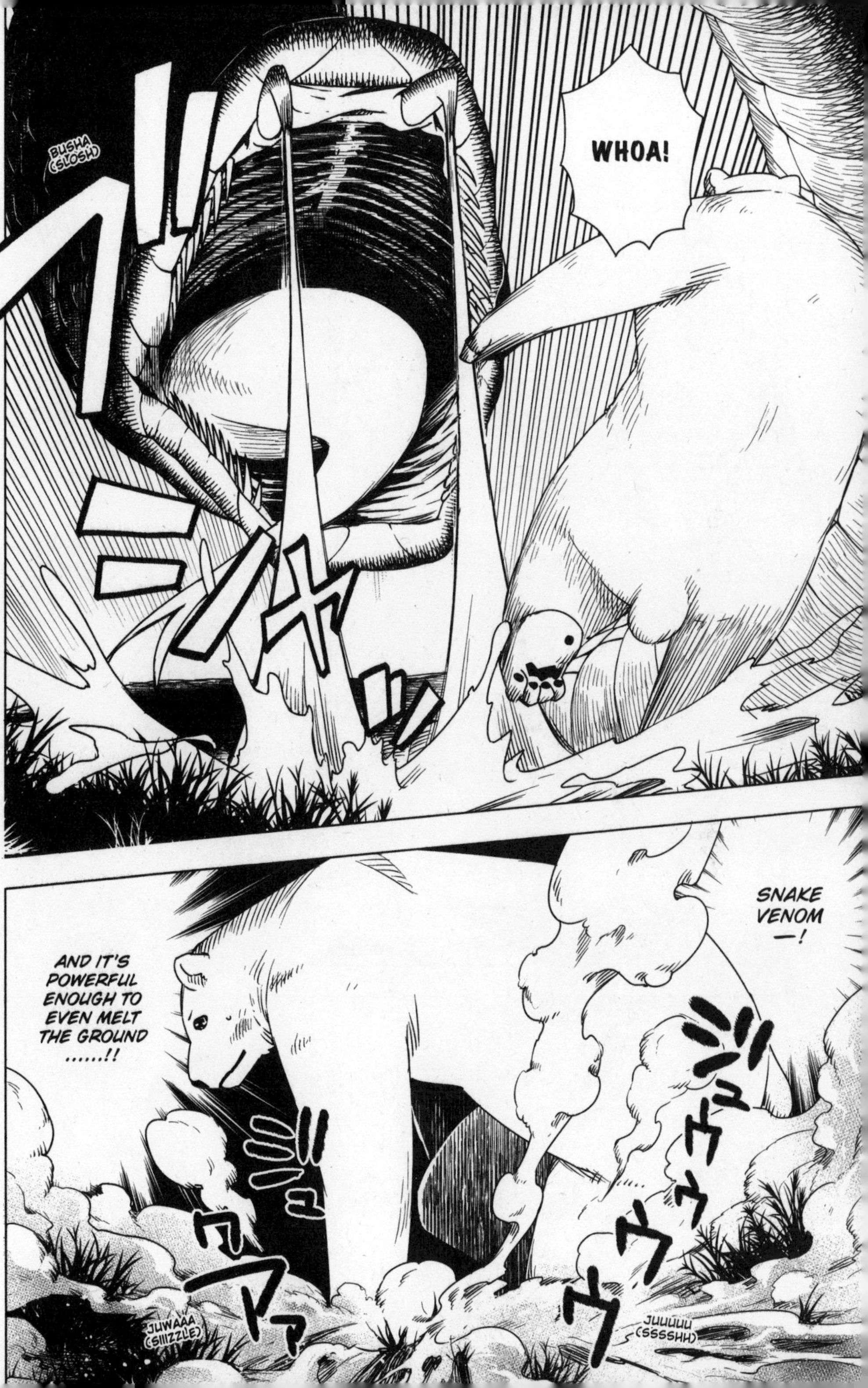
WHOA!
BUSHA (SLOSH)
SNAKE VENOM —!
AND IT'S POWERFUL ENOUGH TO EVEN MELT THE GROUND ......!!
JUUUUU (SSSSHH)
JUWAAA (SIIIZZLE)

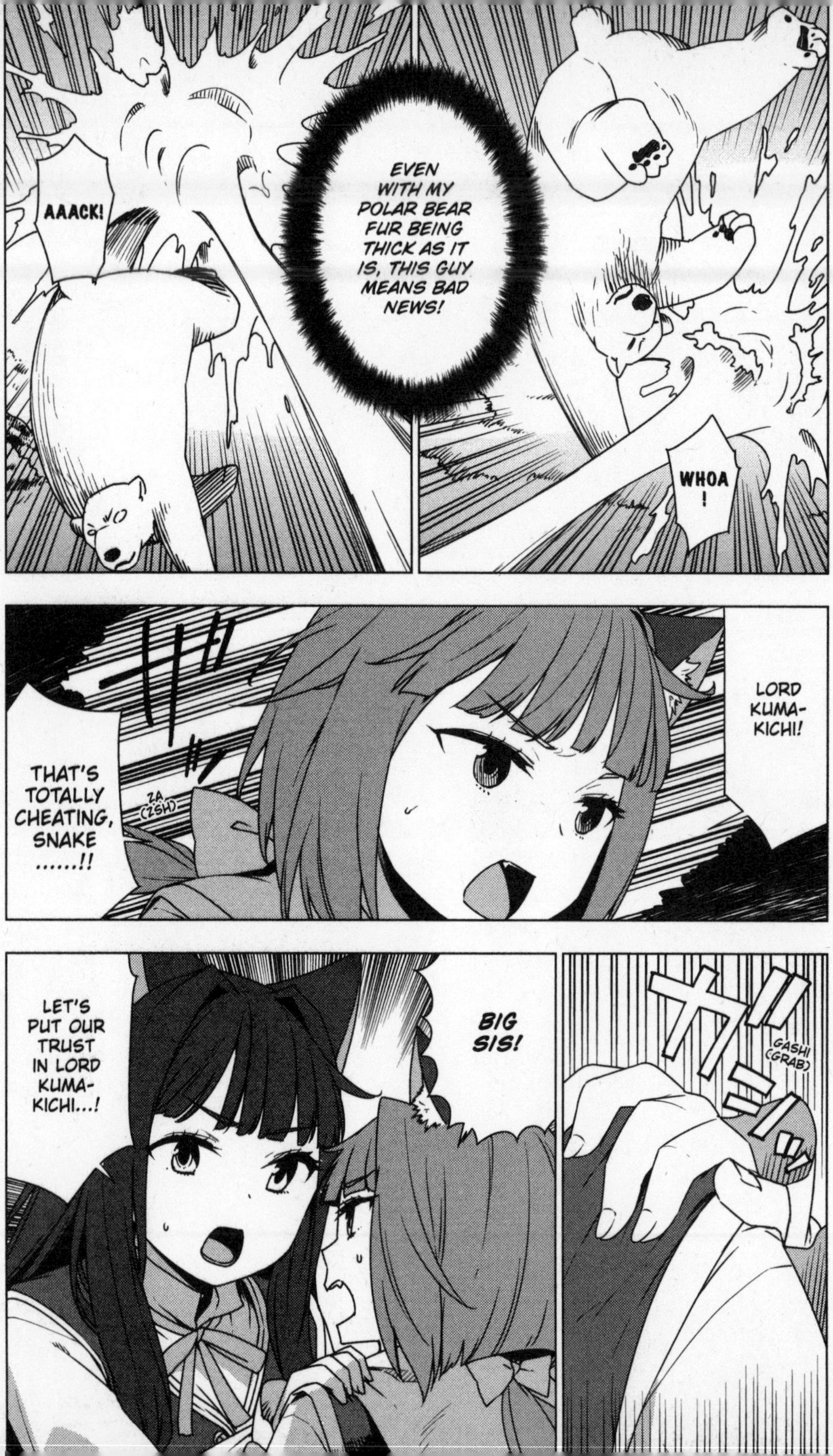
EVEN WITH MY POLAR BEAR FUR BEING THICK AS IT IS, THIS GUY MEANS BAD NEWS!
WHOA!
AAACK!
LORD KUMA-KICHI!
ZA (ZSH)
THAT'S TOTALLY CHEATING, SNAKE ......!!
GASHI (GRAB)
BIG SIS!
LET'S PUT OUR TRUST IN LORD KUMA-KICHI...!

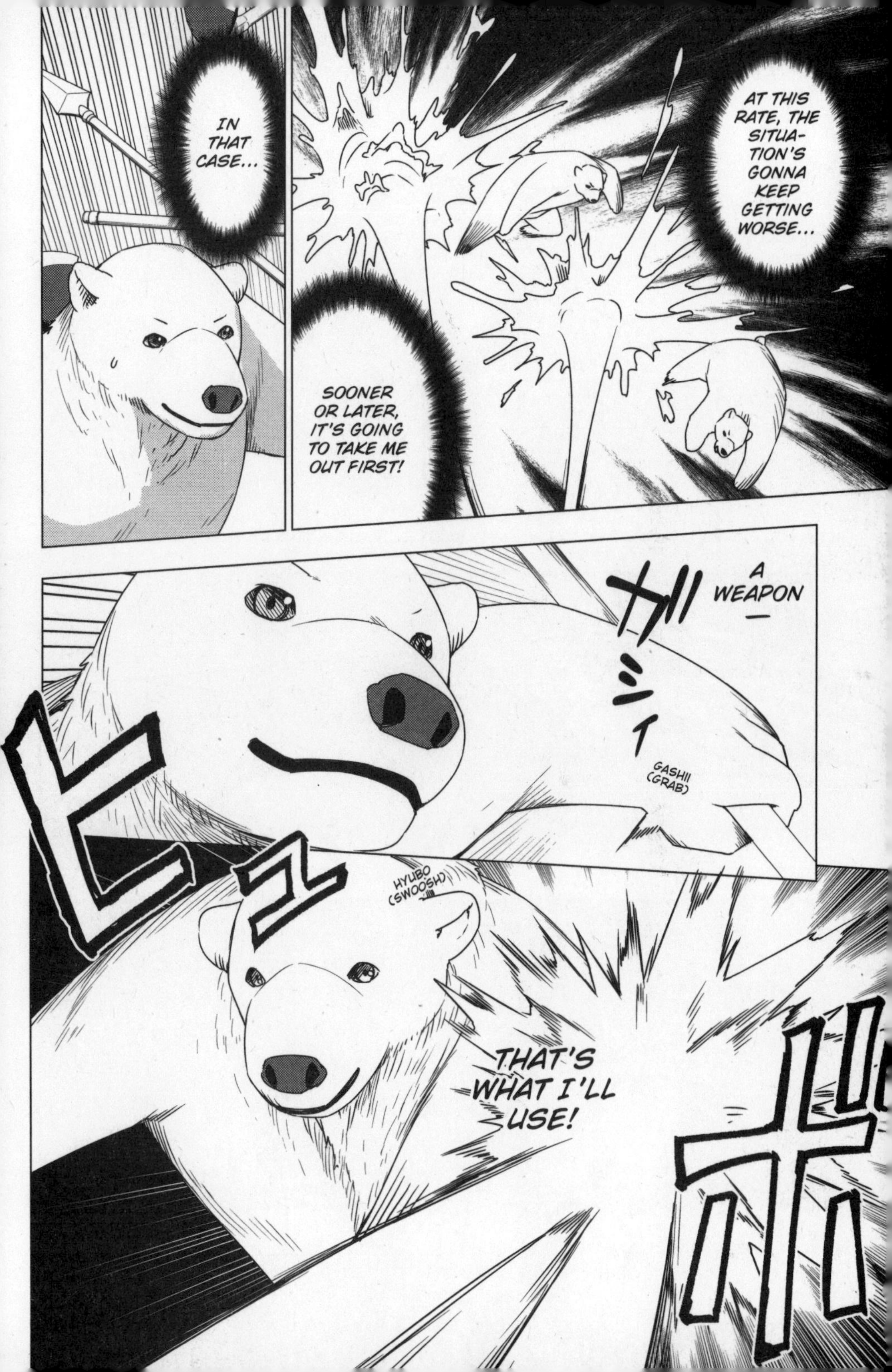
AT THIS RATE, THE SITUATION'S GONNA KEEP GETTING WORSE...
SOONER OR LATER, IT'S GOING TO TAKE ME OUT FIRST!
IN THAT CASE...
A WEAPON —
GASHII (GRAB)
HYUBO (SWOOSH)
THAT'S WHAT I'LL USE!

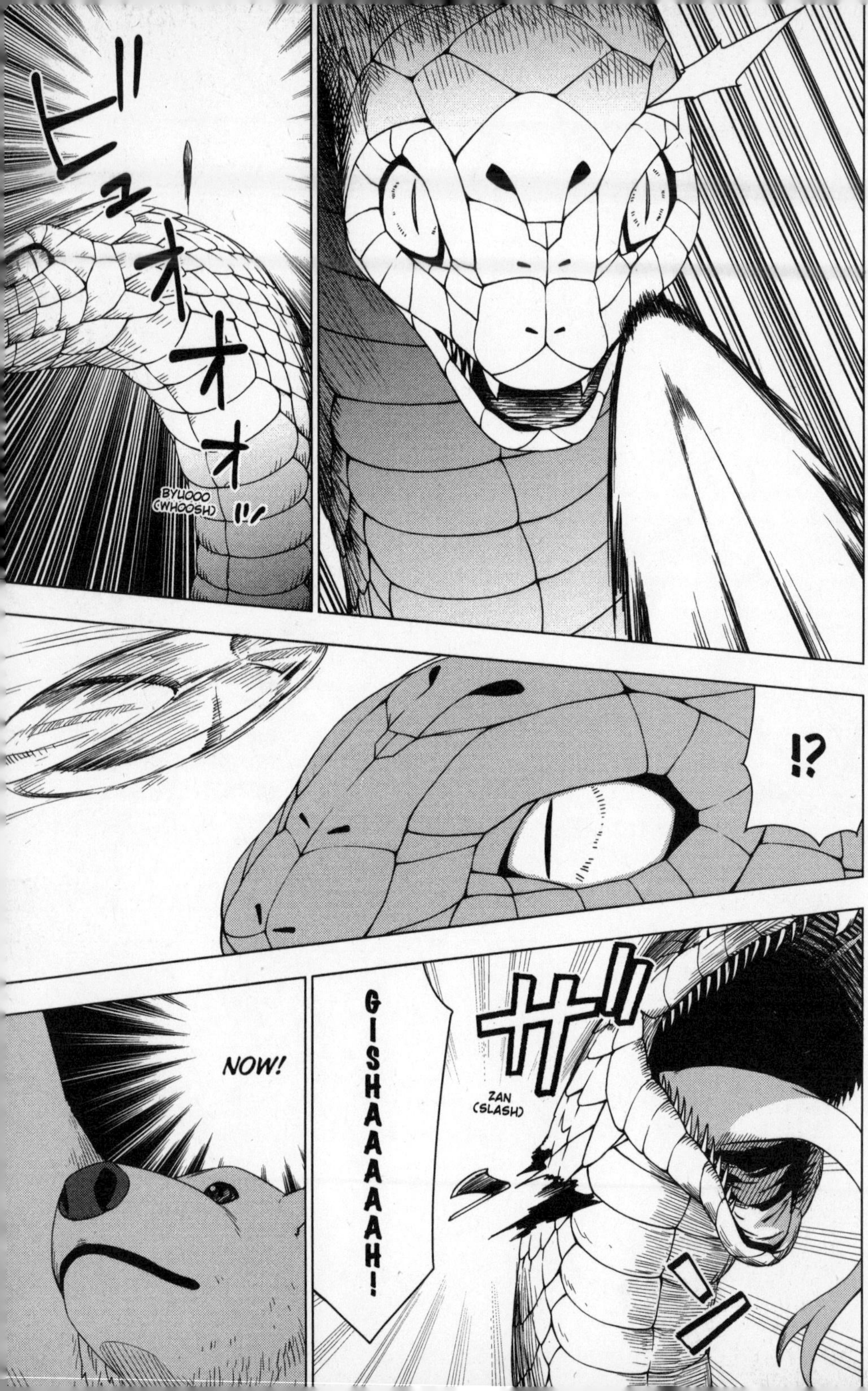
ビュオオオ!!
BYUOOO (WHOOSH)
!?
ZAN (SLASH)
GISHAAAAAAH!
NOW!

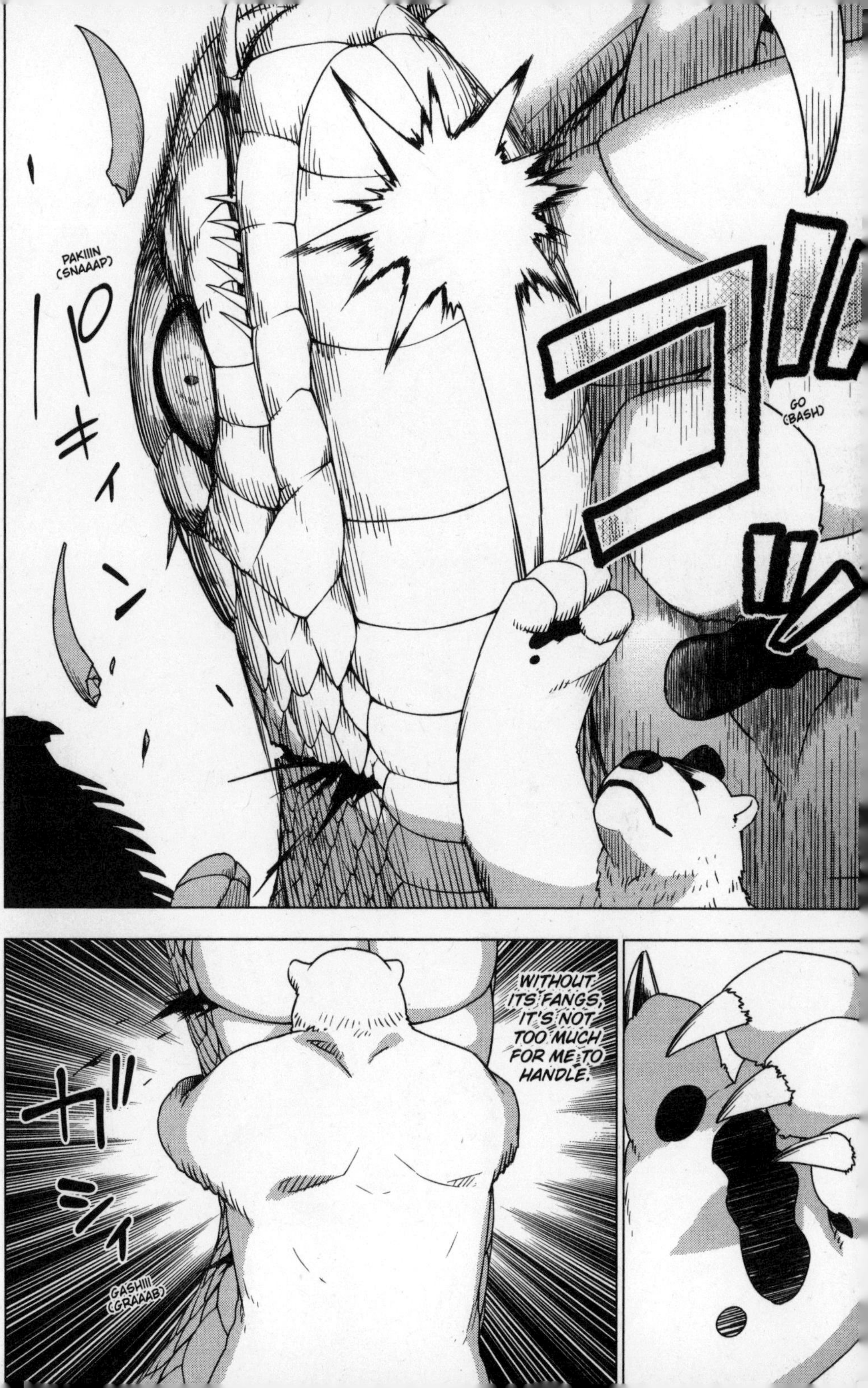
ゴッ
GO (BASH)
パキィン
PAKIIIN (SNAAAP)
WITHOUT ITS FANGS, IT'S NOT TOO MUCH FOR ME TO HANDLE.
ガシィ
GASHIII (GRAAAB)

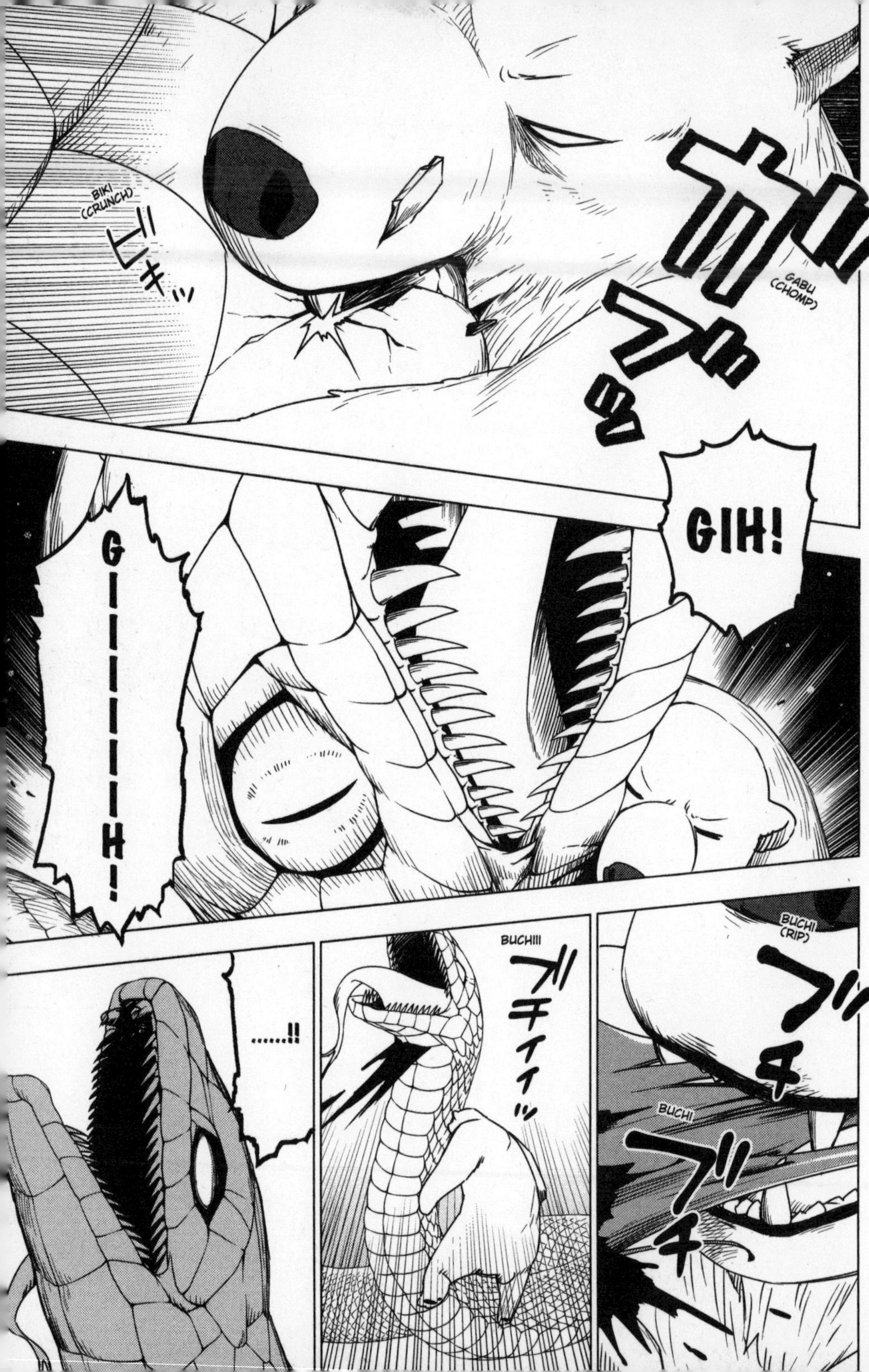
GABU (CHOMP)
BIKI (CRUNCH)
GIH!
GIIIIIIH!
BUCHI (RIP)
BUCHI
BUCHIII
......!!

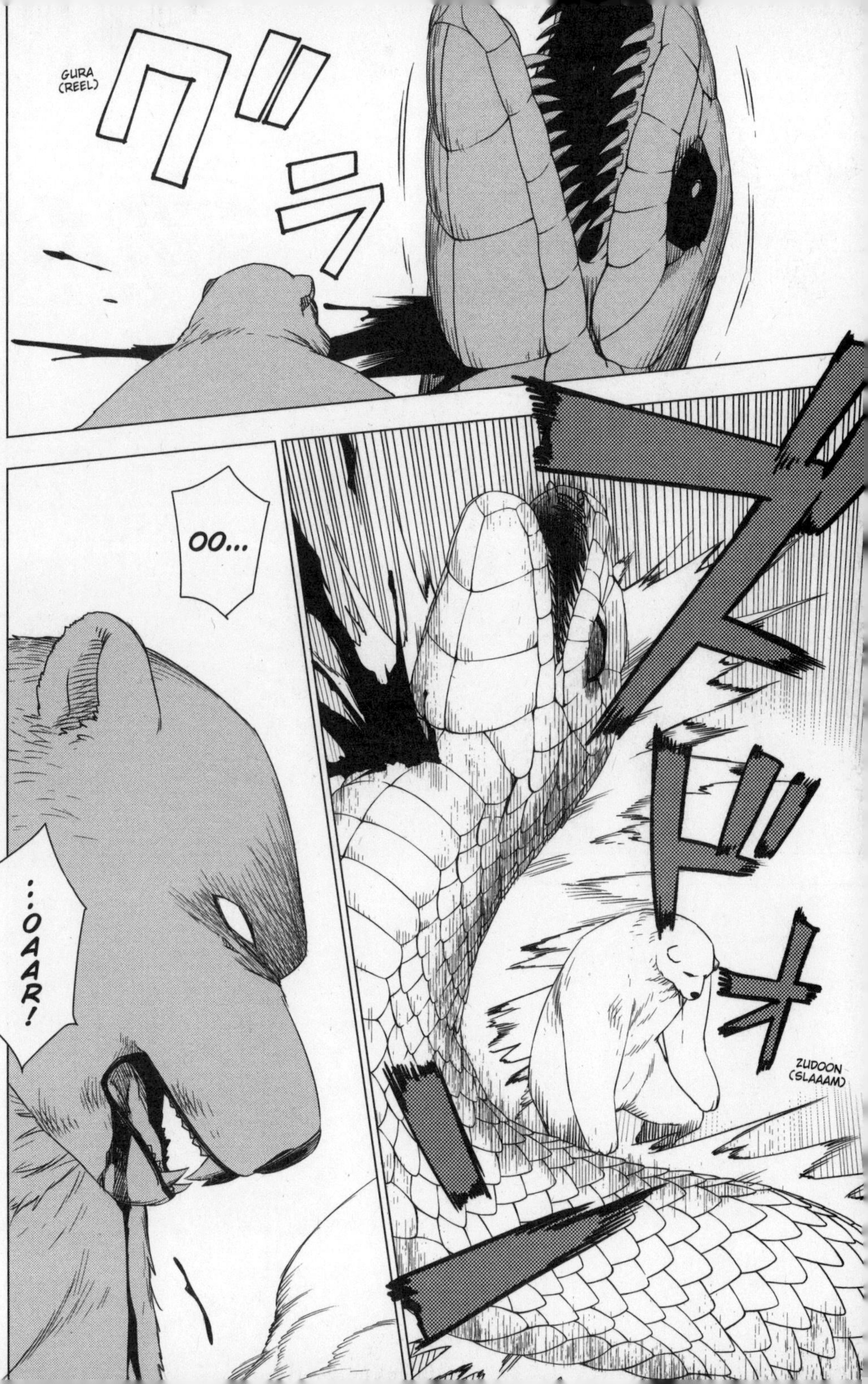
GURA (REEL)
ZUDOON (SLAAAM)
OO...
...OAAR!

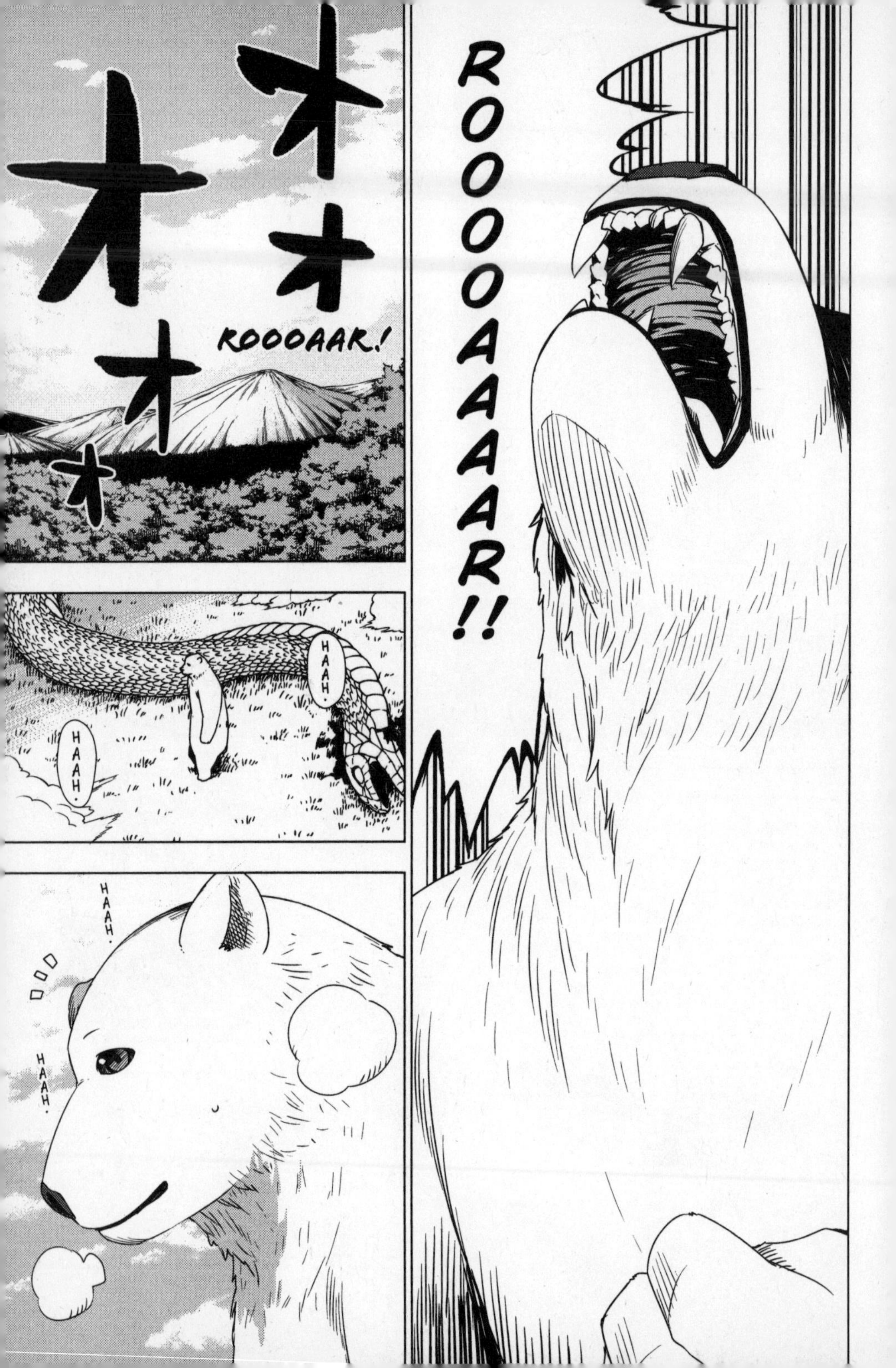
ROOOOAAAAAR!!
オオオオ
ROOOAAR!
HAAH.
HAAH.
HAAH.
HAAH.

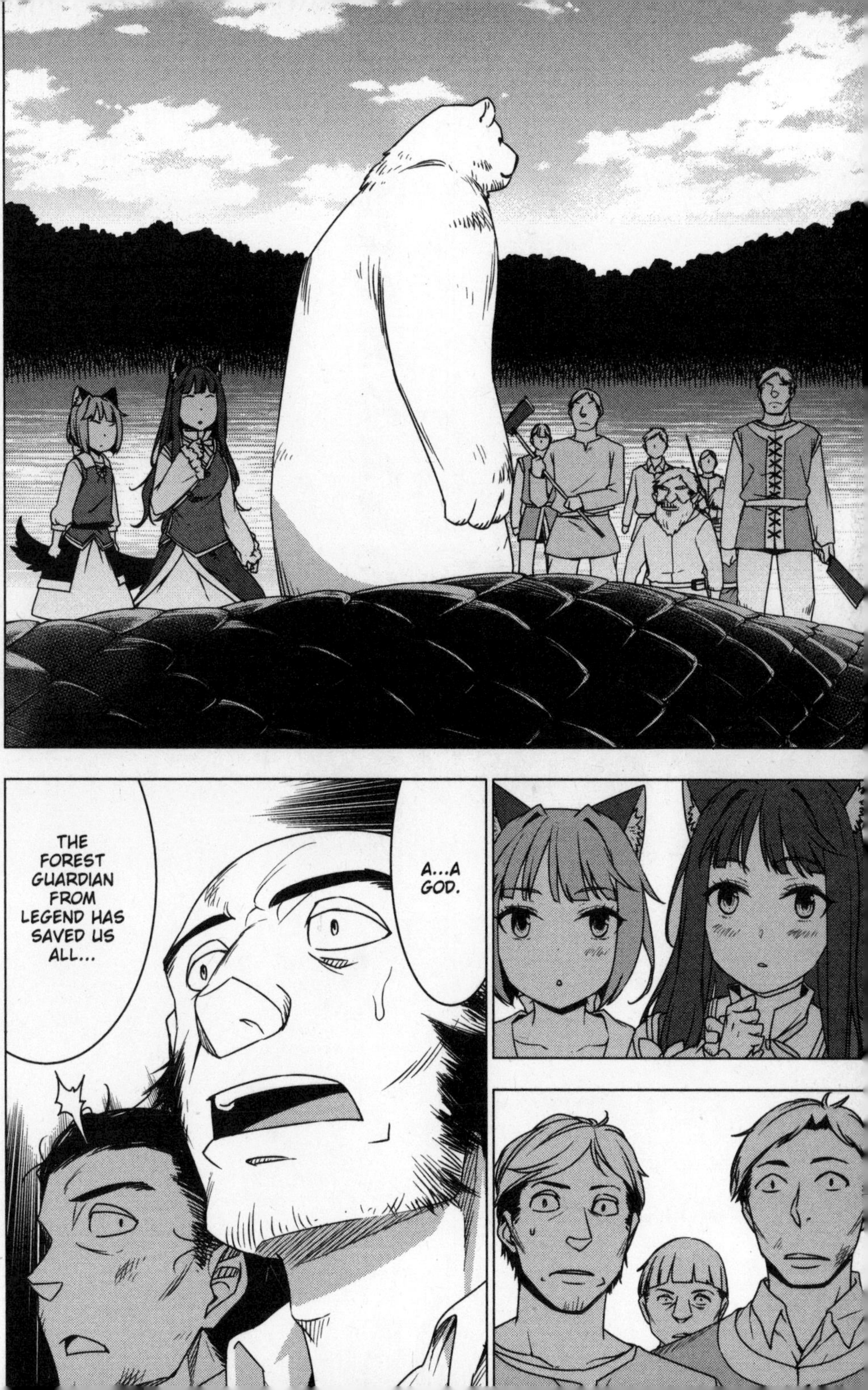
A...A GOD.
THE FOREST GUARDIAN FROM LEGEND HAS SAVED US ALL...

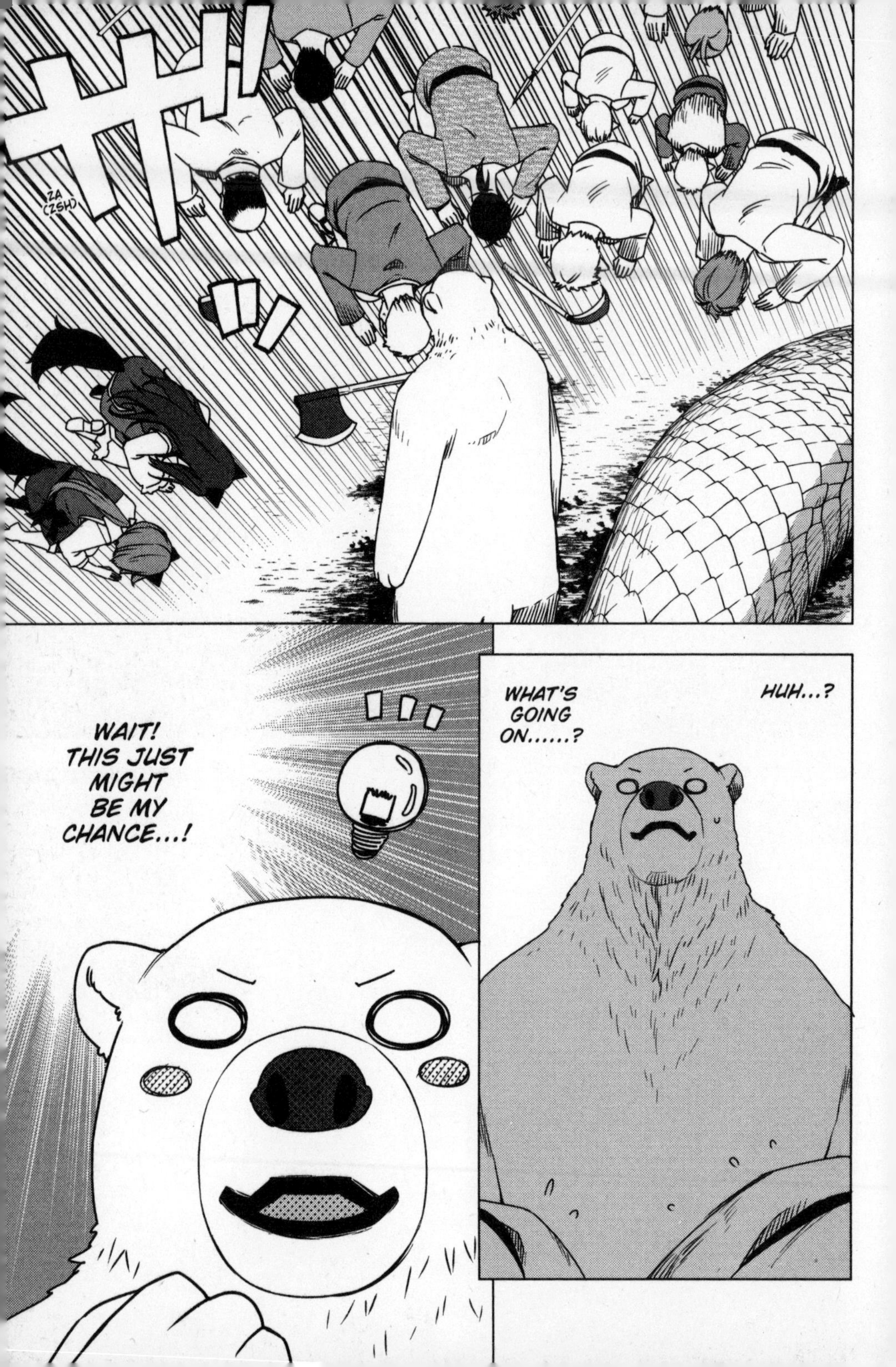
ZA (ZSH)
HUH...?
WHAT'S GOING ON......?
WAIT! THIS JUST MIGHT BE MY CHANCE...!

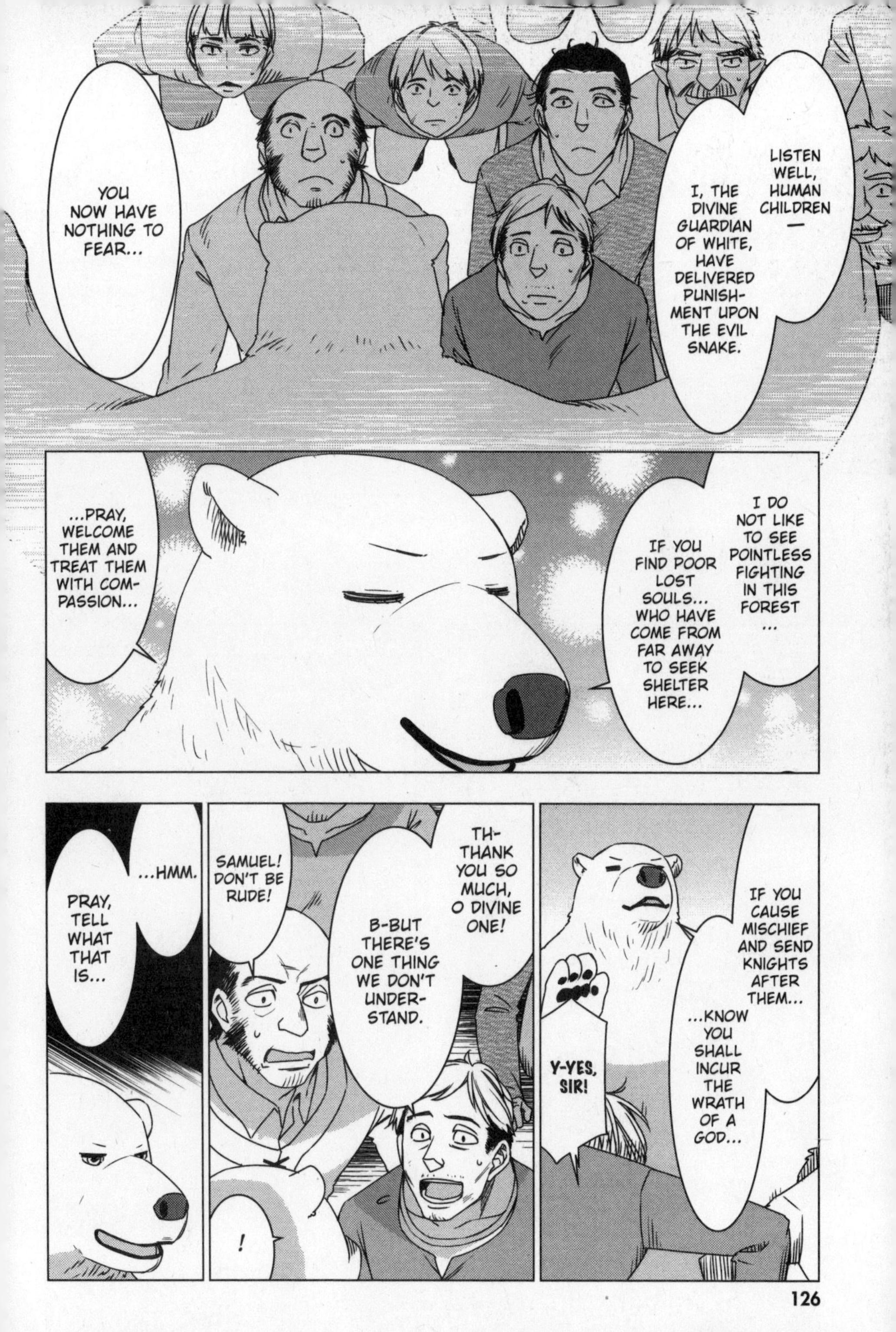
LISTEN WELL, HUMAN CHILDREN —
I, THE DIVINE GUARDIAN OF WHITE, HAVE DELIVERED PUNISHMENT UPON THE EVIL SNAKE.
YOU NOW HAVE NOTHING TO FEAR...
I DO NOT LIKE TO SEE POINTLESS FIGHTING IN THIS FOREST...
IF YOU FIND POOR LOST SOULS... WHO HAVE COME FROM FAR AWAY TO SEEK SHELTER HERE...
...PRAY, WELCOME THEM AND TREAT THEM WITH COMPASSION...
IF YOU CAUSE MISCHIEF AND SEND KNIGHTS AFTER THEM...
...KNOW YOU SHALL INCUR THE WRATH OF A GOD...
Y-YES, SIR!
TH-THANK YOU SO MUCH, O DIVINE ONE!
B-BUT THERE'S ONE THING WE DON'T UNDERSTAND.
SAMUEL! DON'T BE RUDE!
!
...HMM.
PRAY, TELL WHAT THAT IS...

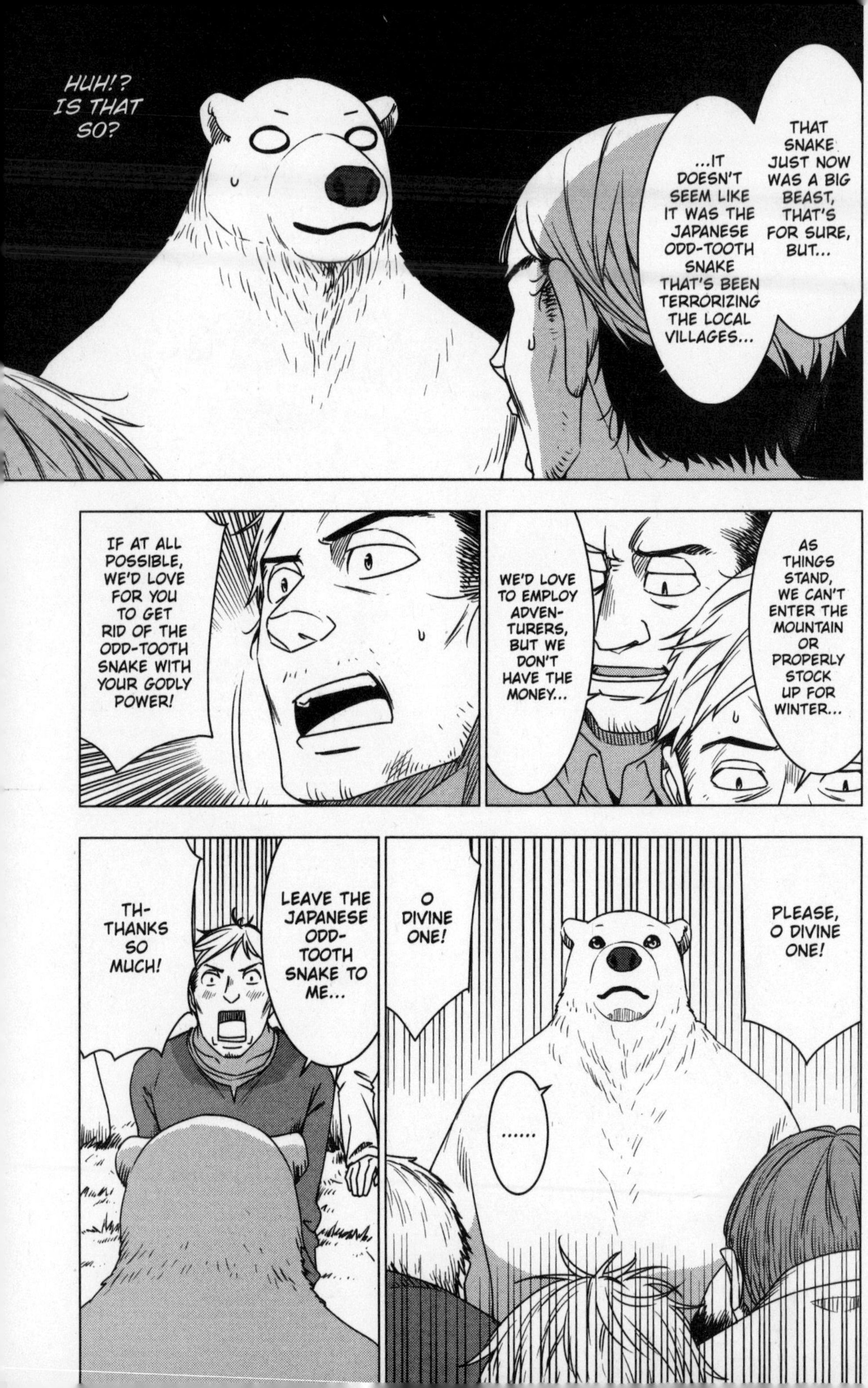
THAT SNAKE JUST NOW WAS A BIG BEAST, THAT'S FOR SURE, BUT...
...IT DOESN'T SEEM LIKE IT WAS THE JAPANESE ODD-TOOTH SNAKE THAT'S BEEN TERRORIZING THE LOCAL VILLAGES...
HUH!? IS THAT SO?
AS THINGS STAND, WE CAN'T ENTER THE MOUNTAIN OR PROPERLY STOCK UP FOR WINTER...
WE'D LOVE TO EMPLOY ADVEN-TURERS, BUT WE DON'T HAVE THE MONEY...
IF AT ALL POSSIBLE, WE'D LOVE FOR YOU TO GET RID OF THE ODD-TOOTH SNAKE WITH YOUR GODLY POWER!
PLEASE, O DIVINE ONE!
O DIVINE ONE!
......
LEAVE THE JAPANESE ODD-TOOTH SNAKE TO ME...
TH-THANKS SO MUCH!

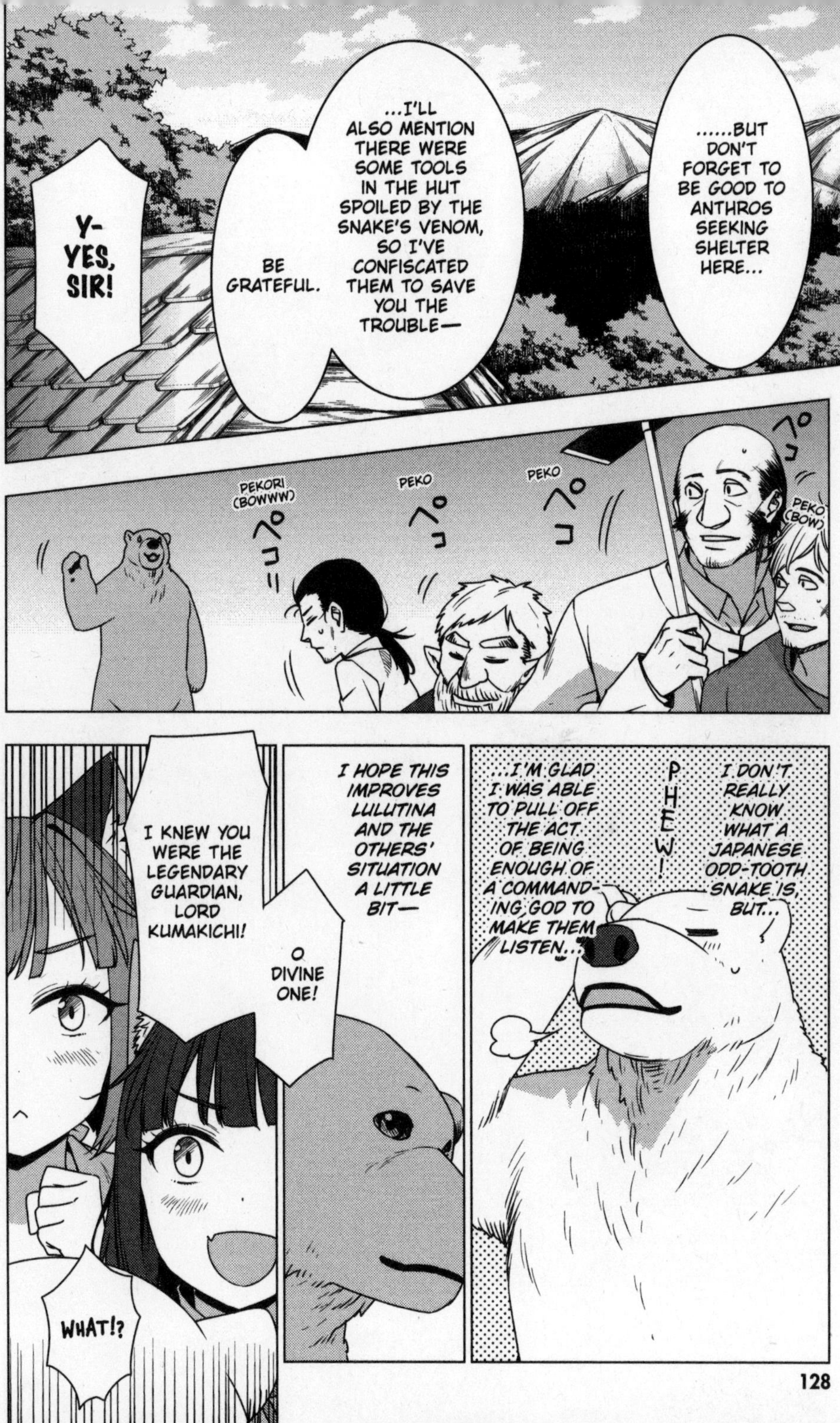
......BUT DON'T FORGET TO BE GOOD TO ANTHROS SEEKING SHELTER HERE...
...I'LL ALSO MENTION THERE WERE SOME TOOLS IN THE HUT SPOILED BY THE SNAKE'S VENOM, SO I'VE CONFISCATED THEM TO SAVE YOU THE TROUBLE—
BE GRATEFUL.
Y- YES, SIR!
ペコ
PEKO (BOW)
PEKO
ペコ
PEKO
ペコ
PEKORI (BOWWW)
ペコリ
I DON'T REALLY KNOW WHAT A JAPANESE ODD-TOOTH SNAKE IS, BUT...
PHEW!
...I'M GLAD I WAS ABLE TO PULL OFF THE ACT OF BEING ENOUGH OF A COMMANDING GOD TO MAKE THEM LISTEN...
I HOPE THIS IMPROVES LULUTINA AND THE OTHERS' SITUATION A LITTLE BIT—
I KNEW YOU WERE THE LEGENDARY GUARDIAN, LORD KUMAKICHI!
O DIVINE ONE!
WHAT!?

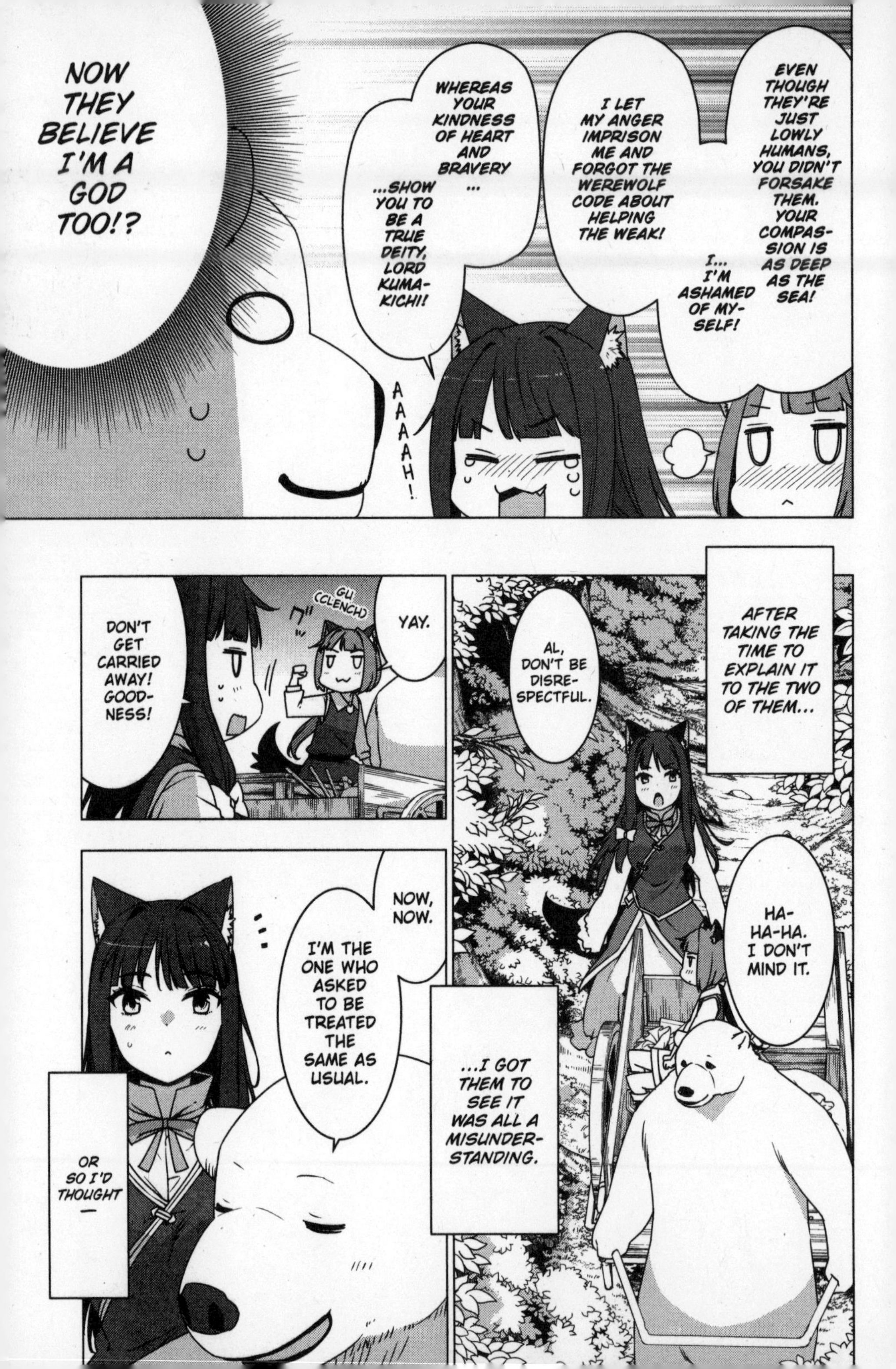

EVEN THOUGH THEY'RE JUST LOWLY HUMANS, YOU DIDN'T FORSAKE THEM. YOUR COMPASSION IS AS DEEP AS THE SEA!
I... I'M ASHAMED OF MYSELF!
I LET MY ANGER IMPRISON ME AND FORGOT THE WEREWOLF CODE ABOUT HELPING THE WEAK!
WHEREAS YOUR KINDNESS OF HEART AND BRAVERY...
...SHOW YOU TO BE A TRUE DEITY, LORD KUMAKICHI!
AAAAAH!
NOW THEY BELIEVE I'M A GOD TOO!?
AFTER TAKING THE TIME TO EXPLAIN IT TO THE TWO OF THEM...
AL, DON'T BE DISRESPECTFUL.
HA-HA-HA. I DON'T MIND IT.
YAY.
GU (CLENCH)
DON'T GET CARRIED AWAY! GOODNESS!
NOW, NOW.
I'M THE ONE WHO ASKED TO BE TREATED THE SAME AS USUAL.
...I GOT THEM TO SEE IT WAS ALL A MISUNDERSTANDING.
OR SO I'D THOUGHT—

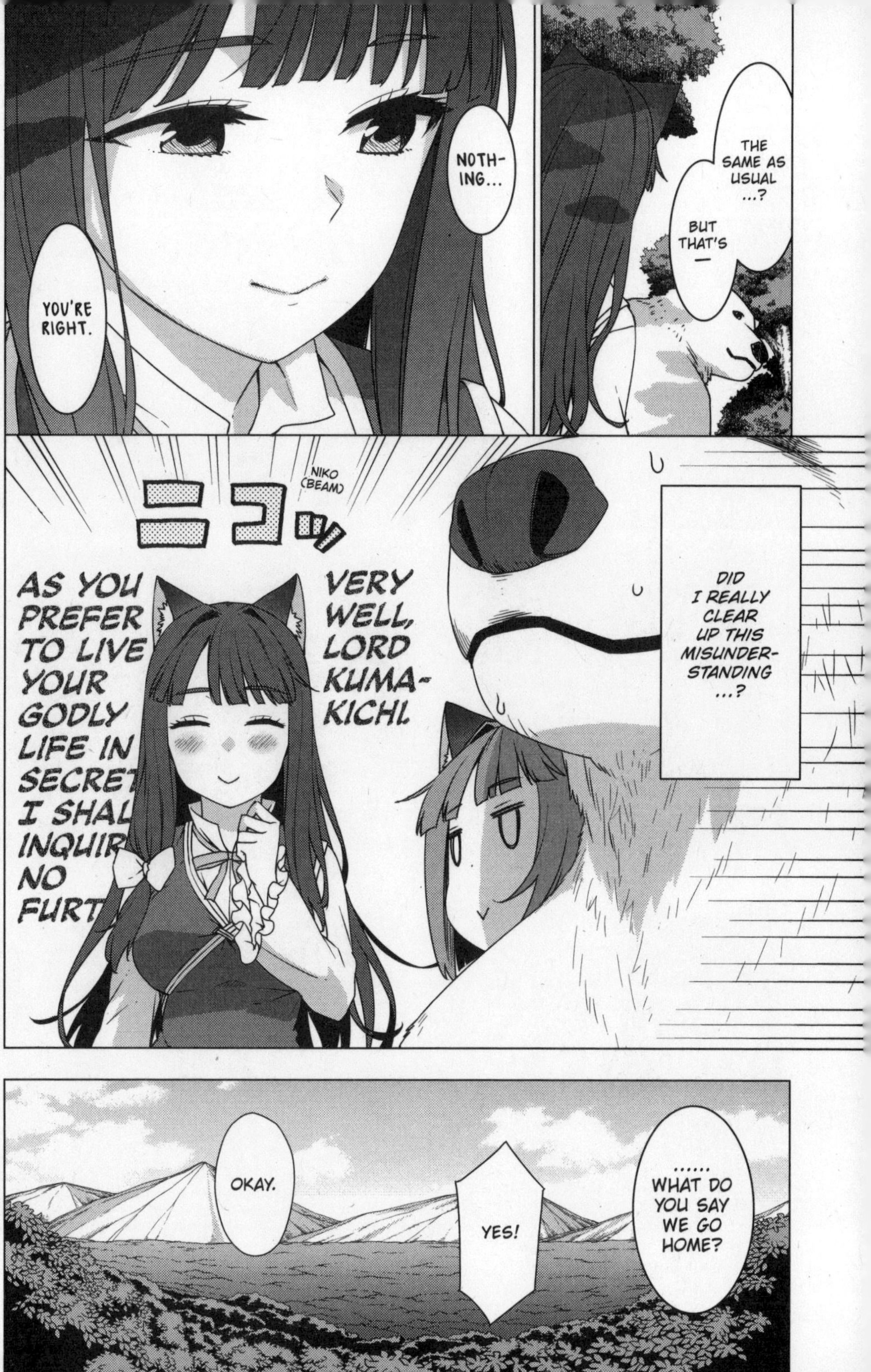
THE SAME AS USUAL ...?
BUT THAT'S —
NOTH-ING...
YOU'RE RIGHT.
NIKO (BEAM)
ニコッ
VERY WELL, LORD KUMA-KICHI.
AS YOU PREFER TO LIVE YOUR GODLY LIFE IN SECRET I SHAL INQUIR NO FURT
DID I REALLY CLEAR UP THIS MISUNDER-STANDING ...?
...... WHAT DO YOU SAY WE GO HOME?
YES!
OKAY.

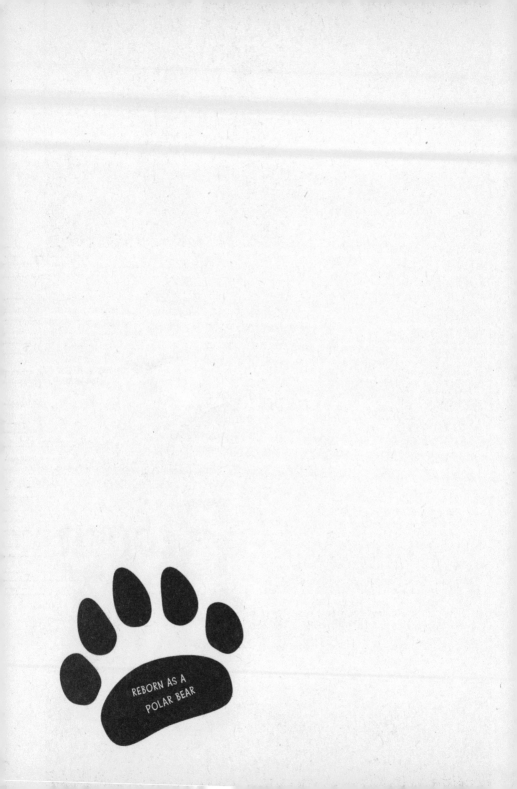

REBORN AS A
POLAR BEAR

Reborn as a Polar Bear

The Legend of How I Became a Forest Guardian

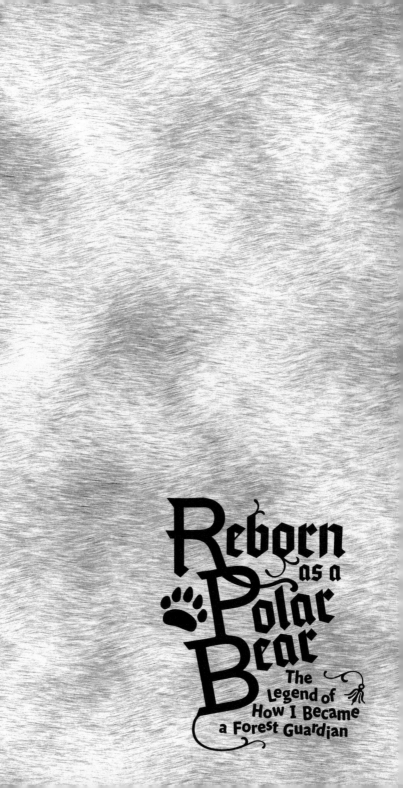

Chapter 4 Woodcutting

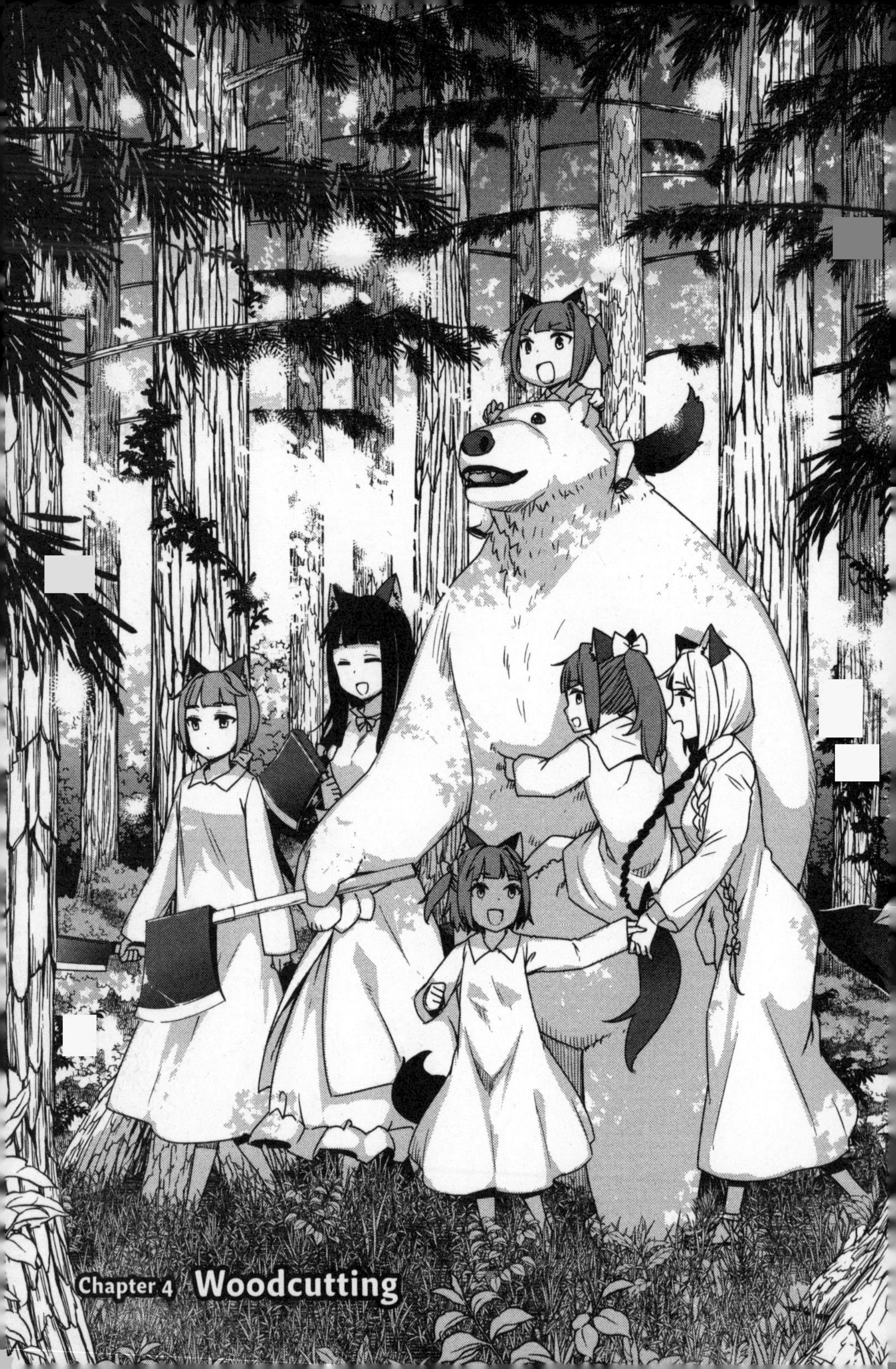

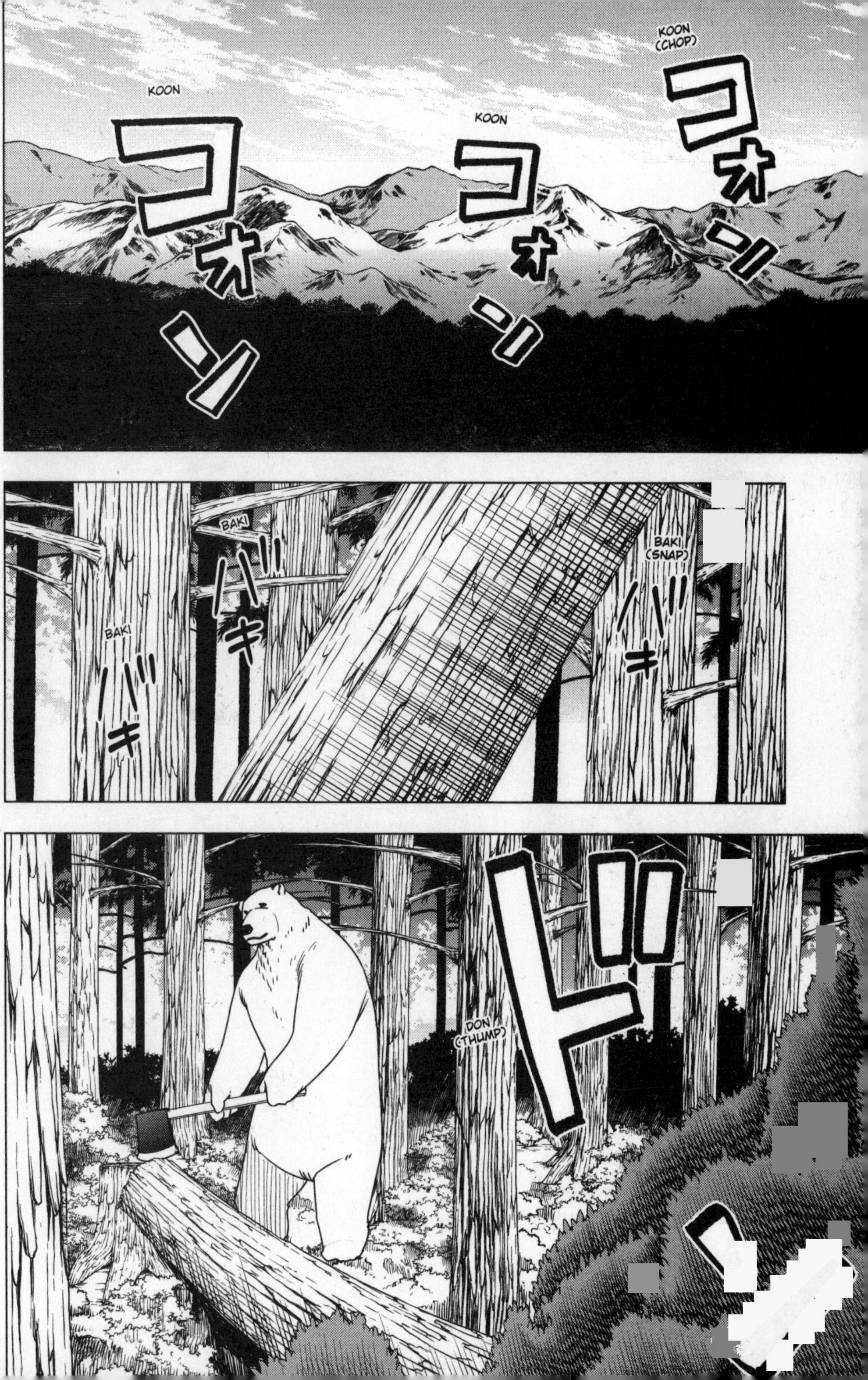
KOON (CHOP)
KOON
KOON
BAKI (SNAP)
BAKI
BAKI
DON (THUMP)

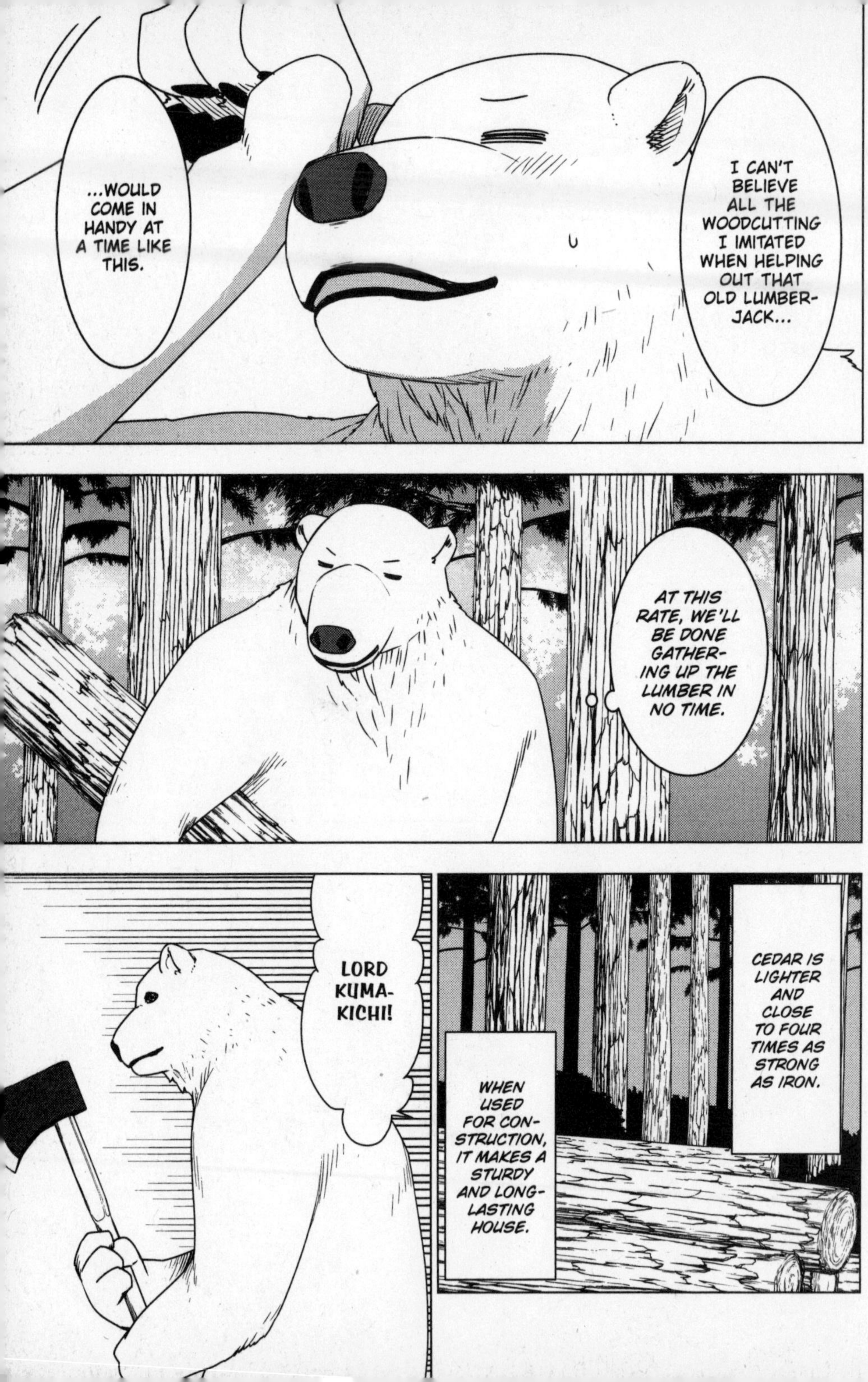
I CAN'T BELIEVE ALL THE WOODCUTTING I IMITATED WHEN HELPING OUT THAT OLD LUMBER-JACK...
...WOULD COME IN HANDY AT A TIME LIKE THIS.
AT THIS RATE, WE'LL BE DONE GATHER-ING UP THE LUMBER IN NO TIME.
CEDAR IS LIGHTER AND CLOSE TO FOUR TIMES AS STRONG AS IRON.
WHEN USED FOR CON-STRUCTION, IT MAKES A STURDY AND LONG-LASTING HOUSE.
LORD KUMA-KICHI!

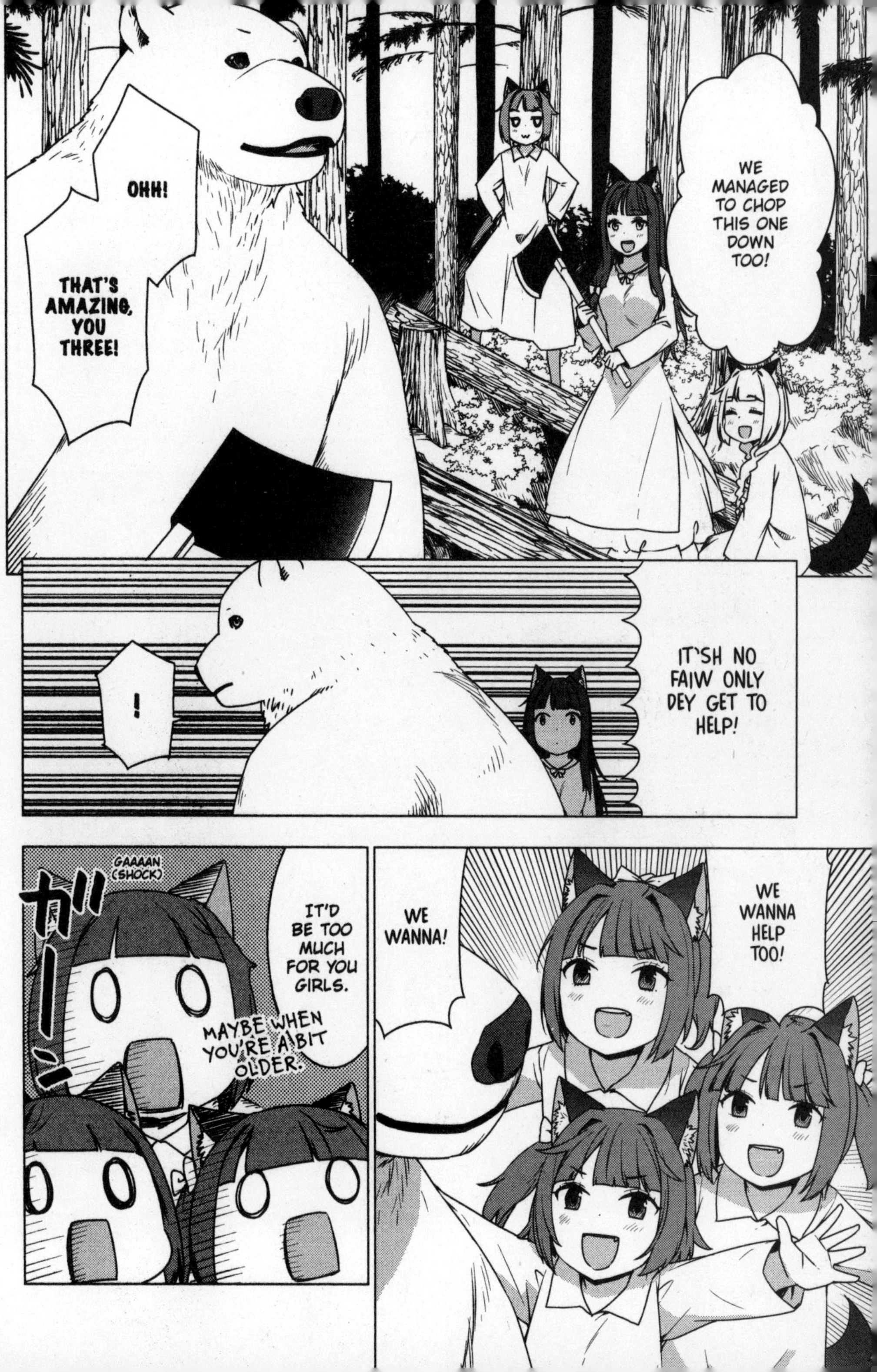
WE MANAGED TO CHOP THIS ONE DOWN TOO!
OHH!
THAT'S AMAZING, YOU THREE!
IT'SH NO FAIW ONLY DEY GET TO HELP!
!
WE WANNA HELP TOO!
WE WANNA!
IT'D BE TOO MUCH FOR YOU GIRLS.
MAYBE WHEN YOU'RE A BIT OLDER.
GAAAAN (SHOCK)

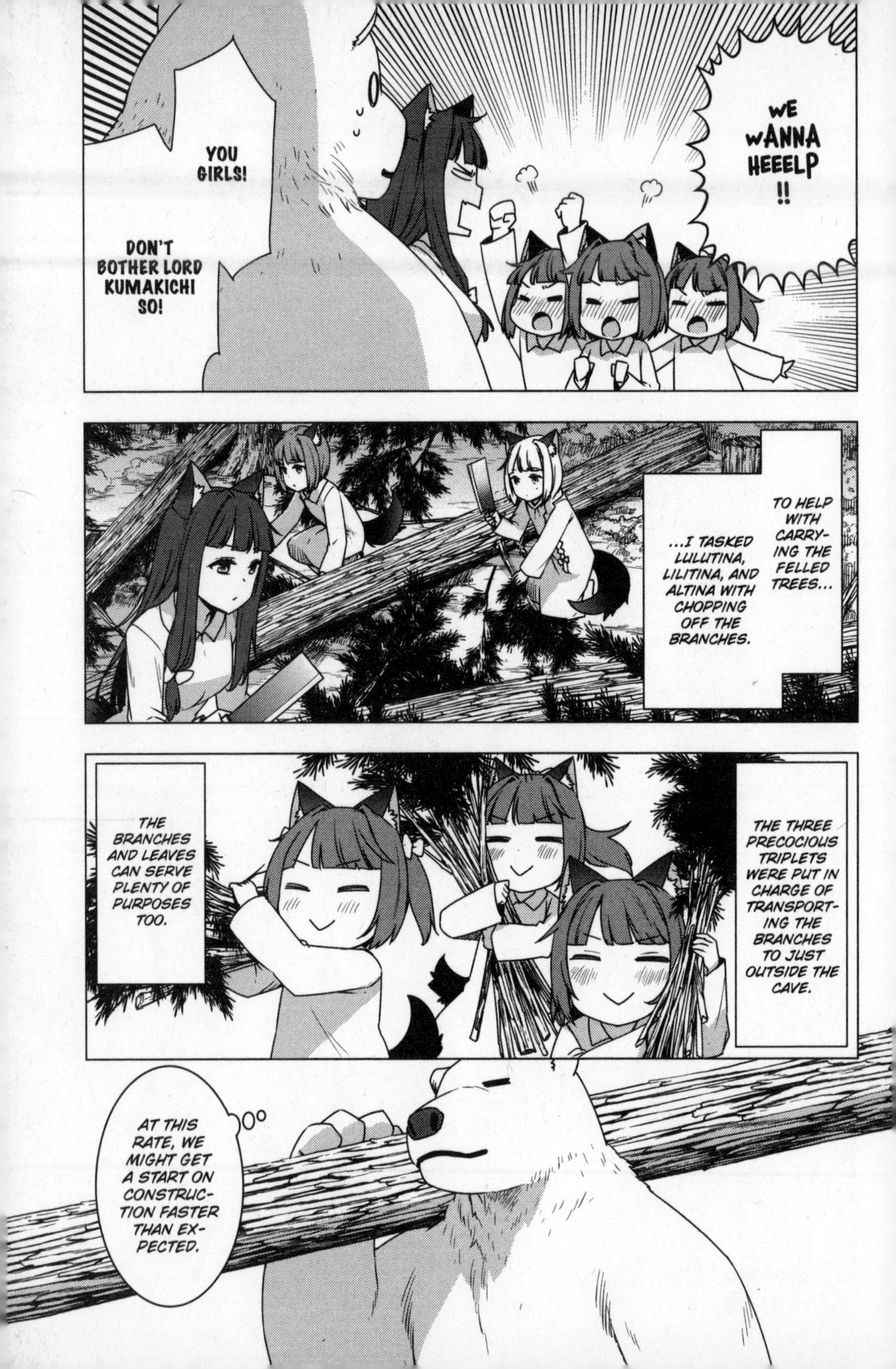
WE wANNA HEEELP !!
YOU GIRLS!
DON'T BOTHER LORD KUMAKICHI SO!
TO HELP WITH CARRYING THE FELLED TREES...
...I TASKED LULUTINA, LILITINA, AND ALTINA WITH CHOPPING OFF THE BRANCHES.
THE THREE PRECOCIOUS TRIPLETS WERE PUT IN CHARGE OF TRANSPORTING THE BRANCHES TO JUST OUTSIDE THE CAVE.
THE BRANCHES AND LEAVES CAN SERVE PLENTY OF PURPOSES TOO.
AT THIS RATE, WE MIGHT GET A START ON CONSTRUCTION FASTER THAN EXPECTED.

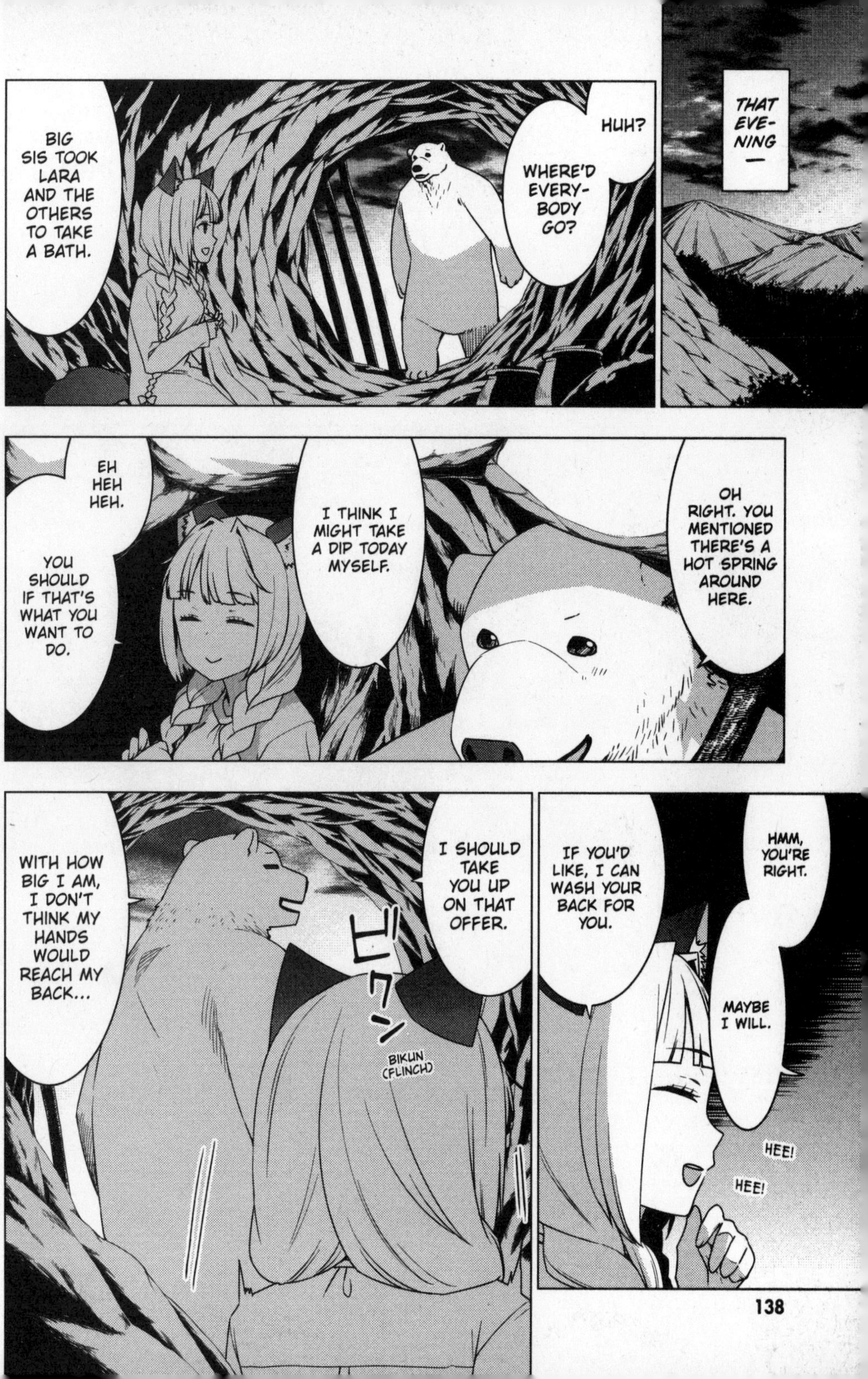
THAT EVENING—
HUH?
WHERE'D EVERYBODY GO?
BIG SIS TOOK LARA AND THE OTHERS TO TAKE A BATH.
OH RIGHT. YOU MENTIONED THERE'S A HOT SPRING AROUND HERE.
I THINK I MIGHT TAKE A DIP TODAY MYSELF.
EH HEH HEH.
YOU SHOULD IF THAT'S WHAT YOU WANT TO DO.
HMM, YOU'RE RIGHT.
MAYBE I WILL.
IF YOU'D LIKE, I CAN WASH YOUR BACK FOR YOU.
HEE!
HEE!
I SHOULD TAKE YOU UP ON THAT OFFER.
ビクン
BIKUN (FLINCH)
WITH HOW BIG I AM, I DON'T THINK MY HANDS WOULD REACH MY BACK...

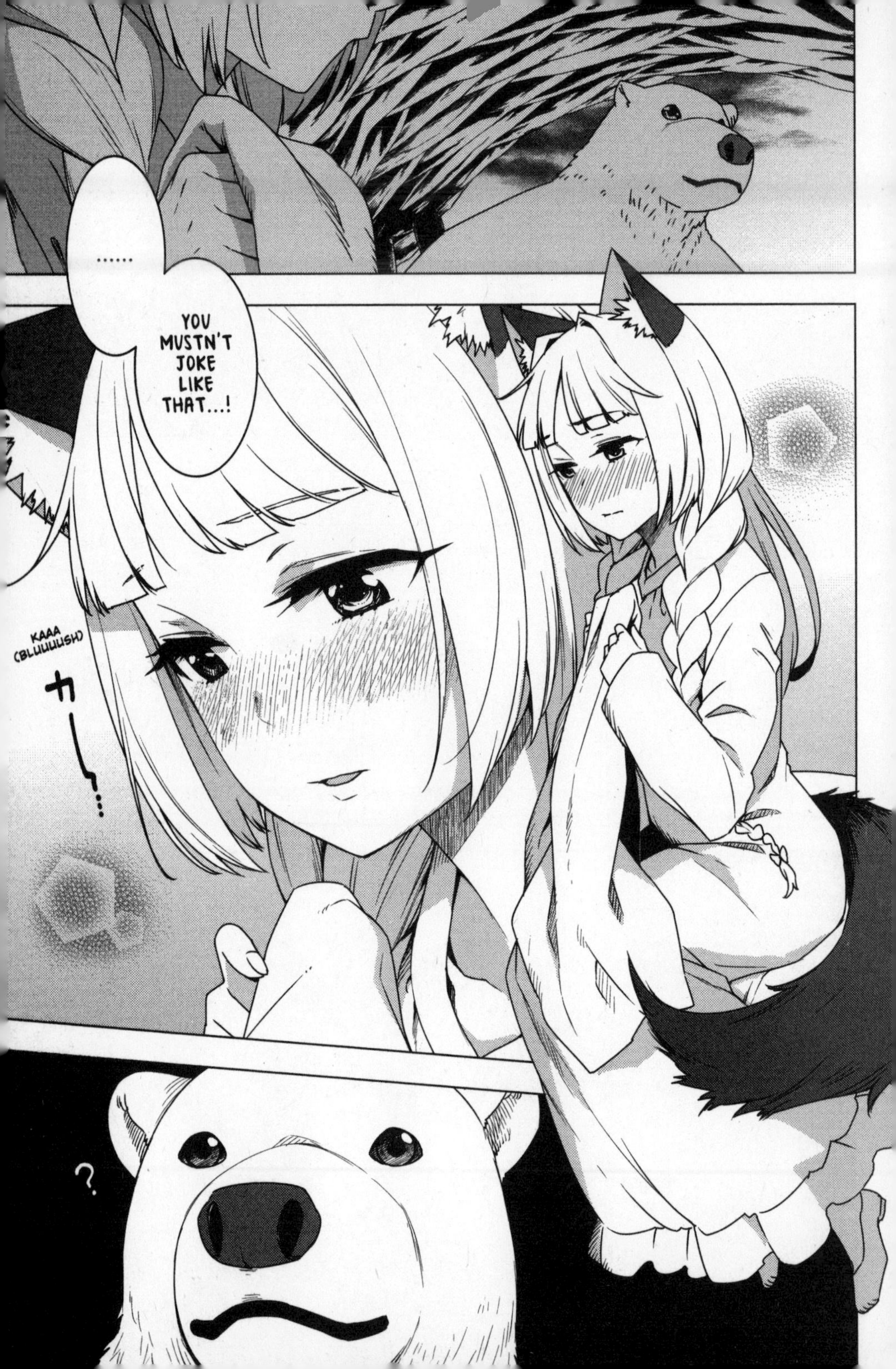

......
YOU MUSTN'T JOKE LIKE THAT...!
KAAA (BLUUUUSH)
カーん…
?

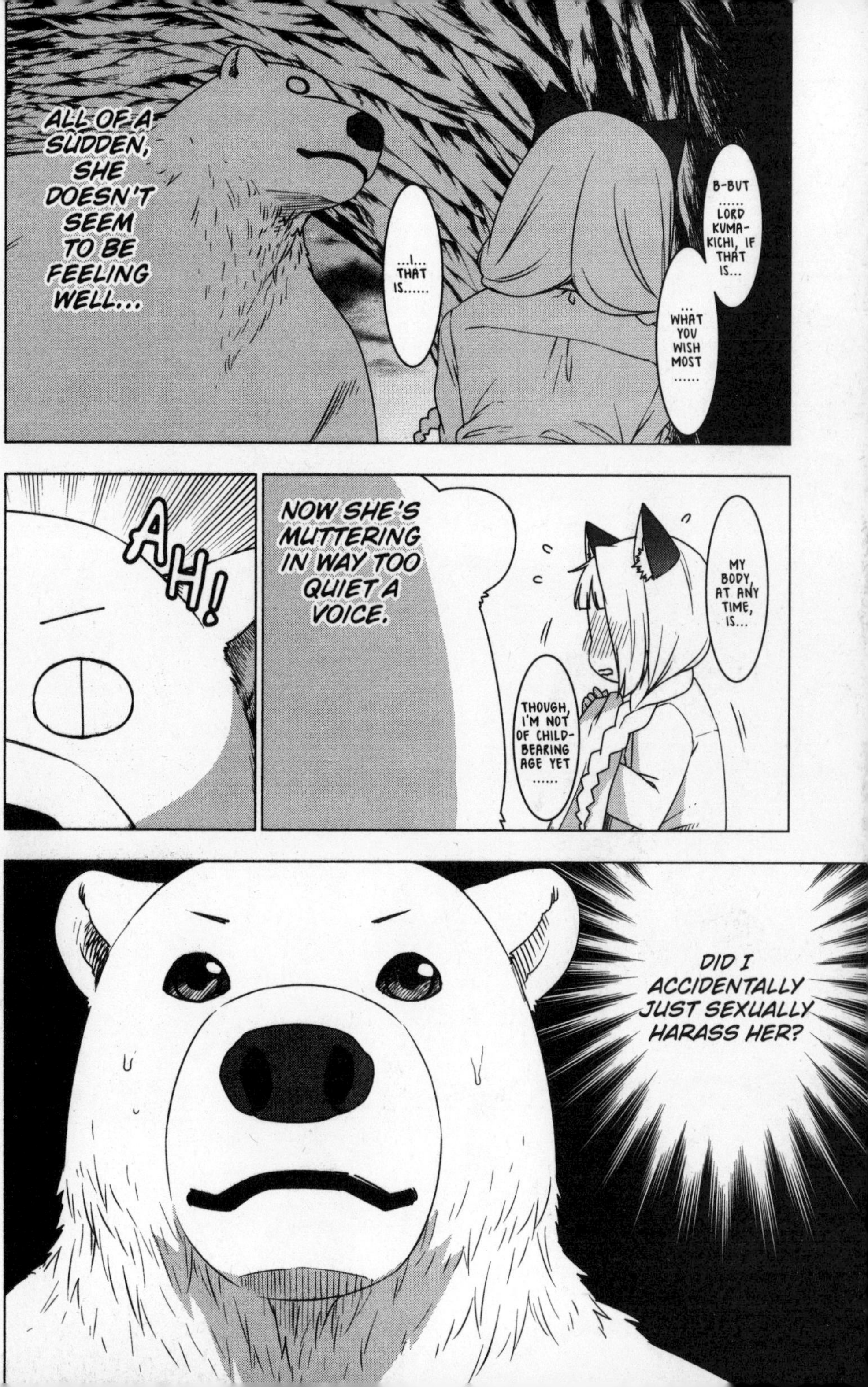

B-BUT ...... LORD KUMA-KICHI, IF THAT IS...
... WHAT YOU WISH MOST ......
...I... THAT IS......
ALL OF A SUDDEN, SHE DOESN'T SEEM TO BE FEELING WELL...
MY BODY, AT ANY TIME, IS...
THOUGH, I'M NOT OF CHILD-BEARING AGE YET ......
NOW SHE'S MUTTERING IN WAY TOO QUIET A VOICE.
AH!
DID I ACCIDENTALLY JUST SEXUALLY HARASS HER?

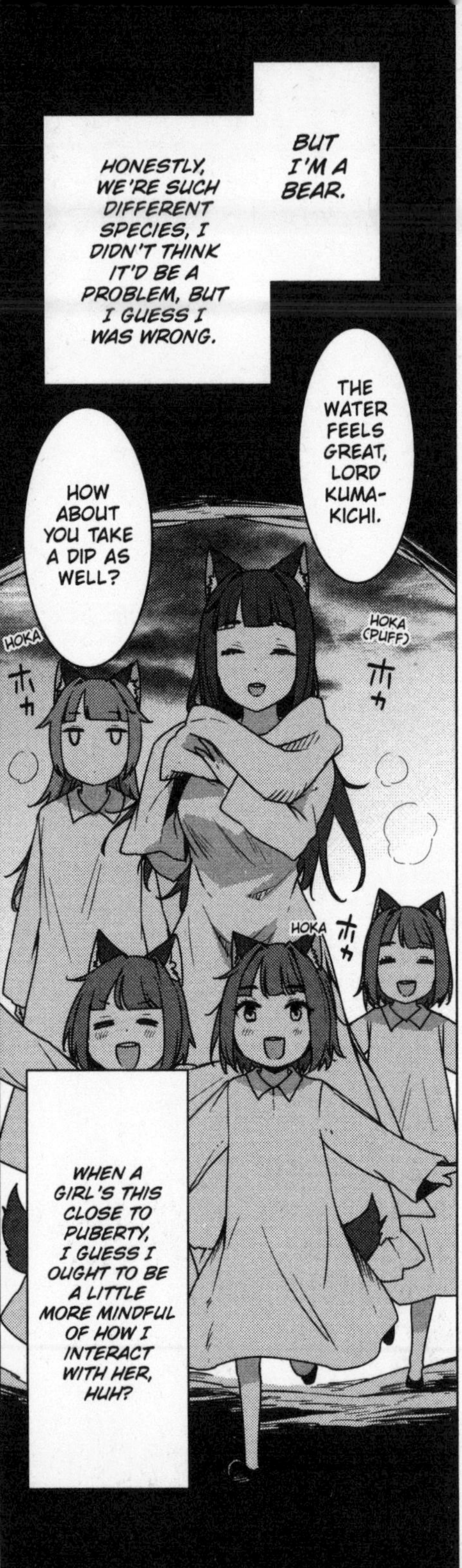
BUT I'M A BEAR.
HONESTLY, WE'RE SUCH DIFFERENT SPECIES, I DIDN'T THINK IT'D BE A PROBLEM, BUT I GUESS I WAS WRONG.
THE WATER FEELS GREAT, LORD KUMAKICHI.
HOW ABOUT YOU TAKE A DIP AS WELL?
HOKA (PUFF)
HOKA
HOKA
WHEN A GIRL'S THIS CLOSE TO PUBERTY, I GUESS I OUGHT TO BE A LITTLE MORE MINDFUL OF HOW I INTERACT WITH HER, HUH?

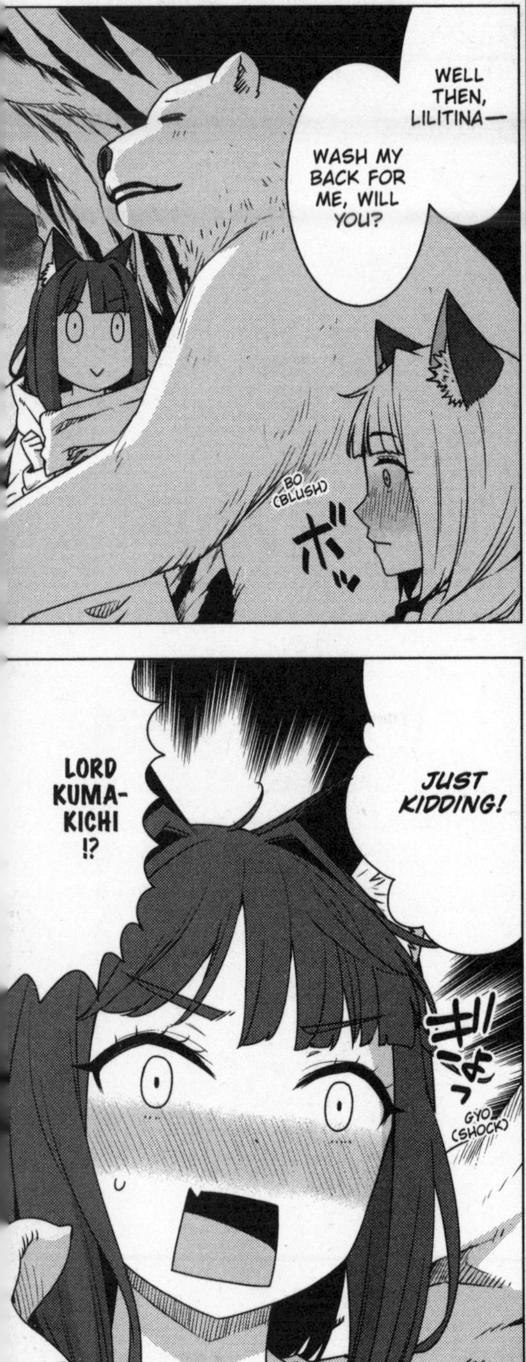
WELL THEN, LILITINA—
WASH MY BACK FOR ME, WILL YOU?
BO (BLUSH)
JUST KIDDING!
LORD KUMA-KICHI !?
GYO (SHOCK)

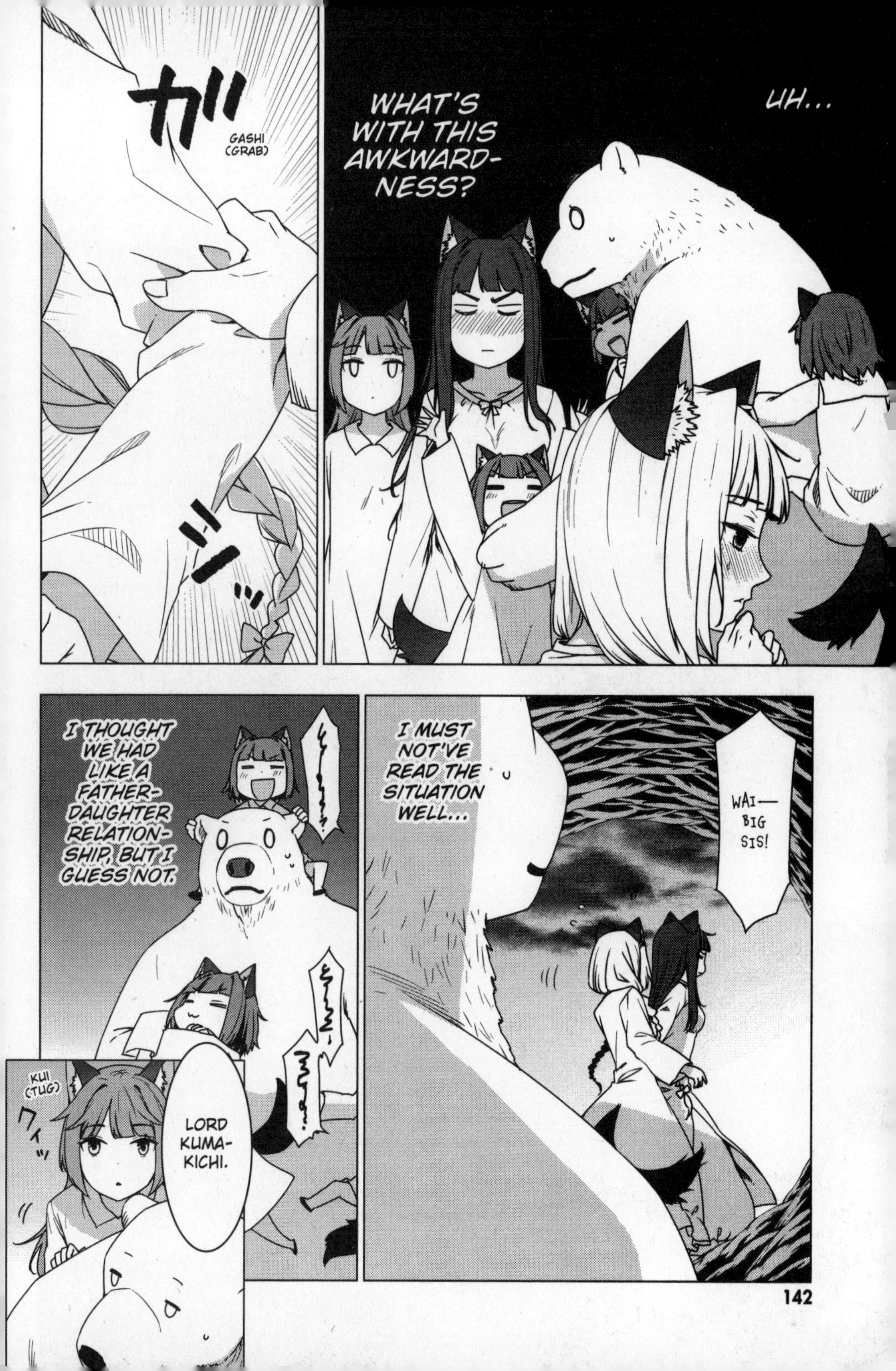
UH...
WHAT'S WITH THIS AWKWARD-NESS?
ガシ
GASHI (GRAB)
WAI— BIG SIS!
I MUST NOT'VE READ THE SITUATION WELL...
I THOUGHT WE HAD LIKE A FATHER-DAUGHTER RELATION-SHIP, BUT I GUESS NOT.
KUI (TUG)
LORD KUMA-KICHI.

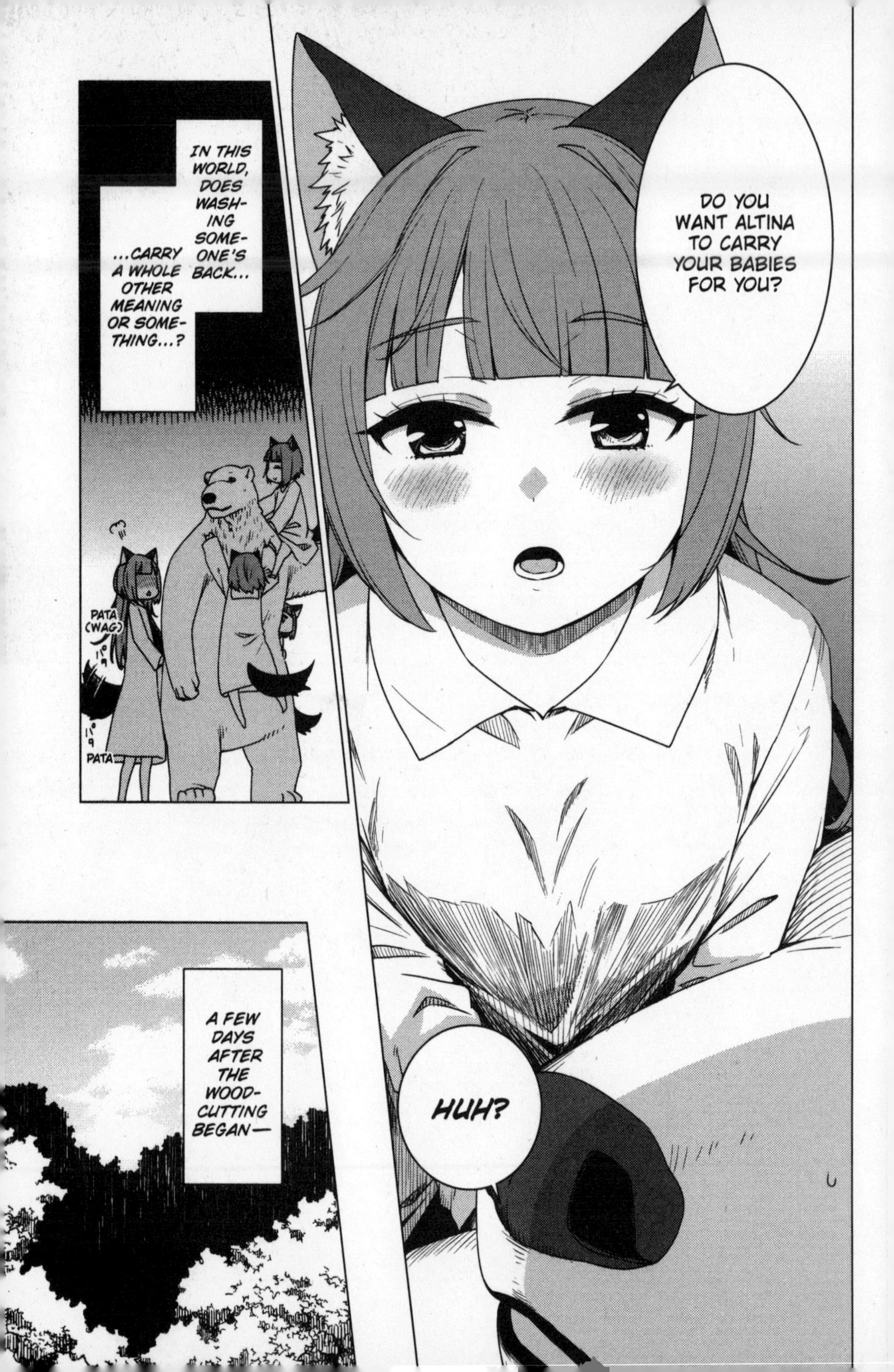
DO YOU WANT ALTINA TO CARRY YOUR BABIES FOR YOU?
HUH?
IN THIS WORLD, DOES WASHING SOME-ONE'S BACK...
...CARRY A WHOLE OTHER MEANING OR SOME-THING...?
PATA (WAG)
PATA
A FEW DAYS AFTER THE WOOD-CUTTING BEGAN—

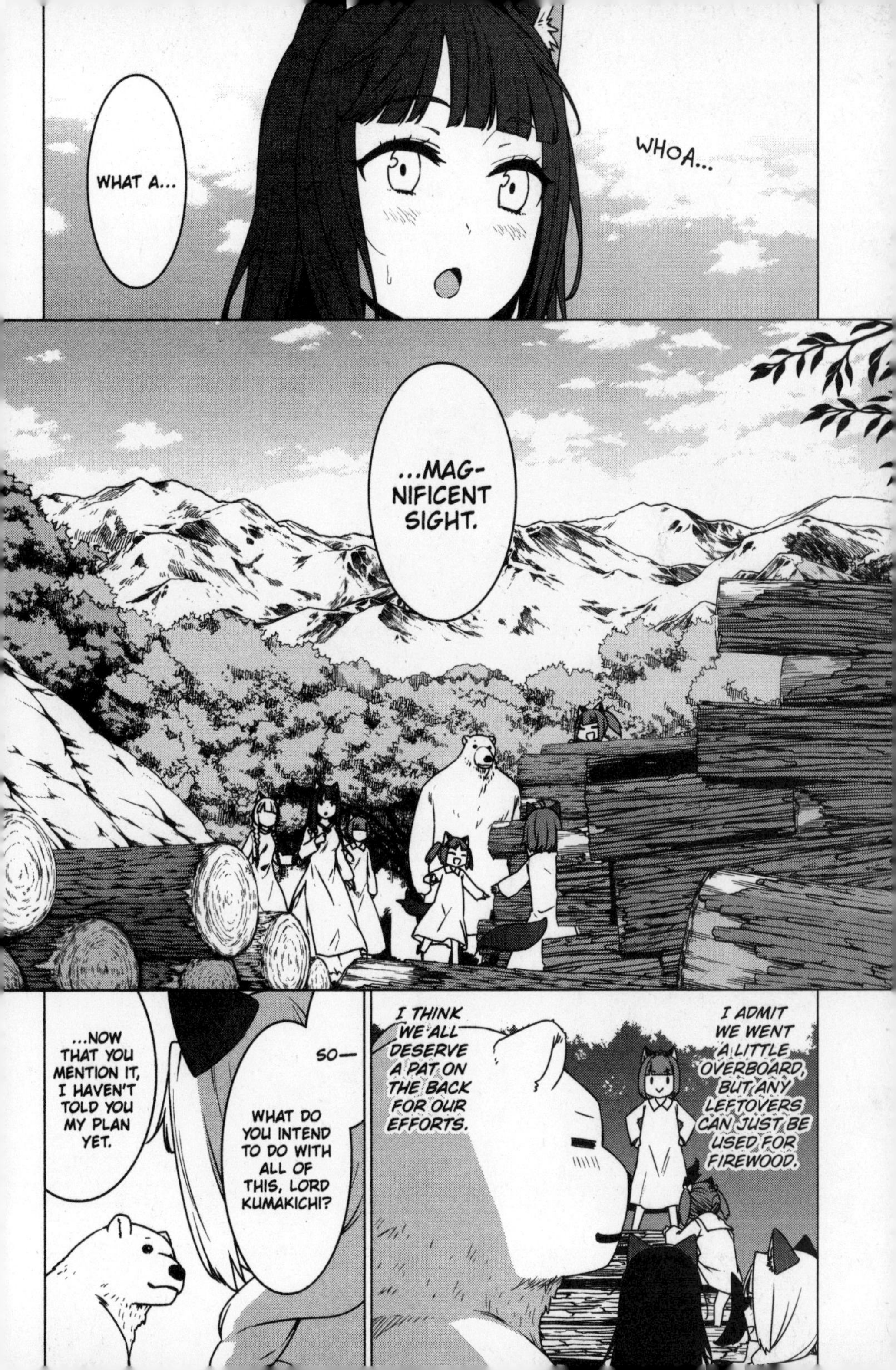
WHOA...
WHAT A...
...MAG-NIFICENT SIGHT.
I ADMIT WE WENT A LITTLE OVERBOARD, BUT ANY LEFTOVERS CAN JUST BE USED FOR FIREWOOD.
I THINK WE ALL DESERVE A PAT ON THE BACK FOR OUR EFFORTS.
SO—
WHAT DO YOU INTEND TO DO WITH ALL OF THIS, LORD KUMAKICHI?
...NOW THAT YOU MENTION IT, I HAVEN'T TOLD YOU MY PLAN YET.

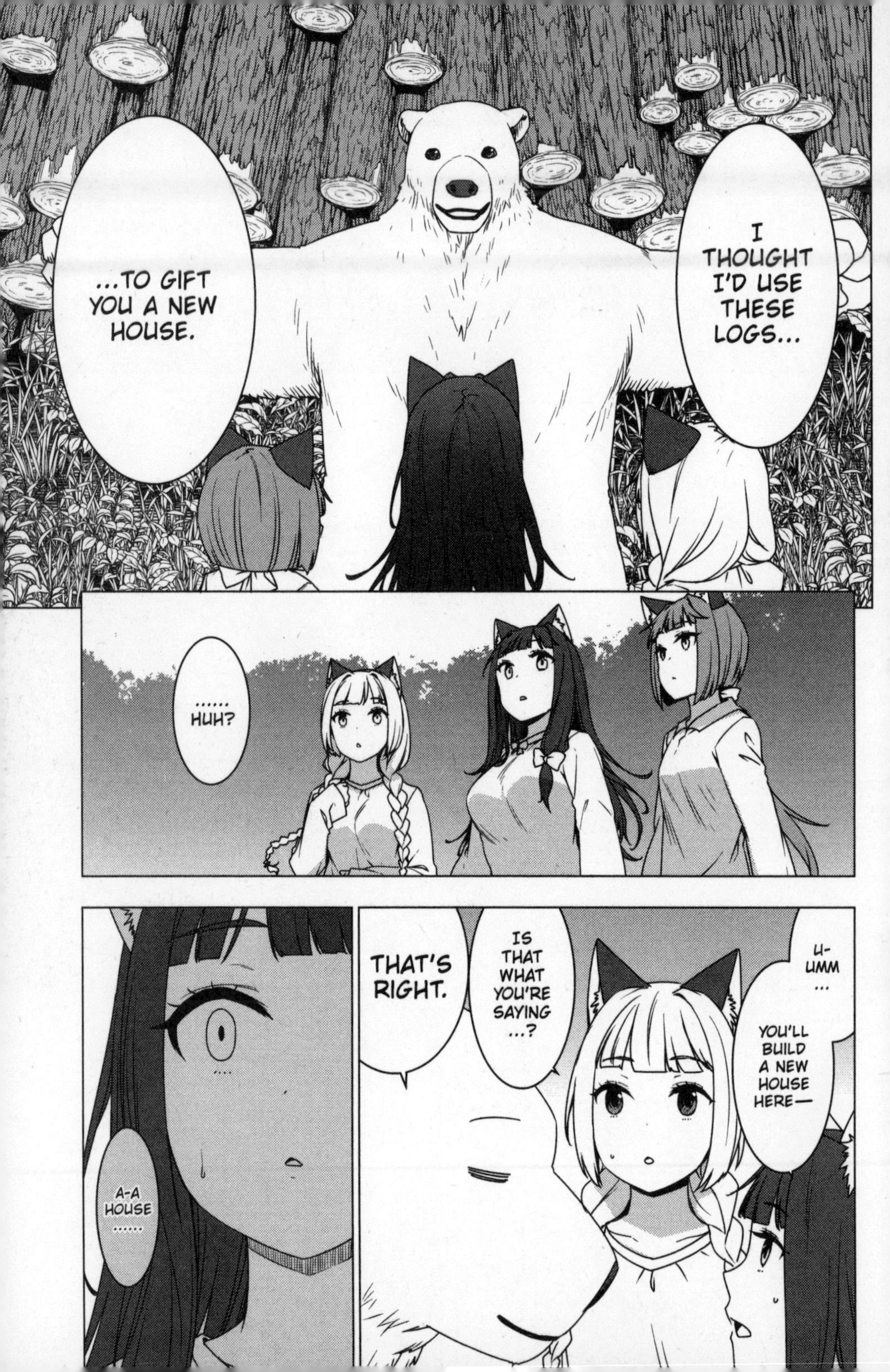
I THOUGHT I'D USE THESE LOGS...
...TO GIFT YOU A NEW HOUSE.
...... HUH?
U-UMM ... YOU'LL BUILD A NEW HOUSE HERE—
IS THAT WHAT YOU'RE SAYING ...?
THAT'S RIGHT.
A-A HOUSE ......

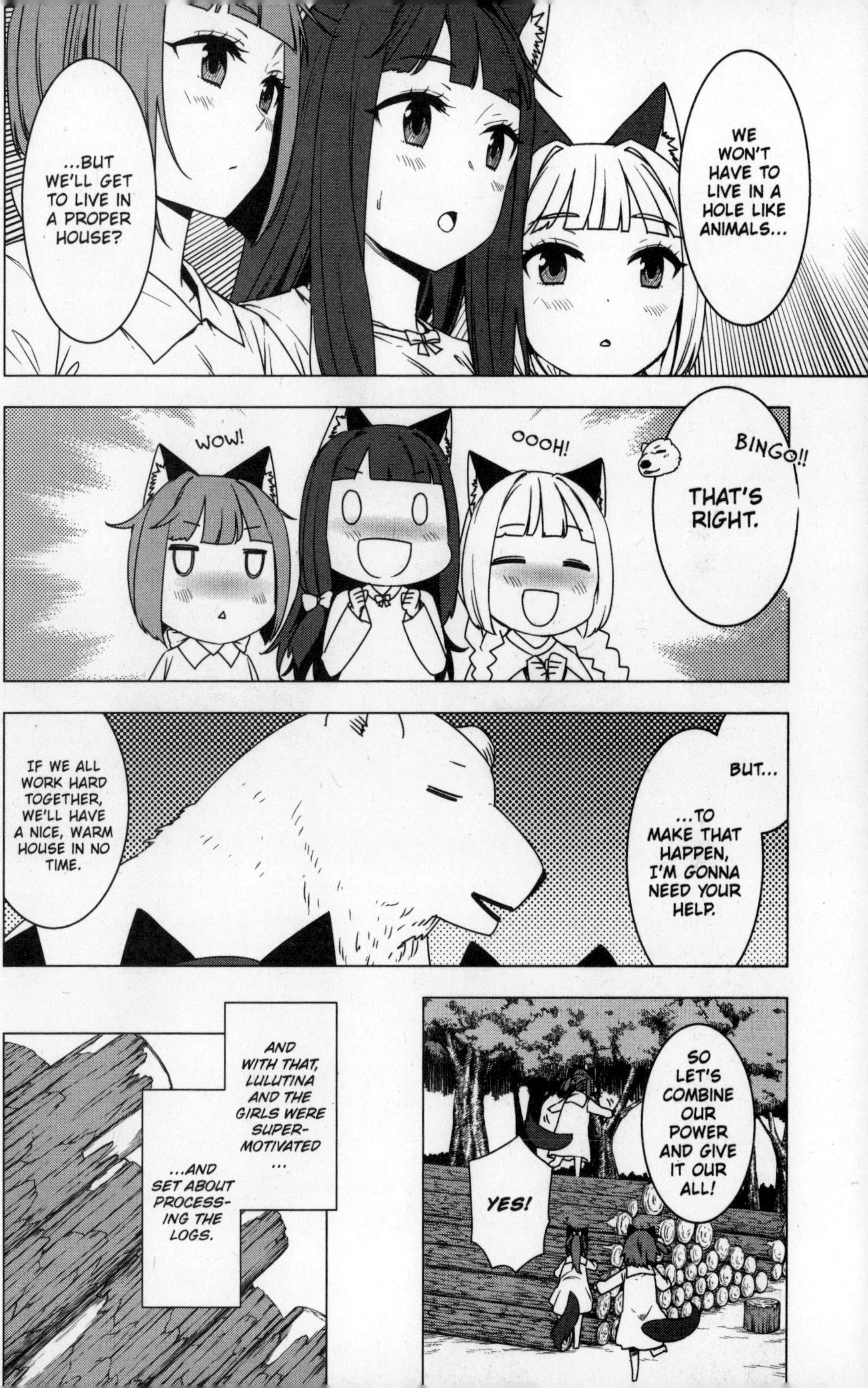
WE WON'T HAVE TO LIVE IN A HOLE LIKE ANIMALS...
...BUT WE'LL GET TO LIVE IN A PROPER HOUSE?
BINGO!!
THAT'S RIGHT.
OOOH!
WOW!
BUT...
...TO MAKE THAT HAPPEN, I'M GONNA NEED YOUR HELP.
IF WE ALL WORK HARD TOGETHER, WE'LL HAVE A NICE, WARM HOUSE IN NO TIME.
SO LET'S COMBINE OUR POWER AND GIVE IT OUR ALL!
YES!
AND WITH THAT, LULUTINA AND THE GIRLS WERE SUPER-MOTIVATED...
...AND SET ABOUT PROCESS-ING THE LOGS.

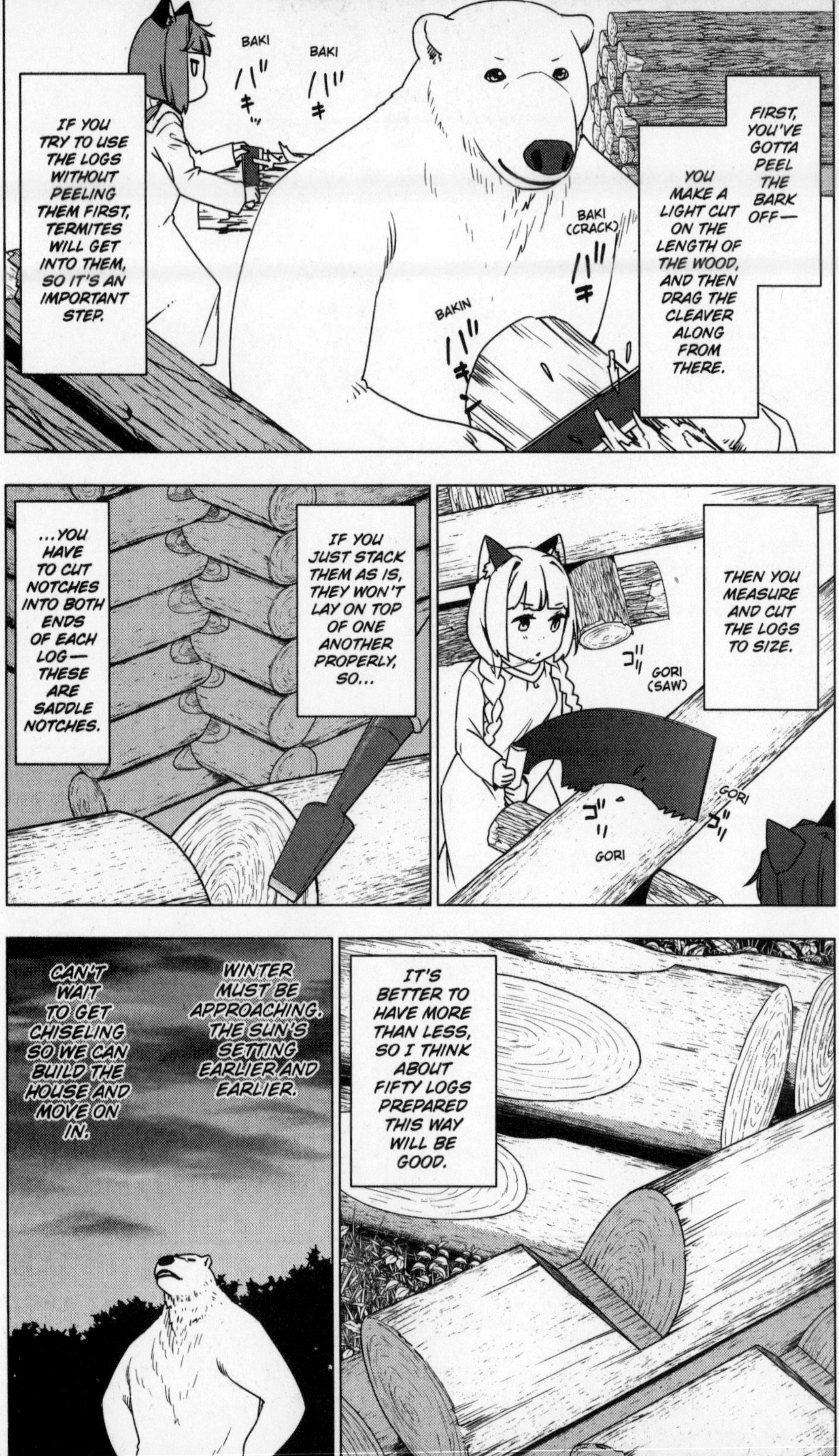

FIRST, YOU'VE GOTTA PEEL THE BARK OFF—
YOU MAKE A LIGHT CUT ON THE LENGTH OF THE WOOD, AND THEN DRAG THE CLEAVER ALONG FROM THERE.
BAKI (CRACK)
BAKIN
BAKI
BAKI
IF YOU TRY TO USE THE LOGS WITHOUT PEELING THEM FIRST, TERMITES WILL GET INTO THEM, SO IT'S AN IMPORTANT STEP.
THEN YOU MEASURE AND CUT THE LOGS TO SIZE.
GORI (SAW)
GORI
GORI
IF YOU JUST STACK THEM AS IS, THEY WON'T LAY ON TOP OF ONE ANOTHER PROPERLY, SO...
...YOU HAVE TO CUT NOTCHES INTO BOTH ENDS OF EACH LOG— THESE ARE SADDLE NOTCHES.
IT'S BETTER TO HAVE MORE THAN LESS, SO I THINK ABOUT FIFTY LOGS PREPARED THIS WAY WILL BE GOOD.
WINTER MUST BE APPROACHING. THE SUN'S SETTING EARLIER AND EARLIER.
CAN'T WAIT TO GET CHISELING SO WE CAN BUILD THE HOUSE AND MOVE ON IN.

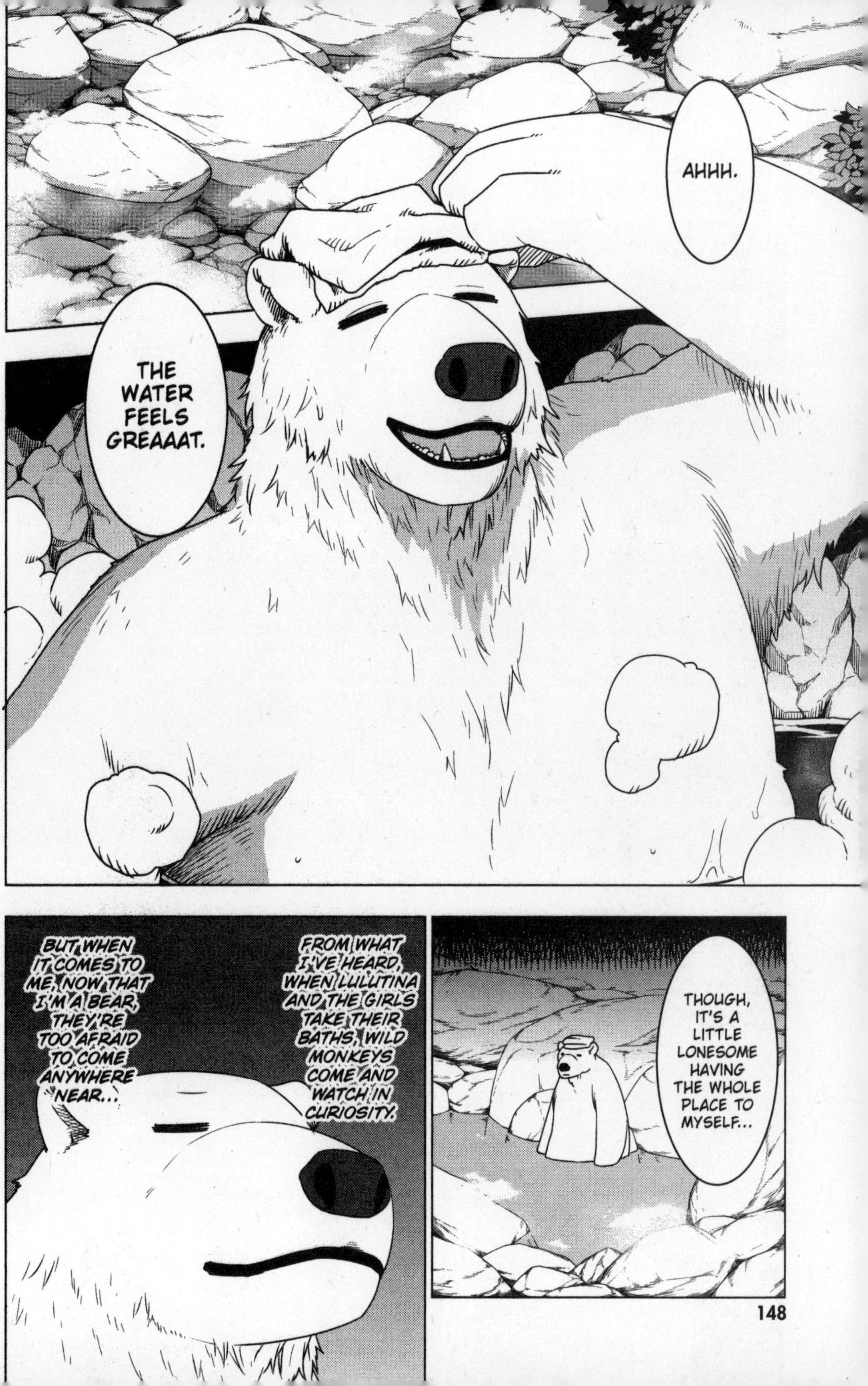
AHHH.
THE WATER FEELS GREAAAT.
THOUGH, IT'S A LITTLE LONESOME HAVING THE WHOLE PLACE TO MYSELF...
FROM WHAT I'VE HEARD, WHEN LULUTINA AND THE GIRLS TAKE THEIR BATHS, WILD MONKEYS COME AND WATCH IN CURIOSITY.
BUT WHEN IT COMES TO ME, NOW THAT I'M A BEAR, THEY'RE TOO AFRAID TO COME ANYWHERE NEAR...

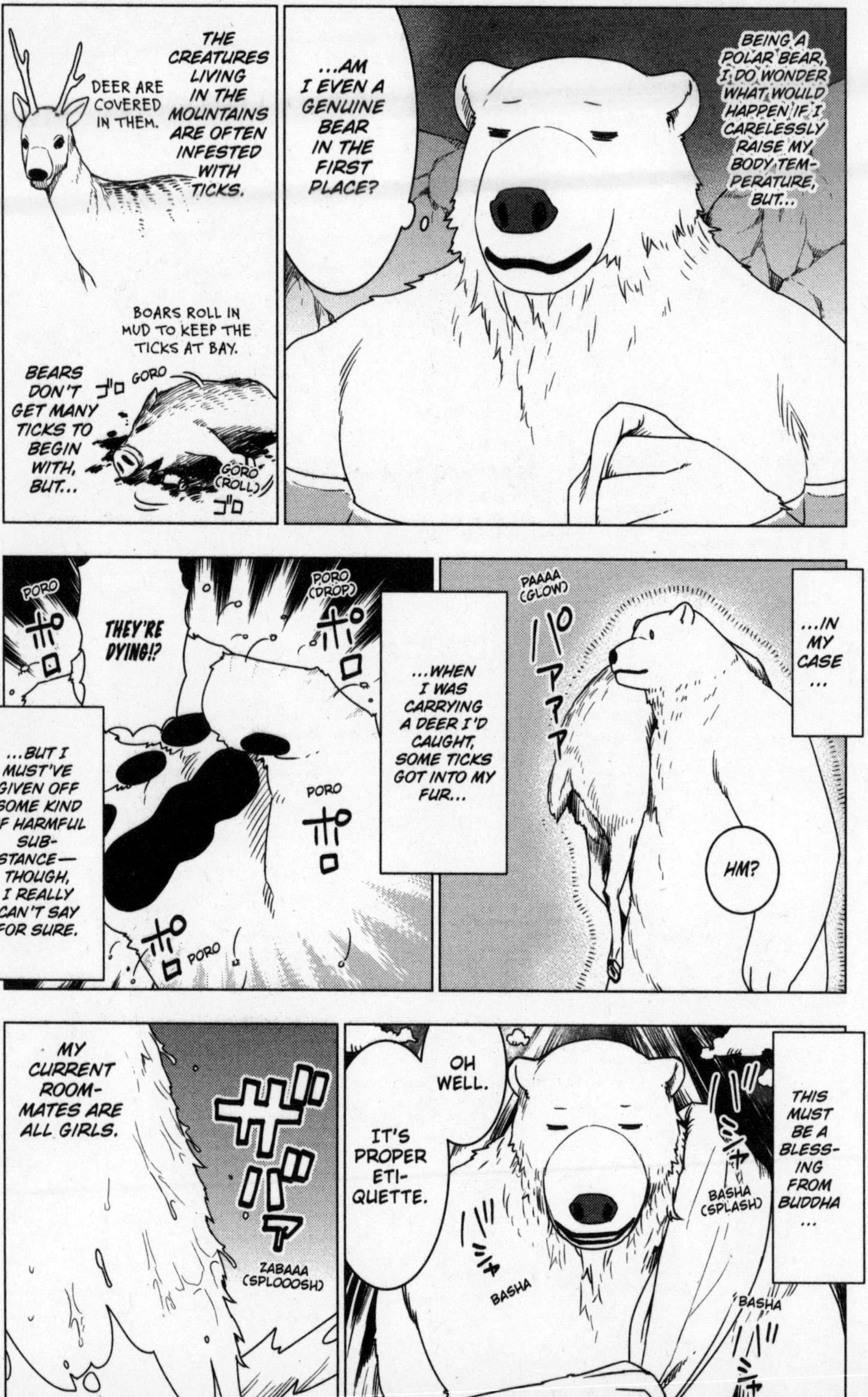
BEING A POLAR BEAR, I DO WONDER WHAT WOULD HAPPEN IF I CARELESSLY RAISE MY BODY TEMPERATURE, BUT...
...AM I EVEN A GENUINE BEAR IN THE FIRST PLACE?
THE CREATURES LIVING IN THE MOUNTAINS ARE OFTEN INFESTED WITH TICKS.
DEER ARE COVERED IN THEM.
BOARS ROLL IN MUD TO KEEP THE TICKS AT BAY.
GORO
BEARS DON'T GET MANY TICKS TO BEGIN WITH, BUT...
GORO (ROLL)
...IN MY CASE...
PAAAA (GLOW)
HM?
...WHEN I WAS CARRYING A DEER I'D CAUGHT, SOME TICKS GOT INTO MY FUR...
PORO (DROP)
THEY'RE DYING!?
PORO
PORO
...BUT I MUST'VE GIVEN OFF SOME KIND OF HARMFUL SUB-STANCE—THOUGH, I REALLY CAN'T SAY FOR SURE.
PORO
THIS MUST BE A BLESS-ING FROM BUDDHA...
BASHA (SPLASH)
OH WELL.
IT'S PROPER ETI-QUETTE.
BASHA
BASHA
MY CURRENT ROOM-MATES ARE ALL GIRLS.
ZABAAA (SPLOOOSH)

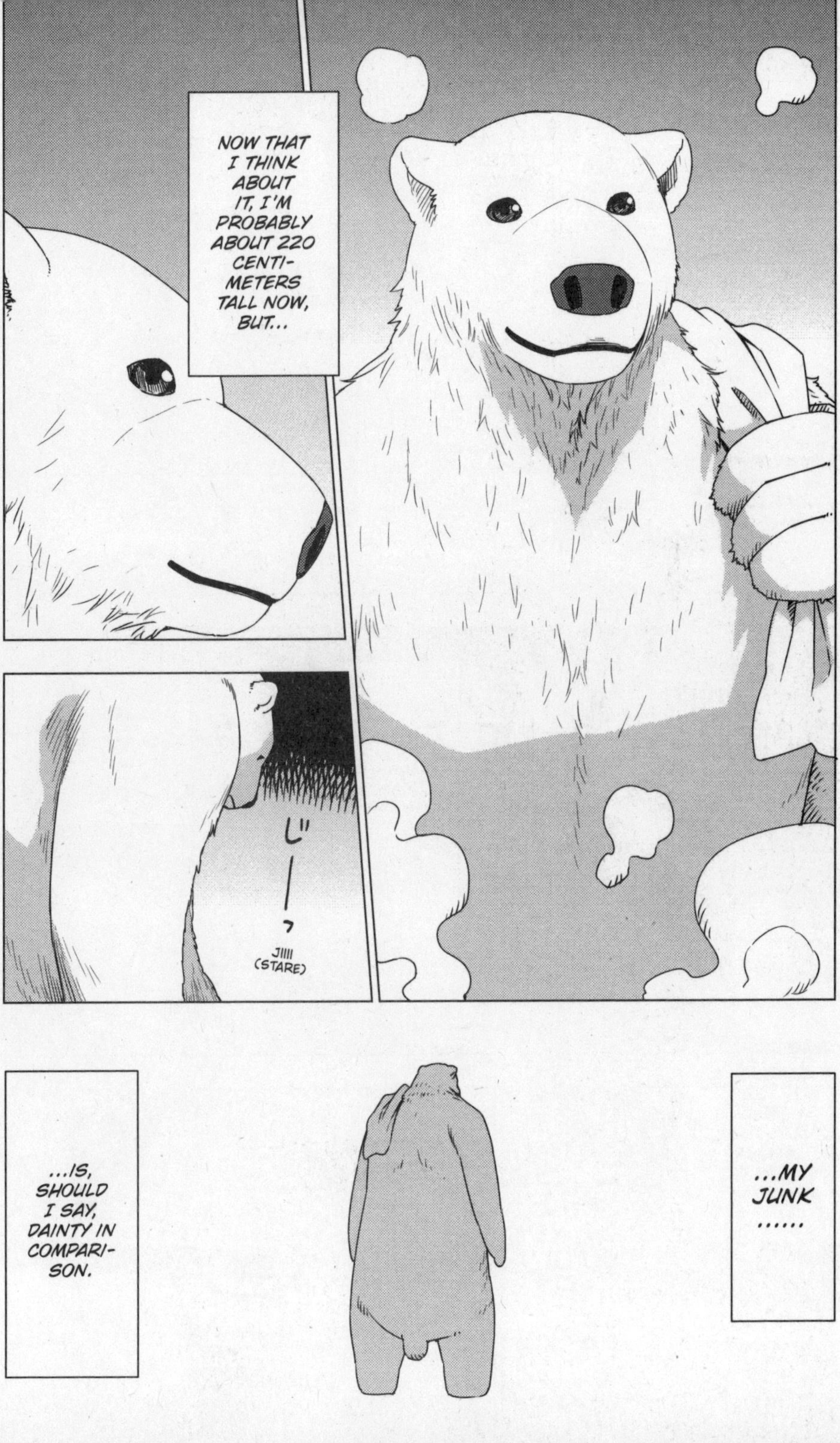
NOW THAT I THINK ABOUT IT, I'M PROBABLY ABOUT 220 CENTIMETERS TALL NOW, BUT...
じーっ
JIIII (STARE)
...MY JUNK......
...IS, SHOULD I SAY, DAINTY IN COMPARISON.

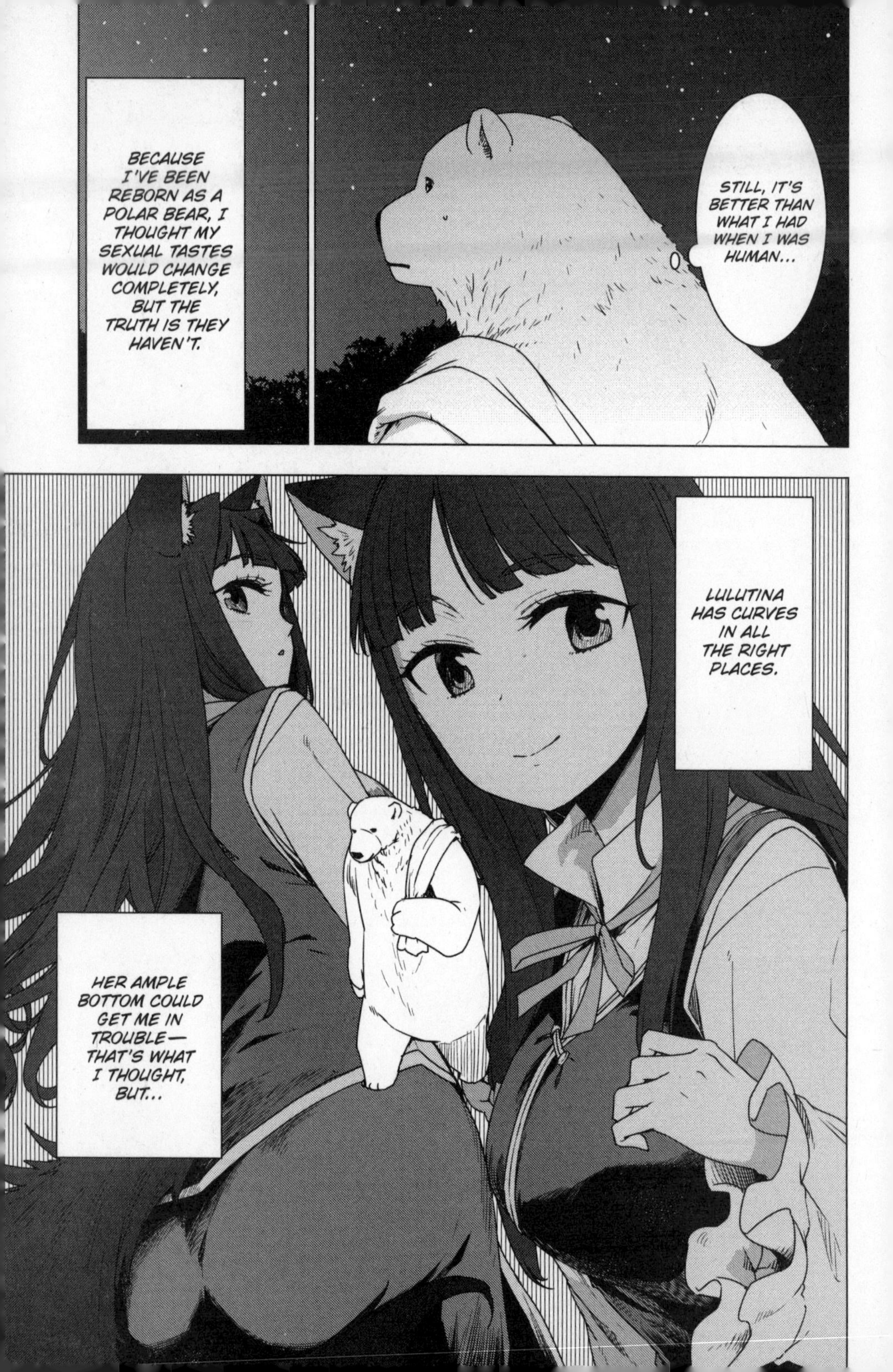
STILL, IT'S BETTER THAN WHAT I HAD WHEN I WAS HUMAN...
BECAUSE I'VE BEEN REBORN AS A POLAR BEAR, I THOUGHT MY SEXUAL TASTES WOULD CHANGE COMPLETELY, BUT THE TRUTH IS THEY HAVEN'T.
LULUTINA HAS CURVES IN ALL THE RIGHT PLACES.
HER AMPLE BOTTOM COULD GET ME IN TROUBLE—THAT'S WHAT I THOUGHT, BUT...

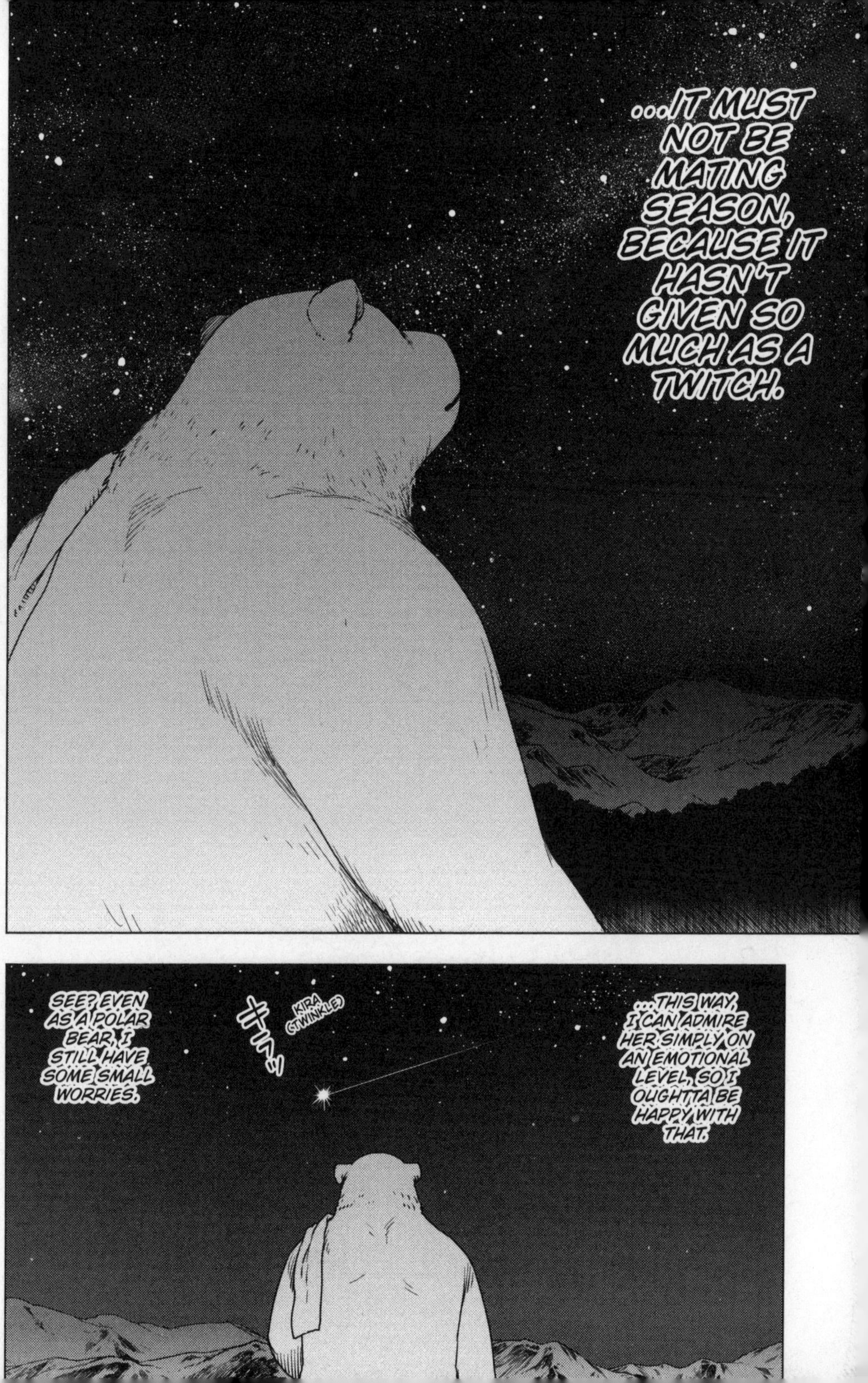
...IT MUST NOT BE MATING SEASON, BECAUSE IT HASN'T GIVEN SO MUCH AS A TWITCH.
...THIS WAY, I CAN ADMIRE HER SIMPLY ON AN EMOTIONAL LEVEL, SO I OUGHTTA BE HAPPY WITH THAT.
KIRA (TWINKLE)
SEE? EVEN AS A POLAR BEAR, I STILL HAVE SOME SMALL WORRIES.

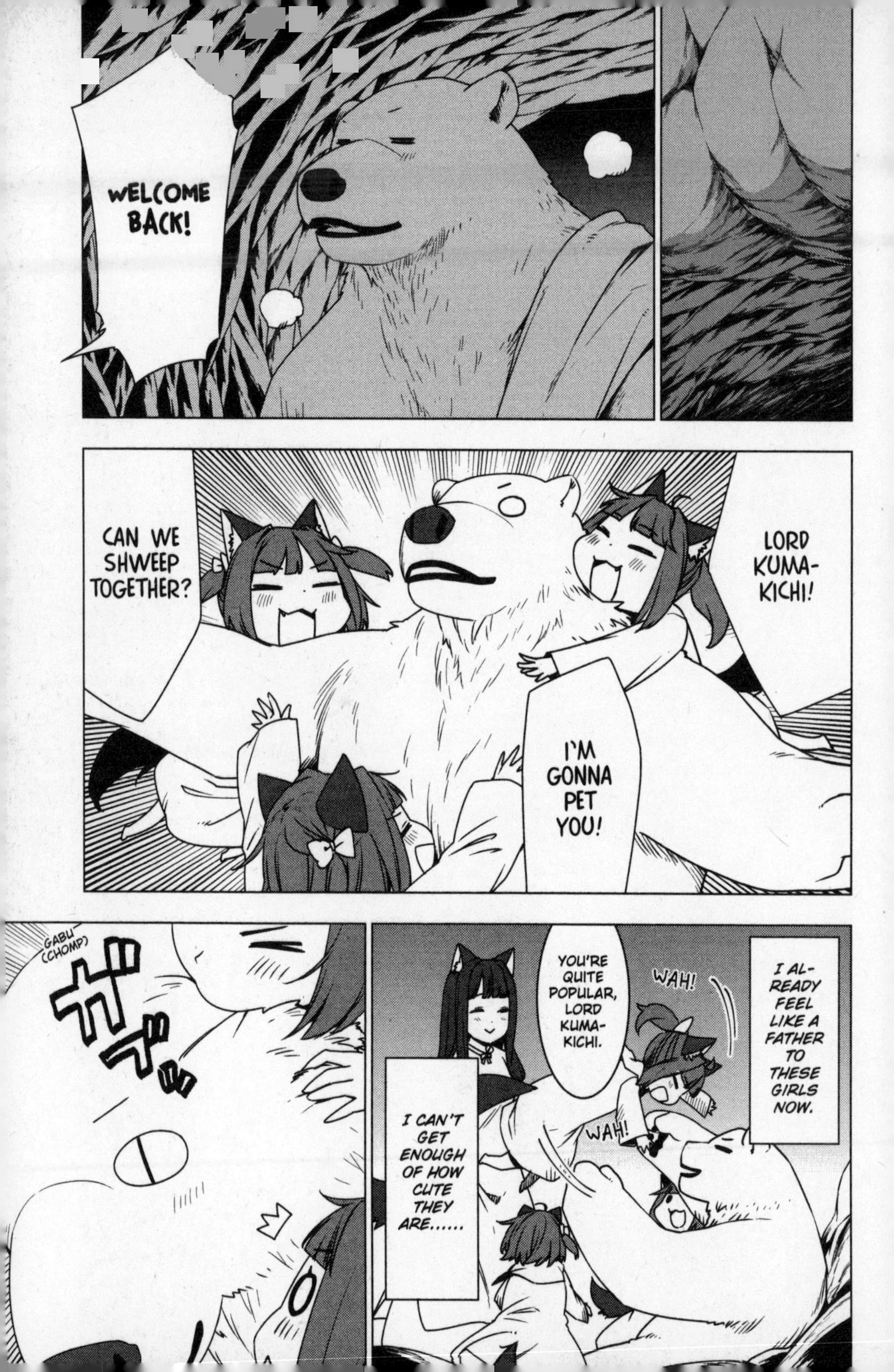
WELCOME BACK!
LORD KUMA-KICHI!
CAN WE SHWEEP TOGETHER?
I'M GONNA PET YOU!
I AL-READY FEEL LIKE A FATHER TO THESE GIRLS NOW.
YOU'RE QUITE POPULAR, LORD KUMA-KICHI.
WAH!
WAH!
I CAN'T GET ENOUGH OF HOW CUTE THEY ARE......
GABU (CHOMP)
ガブッ

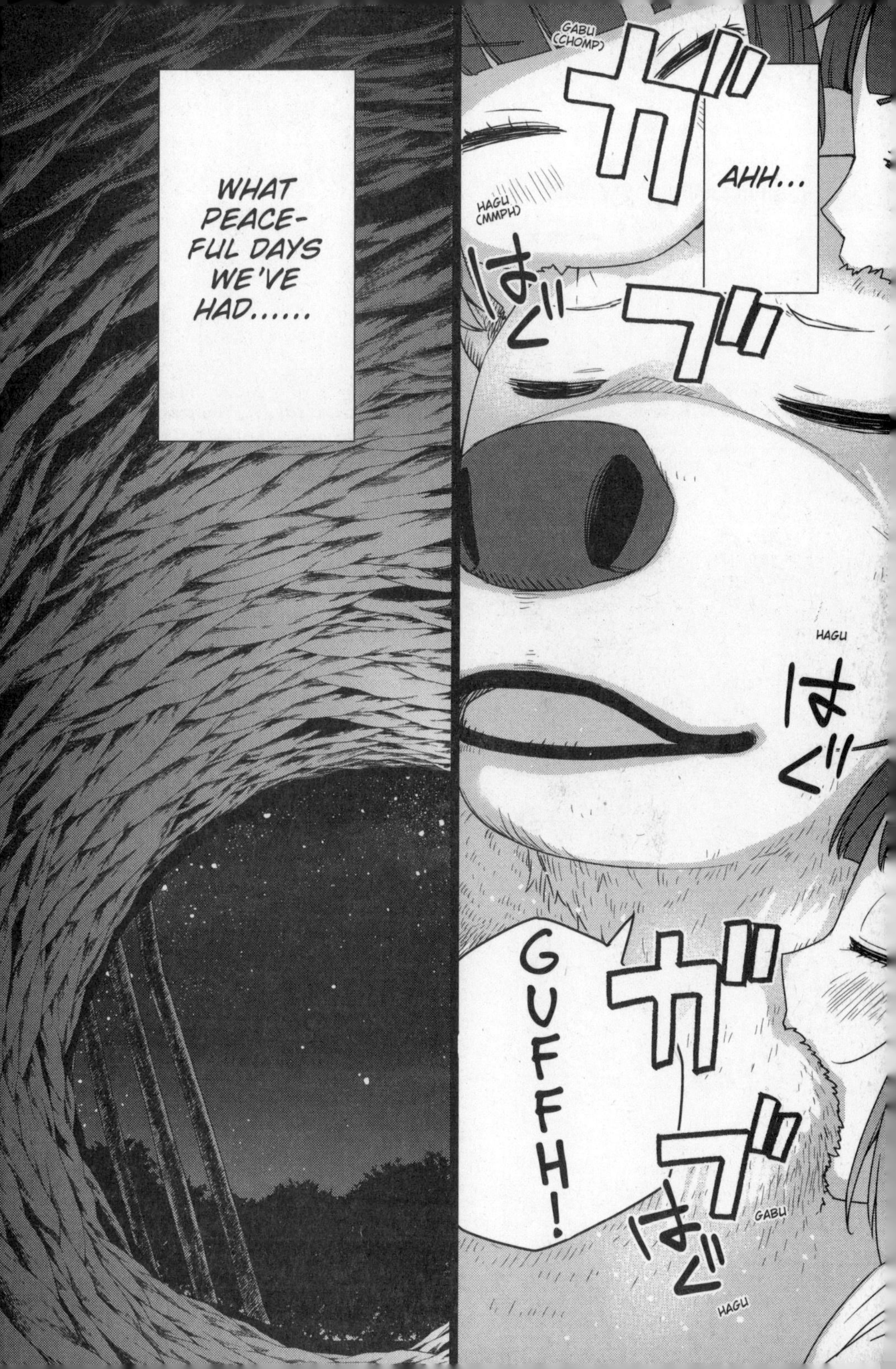
GABU (CHOMP)
ガブ
AHH...
HAGU (MMPH)
はぐ
HAGU
はぐ
ガブ
GUFFH!
GABU
はぐ
HAGU
WHAT PEACE-FUL DAYS WE'VE HAD......

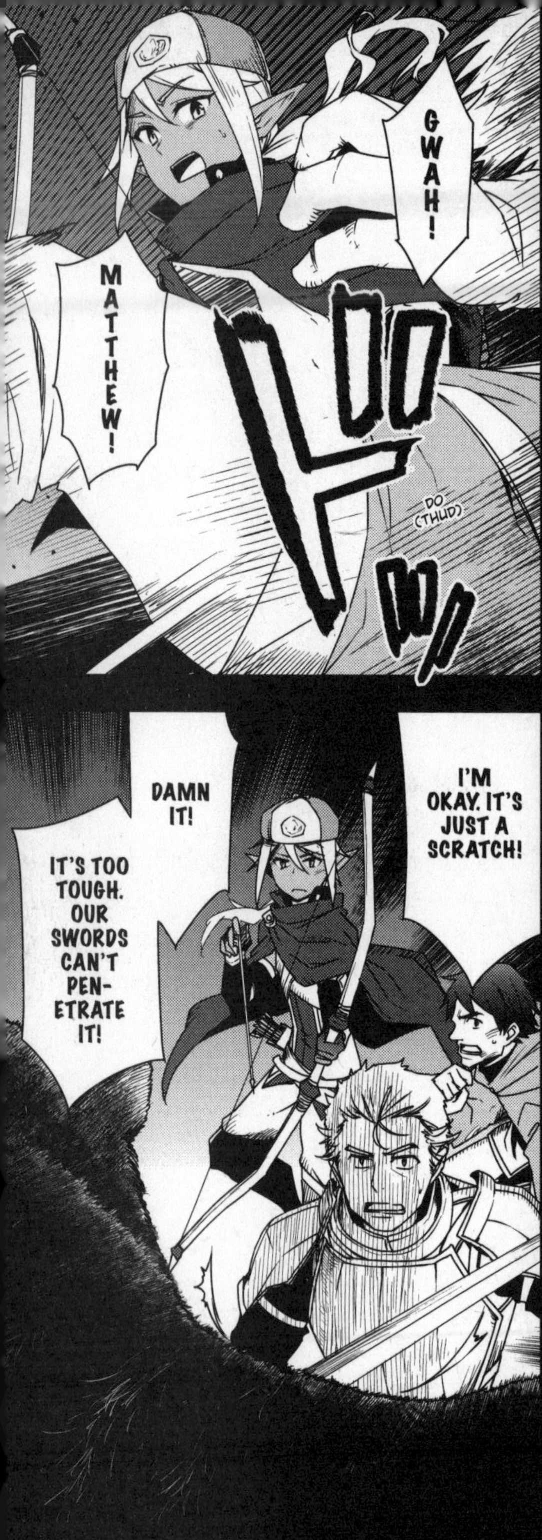
GWAH!
MATTHEW!
DO (THUD)
I'M OKAY. IT'S JUST A SCRATCH!
DAMN IT!
IT'S TOO TOUGH. OUR SWORDS CAN'T PEN-ETRATE IT!

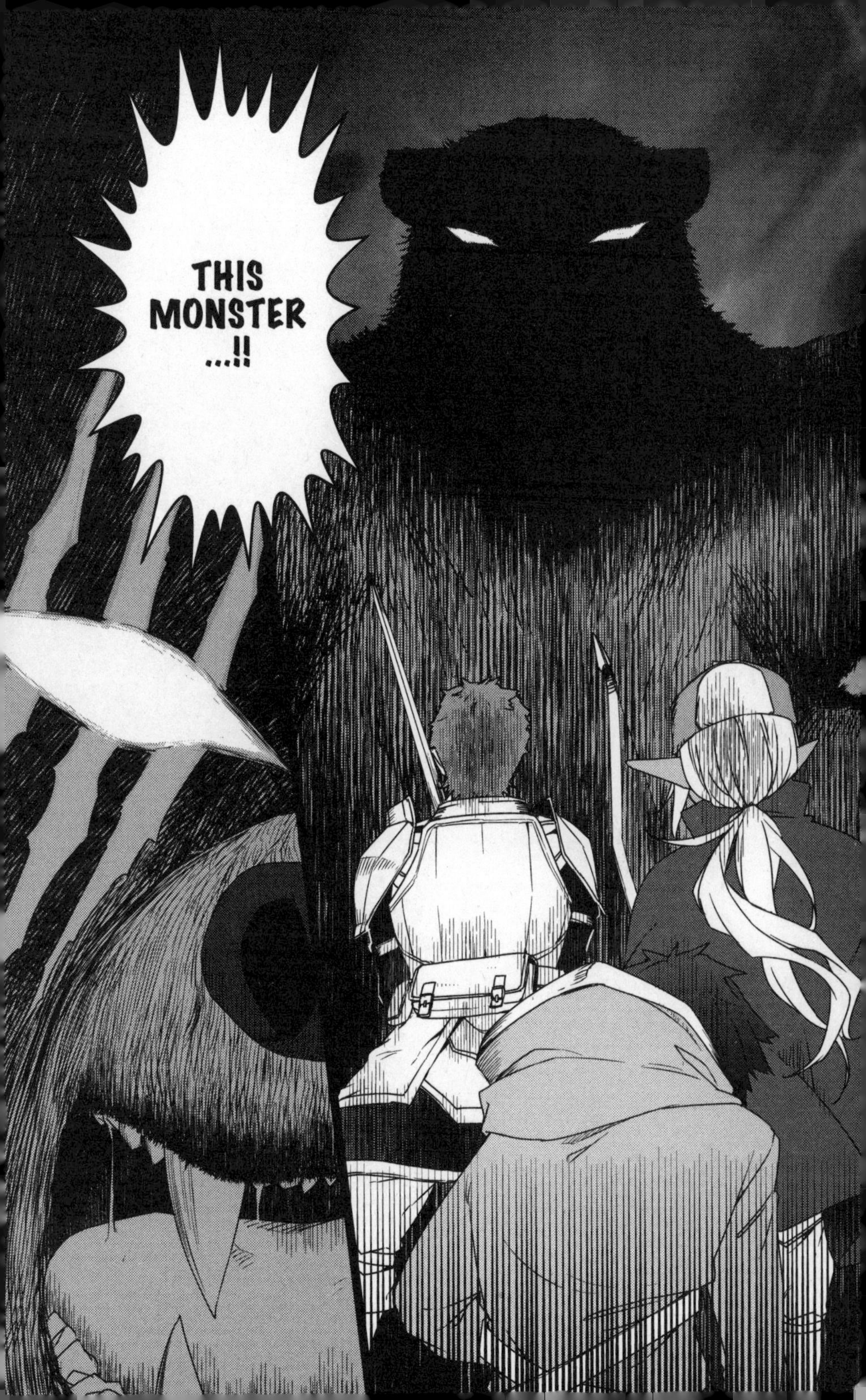
THIS MONSTER ...!!

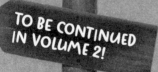
TO BE CONTINUED
IN VOLUME 2!

Reborn as a Polar Bear

The Legend of How I Became a Forest Guardian

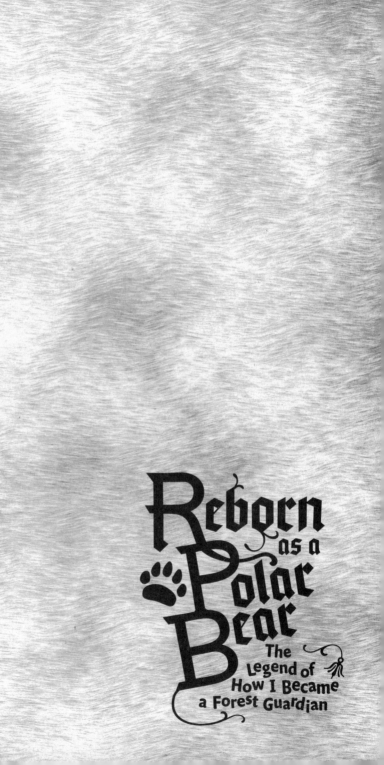

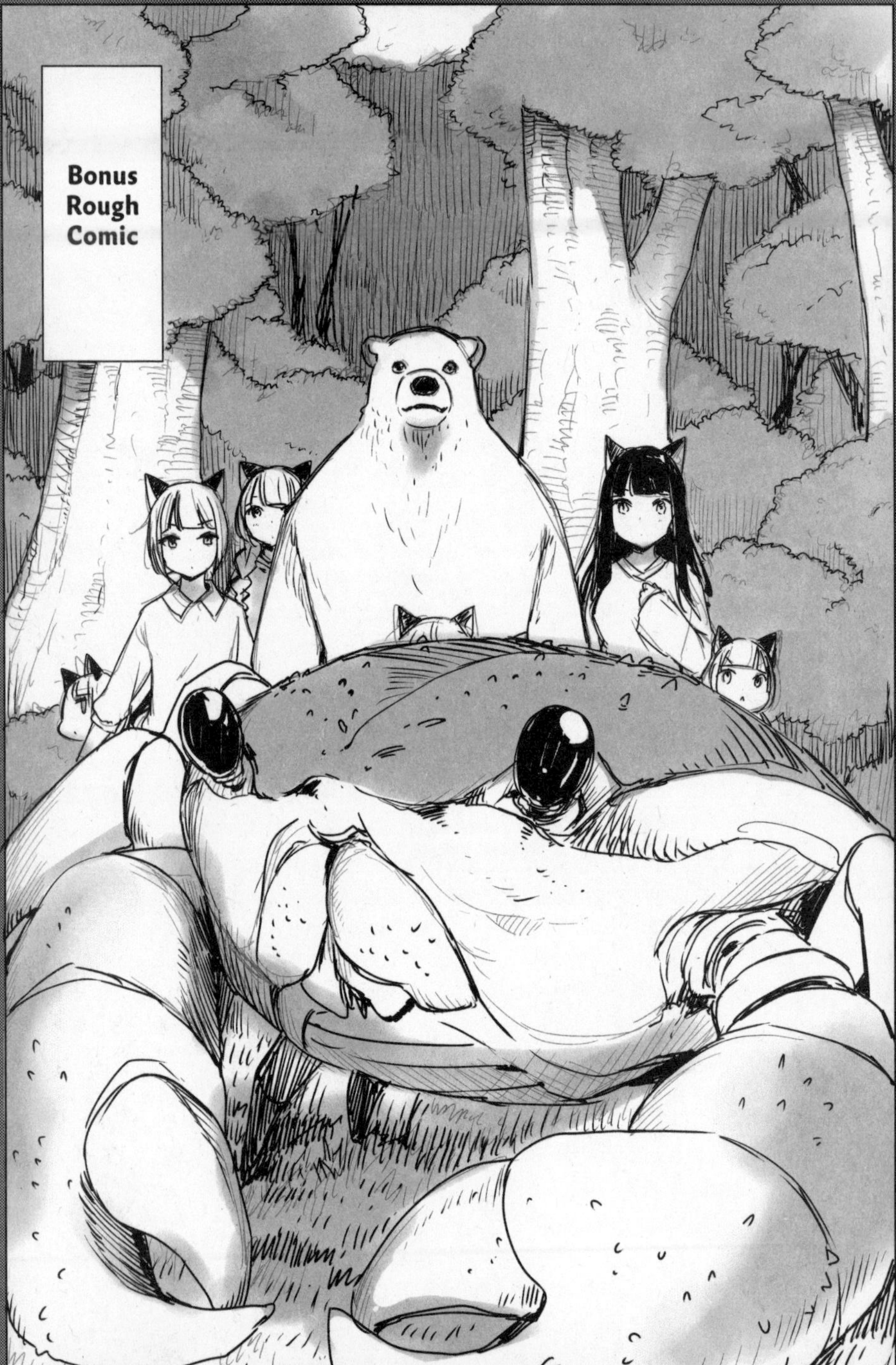
Bonus Rough Comic

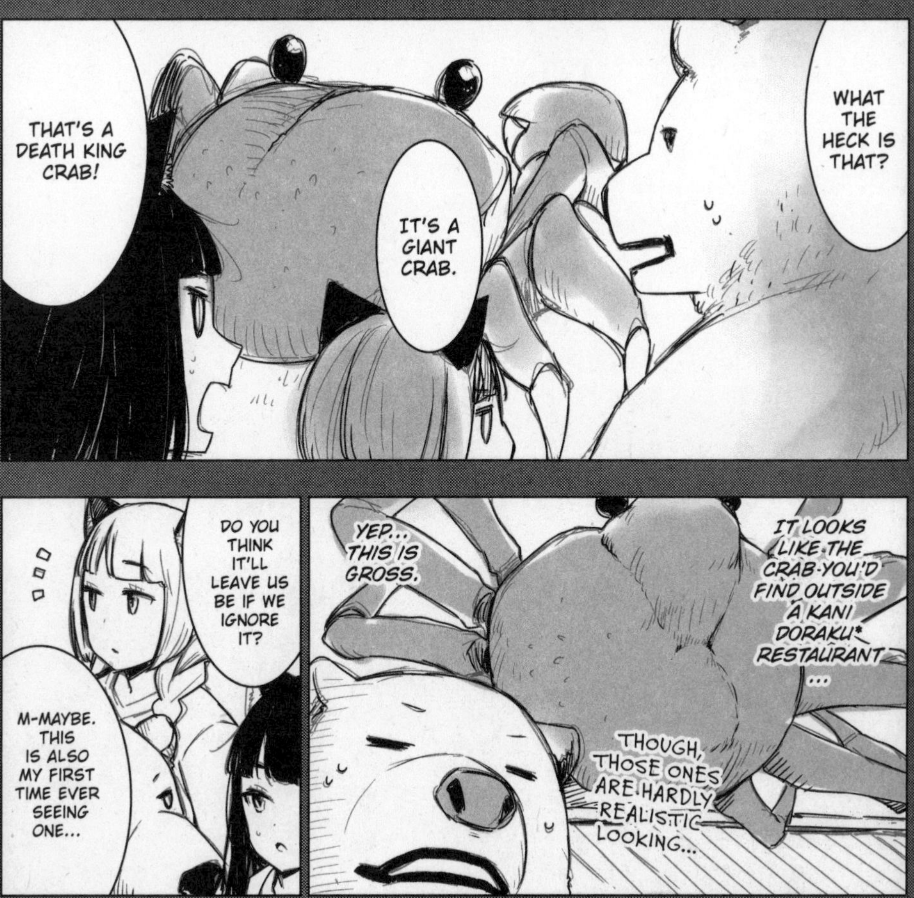
WHAT THE HECK IS THAT?
IT'S A GIANT CRAB.
THAT'S A DEATH KING CRAB!
IT LOOKS LIKE THE CRAB YOU'D FIND OUTSIDE A KANI DORAKU* RESTAURANT...
YEP... THIS IS GROSS.
THOUGH, THOSE ONES ARE HARDLY REALISTIC LOOKING...
DO YOU THINK IT'LL LEAVE US BE IF WE IGNORE IT?
M-MAYBE. THIS IS ALSO MY FIRST TIME EVER SEEING ONE...

*KANI DORAKU: A CHAIN OF SEAFOOD RESTAURANTS IN JAPAN KNOWN FOR THEIR LARGE MECHANICAL CRABS ABOVE THE MAIN ENTRANCES.

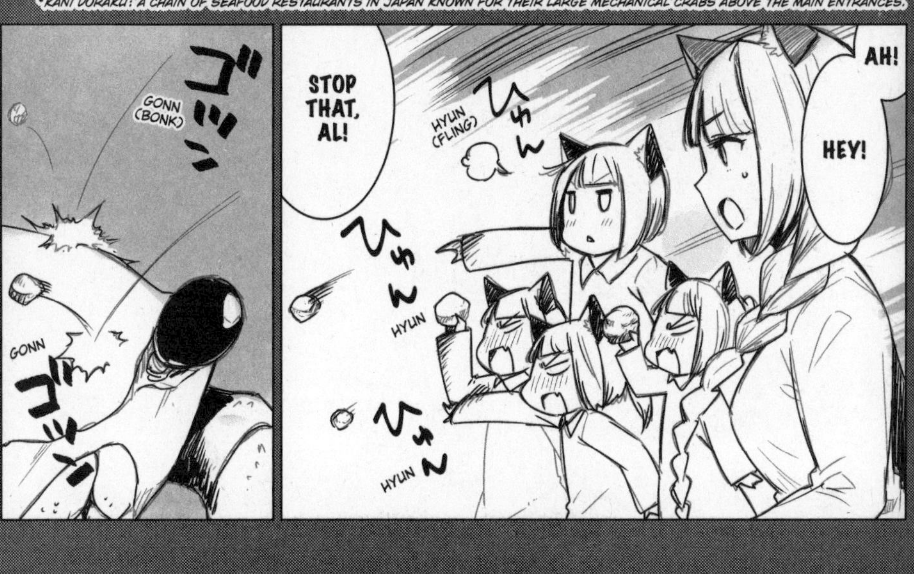
AH!
HEY!
STOP THAT, AL!
ひゅん
HYUN (FLING)
ひゅん
HYUN
ひゅん
HYUN
ゴッ
GONN (BONK)
ゴッ
GONN

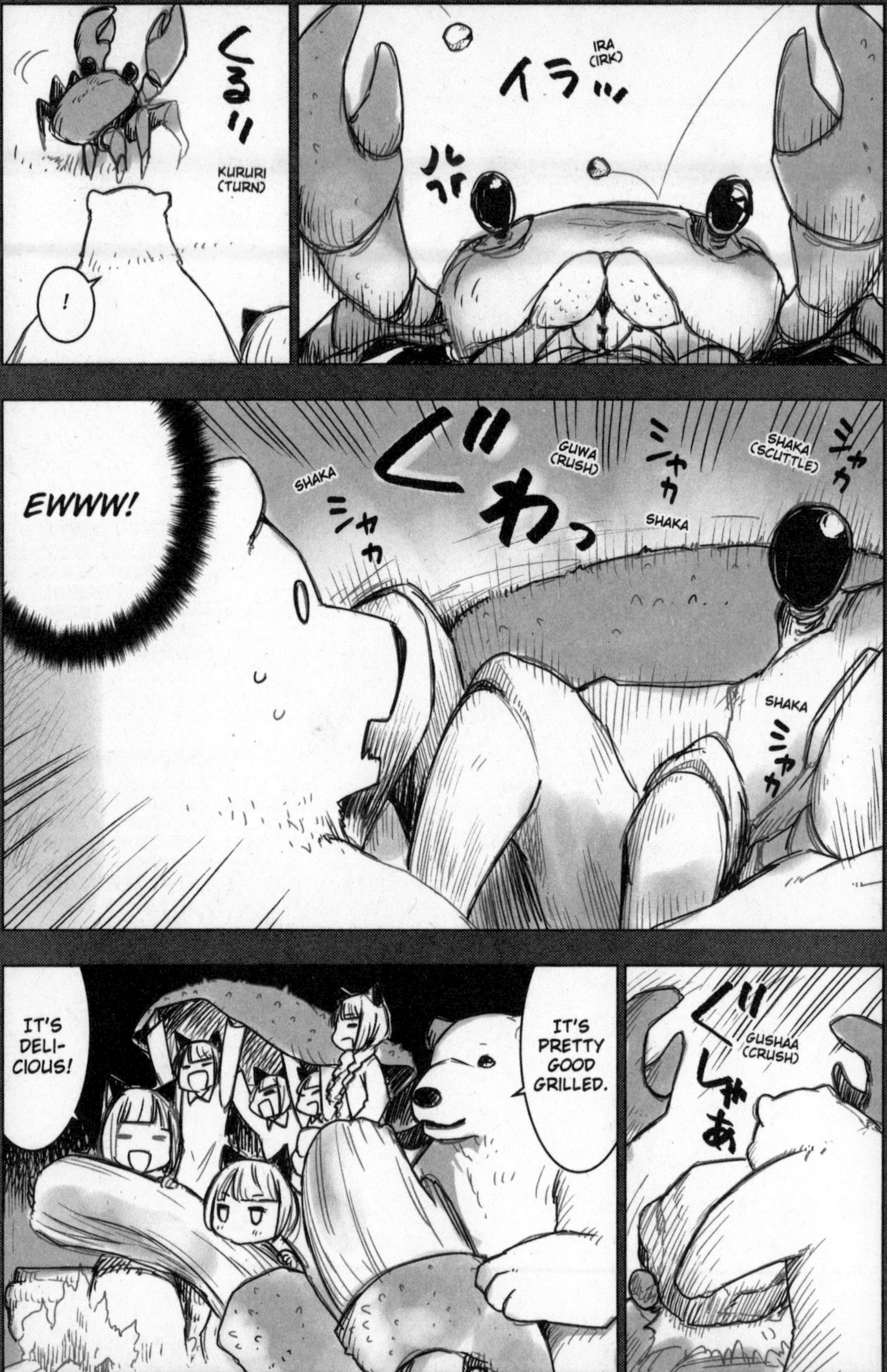

イラッ
IRA (IRK)
くるッ
KURURI (TURN)
!
シャカ
SHAKA (SCUTTLE)
ぐわっ
GUWA (RUSH)
シャカ
SHAKA
シャカ
SHAKA
EWWW!
シャカ
SHAKA
ぐしゃあ
GUSHAA (CRUSH)
IT'S PRETTY GOOD GRILLED.
IT'S DELI-CIOUS!

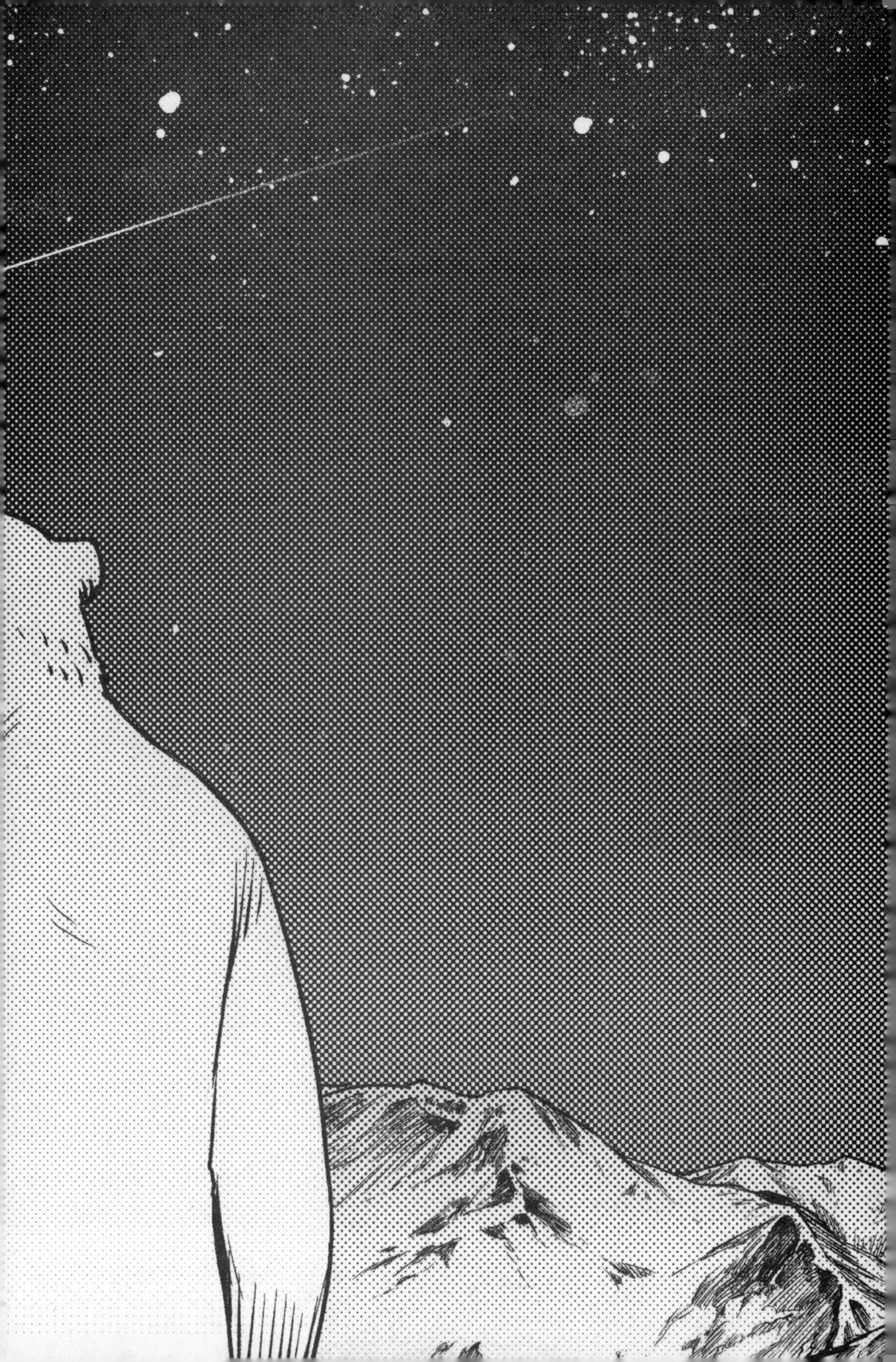

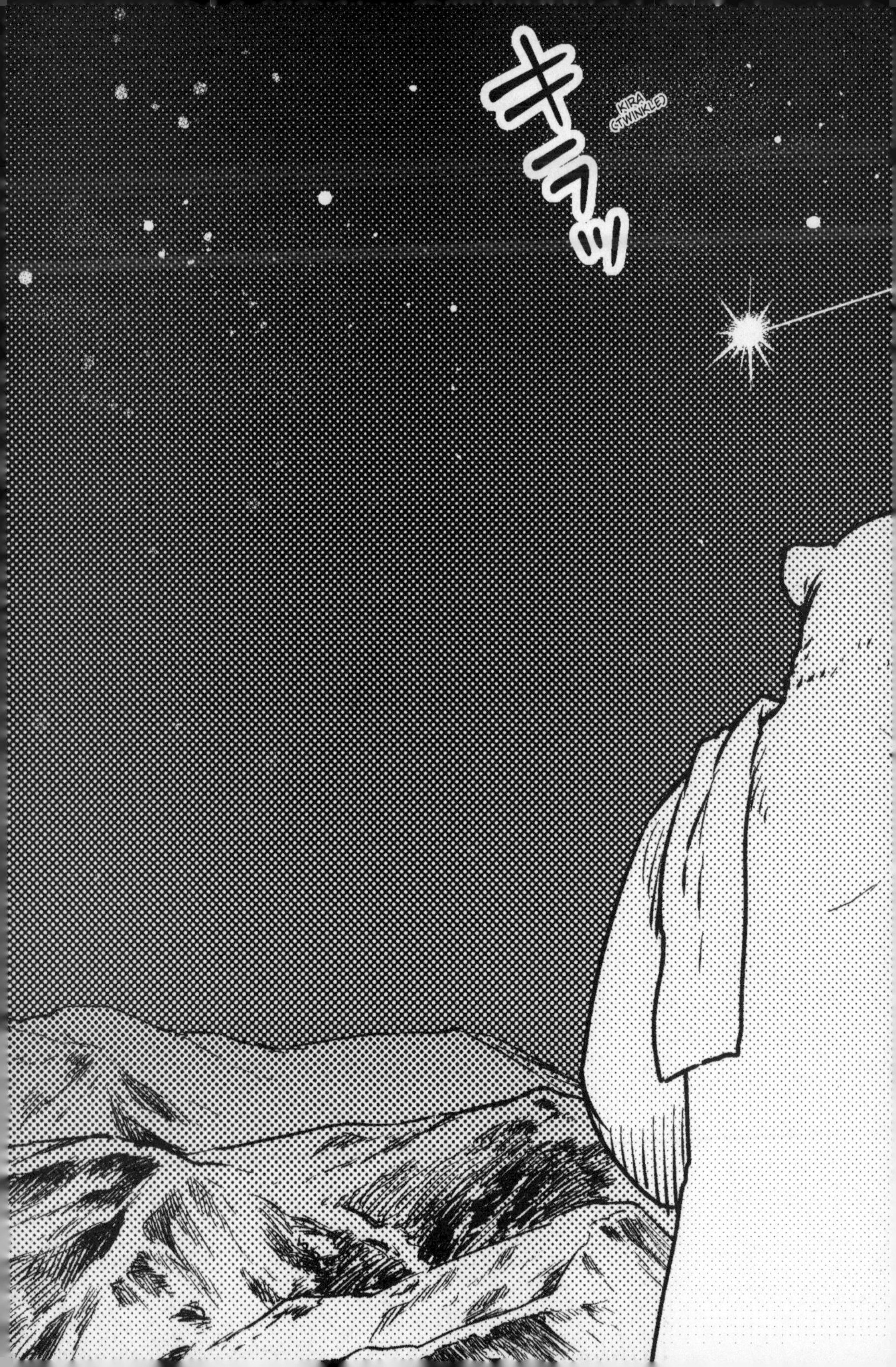
キラッ
KIRA
(TWINKLE)

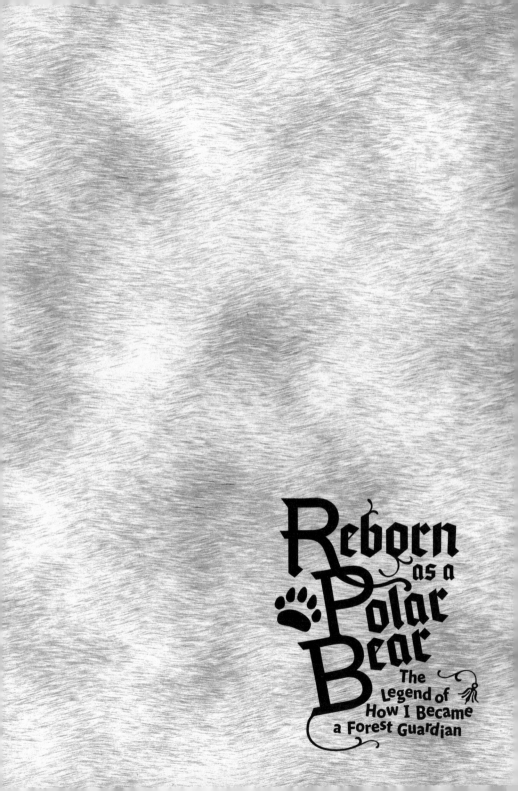

Reborn
as a
Polar
Bear

The
Legend of
How I Became
a Forest Guardian

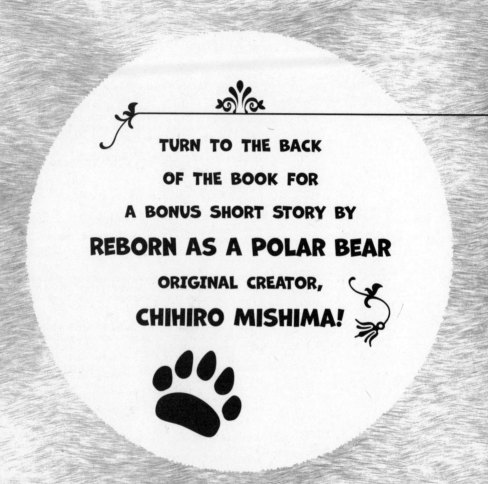

TURN TO THE BACK
OF THE BOOK FOR
A BONUS SHORT STORY BY

REBORN AS A POLAR BEAR

ORIGINAL CREATOR,

CHIHIRO MISHIMA!

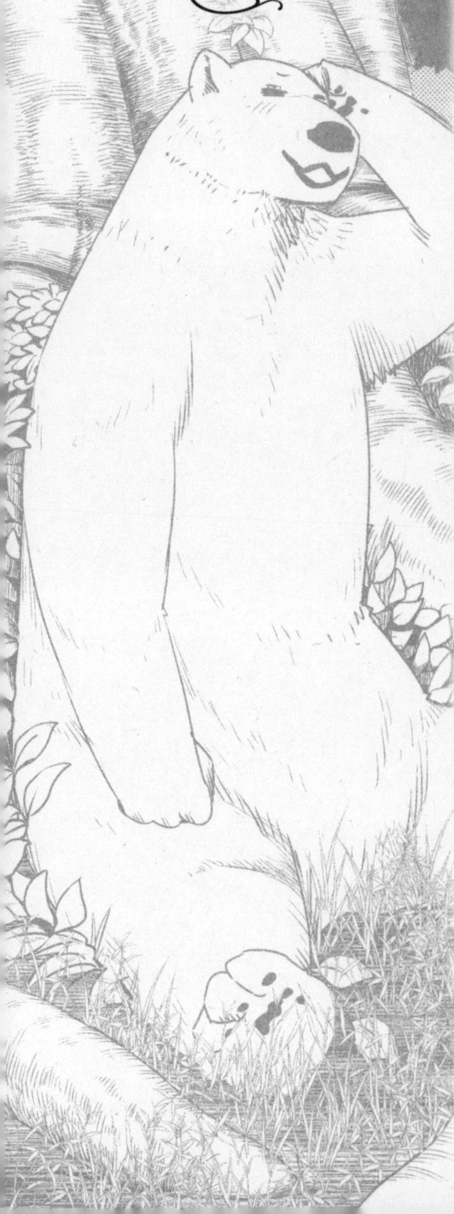

Reborn as a Polar Bear

1

The Legend of How I Became a Forest Guardian

ART: **Houki Kusano**

ORIGINAL STORY: **Chihiro Mishima**

CHARACTER DESIGN: **Kururi**

Translation: Christine Dashiell
Lettering: Thalia Sutton

SHIROKUMA TENSEI MORI NO SHUGOSHIN NI NATTAZO DENSETSU Volume 1
© Houki Kusano 2018
© Chihiro Mishima 2018
First published in Japan in 2018 by KADOKAWA CORPORATION, Tokyo.
English translation rights arranged with KADOKAWA CORPORATION,
Tokyo through TUTTLE-MORI AGENCY, INC., Tokyo.

English translation © 2019 by Yen Press, LLC

Yen Press
150 West 30th Street, 19th Floor
New York, NY 10001

Visit us at yenpress.com
facebook.com/yenpress
twitter.com/yenpress
yenpress.tumblr.com
instagram.com/yenpress

First Yen Press Edition: August 2019

Yen Press is an imprint of Yen Press, LLC.
The Yen Press name and logo are trademarks of Yen Press, LLC.

The publisher is not responsible for websites (or their content) that are not owned by the publisher.

Library of Congress Control Number: 2019942575
ISBNs: 978-1-9753-0552-9 (paperback)
       978-1-9753-5879-2 (ebook)

10 9 8 7 6 5 4 3 2 1

WOR

Printed in the United States of America

Reborn as a Polar Bear

The Legend of How I Became a Forest Guardian

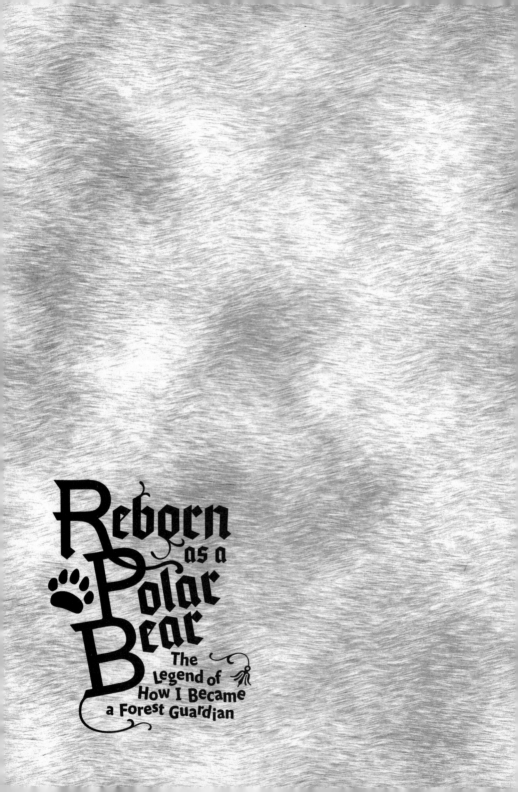

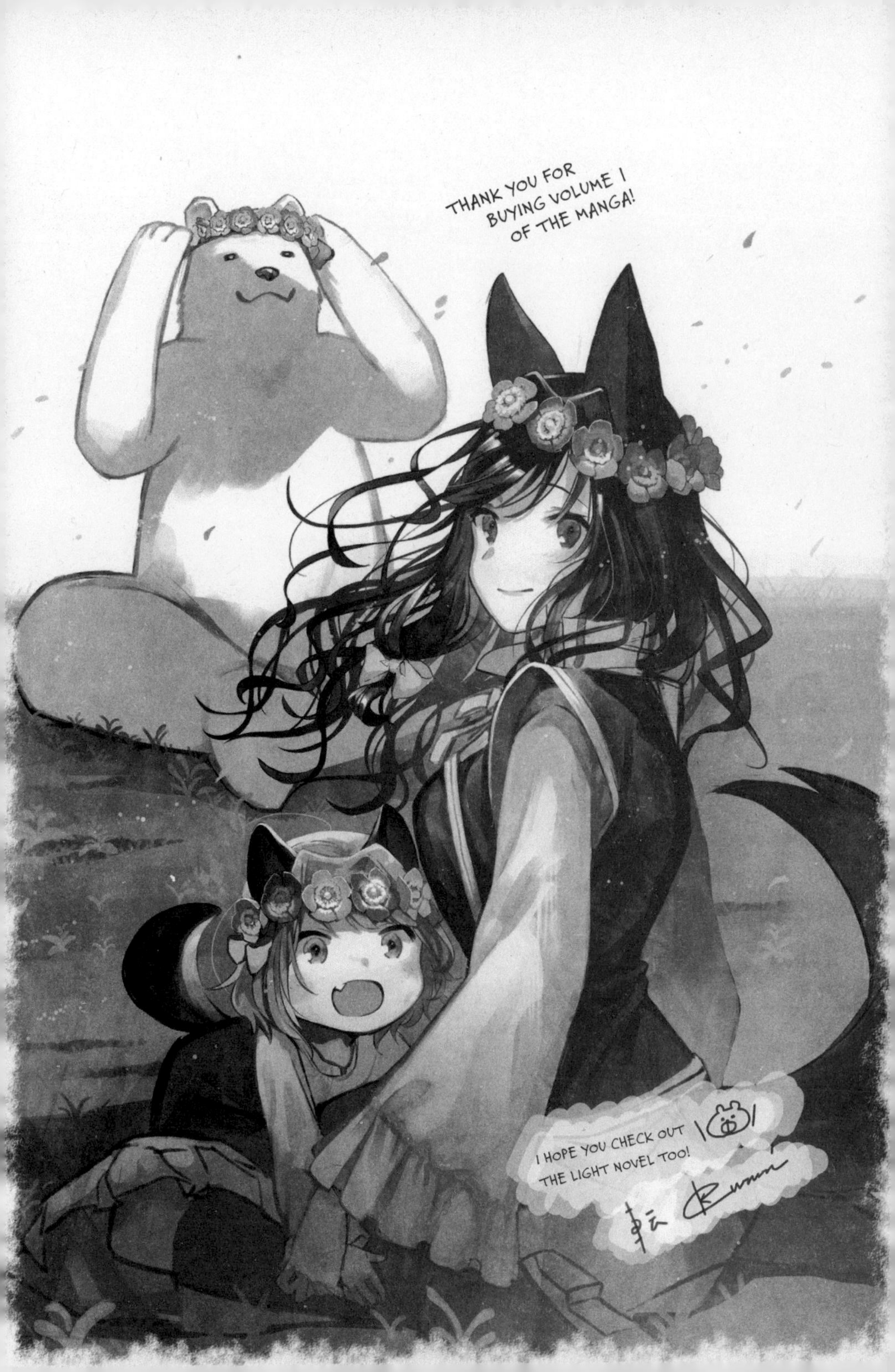
THANK YOU FOR
BUYING VOLUME 1
OF THE MANGA!
I HOPE YOU CHECK OUT
THE LIGHT NOVEL TOO!

Reborn as a Polar Bear

The Legend of How I Became a Forest Guardian

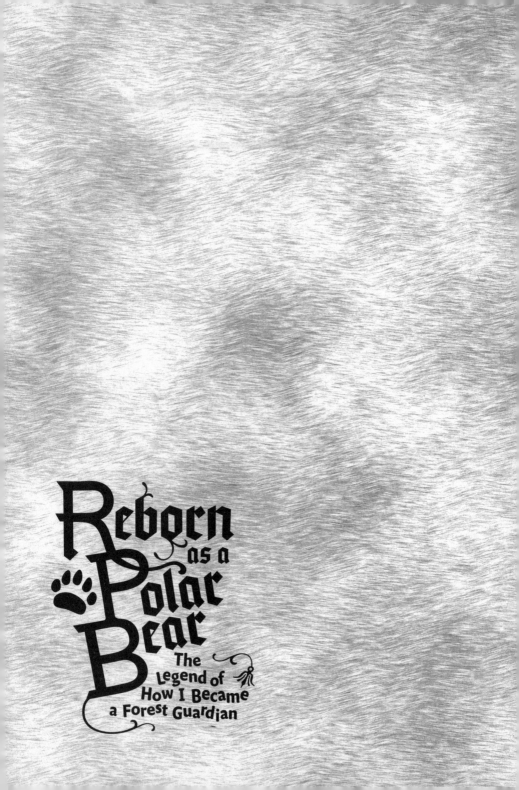

But it was so unnatural, Kumakichi only became even more frightened.

"Aww! Come on, Al, don't sneak a bite before everyone gets to eat!"

"Needs more salt."

While Lulutina was still trying to maintain her fake smile for Kumakichi, Lilitina scolded Altina, her voice ringing out.

And Kumakichi thought to himself that life as a polar bear wasn't so bad.

"Waaah!"

The real problem was that sounds echoed more easily in the cramped little cave, and it was unusual for Lulutina to raise her voice in true anger.

Oof, my ears are ringing.

Her voice was loud enough to make even a polar bear like Kumakichi flinch.

Even the spoiled little pups must have felt true terror when they heard it. Though the trio raised pitiful cries of protest, with Lulutina having closed the distance between them in an instant and glaring at them, they were essentially rooted to the spot.

"No crying. If you understand, then get a move on."

With both hands on her hips, Lulutina delivered her instructions calmly, and the three pups could do nothing but nod in surrender with tears in their eyes.

Come on, Kumakichi. Don't misunderstand. This is disciplining. This is just how she keeps the kids in line. The real Lulutina is gentle, kind, and delicate. A good kid......

"Sister. Lord Kumakichi is totally terrified by you. I really don't think you should be yelling in such cramped quarters."

Lilitina, who had been grilling the dried meats, offered a succinct warning, bringing Lulutina to her senses and prompting her to flash a quick smile at Kumakichi.

"S-see? I'm smiling."

Kumakichi.

"Come now, girls. Breakfast will be ready soon, so hurry up and give Lord Kumakichi some space while you go and wash your faces."

While Kumakichi soothed the three girls, Lulutina was quickly getting the things in order to have breakfast ready.

"Awww!"

"It's too cowld!"

"I don't wanna!"

It had become standard practice for the three pups to disobey Lulutina's orders every morning.

That's right. It's okay like this. This is happiness.

"Now see here, you three. If you don't listen to what Lulutina says, you'll all be naughty children!"

"Mm. But Laro wants to pway with Lord Kuma."

When Kumakichi lifted his right arm, Laro clung to it, still whining.

"They're just like puppies," mused Kumakuchi, but Lulutina, who was stirring the pot of food, barked impatiently at them:

"That's quite enough! You're really going to make your sister mad!"

"Eeeek!"

"Ack!"

"Ah! Lord Kumakichi, let me do that."

"Now, now. You can take it easy."

Kumakichi did Lulutina and the others the favor of quickly building a fire.

Since there were still leftover embers from last night's fire, it was a simple matter to start a new fire.

I have those knights to thank. If not for them, things would be a lot more difficult around here.

Shortly after being reincarnated, Kumakichi had run into and defeated some knights from Romles. The weapons and tools he stole from them were constantly coming in handy.

"Meeew."

"I'm shweepy."

"Brrr!"

As the cave warmed up thanks to the crackling little fire, the triplets finally shook off the remaining dregs of sleep. While clutching their bodies tightly, they mewled and stuck fast to Kumakichi's body.

"Aww. There, there. I know it's cold."

"Brrr. Lord Kumakichi, we're cowld."

Lana climbed up onto Kumakichi until she reached his knee, where she sat cross-legged. Then, almost as if they had a mutual agreement on what to do, Lara and Laro buried their faces on either side of his lap, tickling

Well, it is good luck to let children sleep as long as they want.

Perking his ears up, he could hear the twittering of little birds.

This place was deep in the heart of the forest.

There was no noise pollution from automobiles nor any other sounds of human activity.

"Ah, Lord Kumakichi. Good morning. You're up early."

After a short while, Lulutina woke up, rubbing her eyes. Next came Lilitina, and then Altina. Altina gave a great yawn and stretched on all fours the way a dog or cat might. It was a heartwarming sight. Kumakichi scratched at his cheek and then raised his paw to greet them.

"Good morning, Lulutina. It's a beautiful morning."

"Y-yes, it is."

Huh. She's shivering. For a polar bear, this weather is nothing, but I guess it's hard for her to endure.

Lulutina was doing her best to smile, but her lip was quivering, probably because she was trying to bear the early morning cold.

She must have a hard time having to deal with this right after waking up. Time to show how gentle this polar bear can be.

Especially in this cave made of rock that had no source of heat; it felt like the cold seeped into their very bones.

Kumakichi, familiar with mountains and using his senses, guessed the temperature must have been close to below freezing.

Your average human wouldn't be able to sleep soundly under such conditions.

But that's what made this a fantasy world.

Lulutina and the others, being anthros descended from wild animals, were apparently able to handle a little cold if their success in falling fast asleep was any indication.

"Uungh. Meeew."

"I'm cowld."

"Brr!"

Whoops. Well, that didn't go as planned.

When Kumakichi tried shifting his body even a little, the three little pups, who'd been using his snow-white fur as a blanket, disrupted the peace and quiet with their sleepy murmurs of protest.

True, the cave was pretty cold, but as a polar bear, Kumakichi could barely feel it.

Since the three pups clung to him for his body heat, he stayed absolutely still, granting them their wish.

He often woke with memories of his previous life as a human.

And it always perplexed him how the dull days of his previous life could kindle such nostalgia.

His five senses were almost certainly sharper now that he was a polar bear, because even in the dim light, he could see clearly.

He was in a cave.

He could make out the jagged rocks and his meager household items perfectly.

All told, there wasn't much.

But that was natural, given how this place was never meant to be occupied.

Kumakichi had been slumbering deeply with the werewolf sisters.

I'm happy with my life now. This must be what it means to be a winner. And as proof...

The gentle sensation he felt on his fur was the three wolf pups—Lara, Laro, and Lana—having buried their faces in his fur as they slept.

I'm a pretty big hit with the younguns.

Leaving such distracting thoughts aside...

With winter on its way, mornings in the forest were chilly.

expensive, and the average office worker doesn't earn the kind of money that makes it possible to afford the luxury of owning a car.

As a result, traveling to prefectures with mountains requires taking the train. It's more restrictive than traveling by car but, on the whole, leaves almost nothing to be desired.

Mountains.

Japan is a country rich in greenery with two-thirds of the land covered in forest.

Whenever he stood at the peak of a mountain and gazed down at the scenery below, this thought crossed Kumakichi's mind many a time:

If I'm ever reborn, I'd like to come back as a woodland creature.

Who knows whether God saw what was in Kumakichi Kumada's heart...? In any case, he was reborn. As a polar bear, bizarrely enough.

Kumakichi suddenly awoke, feeling faintly warm all over his body.

I dreamed about back when I was a human. I can't believe how real it all felt.

A dream...

A far-off fantasy.

Satisfied Days

The last train, the last train, the last train...

It never ends.

Like a spiral forever winding down into hell.

On the train at the end of a full workday, there's always people who are absolutely wiped out sitting down with their arms crossed or with their eyes closed and their heads bowed.

The company Kumakichi worked for wasn't all that particularly demanding, but during crunch time, the workload could get a little—or, rather, excessively—heavy. But that was par for the course.

Once people reach their late twenties, a single night's worth of sleep no longer restores energy like it used to.

At the same time, it's only with age that anyone gets a chance to experience the joy and relief that comes when the dreaded Friday workday is over and everyone suddenly finds themselves standing on the station platform.

Days off aren't remarkably special, but the moment Kumakichi's workweek ended, it's hard to put into words how he felt. "Joy," "excitement," or "a sense of freedom"? None of those words could even begin to do it justice.

In his spare moments away from work, Kumakichi enjoyed going to the mountains.

Unlike in the countryside, parking in the city is

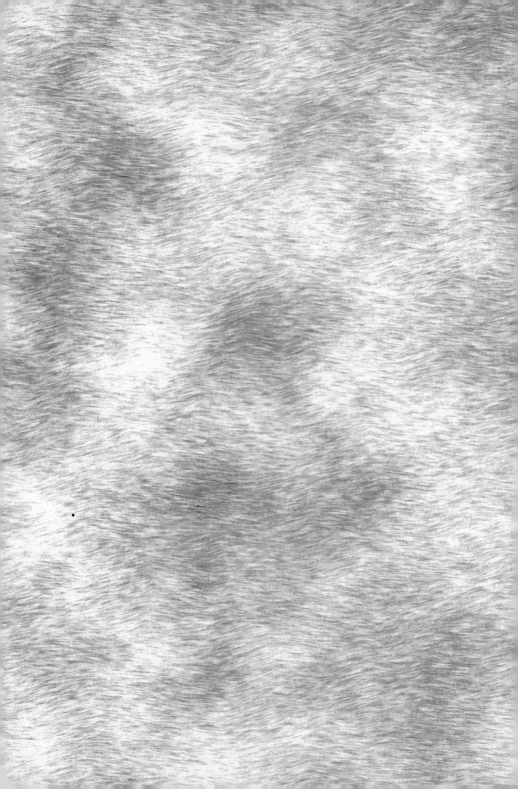

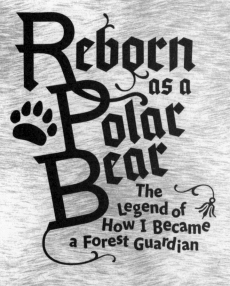

Reborn as a Polar Bear

The Legend of How I Became a Forest Guardian

BONUS SIDE STORY

Chihiro Mishima